D1558720

Woody, From *Antz* to *Zelig*

Woody, From *Antz* to *Zelig*

A Reference Guide to Woody Allen's
Creative Work, 1964–1998

RICHARD A. SCHWARTZ

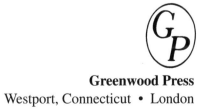

Greenwood Press
Westport, Connecticut • London

Library of Congress Cataloging-in-Publication Data

Schwartz, Richard A., 1951–
  Woody, from Antz to Zelig : a reference guide to Woody Allen's creative work,
  1964–1998 / Richard A. Schwartz.
    p. cm.
  Filmography: p.
  Includes bibliographical references and index.
  ISBN 0–313–31133–1 (alk. paper)
    1. Allen, Woody—Criticism and interpretation.   I. Title.
  PN1998.3.A455S38   2000
  791.43′092—dc21   99–045566

British Library Cataloguing in Publication Data is available.

Library of Congress Catalog Card Number: 99–045566
ISBN: 0–313–31133–1

First published in 2000

Greenwood Press, 88 Post Road West, Westport, CT 06881
An imprint of Greenwood Publishing Group, Inc.
www.greenwood.com

Printed in the United States of America

The paper used in this book complies with the
Permanent Paper Standard issued by the National
Information Standards Organization (Z39.48–1984).

10 9 8 7 6 5 4 3 2 1

To Ana-Maria,
My loving wife, mother to our cats and dogs,
teacher, entrepreneur, artist, nature worshiper,
and Woody Allen aficionado

Know Thyself

—*The Oracle of Apollo at Delphi*

Whimsic fantasy, grub fact, pure senseless music—none in itself would do; to embody *all* and rise above each, in a work neither longfaced nor idiotly grinning, but adventuresome, passionately humored, merry with the pain of insight, wise and smiling in the terror of our life—that was my calm ambition.

—John Barth's "Anonymiad" in *Lost in the Funhouse*

Contents

Illustrations

Introduction

Although Woody Allen remains a major celebrity in American culture and retains a devoted following that spans generations, genders, and some ethnic lines, the vast scope of his artistic accomplishment over the past three and a half decades is not always fully recognized. Few artists of any era can match Allen's prodigious output. Since 1964, he has written, directed, and/or acted in thirty-four films; made one film for television; written three full-length Broadway plays, one one-act Broadway play, and five additional one-act plays; published three books of stories and sketches; issued five record albums; performed internationally as a jazz musician; and appeared as a comic strip character. Although Allen disdains awards because he feels they too often overlook truly great accomplishments and reward inferior ones, the fact that Allen has repeatedly been recognized by award-granting institutions throughout the world indicates that his work has been widely appreciated and has earned deep international respect.

Allen's success extends to several genres beyond film, and his creative genius appeals to a vast spectrum of audiences. A top television writer in the late 1950s, Allen quit in 1959 to pursue a career as a stand-up comedian. Initially working for free as he honed his craft, he soon became one of the highest-paid comic performers in America. During the divisive Vietnam War era, he won followings first among college students, the antiwar counterculture, and the hip Greenwich Village crowd, and then subsequently drew large middle American audiences that frequented Las Vegas and other popular entertainment spots. During that period Allen wrote his first Broadway play, *Don't Drink the Water*; wrote and acted in his second Broadway play, the highly successful *Play It Again, Sam*; published short stories in such respected magazines as *New Yorker, Playboy,* and *Evergreen Re-*

view—later collected in his first book, *Getting Even*—and wrote his first screenplay: *What's New, Pussycat?*, a huge box office success that gave Allen the necessary credibility in Hollywood to become a director. Since then, he has focused most of his efforts on filmmaking—writing, directing, and acting. But he remained enough involved in other media to write two additional books of stories and plays, two additional Broadway plays, and an occasional essay or television movie.

The range of Allen's accomplishments and his ability to attract such diverse audiences for so many years would alone merit another study of his work. Moreover, recent criticism has focused on the autobiographical elements in Allen's films, especially since his scandalous breakup with Mia Farrow in 1992, and has been dominated by discourse about the supposed misogyny in his work. Accordingly, there have been comparatively few attempts to take his work on its own terms and explore the complete vision that Allen realizes in his art, as *Woody, From* Antz *to* Zelig attempts to do.

When we do take Allen's work on its own terms, many of the charges of misogyny become mystifying. Indeed, one can argue just as readily that Allen addresses feminist concerns and projects feminist values more consistently than any other major American director. Allen, who maintains that he greatly admires women and numbers several women among his closest friends, advisers, and professional colleagues, frequently features women as protagonists in his stories—something rare in American films since the 1980s. Moreover, he typically represents women as intelligent and emotionally complex individuals who have sexual desires but are much more than mere sexual objects. Many of his female characters, like his male characters, are articulate, independent, self-motivated, and assertive. Many are accomplished professionals; several are women in their forties or older—something even rarer in American films.

Like his men, Allen's female characters are often emotionally flawed but never in stereotypical ways. He develops his female characters more fully than most other directors and features few hysterical women and fewer bimbos. When Allen does show hysteria, he explores it in depth, as with Dorrie in *Stardust Memories* and Delores in *Crimes and Misdemeanors*. And even attractive but shallow women, like Flyn in *Interiors* and Sam in *Husbands and Wives*, are more than just pretty faces. Moreover, as Aristotle reminds us, character flaws are the stuff of literature. Indeed, such films as *Annie Hall, Interiors, Hannah and Her Sisters, Another Woman, Alice, Husbands and Wives*, and *Celebrity* center around the personal growth of female protagonists as they come to know themselves better, reverse their character flaws, and alter their lives so they can live in greater harmony with their personal values. *Alice*, for instance, can easily be read as a Felliniesque remake of Kate Chopin's *The Awakening* (1899), a book that is rightfully celebrated by feminists for these identical qualities.

In addition, Allen explores women's relationships with other women and with family members more deeply than most other directors do. Which film, for instance, truly explores mother-daughter relationships more fully: *Interiors* or *Steel Magnolias*? Which offers a more thorough exploration of sisterly relationships: *Hannah and Her Sisters* or *Like Water for Chocolate*? Which provides a deeper study of the dynamics of female friendship: *September* or *Thelma and Louise*? Moreover, Allen rarely subjects women to violence in his movies. And when he does, such as in *The Purple Rose of Cairo, Crimes and Misdemeanors, Husbands and Wives*, or *Bullets over Broadway*, it is neither gratuitous nor glorified but always integral to the story.

It is true, as Allen's critics point out, that he often pairs himself as a romantic lead with much younger women, but this is neither unique to Allen nor necessarily a fault. American cinema is filled with pairings of older men and younger women, from *Casablanca, To Have and Have Not, Ninotchka, Sabrina* (both the original and remake), *Love in the Afternoon*, and *To Catch a Thief* to *Lolita* and *Pretty Woman*. World literature abounds in such pairings. Even Jane Austen celebrates them: Mr. Knightley presumably is old enough to be the protagonist's father in *Emma*. Thus it seems odd to single out Allen for criticism on this score.

Moreover, Allen's critics employ a dubious premise when they maintain that any romantic relationship between a much older man and a younger woman is necessarily exploitive or perverse. It may be that many such couplings are inappropriate, and skeptics are justified in viewing them suspiciously. But great literature teaches us that all personal relationships have their own unique dynamics, and we must evaluate them one at a time. In a hostile, confusing, irrational world such as Allen depicts, some improbable pairings do prove mutually beneficial, at least temporarily, and this is how Allen typically represents most of his May–December relationships. He presents them in affectionate terms that respect the woman's character, intelligence, and independence and insist on her deriving satisfaction from the relationship. When the interaction ceases to satisfy the young woman, the relationship dissolves, such as in *Annie Hall* or *Hannah and Her Sisters*. In *Manhattan* teenaged Tracy proves the most self-possessed and emotionally healthy character in the story, and Ike learns at least as much from her as she does from him. Moreover, Allen manipulates the story so we applaud Tracy's strength, self-knowledge, and independence at the end of the film when she leaves Ike for England. In *Mighty Aphrodite* both Lenny and Linda Ash grow from their relationship, which is primarily a caring friendship, not a sexual romance. And in *Everyone Says I Love You* Joe facilitates

Von's maturation, while satisfying all of her fantasies in the process. In the end Joe proves to be an inappropriate partner for Von, suggesting that Allen is aware that relationships based on duplicity inevitably fail. Where is the misogyny in this?

Therefore, rather than approach Allen's work from a sociopolitical perspective or as a series of autobiographical statements, which it mostly is not, despite Allen's proclivity for drawing heavily from his own life experiences, *Woody, From* Antz *to* Zelig examines Allen's artistic endeavor. The literary analyses discuss how Allen develops his themes and generates humor from the process. They describe Allen's insights into the human condition and consider how these insights apply to his characters. They explore how he examines human behavior, family dynamics, and male-female relationships. Allen routinely experiments with the cinematic medium, and the book considers how and why Allen develops new narrative forms for conveying his stories. It also places Allen within the contexts of film and literary history.

Taken as a whole *Woody, From* Antz *to* Zelig shows Woody Allen to be a serious and substantial artist who works within and plays off the great traditions of Western literature. The writers he most respects—Shakespeare, Dostoyevsky, and Chekhov—deal with the great existential questions of human existence: Is there a God? What happens to us after we die? What are the meaning and purpose of life? Allen too addresses these issues, sometimes seriously but often playfully, and his playfulness becomes a crucial part of his response to the human condition.

Although the characters he portrays do not always possess these qualities—those who do not suffer for their deficiency—Allen repeatedly reminds us that self-respect, personal integrity, self-knowledge, and self-acceptance are essential if we are to be happy. He shows how crucial it is for us first to know what really excites us in life and then to have the courage to pursue it. Moreover, Allen repeatedly asks what constitutes proper action in an absurd, atheistic universe in which we cannot expect to be held accountable for our behavior in an afterlife, and in which we are in a perpetual state of uncertainty, as we can never take it for granted that things are as we believe them to be or that we have access to complete and fully accurate information. In one way or another, this has been a dominant question in twentieth-century Western literature, from James Joyce, Franz Kafka, and T. S. Eliot to William Faulkner, Luigi Pirandello, and Virginia Woolf, to Ralph Ellison and Ishmael Reed, to John Barth, Thomas Pynchon, and Tom Stoppard, to the films of Orson Welles, Akira Kurosawa, Federico Fellini, and Ingmar Bergman. *Woody, From* Antz *to* Zelig thus strives to shows how Woody Allen draws from and contributes to this great literary and cinematic tradition.

Woody, From *Antz* to *Zelig*

A

Academy Awards. Allen's disdain for awards is well known; he regards them largely as popularity contests that do not consistently reward true artistic achievement. Alvy Singer, apparently speaking for Allen in *Annie Hall*, complains that in Hollywood, everyone is always receiving an award for something, and he scornfully proposes to give an award to Adolf Hitler for best fascist dictator. As a matter of principle, Allen has consistently declined to accept his Academy Awards in person.

Nonetheless, Allen's films have reaped numerous honors. *Annie Hall* (1977) won best picture; *Hannah and Her Sisters* (1986) was nominated for that award. Allen won best director for *Annie Hall* and was nominated for *Interiors* (1978), *Broadway Danny Rose* (1984), *Hannah*, *Crimes and Misdemeanors*, and *Bullets over Broadway* (1994). Allen and Marshall Brickman won best screenplay for *Annie Hall*. He later won best original screenplay for *Hannah* and was nominated for *Interiors*, *Manhattan* (with Brickman, 1979), *Broadway Danny Rose*, *The Purple Rose of Cairo* (1985), *Radio Days* (1987), *Crimes and Misdemeanors* (1989), *Alice* (1990), *Husbands and Wives* (1992), *Bullets over Broadway* (with Doug McGrath), *Mighty Aphrodite* (1995), and *Deconstructing Harry* (1997).

Diane Keaton won best actress for *Annie Hall*, and Geraldine Page was nominated for *Interiors*. Allen was nominated best actor for *Annie Hall*. Dianne Wiest won best supporting actress for *Hannah* and again for *Bullets over Broadway*, and Mira Sorvino won for *Mighty Aphrodite*. Maureen Stapleton was nominated best supporting actress for *Interiors*, Mariel Hemingway for *Manhattan*, Judy Davis for *Husbands and Wives*, and Jennifer Tilly for *Bullets over Broadway*. Michael Caine received an Oscar as best supporting actor for *Hannah*. Martin Landau was nominated for *Crimes and Misdemeanors* and Chazz Palminteri for *Bullets over Broadway*.

Allen cites the Academy's failure to recognize the cinematography of Gordon Willis as a glaring example of how the awards do not properly reward real artistic achievement. Notably, Willis was overlooked for his work on *The Godfather* Parts I and II, *Manhattan*, *Interiors*, and *A Midsummer Night's Sex Comedy*. He was finally nominated for *Zelig* (1983), but Allen feels even this nomination was primarily for his technical achievement and not his aesthetic accomplishments. Willis was later nominated for *The Godfather* Part III (1990).

Mel Bourne and Daniel Robert were nominated for art direction in *Interiors*, Stuart Wurtzel and Carol Joffe for *Hannah*, Santo Loquasto and Joffe for *Radio Days*, and Loquasto and Susan Bode for *Bullets over Broadway*. Loquasto was also nominated for costume design in *Zelig* (1983); Jeffrey Kurland received a nomination for costume design in *Bullets over Broadway*. Susan E. Morse was nominated for film editing in *Hannah*.

Alda, Alan. Film and television actor who appears in *Crimes and Misdemeanors*, *Manhattan Murder Mystery*, and *Everyone Says I Love You*. Notable appearances in films by other directors include *The Same Time Next Year* (1978), *California Suite* (1978), *The Seduction of Joe Tynan* (1979; Alda wrote the screenplay), *The Four Seasons* (1981; Alda wrote and directed), *Sweet Liberty* (1986; Alda wrote and directed), and *Betsy's Wedding* (1990; Alda wrote and directed). Alda is probably best known for his role as smart-aleck Korean War surgeon Hawkeye Pierce on *M*A*S*H*, a popular television sitcom that ran on CBS from 1972 to 1982. The role established Alda as humorous and irreverent but sensitive, caring, and inclined to do the right thing.

Alda's collaboration with Allen dates back at least to 1962, when Allen conceived and wrote a television pilot entitled *The Laughmakers*, which was to star Alda, Louise Lasser, and Paul Hampton. ABC declined to pick it up because its sophisticated humor appealed to too limited an audience.

Alice. 1990 film directed and written by Allen. It stars Mia Farrow (Alice Tait), William Hurt (Doug Tait), Alec Baldwin (Eddie), Joe Mantegna (Joe Rufilho), Judy Davis (Joe's ex-wife, Vicki), Bernadette Peters (Muse), Keye Brill (Dr. Yang), Cybill Shepherd (Nancy Brill), Julie Kavner (interior decorator), Blythe Danner (Alice's sister, Dorothy), Gwen Verdon (Alice's mother), Patrick O'Neal (Alice's father), Elle Macpherson (model in dressing room), James Toback (writing professor), Caroline Aaron (Sue), and Bob Balaban (Sid Moscowitz). Robert Greenhut was the producer, Carlo Di

Palma director of photography, Santo Loquasto production designer, Jeffrey Kurland costumer, and Susan E. Morse editor. Randall Balsmeyer and Mimi Evert provided the special effects. Bob Harman of Preston Cinema Systems supervised the flying effects. Orion Pictures was the North American distributor.

One of several ghost-driven films to appear in the late 1980s and early 1990s, *Alice* did not fare well in the United States. Nonetheless, Farrow won the National Board of Review's best actress award, and Allen received an Academy Award nomination for best original screenplay. An overall money loser, *Alice* cost $12 million to produce but grossed only $5.9 million in U.S. and Canadian distribution ($3.3 million net, not including later video rentals and television revenues). The film recouped some of its losses in Europe, especially in Paris, where it was the fifth largest box office draw in 1991.

Alice is loosely based on the life of Mia Farrow. Like the character she plays, Farrow attended Catholic school and is known for her devotion to her children, whom she once took to a film documentary about Mother Teresa. The event stands out in Farrow's autobiography, and it appears as a pivotal moment of illumination in *Alice*. As a younger woman, Farrow, like Alice, traveled to India for spiritual reasons. However, she visited Maharishi Mahesh Yogi, the master of transcendental meditation, not Mother Teresa. In her autobiography Farrow asserts, "I loved my parents with a fierceness and incomprehension that was terrifying" (Farrow 15). Alice, whose mother is also a film actress, demonstrates similar devotion. Like the young Farrow, she idealizes her parents' dysfunctional marriage and fails to see how their flaws have influenced her own view of life.

Another inspiration for the movie was a visit to a Chinese herbalist Allen had made some years earlier to cure a sty in his eye. The herbalist used a cat's whisker to clear Allen's tear duct. Although the effort failed to eradicate the sty, it reinforced Allen's suspicion of practices and beliefs that have not survived close scientific scrutiny. Nonetheless, Allen observed how popular such unproven forms of alternative medicine are among wealthy socialite women, and he conceived the idea of writing a story about a woman who squanders her life by indulging in material comforts instead of applying her talents more productively. "I thought it would be a funny story that she goes to an acupuncturist, but he's really a magician. Because what's bothering her is nothing physical. There's nothing physically wrong with her. It's all emotional" (*Woody Allen on Woody Allen* 228).

Like Kate Chopin's *The Awakening* (1899), which had recently been revived to great acclaim by feminist scholars, *Alice* centers around an affluent woman who awakens to her "inner life," as Allen calls it. In many ways a comic remake of his *Another Woman*, which Allen himself criticized as cold and emotionally distant, *Alice* shows how the protagonist's awakening results from removing layers of self-deception and rediscovering what she truly values.

By the end of her saga, Alice learns that her marriage is a sham; her friends ridicule her sexuality and finally betray her; and she no longer lives in harmony with what she most values or what most excites and animates her. In addition, Alice recognizes that she has deluded herself by idealizing her flawed parents, and she has debilitated herself by heeding her mother's advice to sacrifice passionate love, creativity, and spiritual connection in favor of stability and financial security.

A nagging backache initiates Alice's voyage of self-discovery. Hypnotherapist Nicholas Mason, Ph.D., points out that physical symptoms are sometimes expressions by the subconscious intended to make us aware of deeper problems. Back pain in particular often signals a spiritual imbalance of some kind. Alice's backache comes about because her lifestyle has become too detached from what she values, and she is turning into someone she does not fully respect. As she begins to become aware of this transformation and takes steps to rectify it, the pain disappears.

Dr. Yang, the Chinese acupuncturist whom Alice consults, immediately recognizes that her problem is spiritual, not physical. He tells her in his broken English, "Problem is not back. Problem is here [pointing to his head] and here [pointing to his heart]." He induces an hypnotic trance that reveals Alice's basic problem: her life lacks passion and meaning.

Under hypnosis Alice states that she is at a crossroads in her life and feels lost. She admits fantasizing about Joe, a man whose child attends the same school as hers. She says that the fantasy has reawakened passions she has felt only once in her life, before she met her husband, Doug. As she recalls her first date with Doug, we learn that he proposed shortly after meeting her and that she accepted because he was wealthy and good looking. Now she feels as if she is squandering her life with frivolous shopping and failing to live up to her potential. Instead of pursuing meaningful activities, she is simply struggling to maintain her youth—and Doug does not even notice.

Nor does Doug encourage Alice when she says she wants to do something more significant. In her trance, Alice sees Doug treating her condescendingly, using his highly honed reasoning skills to make her feel ineffectual and insignificant. Like Marion from *Another Woman*, who sacrificed her passion for painting watercolors in order to appease her father's image of who she should be, Alice dropped her fledgling dream to be a fashion designer in order marry Doug and fulfill the role of wife for the successful businessman. In both instances, the young women surrender their creative passion in order to appease a parent, as Alice is obeying her mother's admonition when she rejects the artist she loves in favor of the security Doug offers.

Although the hypnosis yields all of these insights to Yang and to us on the first visit, Yang instructs Alice not to remember them when she awakens. Thus through the hypnosis sequence, the audience gains more information than Alice consciously possesses. This serves a rhetorical purpose by enabling viewers more readily to identify the issues Alice struggles with in later scenes, and it creates a context for judging her actions. For instance, our knowledge that she has no passion for Doug and that he does not respect her individual capabilities allows us to regard Alice's adultery with Joe more sympathetically.

On subsequent visits, Yang gives Alice magic herbs that facilitate her conscious recognition of the same things she has already acknowledged subconsciously. The herbs enable her repressed sexual desire to express itself, allow her to see how her husband and friends actually regard her, and cause her to recognize the truth about her parents. We know her cure is complete when she no longer requires Yang or his magic. She takes control of her life and creates a new, more spiritually balanced existence that manifests who she is and what she believes in.

Her sexual passion is the first to surface. The film opens with Alice daydreaming about kissing Joe by the penguin cages at the zoo, and after she takes Yang's herbs for the first time, she gives voice to the earthy, flirtatious, sexually assertive side of herself. The incongruity between the sweet, repressed Alice we usually see and this bold, assertive persona produces one of the funniest scenes in the movie, as Joe is overwhelmed by her come-on. At the same time, the scene compels Alice to acknowledge that this confident, aggressive side of herself exists and wants to come out. (The tango on the soundtrack and Alice's expressed weakness for tenor saxophone players evoke Marilyn Monroe, Tony Curtis, and Jack Lemmon in an earlier comedy, *Some Like It Hot*, 1959.)

On several occasions Alice takes an herbal tea that makes her invisible and allows her to spy on others. Her invisibility enables her to discover what kind of man Joe really is, how her friends really feel about her, and that her husband has long been cheating on her. She first drinks the tea after coming on to Joe. Observing him at his ex-wife's studio, Alice learns that during their marriage, Joe lied, gambled, and flirted with his wife's friends, but now he behaves maturely and seems sensitive, creative, passionate, and fundamentally decent. In these respects he appears as Allen's ideal man. He graciously accommodates his ex-wife's requests to rearrange his visitation dates, shows concern for his daughter's safety and happiness, appreciates his ex-wife's achievements, respects her capabilities, and is highly sexed.

Later, Alice uses her power of invisibility to discover that her friends consider her mousy and incapable of satisfying Doug, who has a long-standing reputation for womanizing. (Joe, who accompanies Alice, uses his invisibility for happier, if shallower, purposes: he watches fashion model Elle Macpherson undress in a clothing changing room.)

Alice's final use of the invisibility herb allows her to catch Doug with another woman at his office Christmas party. Collectively, Yang's herbs enable Alice to see not only Doug's infidelity, even with her best friends, but also that he has little regard for her intelligence, creative capabilities, or capacity for independent action. She further realizes that she feels no deep passion for him either.

Burning a different herb in a teacup makes Alice more acutely aware of the absence of passion in her life and allows her to see more clearly the mistake she made twenty years earlier when she followed her mother's advice and ended a loving relationship because it offered no long-term security. The burning herb enables Alice to conjure Eddie, an artist whom she once loved but broke up with because he was irresponsible. Eddie, who died years later in an automobile accident, now visits her from the grave. (His otherworldly presence and powers occasion the special effects for which the film was praised.) Eddie observes Alice's materialism with mild sarcasm, asks with genuine concern about her now nonexistent career, and encourages her to explore her feelings for Joe, who reminds her of Eddie. We learn that unlike her marriage with Doug, Eddie and Alice's romance had been intense and passionate. He made love so recklessly that Alice, who once aspired to be a nun, sometimes felt guilty. But in the end, Alice terminated the relationship because her mother insisted Eddie would never be a good provider.

An opium dream provokes additional insights about her failure to live by the values she cherishes. Alice accepts some opium during an after-hours visit with Yang, and in the subsequent dream her sister condemns her for her shallow materialism. The dream takes on a Fellini-like quality as Alice enters a Catholic confessional that suddenly appears on the front yard of her childhood home. In her confession, she admits spoiling her children and failing to expose them to the things that matter most. Alice remembers that as a child, she was happiest when she helped other people, and she wonders, "Where did that part of me go?" After she comes down from the opium, Alice tries to reconcile with her sister, and she takes her children to see a documentary about Mother Teresa. (An earlier reference to Mother Teresa had sparked the strongest show of enthusiasm Alice demonstrates in the entire movie.)

An herbal tea taken to dispel writing block helps Alice see her friends and parents more clearly. It produces a straight-talking Muse that acts like the voice of her subconscious and makes her admit to herself several facts she has refused to acknowledge consciously: a friend she had helped in the past now resents her and wants to disassociate from her, and her creative writing professor wants to seduce her. Most important, Alice concedes that her mother was not a gifted actress who sacrificed her career for marriage. Instead, she was a loser who depended on others to care for her. In this new context, her admonition that Alice "marry a substantial man, not some struggling, left-wing, Greenwich Village artist" appears as a reflection of her mother's weakness, not as the responsible advice Alice believed it was.

As in *Another Woman*, Alice finally becomes free to explore herself after she catches Doug cheating and the dissolution of her unloving marriage becomes evident. A comic fiasco with Yang's last herb induces her to repudiate magic and rededicate herself to what she really cherishes. Over Doug's objections—and his accusation that she cannot survive without the amenities to which she has grown accustomed—Alice flies to India to work with Mother Teresa. When she returns to New York, she is a different person. No longer living in a fancy apartment or wearing designer clothes, she dresses in jeans, lives in a humble flat, and befriends the people on her street. Most important, she no longer entrusts her children to the care of others but raises them herself. In this way she not only ensures they will be raised with meaningful values, she also is able to know them better and enjoy them more.

The final shot shows Alice pushing her kids on the swings in a public park and smiling. She has rediscovered what matters most to her and has restructured her life accordingly. Only in this way is she able to discover true happiness.

Allen, Woody. Woody Allen has had a prolific career. By spring 1999, Allen had written, directed, and/or acted in thirty-four films; made one film for television; written three full-length Broadway plays, one one-act Broadway play, and five additional one-act plays; published three books of stories and sketches, issued five record albums; performed internationally as a jazz musician; been the subject of one full-length documentary film and numerous shorter ones; and appeared as a comic strip character.

He was born Allan Stewart Konigsberg on December 1, 1935, in the Bronx, New York. His parents, Martin and Netti Konigsberg, were first-generation Americans of Austrian Jewish and Russian Jewish descent. His only sibling, Letty, was born in 1943, the same year Allen saw his first Marx Brothers movie. The Marx Brothers subsequently became a major source of joy and inspiration. (See **Marx Brothers**.) Allen and Letty (now Letty Aronson) were close growing up, and she has been involved in the production of several of Allen's more recent films. Although he was bright and adept at sports, Allen disliked school, which he found boring and demeaning, and his performance was indifferent. As a teenager, he took up the clarinet, which became a lifelong passion, and he began performing magic tricks. At the age of sixteen he first performed at Weinstein's Majestic Bungalow Colony in the Catskills. Allen has remained interested in magic throughout his life, and supernatural events play prominent roles in many of his works. (See **Magic**.)

When Allen was seventeen he began sending jokes to New York newspaper columnists under the pen name Woody Allen. His first published joke appeared on November 25, 1952, in Walter Winchell's column: "Woody Allen says he ate at a restaurant that had OPS prices—over people's salaries" (Lax 69). That year he saw his first Bergman film, *Summer with Monika* (1952), and performed his first stand-up routine at a Young Israel social club. Allen graduated from high school the following year and began writing jokes for David Alber for twenty dollars a week. He enrolled in New York University to study film but dropped out. He then enrolled in and dropped out from City College of New York.

In 1955, Allen began working in NBC's Writers Development Program and moved to Hollywood to write for the *Colgate Comedy Hour*. There he met fellow writer Danny Simon (Neil's brother), who, according to Allen, taught him how to structure a comedy script. The following year Allen began writing comedy skits at the Camp Tamiment Resort and married Harlene Rosen, his seventeen-year-old girlfriend who encouraged him to continue his education. Allen describes Rosen as a very nice person who became a well educated and formidable woman (Lax 168). However, his treatment of her in his stand-up comedy was less kind, and Rosen later sued him over his jokes about her. Julian Fox suggests that many of the less appealing characteristics of Nancy, Allan Felix's ex-wife in *Play It Again, Sam*, are based on Rosen.

In 1958, Sid Caesar hired Allen to write for NBC's *Sid Caesar's Chevy Show*, and with cowriter Larry Gelbart, Allen won a Sylvania Award and received an Emmy nomination. (See **Television**.) That year he also formed an enduring business relationship with the management team of Jack Rollins and Charles Joffe, who developed his early career, helped him hone his skills as a performer, and later produced his films.

In 1959, Allen began psychoanalysis and remained in therapy through 1998, when he quit after declaring he no longer needed it following his marriage to his third wife, Soon-Yi Previn. Allen's experience in therapy informs much of his work, either as the target of his humor or the basis for his exploration of character and human interaction.

In 1959, Allen quit his job as one of the highest-paid television comedy writers in order to begin a more personally satisfying career as a stand-up comedian. Initially working for free as he developed his craft, Allen started at the Upstairs at the Duplex in Greenwich Village, where he did two shows a night for six days a week. In 1960, Allen met Louise Lasser and had his Broadway debut as the writer of two skits in the revue *From A to Z*, which ran for twenty-one performances at the Plymouth Theater. He separated from his wife in 1961 and made his first appearance on *The Ed Sullivan Show*. He divorced Harlene in 1962 and the following year appeared at such major venue's as Mr. Kelly's in Chicago and New York's Carnegie Hall, where he was on the same billing with Count Basie. During these early days of his stand-up career, Allen befriended banjo player Marshall Brickman, with whom he later collaborated on four screenplays, and other rising comedians such as Bill Cosby and Dick Cavett, a lifelong friend. (See **Stand-Up Comedy**.)

By 1964, Allen was earning up to $10,000 per performance and guest hosting on Johnny Carson's *Tonight Show*. That year Charles K. Feldman approached him to write the script for and act in *What's New, Pussycat?* The financial success of that film in 1965 established Allen's credibility in Hollywood and opened new possibilities for him in film, on stage, and in print. In 1966, he published his first story in *The New Yorker*, "The Gossage-Vardebedian Papers"; wrote his first full-length Broadway play, *Don't Drink the Water*, which enjoyed 598 performances; and had his debut as a film director with *What's Up, Tiger Lily?* He also married Louise Lasser that year, the same year Mia Farrow married Frank Sinatra. (See **Louise Lasser**.)

Between 1966 and 1969 Allen became one of the top-paid nightclub performers in the country. He issued his first three record albums, published additional stories, and acted as James Bond's evil nephew in *Casino Royale*. In 1968, he met Diane Keaton when she auditioned for the female lead in *Play It Again, Sam*. The following year Allen divorced Lasser and lived with Keaton while they starred together with Tony Roberts in the successful run of *Play It Again, Sam*. (See **Diane Keaton**.) That year he directed his first fully original film, *Take the Money and Run*.

The 1972 release of *Play It Again, Sam* brought Allen his first major success as a film director and began his cinematic collaboration with Keaton. (Their romantic relationship had ended about 1970.) Between 1972 and 1977, Allen and Keaton costarred in three additional comedies: *Sleeper*, *Love and Death*, and *Annie Hall*, which is based loosely on their relation-

Woody Allen on the set of *The Front*. Courtesy of Photofest.

ship. *Sleeper* first paired Allen with Ralph Rosenblum, a gifted editor, and *Annie Hall* first united him with Gordon Willis, whom Allen regards as a master cinematographer. (See **Gordon Willis**.) Allen continued to work with Rosenblum through *Annie Hall* (filmed in 1976), after which Rosenblum's assistant, Susan E. Morse, replaced him. Morse has edited all of Allen's subsequent films to date. Willis worked with Allen through *The Purple Rose of Cairo*. Their schedules conflicted when Allen was ready to film *Hannah and Her Sisters* in 1984, and Allen began a new collaboration with Carlo Di Palma, which still continues. He later also collaborated with Sven Nykvist, who had been Bergman's cinematographer. (See **Carlo Di Palma** and **Sven Nykvist**.) Allen considers both Rosenblum and Willis outstanding professionals from whom he learned many important elements of his craft.

 Annie Hall further established Keaton as a major performer and Allen as a major filmmaker. She received an Academy Award for best actress, he for best director, and the movie for best film. *Annie Hall* also began a transition in Allen's work from pure comedy to films with deeper content that explore human longings and personal relationships. It also marked the shift from movies in which Allen's character is the central figure to films in which the female lead shares or exclusively possesses the central focus.

The early and mid-1970s were also a fruitful time for Allen's other creative work; he published his first two books, *Getting Even* and *Without Feathers*, wrote the plays *Death* and *God*, and debuted as a comic strip character in Stuart Hample's *Inside Woody Allen* (See **Inside Woody Allen**).

In 1978, Allen's work turned more serious, visually compelling, and cinematically sophisticated as he released the Bergman-like *Interiors*, followed in successive years by *Manhattan* and *Stardust Memories*, which along with *Deconstructing Harry* is his most experimental and postmodern film. *Stardust Memories* also inaugurated Allen's long-standing collaborations with music director Dick Hyman and Santo Loquasto, who began as a costumer and subsequently became the production designer for all of Allen's films from *Radio Days*, shot in 1985, to the present. Mel Bourne designed the films between *Annie Hall* and *Broadway Danny Rose*, and Stuart Wurtzel designed *The Purple Rose of Cairo* and *Hannah and Her Sisters*.

Allen's contract with United Artists ended after he completed *Stardust Memories*, and in 1980, he entered into a contract with Orion Pictures that granted him almost unprecedented artistic control. As long as he restricted his budgets to $8 to $10 million, then considered a moderate amount, Allen was free to make any film he wanted without having to submit a script for approval. Moreover, he retained complete control over all aspects of production and postproduction. Allen remained with Orion until 1991, when Orion filed for bankruptcy. He moved to TriStar to film *Husbands and Wives* and *Manhattan Murder Mystery*, and then to Sweetland Films and Miramax, which have distributed his movies since.

Allen met Mia Farrow in late 1979, and in 1980 they became a couple, although they never married and maintained separate apartments on opposite sides of Central Park. Farrow starred in thirteen of Allen's films between 1982 and 1992, from *A Midsummer Night's Sex Comedy* to *Husbands and Wives*. These include some of Allen's finest and most widely enjoyed films, such as *The Purple Rose of Cairo, Broadway Danny Rose, Hannah and Her Sisters, Radio Days*, and *Crimes and Misdemeanors*. *Hannah*, which was also nominated for best picture, won an Academy Award for best original screenplay, and Michael Caine and Dianne Wiest won as best supporting actor and actress, respectively. (Wiest received the award again for her performance in *Bullets over Broadway*.) Altogether, eleven of the seventeen films Allen released between 1977 and 1992 received at least one Academy Award nomination. (See **Academy Awards**.)

In 1980, Allen's third book of fiction, *Side Effects*, was published; in 1981, his play *The Floating Light Bulb* appeared on Broadway; and in 1987, Allen played a small role as the Professor in Jean-Luc Godard's *King Lear*.

His personal life also underwent significant changes. In 1985, he and Farrow adopted a newborn Texas girl, Dylan O'Sullivan Farrow, and two years later Farrow gave birth to Allen's son, Satchel O'Sullivan Farrow, named after Satchel Paige, the great baseball pitcher from the Negro League.

Allen's romantic and cinematic relationship with Farrow terminated in 1992, after Farrow discovered Allen's affair with her adopted daughter, Soon-Yi Previn. Farrow learned of the relationship while she and Allen were filming *Husbands and Wives*. Farrow subsequently accused Allen of sexually molesting Dylan. The resulting scandal became a media event that pushed the normally private Allen into the headlines and made his personal life the topic of conversation throughout the world. An investigation found insufficient grounds for criminal charges against Allen, but the judge presiding over the later custody trial was highly critical and denied Allen custody or visitation rights to the children. (See **Mia Farrow**.) Allen and Previn married in December 1997, and they have a adopted child, Bechet Dumaine Allen, named after jazz clarinetist Sidney Bechet.

Since the breakup with Farrow, Allen's career has continued in full force. Several of the post-Farrow films are happier and less serious, especially *Manhattan Murder Mystery*, *Mighty Aphrodite*, and *Everyone Says I Love You*, Allen's only musical comedy. Beautifully filmed in art deco settings, *Bullets over Broadway* raises some of the philosophical questions about morality in an absurd universe that Allen addresses in earlier films like *Crimes and Misdemeanors*. However, the tone in the later film is much lighter, more akin to *Broadway Danny Rose*, which is also a gangster comedy. On the other hand, *Deconstructing Harry* is uncharacteristically harsh; Allen answers his critics by presenting a caricature of himself that exaggerates all the negative things he has been accused of: being misogynistic, selfish and self-absorbed, anti-Jewish, sexually exploitive and perverse, and fundamentally unable to connect to other people. Echoing *Manhattan* and Federico Fellini's *La Dolce Vita* (1959), *Celebrity* returns to the familiar theme of a protagonist who suffers because of a failure in self-knowledge that results in misplaced priorities. At the same time, it reveals the shallowness and excess of the American culture of celebrity.

During the 1990s Allen remained productive in other areas too. In 1991, he appeared in Paul Mazursky's *Scenes from a Mall* with Bette Midler. In 1994, Allen aired his made-for-television remake of *Don't Drink the Water*, in which he plays the father. His play *Central Park West* enjoyed 343 performances on Broadway in 1995, as part of *Death Defying Acts*, a trilogy of one-act plays by Allen, Elaine May, and David Mamet. In 1996, he appeared again on television in Neil Simon's *The Sunshine Boys*, reviving the

role of a retired vaudeville performer originated by George Burns in 1975. Allen's 1996 jazz tour of Europe, in which he soloed as clarinetist, was the subject of Barbara Kopple's 1998 documentary, *Wild Man Blues*. That year Allen provided the voice of Z, a "little man" ant, in the animated film *Antz*.

Throughout his career Allen has returned to several basic themes and concerns, notably anxiety about death and the meaning of life; the question of proper, moral action in a meaningless universe; problems of loyalty and betrayal; the effects of neuroses on family dynamics and romantic relationships; the problem of sustaining love and passion simultaneously; and the problems that ensue when people fail to know themselves adequately and shape their lives around warped priorities. Moreover, the Holocaust is never far from his mind. (See **Death**; **Holocaust**; **"Random Reflections of a Second-Rate Mind."**)

The humor in his films often springs from the incongruities that arise because of these failures in self-knowledge or from other incongruities stemming from the problems that concern him. Allen's early characters, especially, are "little men" whose fears and ineptitude are the basis of the comedy. (See **Little-Man Humor**.) Allen also develops new cinematic forms and invents modernist and postmodernist structures to render his explorations in ways that reflect his belief that reality is irrational, inconsistent, subjective, and absurd. (See **Metafiction**; **Modernist Worldview**.) His screenplays are more word centered than those of most Hollywood movies, but especially since the late 1970s he has continued to develop his visual awareness and make visually interesting and sophisticated films. His fiction is playful, imaginative, and filled with literary and artistic allusions that he twists to humorous effect. (See **Literary Comedy**.)

The laughter that colors most of his work is integral to their aesthetic sensibility and final meaning. In the long run, Allen's artistic aspirations appear identical to those articulated by the abandoned minstrel in John Barth's story "Anonymiad":

Whimsic fantasy, grub fact, pure senseless music—none in itself would do; to embody *all* and rise above each, in a work neither longfaced nor idiotly grinning, but adventuresome, passionately humored, merry with the pain of insight, wise and smiling in the terror of our life—that was my calm ambition. (Barth, *Lost in the Funhouse* 198)

Annie Hall. A 1977 film directed by, written by, and starring Allen, who plays comedian Alvy Singer. It costars Diane Keaton (Annie Hall), Shelley Duvall (Pam), Colleen Dewhurst (Mother Hall), Carol Kane (Allison), Tony Roberts (Rob), Paul Simon (Tony Lacy), Christopher Walken (Annie's brother, Duane), and Marshall McLuhan, Dick Cavett, and Truman

Capote as themselves. Charles Joffe was the producer, Gordon Willis director of photography, Mel Bourne production designer, Ruth Morley costumer, and Ralph Rosenblum editor. Chris Ishii was responsible for the animation, and Marshall Brickman collaborated on the screenplay with Allen. The film has no musical soundtrack. United Artists was the North American distributor.

Annie Hall was the pivotal movie in Allen's career, and it was his first film to focus on the female protagonist instead of the male lead. It cost approximately $4 million to produce and grossed $19 million in U.S. and Canadian revenues (not including later video rentals and television revenues). *Annie Hall* was both a critical and financial success in the United States and Europe, and it established Allen as a major film director. It won Academy Awards for best picture, best screenplay, and best director. However, Allen, who was also nominated for best actor, declined to accept the award, because he believes awards ceremonies lack credibility. Indeed, in the movie, Alvy Singer, apparently speaking for Allen, denounces awards ceremonies and scornfully proposes to give an award to Adolf Hitler for best fascist dictator. Keaton, whose Annie Hall look created a fashion sensation, won an Academy Award for best actress.

Annie Hall explores the relationship between a forty-year-old neurotic New York Jewish man and a younger, insecure, midwestern, Protestant woman. Although humor still plays a substantial role in shaping the film's overall tone, in *Annie Hall*, for the first time, Allen's artistic intention as a writer-director extends beyond comedy alone. "It was a major turning point for me. I had the courage to abandon . . . just clowning around and the safety of complete broad comedy. I said to myself, 'I think I will try and make some deeper film and not be as funny in the same way. And maybe there will be other values that will emerge, that will be interesting or nourishing for the audience'" (*Woody Allen on Woody Allen* 75).

The script went through several incarnations before Allen settled on the final version. Originally the story was to be a murder mystery in which Annie Hall and her boyfriend, Alvy Singer, prove that the apparent suicide of a life-affirming philosophy professor was actually murder. In the next version the professor was replaced by a neighbor, an idea Allen later returned to in *Manhattan Murder Mystery*. (He returned to the suicidal philosopher in *Crimes and Misdemeanors*.) Next, the story became a farce set in Victorian England and then a stream-of-consciousness exploration of Alvy's mind as he turns forty and tries to understand his life. In that version, his relationship with Annie Hall was only one aspect of the story. Allen filmed and edited this version, which he entitled *Anhedonia*—a condition whose symptom, the inability to experience pleasure, is characteristic of Alvy but not Annie.

However, test audiences felt the Proustian free associations in this version lacked dramatic tension and failed to sustain interest. On the other hand, they were engaged by the love story between Annie and Alvy, which subsequently became the film's central focus.

In *Annie Hall* Allen begins the exploration of character and human relations that characterizes much of his subsequent work. As Sander H. Lee points out, the film introduces several new themes, notably a preoccupation with matters of freedom, responsibility, and proper action; an obsession with death; concern about gender roles; and interest in and suspicion of Freudian psychotherapy. *Annie Hall* also sustains Allen's practice of creating characters easily identified with himself, even though he insists that his films are not inherently autobiographical and that his real-life differences from these characters are more substantial than the similarities they share.

Like the real-life Allen, Alvy is a divorced, Jewish comedian who has appeared on popular late-night talk shows. He is a committed New Yorker who had been in therapy for many years. Alvy and Allen share similar tastes in music, similar disdain for cocaine and California, and similar appreciation of great literature. Moreover, the relationship between Alvy and Annie clearly mirrors Allen and Keaton's yearlong love affair in 1969–1970, before their developing interests took them in different directions. (In fact, Keaton's family name is Diane Hall.)

But Allen's admonition not to equate him with his character is well taken. Allen's perspective on Alvy far exceeds Alvy's perspective on himself. Indeed, Alvy's tragic flaw is that he lacks the insight about his neurosis that Allen possesses and presents before his audience. Presumably the real-life Allen, armed with this wisdom, is far more capable of constructive change, while Alvy remains not only mired in but completely identified with his anhedonia.

Annie, on the other hand, proves capable of growth as she evolves from a limited, insecure, and unaccomplished would-be singer to a cosmopolitan, self-assured, successful performing artist. Alvy plays both constructive and destructive roles in her evolution. Initially he assumes a paternal role, mentoring her as well as being her lover. And initially Annie thrives in her subservient, daughterly role, where she benefits from Alvy's greater knowledge about New York, literature, and high culture. Moreover, Alvy convinces Annie to begin psychological counseling, and he pays for her sessions.

Annie benefits significantly from her therapy, but as she becomes a healthier, more autonomous, and more fully actualized person—more accomplished, experienced, and independent—they are unable to manage the transition from their initial parent-child/mentor-apprentice relationship to one in which they function as equals. Sam Girgus points out in *The Films of*

Diane Keaton and Woody Allen in *Annie Hall*. Courtesy of
Photofest.

Woody Allen that Alvy's response to Annie's dream about being smothered
by Frank Sinatra captures the essence of the film. Alvy interprets the dream
to mean that Annie's singing career is making her feel threatened, but Annie's therapist has suggested that Sinatra symbolizes Alvy, whose last name
is Singer. Alvy finally gets the point, reluctantly. "So whatta you saying that
I—I'm suffocating you?" The scene underscores not only that Alvy is sti-
fling Annie but also his refusal to acknowledge this, even to himself. As
Girgus points out, "Even as Alvy confronts the truth, he avoids and represses it with a joke that follows about Annie's implied desire to castrate
the singer in the dream" (Girgus, *The Films of Woody Allen* 33).

Indeed, both Annie and Alvy fail to recognize that managing the transition from a mentor-student relationship to a partnership of equals is their
central challenge, though Annie intuits this from time to time. Consequently the relationship falls apart as Alvy refuses to try new experiences,
because these threaten to disrupt the security of familiar people and places
and undermine his role as the wiser, more knowledgeable, and more experi-

enced partner. At the same Annie, her eyes opened by her therapy and Alvy's tutelage, feels compelled to assert herself and explore new possibilities beyond those offered within Alvy's limited sphere. When it becomes apparent that Alvy cannot handle this, she finally leaves him, though they remain friends. The movie concludes by reminding us that even though the breakup was necessary in order for Annie to retain her spirit intact, Alvy was in many ways a positive influence in her life.

Because *Annie Hall* is fundamentally the story of a failed relationship between two likable, if imperfect, characters, it is difficult to call the film a comedy. But *Annie Hall* is a very funny movie. Because both Annie and Alvy are neurotic at the beginning of the film, their obsessions and insecurities make easy comic targets. However, as Annie begins to overcome her neuroses and become a stronger, more centered person, she becomes less the butt of the humor, and Alvy becomes more so. Thus, when he flies out to unfamiliar Los Angeles to try to retrieve her at the end of the movie, the jokes are entirely at Alvy's expense, or at California's, but never at Annie's. Their roles have become emphatically reversed; Annie now seems cosmopolitan and mature, and Alvy is whiny and infantile. When Alvy, a notoriously poor driver, creates mayhem in a parking lot and then loses his composure before a policeman because figures of authority intimidate him, he is reduced to a farcical figure.

Allen uses several innovative cinematic techniques to expose the humor of courtship, including voice-overs that contrast characters' thoughts to their words, animations that depict Annie and Alvy as characters from *Snow White*,[1] and a split screen that underscores the differences in their background—contrasting the placid, innocuous conversation at Annie's Wisconsin, Protestant family dinner to the passionate declarations, curses, and oaths at Alvy's New York, Jewish family table. Split screens also highlight comic incongruities between Annie and Alvy as they discuss their sex life with their respective psychiatrists. When asked how often they make love, Alvy declares it is almost never—three times a week; while Annie complains they have sex all the time—three times a week.

By intercutting scenes of Alvy's childhood, Allen also illustrates the Freudian premise that events and relationships from our childhood influence how we experience and respond to the world as adults. Allen uses this technique most effectively when he intercuts shots of young Alvy taking out his aggression in carnival bumper cars into the scene in which grown-up Alvy drives through a Los Angeles parking lot after Annie has turned down his request to get back together.

These innovations are also part of Allen's effort to find new narrative forms for telling his stories. True to the original Proustian conception of the film, the scenes are linked associatively, not causally. The movie begins not at the beginning but at the end, after Annie and Alvy have broken up for good. The scenes do not progress chronologically, but move dreamlike, jumping back and forth among different stages of the relationship. Passage of time is revealed in the improvement in Annie's singing, in her increasing willingness assert her own ideas and challenge Alvy's, in the diminishing joy of the relationship, and finally in Annie's relocation to California. The split screens make us aware of the protagonists' differing cultural heritages, which are always simultaneously present in each of them. Alvy's direct addresses to the audience help characterize him as someone seeking sympathy and understanding, someone who wants others to appreciate his side of the story—another subtle manifestation of his controlling personality.

The direct addresses also violate the traditional separation of the audience from the story found in most films. Instead, the addresses draw the audience members into the film, making them an interactive part of it. Allen and Keaton's own personal identification with Alvy and Annie further confuses the distinction between the inner world of the film and the outer world of real life, as does Allen's interjection of the real Marshall McLuhan as the ultimate authority to settle an argument between two cinematic characters, Alvy and a film professor. (Allen originally sought Federico Fellini for McLuhan's role.)

In fact, Allen uses these disparities between levels of reality to generate humor and highlight certain truths simultaneously. The McLuhan episode, for example, deflates authority. The pretentious professor is ultimately ridiculed for basing his claim to being right not on the soundness of his thoughts but on the authority of his academic position. McLuhan too fails on the same account. He asserts himself as the foremost authority on himself but speaks utter nonsense: "You mean, my whole fallacy is wrong." The conflation of the two levels of reality nonetheless leaves us with a solid sense of how pompous and ludicrous intellectual pretentiousness can be, a common theme of Allen.

Other examples of Allen's layering of reality include the voice-overs revealing the disparity between Annie and Alvy's thoughts and their words when they first become acquainted, Annie's dialogue with herself while she makes love without marijuana, and Alvy's visual projections of Grammy Hall's view of him as a Hasidic rabbi. The same narrative process that spawns the laughter in each of the scenes also reveals the characters' psychological states.

Thus, in *Annie Hall* Allen returns to a formal experiment he began two years earlier in his play *God* and made more central in *Stardust Memories* and *The Purple Rose of Cairo*. That experiment represents reality as layered and multidimensional and suggests that the different layers can become inverted and interwoven through art. Such interplay among the inner and outer layers of narrative date back at least to the play within the play in *Hamlet* and reappear as recently as John Barth's *Chimera* (1972), in which Scheherazade and a Barth-like genie spawn stories "framed from inside, as it were, so that the usual relation between container and contained would be reversed and paradoxically reversible" (Barth, *Chimera* 24). These and other narrative innovations not only place Allen within an ongoing literary tradition concerned with exploring the relationships among characters, authors, and audience members, but also demonstrate Allen's new awareness of form and of the expanded possibilities for presenting a story within the medium of cinema.

NOTE

1. The animations were anticipated by *Inside Woody Allen*, an internationally syndicated comic strip based on the Woody Allen persona that first appeared in 1976. (See **Inside Woody Allen**.)

***Another Woman*.** A 1988 film directed and written by Allen. It stars Gena Rowlands (Marion Post), Mia Farrow (Hope), Ian Holm (Dr. Ken Post), Blythe Danner (Lydia), Gene Hackman (Larry Lewis), Betty Buckley (Ken's ex-wife, Kathy), Martha Plimpton (Laura), John Houseman (Marion's father), David Ogden Stiers (Marion's father as a young man), Sandy Dennis (Claire), Philip Bosco (Marion's first husband, Sam), Harris Yulin (Marion's brother, Paul), Frances Conroy (Paul's wife, Lynn), Kenneth Welsh (Donald), Bruce Jay Friedman (Mark), and Michael Kirby (psychiatrist). Ben Gazzara had originally been cast as Ken, Jane Alexander as Hope, and Mary Steenburgen as Lynn. Robert Greenhut was the producer, Sven Nykvist director of photography, Santo Loquasto production designer, Jeffrey Kurland costumer, and Susan E. Morse editor. (This was the first collaboration between Allen and Nykvist, who was also Ingmar Bergman's regular cinematographer.) Erik Satie's "Gymnopédie no. 3" is the most prominently featured music. Orion Pictures was the North American distributor.

Allen hoped *Another Woman* would be the dramatic breakthrough that would establish him as a writer and director of dramatic films. After his initial screenings, he was enthusiastic, but he subsequently agreed with others that the film was cold. His final assessment is that *Another Woman* is "boring, ball-less. A cure for insomnia. . . . The movie is like [Satie's] music over the titles: wispy, unfocused." In more generous moments he praises the acting and describes the film as improved, but he remains dissatisfied with it

(Lax 342–345, 278). Several critics concur with Allen's negative assessment, including the *New Yorker*'s Pauline Kael, Amy Taubin of the *Village Voice*, and the *New York Times*'s Vincent Canby, a traditional Allen supporter who called the movie a "windy failure." On the other hand, Time's Richard Schickel praised its irony and subtlety. A financial failure as well, the film opened in only four U.S. theaters. It cost $10 million to produce and grossed only $1.6 million in North American rentals (not including later video rentals and television revenues). Though it fared somewhat better in Europe, it remained a significant moneyloser for Orion.

In her autobiography, Mia Farrow claims to have originated the idea of spying on a psychiatrist's sessions, and she states that Allen censured her when she suggested it in jest a year or so before they filmed *Another Woman*: " 'Would you want to define yourself as a person who would do that?' he asked disapprovingly" (Farrow 221–222). However, according to Allen, the plot device came from a humorous story he had worked on several years earlier in which thin walls allow a man to overhear an attractive woman talking to her analyst. He then uses the information she reveals to transform himself into the man of her dreams. Allen dropped the idea because at the time, he found the notion of eavesdropping on a psychiatric session too distasteful. Nonetheless, he returned to this original idea in *Everyone Says I Love You*, where DJ listens in on Von's therapy sessions and reports the results to Joe, who uses the information to seduce Von. And in *Alice*, Joe decides to reconcile with his ex-wife after listening in on her therapy session while he is invisible (*Woody Allen on Woody Allen* 190).

It is appropriate that the plot centers around psychoanalytical sessions because the story shows how Marion, a successful fifty-year-old philosophy professor, strips away layers of self-deception and comes to know her true self. The process requires recognizing and accepting her subconscious desires, and it involves attuning herself to communications from her subconscious, especially those that come in dreams. This Freudian-like experience forces Marion to reevaluate every important relationship in her life: her marriage, parents, brother, friends, and, most important, her own view of herself and her past actions and missed opportunities.

Although the process is painful, the woman who emerges at the end knows herself more fully and is therefore capable of feeling more deeply and enjoying life more completely. She admits to herself that she is lonely; she has wrongly sacrificed her family for her career; she enjoys making art; she judges others severely; she enjoys luring men from her female friends; she wants to have a child; and her abortion years earlier contributed heavily to both her ex-husband's suicidal despair and her own emotional isolation. Humbled by her recognitions, Marion becomes more compassionate and less judgmental of others. She becomes filled with new creative energy and achieves a level of self-acceptance she had not even known she was lacking.[1]

The opening shot suggests Marion's eventual illumination and rebirth. It shows Marion walking down a long, enclosed corridor that leads to the apartment she has just sublet. As she approaches the camera, her image grows, and she progresses from darkness into light. Her motion suggests both passage down a birth canal and the movement from the unconscious, which is traditionally associated with shadows, to consciousness, more often associated with light.

The story alternates between Marion's apartment and scenes from her private life. Although she has rented the apartment so she can write a new philosophical treatise without distractions, Marion quickly becomes caught up in a therapy session she overhears through the ventilation ducts. She becomes compelled by the story of Hope, a woman whose own life does not seem real to her. It is filled with deceptions that "had become so many and so much a part of me now that I couldn't even tell who I really was." Hope, who we later learn is pregnant, claims that she has nothing to look forward to, and she is considering suicide. (Farrow was pregnant with Allen's son, Satchel, at the time she played Hope. Her character's name appears only in the credits.)

Although Marion expresses sympathy for Hope's evident despair, initially she believes she has nothing in common with the younger woman, who seems utterly lost. By all external criteria, Marion epitomizes direction and success; younger women in particular admire her for her intellectual and professional accomplishments. Marion chairs the philosophy department at a prestigious woman's college; she is married to a capable cardiologist, and they are financially well off. She is surrounded by friends and seems comfortable with her family.

But the glimpses of Hope's despair spark within Marion an unconscious exploration of her own life. They initiate a process by which Marion becomes more aware of herself and her surroundings. Initially Marion resists such self-exploration. When she first describes herself, she is very controlled and emotionally guarded. She gives facts but expresses no feelings about them. Marion mentions dispassionately that her mother died recently and adds with relief that her father is all right. And she states that although she is not afraid of what she might find, she does not believe in looking too deeply into her life because "I've always felt that one should let things be as they are, if they work." Presumably Marion acquired these sentiments from her father, a scholar who asserts about his recently deceased wife, "There are times even an historian shouldn't look at the past."[2]

The early scenes establish that Marion thinks she has a warm relationship with her father, a loving one with her brother, a close one with her childhood friend, and a passionate one with her husband. But Hope's story attunes Marion to see these relationships, and herself, with new eyes.

Marion's initial association between Hope's life and her own comes after Marion awakens from a nap and hears Hope declaring how emotionally empty her marriage feels. Marion is in a foggy state between sleep and wakefulness when she first hears Hope's story, a state of consciousness wherein people are known to be especially susceptible to subconscious suggestion. Hope's words bypass the rational filters of Marion's consciousness that would normally inhibit any projection of herself into Hope's situation. Instead, in this hypnotic state, Hope's statements appeal directly to Marion's subconscious, and Marion's identification with Hope is allowed to take root.

The first indication that Marion is beginning to identify with Hope comes that evening at a party, when another couple describes an impulsive sexual episode. For the first time, Marion becomes aware of the absence of any such passion in her own marriage, even though it had been present years earlier when Ken was still married to someone else and they conducted an adulterous affair.

Marion's next inkling comes when her sister-in-law Lynn accuses her of being distant and blind to how much Marion's brother, Paul, hates Marion, as well as idolizes her. Declaring "I don't accept that," Marion refuses consciously even to consider the possibility that she and her brother are not "very close," as she believes. Instead, she quickly terminates the conversation in an emotionally detached, businesslike fashion. Nonetheless, Lynn has subconsciously planted the suggestion that Marion's relationship with Paul, a failed writer, failing entrepreneur, and poor provider, is not as loving as she believes.

Overhearing Hope confess that she had married the wrong man sparks in Marion a flashback to Larry Lewis, a passionate writer who rivaled Ken for Marion's affection. In her memory, Larry tries to point out that Ken is cold, but Marion sees her future husband as being emotionally in control. She recalls a toast in which Ken calls for good health and happiness but is taken to task for not saluting Marion, his bride-to-be. Although Ken extricates himself smoothly, declaring that he drinks to Marion with his eyes, it begins to become apparent to us and subconsciously to Marion that he is less than head over heels in love. According to Allen, Marion has married Ken because "she made safe choices and cold choices, but never the right ones," and these flashbacks provide her first vague awareness of this fact (*Woody Allen on Woody Allen* 196).

Hope's declaration that she keeps herself from thinking about real love restores Marion from her reverie and causes her to block out the therapy session by placing pillows over the vents. Nonetheless, Marion is noticeably flustered when her stepdaughter, Laura, arrives to join her for a visit to Marion's father's house in the country.

The visit stirs further memories and provides additional material for Marion to reevaluate, at least subconsciously. The scene also establishes how much Marion has modeled herself after her father and how much she seeks his approval. Her father's emotional detachment becomes evident in his desire to rid his house of all pictures, mementos, and other evidence of his late wife. When Laura asks him if, at his advanced age, he would like to fall in love again, he replies coldly that he hopes to build an "immunity to love." The exchange clearly disturbs Marion, though she covers her discomfort by taking Laura to task for indelicately pointing out that her father is old.

By suppressing her subconscious and repressing her deepest pleasures in order to win her father's approval, Marion has crushed her own spirit.[3] Marion admires her father, a board member of the Smithsonian, and she has emulated him in pursuing an academic career and placing her professional achievement above family relationships. She also adopts her father's no-nonsense approach to life that insists on individual responsibility and disapproves of any kind of dependency or frivolous behavior. In short, Marion has disassociated from her passions. And this denial of her bliss, as Joseph Campbell would call it, lies at the heart of her despair and emotional emptiness.

The soon-to-be-discarded photos occasion recollections that implicitly undermine Marion's placid view of her family life. Flashbacks show how their father made Paul work at a job that demoralized him, so Marion could attend college on scholarship and her father could take a sabbatical to complete an academic study. In shots evocative of Bergman's *Cries and Whispers* (1972) we see Marion's mother as a young woman, a lovely, romantic figure who cared only for nature, music, and poetry. Although Marion shared some of these sensibilities, her father criticized her for them, especially for "daydreaming in the woods with her beloved watercolors." As an adult, Marion has put these passions behind her, though she later identifies herself as an artist to Hope, who has also turned her back on her love for painting. The repudiation of their artistic inclinations is another rejection of their unconscious desires that contributes to the spiritual deprivation both women feel.

Although Marion does not acknowledge it, both she and her father censure Paul, who seems idle, without direction, and embarrassingly open in his expression of emotion. Reviewing the pictures, Marion remembers how Paul recognized and resented both parents' self-absorption, something Marion had apparently failed to see. Young Paul accused them of being so caught up in their own worlds that they neglected their children, a charge borne out by Marion's recollection that the maid, not her parents, sat up with her when she was sick as a child.

Marion has no great revelation during her visit, but it provides raw material for the dream sequence that stands at the heart of the movie and crystallizes her newly emerging view of her father and herself. In the dream, her father confesses to a psychiatrist that he had inverted his priorities by putting his scholarship ahead of his family and that he had wrongly closed off his family and cultivated a loveless life. He specifically regrets his cold treatment of his children and that the woman he shared his life with was not the one he loved most deeply.

After visiting her father, Marion runs into her childhood friend Clair, who opens Marion's eyes on another score. Though Marion has never recognized this in herself before, Clair tries to make her see how she has enjoyed stealing men from other women, even when Marion does not actually sleep with the men or pursue any relationship with them. In essence, her pleasure has come not from any passion or intimacy the men might offer—in fact Marion pointedly rejects their intimacy. Instead, she enjoys demonstrating that she is so fascinating and attractive that these men will abandon other women for her. Marion initially resists acknowledging this unpleasant aspect of herself, but eventually she does.

Marion's discomfort and her need for self-scrutiny are further provoked that night when she picks up a book of poems by Rainer Rilke, her mother's favorite poet, and reads the admonition of Apollo, stained years earlier by her mother's tears: "For here there is no place that does not see you. You must change your life" (from Rilke's "Archaic Torso of Apollo." Apollo is the Greek god who declares through the Delphic Oracle, "Know thyself!").

The cumulative effect of her sister-in-law's accusation, the visit to her father, the encounter with Clair, and the review of Rilke leaves the normally confident Marion feeling unusually vulnerable. A therapy session in which Hope remains silent provokes additional images of death from Rilke and then a recollection of Laura telling her boyfriend, after Marion has inadvertently caught them making love, that Marion is judgmental. Though the comment apparently had little impact at the time, Marion is now disturbed by Laura's fear that Marion will make her feel cheap by looking at her with the same censuring gaze that Marion gives her own brother.

Too troubled to write, Marion surrenders further to her subconscious. She wanders the streets with uncharacteristic aimlessness and finds herself visiting Paul, who points out how she has pushed him away, discouraged his creative expression, and rejected his expressions of deep feeling as embarrassing.

A second sleepless night leads to the nap that occasions her pivotal dream. As the dream unfolds, each new sequence focuses on someone increasingly closer to Marion's heart. It moves from Hope to her father to Ken to Larry Lewis and finally to her first husband, Sam. First Marion dreams she is discussing Hope's case with the psychiatrist, who asks Marion for her assessment. Marion's response that Hope suffers from self-delusion clearly applies to herself as well. So does the analyst's remark that Hope will drop her self-deceptions only when she is ready; until she does, she is slowly killing herself.

After her father admits his regrets, the dream features episodes from Marion's own life that reveal Marion's anger at Ken's lack of passion and her recognition that their sexual attraction has dissipated. By contrast, Larry Lewis's depth of feeling now looks appealing, but he has married someone else.

Larry's description in the dream of his daughter as "the greatest, most beautiful experience in my life" triggers new associations to Marion's first husband, Sam, and finally to her own long-repressed desire to have a child. Marion recognizes Sam's tenderness and her own detachment, and for the first time she entertains the possibility that his death was not an accidental mixture of drugs and alcohol, but suicide brought about by her rejection of him and his desire for a child.

The next day, when she actually meets Hope and takes her to lunch, Marion admits that she wishes she had had a child, something she has never said to anyone before, not even to herself. Then she remembers how her unilateral decision to abort Sam's baby, made over his objections and enacted without his knowledge, was ultimately an act intended to destroy his passion for her and leave her free to pursue her career ambitions without distraction. Later, Marion overhears Hope telling her therapist that Marion is afraid of passion and that behind Marion's abortion was a fear of the emotions she would feel for a baby.

Finally, Marion's journey into the recesses of her subconscious causes her to reassess her marriage to Ken. The evening after her dream, she accuses him of wanting to be alone and asks why he no longer sleeps with her. As in her dream, Ken avoids giving a straight answer, and she asserts, "I hadn't realized how much of that had slipped away until today." The next day, while she is dining with Hope, Marion accidentally spies Ken having a romantic lunch with her close friend Lydia. When Marion later confronts him, she admits that they have both been lonely within their marriage. After he questions this, she proclaims her new level of insight: "At least I've come to recognize it."

By the end of the story Marion not only identifies with Hope; she has reversed roles with her. At her final session, Hope describes Marion's despair with the same detached sympathy Marion expressed for her at the beginning. Hope believes Marion has nothing, leads a cold cerebral life, cannot allow herself to feel, and has alienated everyone around her. She says that Marion pretends everything is fine but that Marion is actually lost. She accuses Marion of being terrified of passion.

The fact that Hope terminates her therapy shortly after meeting Marion and hearing her story suggests that Hope too may have grown from her encounter with Marion. In recognizing Marion's fear of passion and the despair that results from it, Hope may have finally learned to address these issues in her own life.

However, Allen leaves this an open question. It is also possible that Hope's terminated psychotherapy implies that she has terminated her life or her fetus's, or that some other crisis has ensued. The therapist says only that Hope has moved away, and certainly the sentiments she had expressed before the final session compel us to consider these unhappy possibilities. But the young woman's newly revealed ability to sympathize with someone else's plight leaves her less self-absorbed and creates a broader context for viewing her own life. And this leaves us with "hope" for a happier ending. Allen's modernist worldview, which asserts that we live in a basic state of uncertainty, precludes him from resolving the question either way. In the end, viewers must make a leap of faith if they are to believe that Hope is now willing to surrender her own self-deceptions and become healthier and happier.

The prospects for Marion, on the other hand, are brighter. Though humbled and pained by her journey of self-enlightenment, she is open for the first time since childhood to forming closer bonds to people she loves and to experiencing real intimacy and passion. She reconciles with her brother, regards Laura less condescendingly, and finally looks through Larry Lewis's novel, which contains a character based on her. After reading his description of herself as someone "capable of intense passion if she would one day just allow herself to feel," Marion admits to experiencing "a strange mixture of wistfulness and hope. . . . For the first time in a long time, I felt at peace."

NOTES

1. Marion's central revelation that her life, which she thought had achieved the epitome of success, is actually empty, cold, and lonely parallels the major insight gleaned by the protagonist of Bergman's *Wild Strawberries* (1957). Richard

A. Blake elaborates: "Marion's confident affirmation of interior peace and her smile in the final scene are reminiscent of Prof. Isak Borg's peaceful vision at the end of Ingmar Bergman's *Wild Strawberries*, after which Allen clearly modeled *Another Woman*. Both [protagonists] . . . discover that the loneliness they find in their later years is really the result of their own coldness. . . . Allen seems not only to have reached a truce with the universe, but to have acknowledged his past exaggeration of its hostility. One who finds the world an unloving place may in fact simply be an unloving person" (Blake 164).

Bergman's *Persona* (1966) is another influence. Like *Another Woman*, it shows how the lives of two women mirror each other, although one is presumably healthy and the other mentally disturbed.

2. Allen claims to share this lack of introspection and to identify with Marion, a character who avoids intimacy by immersing herself in her work. Even though he spent many years in psychoanalysis (he discontinued it soon after marrying Soon-Yi Previn in 1997), Allen states, "I've never re-evaluated my life! I've always kept my nose to the grindstone. All I do is work, and my philosophy has always been that if I . . . just focus on my work everything else will fall into place" (*Woody Allen on Woody Allen* 192).

3. Sander H. Lee discusses the significance of Marion's apparent professional rejection of the philosophy of Martin Heidegger. Heidegger "describes how one is faced with the choice of either becoming authentic or inauthentic. The authentic person chooses to fulfill her caring nature, even though this means exposing the vulnerable parts of herself to a world of others who can sometimes treat her harshly. On the other hand, the inauthentic person . . . hides one's real nature behind a mask designed to superficially satisfy the demands of others without exposing one's true self to the inspection of the world." In these terms, *Another Woman* becomes the story of Marion's transformation from an inauthentic person to an authentic one (Lee 238).

Antz. A 1998 animated film in which Allen narrates the voice of Z, the film's protagonist. It also features the voices of Sharon Stone (Princess Bala), Sylvester Stallone (Weaver), Gene Hackman (General Mandible), Jennifer Lopez (Azteca), Christopher Walken (Colonel Cutter), Dan Aykroyd (Chip, Wasp #1), Anne Bancroft (queen), Jane Curtin (Muffy, Wasp #2), Danny Glover (Barbatus), John Mahoney (drunk scout in bar), Paul Mazursky (psychologist), and Grant Shaud (foreman). Eric Darnell and Tim Johnson directed, and Todd Alcott, Chris Weitz, and Paul Weitz wrote the screenplay. Brad Lewis, Aron Warner, and Patty Wooton were the producers; Harry Gregson-Williams and John Powell music directors, John Bell production designer, Kendal Cronkhite art director, and Stan Webb editor. Lawrence Guterman directed additional sequences. The soundtrack includes "Give Peace a Chance," "Almost Like Being in Love," "I Can See Clearly Now," "High Hopes," and "Guantanamera." Ellen Weiss has pub-

lished a junior novelization (1998) and an *Antz Storybook* (1998). Dream-
Works was the North American distributor.

The computer-animated film was rated PG and directed at a mixed audience of adults and children. Budgeted at $65 million, it was the Dream-
Works studio's attempt to elevate film animation to a new plateau. *Antz* was
highly praised for its visual effects. The characters appear more as carved
wooden figures than drawn ones, and their facial expressions enable them to
"act" by revealing emotions, attitudes, and intentions with nuanced ges-
tures. Bruce Kirkland of the *Toronto Sun* praised the film as having superior
visual scope, social commentary, and star power than Disney's animated
Toy Story (1995), which had set the new standard for animated film. Shortly
after the release of *Antz*, Disney issued its rival film, *A Bug's Life* (1998).
Cosponsored by Pepsi Cola, whose products are featured in the movie, *Antz*
did well at the box office, though some reviewers found its content and language somewhat advanced for children. Allen was considered especially
well cast for his role.

A tribute in many ways to Fritz Lang's *Metropolis* (1926) and George
Lucas's *Star Wars* (1977), *Antz* promotes individual expression, original
thought, and independent action over mass conformity. In this respect it recalls the antiestablishment, "do your own thing" sentiments of the Vietnam
War–era counterculture, as represented in such films as Robert Altman's
M*A*S*H (1970), Robert Rush's *Getting Straight* (1970), and Hal Ashby's
Harold and Maude (1971). *Antz* presents similar values to the children and
grandchildren of the counterculture generation. At the same time, its rejection of a controlled society in which individual needs are subordinated to
the greater society and children's destinies are assigned at birth appears as a
Cold War anachronism in which the personal freedoms celebrated by the
West are contrasted to the regimentation of a communist-like police state.

The story centers around a worker ant named Z-4195, whose personality
mirrors Allen's little-man characters. Like Allen's characters, Z has lived
his entire life in the big city; he feels insignificant and seeks fulfillment in
his work and relationships. A middle child in a family of millions, he suffers
from abandonment issues: "My father flew away when I was just a larva."
He is not reassured when his psychiatrist informs him that his feelings of in-
significance stem from the fact that he *is* insignificant, or when his female
coworker Azteca feeds him the party line that "It's not about you. It's about
us, the team."

Z falls in love with Princess Bala when she dons a disguise and goes
slumming in a workers' bar. A strong-willed, independent spirit, Bala is attracted by Z's nonconformity. But they are from different social strata, and
she is engaged to the fascistic General Mandible who, unbeknown to any

but his inner circle, plans to destroy the entire colony and begin a new, stronger one from his union with Bala. His diabolical plot makes obvious reference to Hitler's plans for a master race, as well as to more contemporary proposals based on genetic engineering. Therefore, the ultimate triumph of the ordinary worker ants serves to repudiate such arrogant philosophies of eugenics.

Mandible's cynical manipulation of Bala's mother, the queen, reveals the dangers that arise when excessive and unwarranted fear is interjected into national policy. Moreover, Mandible's Machiavellian use of power contributes to the movie's Cold War subtext and recalls Burt Lancaster's performance as the treacherous General Scott in *Seven Days in May* (1964). By appealing to national security, Mandible convinces the queen to launch a preemptive strike against a nearby termite population with whom the colony had been enjoying good relations. In fact, the general has provoked the termite threat in order to send all of the troops loyal to the queen on a suicide mission, thereby enabling him to pull off his coup.

In order to gain Bala's attention at an official parade, Z has switched jobs for the day with his friend Weaver, a burly soldier ant who subsequently meets and falls in love with Azteca. But Z has the luck of an Allen little man and finds himself assigned to the suicide mission. However, like Boris in *Love and Death*, Z returns an accidental hero, the sole survivor from either side of the battle. He again meets Bala when he is presented to the court for his heroism, but when General Mandible discovers that Z and Bala had danced together, he orders Z arrested. To save himself, Z takes Bala hostage and escapes to the outside world, where he drags the unwilling princess with him as he searches for the legendary Insectopeia.

Bala's character resembles Princess Leia's from *Star Wars*, and her grudging love for Z evolves similarly to Leia's for Han Solo. When Mandible's henchman abducts Bala, Z, like Han, suppresses his selfish inclinations and returns to the nest to rescue her. There they discover Mandible's plan to flood the colony and drown all the workers, but in a sequence evocative of the ending to *Metropolis*, they organize the workers and save the colony. The film thus ends happily with Z back in therapy, this time trying to get in touch with his inner maggot. Z has sacrificed and risked everything for the colony. But even though he is back where he started, subordinating himself to the well-being of the collective, he is now content because this time he chose his destiny.

B

Bananas. A 1971 film directed by, written by, and starring Allen, who plays Fielding Mellish. It costars Louise Lasser (Nancy), Carlos Montalban (General Vargas), Natividad Abascal (Yolanda), Jacobo Morales (Esposito), Miguel Suarez (Luis), David Ortiz (Sanchez), Rene Enriquez (Diaz), Jack Axelrod (Arroyo), Sylvester Stallone (juvenile delinquent on train), Howard Cosell (himself), Roger Grimsby (himself), and Don Dunphy (himself). Jack Grossberg was the producer, Andrew M. Costikyan director of photography, Marvin Hamlisch musical director, Ed Wittstein production designer, Gene Coffin costumer, and Ralph Rosenblum editor. Mickey Rose collaborated on the screenplay, which is loosely suggested by Richard Powell's novel, *Don Quixote, U.S.A.* (1966), and Allen's story "Viva Vargas" from *Getting Even* (first published in *Evergreen Review*, August 1969). United Artists was the North American distributor.

Made during the politically charged Vietnam War era, Allen's second directorial effort was a modest financial and critical success. It was filmed mostly in Puerto Rico, where the production company benefited from facilities and tax incentives offered by the governor. *Bananas* cost $2 million to produce and grossed about $3.5 million in U.S. and Canadian distribution (not including later video rentals and television revenues). American reviewers typically found *Bananas* funny but lightweight; the French were more enthusiastic. Vincent Canby of the *New York Times*, an early supporter of Allen's films, acknowledged its thin plot and noted that the individual gags and skits do not add up to very much, but he maintained that the freestanding scenes were funny enough to make the movie worthwhile. According to Canby, when Allen "is good, [he] is inspired. However, when he's bad, he's not rotten; rather, he just not so hot."

Bananas consists of two very loosely connected plotlines. The film begins and ends with Fielding Mellish's romance with Nancy, a caricature of 1960s liberal, politically active, college coeds. But in the middle of the film, Nancy breaks off the relationship and thereby introduces the second plotline, as Fielding becomes caught up in a populist revolution against a military dictatorship in San Marcos, a thinly disguised comic version of Cuba during the communist revolution of the late 1950s. The two plotlines are joined only by the facts that Nancy campaigns to support the revolution and Fielding goes to San Marcos to sort things out after their breakup. Some critics suggest that the personal growth Fielding experiences while in San Marcos enables him to win Nancy and resolve the first plotline. Nancy Pogel, for instance, believes that Fielding "anticipates a developing self-awareness and concern for personal integrity in Allen's little-man characters" (Pogel 45). However, none of the characters experiences any significant character development—except the rebel leader, who goes insane with power—and the resolutions of both plotlines seem deliberately contrived and do not result from any personal transformations.

The Fielding-Nancy plotline draws its humor primarily by deflating Fielding and depicting him as a "little man," while the revolution scenes rely more heavily on satire, parody, and absurd play. The Fielding-Nancy story characterizes Fielding as inadequate, inept, lonely, and sexually frus-

Woody Allen in *Bananas*. Photo by Brian Hamill. Courtesy of Photofest.

trated. Women will not date him, and his friends will no longer arrange blind dates. He finally scores a date with Nancy, who comes to his door seeking signatures for a political petition, but only because he pretends to share her interests in metaphysics, Eastern philosophy, and revolutionary politics—popular topics in the early 1970s among liberal, intellectual college students and members of the counterculture. Although Fielding eventually seduces Nancy, who apparently also believes in free love—another social cause of the time—she ultimately rejects him because she feels "something is missing." However, when he later returns as president of San Marcos, she agrees to marry him, even though she still notices that something is missing after they make love. Thus, Fielding's inadequacy remains an integral aspect of their relationship.

On the one hand, because Fielding is a little man and we feel superior to him, the exaggerated accounts of his sexual shortcomings seem funny. On the other hand, should we ever think seriously about the prospects for their relationship, we must anticipate its demise, since Fielding is so clearly unable to fulfill Nancy sexually, emotionally, intellectually, or in any other way. However, the farcical nature of the movie does not invite us to consider whether they live happily ever after, only whether they surmount the most immediate obstacles to their love.

His inadequacy and misfortune are also the basis for most of the humor from that section. Fielding is especially inept with machines and appliances. For instance, he works as a product tester, but, in a tribute to Charles Chaplin's *Modern Times* (1936), the exercise machine he demonstrates turns on him and attacks him. His father is a surgeon who dreams, like many other Jewish men of his generation, that someday his son will take over the family practice. However, in this context, the aspiration appears absurd. When Fielding drops by in the middle of an operation, his father insists that Fielding can perform the surgery. Fielding agrees to try, despite his protestations that he has no aptitude, but when he seems likely to botch the entire operation, his mother, the nurse, sends him away before he can do serious harm.

The disparity between who he is and who he pretends to be sparks laughter as Fielding attempts to seem suave, debonair, and accomplished. He tries to disguise his purchase of a sex magazine by buying several highbrow journals as well, but his attempt to disguise his genuine lascivious nature and suggest instead that he cares only for the life of the mind is frustrated when the cashier calls out to his coworker to check the price of *Orgasm*. On the subway, Fielding tries to ignore a gang of juvenile delinquents beating up the old lady beside him until the train stops. Just before the doors close, he pushes the youths out of the car and poses as a hero. But then the doors re-open, and he must flee ignominiously, leaving the old lady to savor his copy of *Orgasm*. Similarly, when he first meets Nancy, he pretends to know more about her interests than he really does, and though he fools her, he does not fool the audience, which enjoys the ineptitude of his deception. His ultimate embodiment as a little man comes when he pretends to be a great and passionate lover but proves to be out of shape and mediocre at best. Nancy expresses her surprise that it all went by so fast, but she concedes to Howard Cosell, who has covered their wedding night for ABC's Wide World of Sports, "He's not the worst I've had. Not the best. But not the worst."

Fielding derives his appeal as a little man from his persistent search for intimacy, community, and acceptance, even though his pretensions undermine those goals. According to Pogel, Fielding "is interested in love, sex, and survival; however, the little soul's instinctive longing for an innocence that requires trust is in constant conflict with the painful realities of modern experience. . . . Fielding's comic struggle to win his girl stresses the quest for intimacy and the importance of personal relationships—the longing for a world where love may still triumph over death" (Pogel 39–40).

Satire, farce, and parody are more characteristic of the San Marcos plotline, and these give the film explicit political content that is absent from most of Allen's other work. Consequently, the San Marcos story, though largely a farce, is darker and more pointed than the Fielding-Nancy romance. Although Fielding's little-man persona accounts for some of the humor in the San Marcos section, such as when he fails to reassemble a rifle while blindfolded or when another soldier urinates on him while he is camouflaged as a tree, political personalities and social institutions become increasingly important objects of ridicule.

The satiric mode gives a harder edge to Allen's absurdist spirit, which until this point in Allen's career had been mostly play purely for play's sake. In *Bananas* even though we laugh, Allen reminds us of atrocities that actually happened and continued to happen throughout the 1970s. But in the long run, Allen rejects political solutions, since they always seem to result in outrageous action, no matter who wields the power.

For instance, Allen renders as farce the mass executions that the revolutionaries conduct following their victory. Fielding announces numbers for the awaiting victims as though he is a deli clerk calling out to customers, and in one slapstick gag, he struggles to get out of the way of a firing squad when his finger becomes stuck in the victim's blindfold. Although it is funny, the scene featuring cheering crowds celebrating the public executions nonetheless evokes the excesses of the French Revolution and Fidel Castro's Cuban revolution. It thus underscores the very real human slaughter that occurs when revolutions go amok, even as it garners laughs. But Allen does not take sides: he reminds us why the revolution was launched in the first place. When one of the dictator's cohorts is charged with committing mass murder and torturing women and children, he ludicrously pleads, "Guilty, with an explanation."

The major personalities Allen satirizes are Castro and Fulgencio Batista, the military dictator of Cuba whom Castro overthrew in 1959. In a cynical attempt to alienate American sympathies for the revolution, General Vargas (Batista's counterpart) tries to arrange Fielding's assassination and blame it on the revolutionaries. This causes the audience's sympathies to flow to the rebels, who befriend Fielding and appear dedicated, self-sacrificing, and committed to the people. This movement of audience sympathies mirrors the actual support Castro enjoyed in the United States during and immediately after his revolution, when he was viewed by many Americans as a reformer replacing a corrupt and abusive regime. But just as Castro eliminated his political opposition, executed members of Batista's government, and made himself sole ruler of Cuba, the rebel leader Ernesto becomes power crazed when the revolutionaries topple Vargas. His manifestos are funny because they are absurd: the official language of San Marcos will now be Swedish; children under sixteen years of age are now sixteen years of age; all citizens must change their underwear every half-hour—and wear it on the outside so the government can check. But at the same time that Ernesto's ridiculous decrees generate laughter, they also make Allen's point that absolute power corrupts absolutely, and they imply that Castro, in particular, has been corrupted.

The scenes of Fielding's prosecution by the U.S. government also point to real-life abuses of political power. Allen ridicules the politically motivated trial of the Chicago Seven—antiwar activists who were charged with conspiring to incite a riot at the 1968 Democratic convention in Chicago. Just as the Chicago Seven tried to point out the unfairness of the trial by turning it into a real-life farce, Allen transforms Fielding's trial into cinematic farce. In particular, Allen highlights the treatment of real-life Black Panther Bobby Seals, whom Judge Julius Hoffman ordered gagged and bound to his chair after Seals's frequent outbursts. In *Bananas* Fielding acts as his own defense attorney and cross-examines a witness while he is bound and gagged. Though he is incoherent, he intimidates her and forces her to retract her testimony. Earlier, Fielding interrogates himself on the witness stand. A police officer calls Fielding "a New York, Jewish, intellectual, Communist crackpot," but adds, "I don't want to cast no aspersions." And a large black woman claiming to be FBI director J. Edgar Hoover in disguise testifies against Fielding, as does Miss America, who sings an operatic aria and then preaches the bland kind of political philosophy commonly expressed in beauty pageants: "Differences of opinion should be tolerated, but not when they are too different. Then he becomes a subversive mother." In addition to providing several funny moments, the trial scene conveys a view of middle America that is smug in its sense of superiority and intolerant of diversity and outsiders.

Allen also satirizes American media. In particular, he uses his humor to highlight the blurring between news and entertainment and the obfuscation of public and private life. The opening sequence, for instance, presents a political killing as though it is simply another hyped sports event that we can watch live on television from the comfort of our homes. It begins with real-life sportscaster Don Dunphy introducing the imminent assassination of the president of San Marcos by Vargas's agents. First, Dunphy comments approvingly on the crowd's excitement and describes how the traditional bombing of the U.S. embassy and beating of the labor leader have already taken place. Next, Dunphy points out where the president will be walking and otherwise clues his viewers about what to anticipate, much as he might instruct them what to watch for in a football game or a basketball match-up.

After the murder, Dunphy cuts to Howard Cosell, another real-life sports announcer known for his aggressive style, grating voice, and brutal "tell it like it is" reporting. Allen satirizes the media's arrogance as Cosell pushes his way through the crowd, ordering them to make way for American television. His attitude takes for granted that his mission—satisfying the curiosity of an uninvolved worldwide audience—is more important than allowing the citizens of San Marcos access to their fallen leader. Allen thus generates humor by incongruously representing the assassination as a sporting event. At the same time, he shows that television has transformed even the most serious aspects of political life into entertainment for passive consumers. Moreover, in an era when the ability to manipulate television coverage translates into political power, Allen makes us aware how television's interests and requirements have come to supersede everyone else's.

Private life, too, becomes fodder for the public's unquenchable appetite for entertainment. The film ends with Cosell announcing Fielding and Nancy's wedding night as though it is a boxing match. The scene is funny because of the lovemaking as prize-fight conceit, but the invasive television camera and Cosell's bombastic commentary about this most intimate aspect of Fielding's life also highlight how tasteless and insensitive television reporting has become as it panders to the public's voyeuristic desires and insistence on being entertained.

As he does frequently in his films, Allen alludes to several film classics, including Sergei Eisenstein's *Battleship Potemkin* (1925) and the Marx Brothers' *Duck Soup* (1933). These references achieve multiple effects, paying homage to the earlier work while simultaneously creating inside jokes for viewers who recognize the allusions. Pogel notes an additional, more pernicious effect: "While creating comic irony, the references suggest how quickly older films and the meaningful responses they originally evoked can become conventionalized. On the one hand, Allen's reflexive film appeals to a nostalgia for great film moments, and on the other, it demonstrates how even this film participates to some extent in the distancing and desensitization of an audience" (Pogel 41).

Allen often mixes absurdist, playful sensibility with satirical attacks. He shows us CIA ineptitude and double-dealing—a favorite target of 1970s liberals and leftists. We learn from American paratroopers en route to San Marcos that this time the agency is taking no chances; it is supporting both sides of the revolution. But Allen's humor becomes more absurd than satiric when Vargas's henchman mistakenly calls in the UJA (United Jewish Appeal) instead of the CIA, and a small army of Hasidic Jews carrying donation cans marches through the streets during the height of the fighting, soliciting change from the soldiers.

Allen sports with Christian images too, mostly in an absurdist fashion that makes no special point. Fielding dreams he has been crucified and is being carried on a cross through the streets of New York. When a parking space appears, the robed men carrying him go to park the cross. But a group carrying another crucified man steals the space, and a fight ensues. In another scene, Fielding evades pursuing soldiers. He camouflages himself by holding up a tire iron as though it is a cross and then joins a passing religious processional. These scenes make no judgments and appear solely in the spirit of irreverent play.

However, the television commercial in which a priest endorses New Testament cigarettes certainly targets the clergy for selling out for financial gain. It also implicitly strikes at other voices of authority that over the years endorsed cigarettes. (In the 1950s, for instance, doctors appeared in cigarette ads.)

A mixture of farce and satire, *Bananas* is Allen's most overtly political film, apart from his never-broadcast satire on the Nixon administration, *Men in Crisis: The Harvey Wallinger Story. Bananas* reflects Allen's liberal politics of the era, as he spoofs such right-wing icons as J. Edgar Hoover, the FBI, the CIA, and the National Rifle Association, which, a news bulletin informs us, has determined death to be "a good thing." At the same time, the movie cautions against liberals and leftists who go too far. Like many other Americans during that turbulent, Cold War–dominated, Vietnam War–dominated time, Allen ultimately expresses his distrust of all political solutions. Instead, like a popular bumper sticker of the period, he encourages us to "Question Authority." But although Allen's own questioning leaves him much to be cynical about, his humor and the happy, if contrived, ending between Fielding and Nancy transforms the latent cynicism into something more life affirming.

See also **Little-Man Humor**.

Bergman, Ingmar. A Swedish film and theater director whom Allen greatly admires and whose work has significantly influenced Allen's. Born in 1918, Bergman is one of the premier twentieth-century directors. His notable films include *The Seventh Seal* (1956), *Wild Strawberries* (1957), *Persona* (1966), *Cries and Whispers* (1972), *Scenes from a Marriage* (originally made for television, 1974), *The Magic Flute* (a cinematic version of the Mozart opera originally made for television, 1975), *Autumn Sonata* (1978), and *Fanny and Alexander* (1982). Like Allen, Bergman repeatedly uses the same actors in his films, notably Bibi Andersson, Harriet Andersson, Liv Ullmann, and Max Von Sydow. Allen played off Bergman's association with Von Sydow by casting the actor to play an alienated, nihilistic artist in *Hannah and Her Sisters*. Allen also employed Sven Nykvist, Bergman's favorite cinematographer, to film *Another Woman*, *Oedipus Wrecks*, *Crimes and Misdemeanors*, and *Celebrity*. As television writers, Allen and Larry Gelbart satirized *Wild Strawberries* in a skit entitled "Strange Strawberries" that they wrote for Art Carney's special, *Hooray for Love*. In *Manhattan* Ike defends Bergman at length against Mary's charge that he belongs in the Academy of Overrated. Apparently speaking for Allen, Ike declares Bergman is "the only genius in cinema today."

Mary complains that Bergman cultivates an adolescent, "fashionable pessimism" that one outgrows: "It's bleak! My God! I mean all that Kierkegaard. . . . I mean the silence, God's silence! OK, OK, OK! . . . I think you absolutely outgrow it." But for Allen, the issues Bergman confronts never vanish, and we do not outgrow them. In this respect, Bergman's appeal is similar to that of Shakespeare, Chekhov, and Dostoyevsky. They all grapple with deep existential questions that probe the meaning of life, proper exercise of free will in an absurd universe, the desirability of moral choices in an absurd universe, and the possibilities of redemption in an afterlife. In addition to these themes, Allen admires Bergman's ability to tell a rich story using visual images and other properties of the camera.

According to Allen, *The Seventh Seal* is "the definitive work on the subject" of death (*Woody Allen on Woody Allen* 210). It thus addresses Allen's anxiety about death more directly than any other work of literature and exerts one of the strongest influences on him. The film asks how it is possible to live an authentic, meaningful life in an absurd universe that has neither inherent meaning nor intrinsic moral structure. Set during the outbreak of the plague during the Middle Ages, the movie centers around a Scandinavian knight who, like Hamlet, is tortured by his need to know what happens to us after death. Is good rewarded and evil punished? The knight's paralyzing obsession with this unanswerable question and its moral implications is contrasted by his action-oriented squire's dismissal of their relevance. It also contrasts the pure love of a young married couple, a pair of traveling carnival performers who are the only ones to survive after the knight sacrifices himself on their behalf in what he hopes is a meaningful act. But in the long run not even Death himself knows what lies beyond life, and each person is left to come to terms with mortality alone.

Allen alludes to *The Seventh Seal* on several occasions, usually by translating it into a joke. His play *Death Knocks*, parodies the film directly. In Bergman's film the knight forestalls Death by offering a game of chess when Death comes to claim him. In *Death Knocks* a Jewish man puts off Death by defeating him in gin rummy. *Love and Death* also parodies *The Seventh Seal*. It too poses the big existential questions, but it spoofs them as it asks them. It also features Death personified, and the final shot is a comic exaggeration of the ending to *The Seventh Seal*. *Deconstructing Harry* likewise personifies Death, who wrongly claims a young reprobate in a case of mistaken identity.

Although Allen characteristically downplays the similarities, several of his films appear to be patterned after or significantly influenced by Bergman movies. In some cases, such as in *A Midsummer Night's Sex Comedy* and *Another Woman*, Allen imitates specific shots from Bergman films. In other instances the similarities are thematic or center around specific conflicts within relationships. For instance, *Interiors* and *Cries and Whispers* both explore the dynamics of a family dominated by an emotionally disturbed mother. In particular, they show how the mother's inability to project love shapes her three daughters' interactions with her, their father, and each other. *A Midsummer Night's Sex Comedy* and *Smiles of a Summer Night* are both loosely based on Shakespeare's *A Midsummer Night's Dream*. Each employs an enchanted outdoor setting to redistribute the pairings of mismatched couples. *September* and *Autumn Sonata* (1978) both center around a dysfunctional daughter who loves, hates, and is in awe of her accomplished but emotionally distant mother. Like *Persona*, *Another Woman* shows how the lives of two women mirror each other, although one is presumably healthy and the other mentally disturbed. Furthermore, Marion's central revelation that her life, which she thought had achieved the epitome of success, is actually empty, cold, and lonely, parallels the major insight gleaned by the protagonist of *Wild Strawberries*. And *Husbands and Wives* appears to be patterned after *Scenes from a Marriage*. In both films, close friends' decision to divorce leads to the dissolution of the marriage of an apparently happy couple. The title of Paul Mazursky's *Scenes from a Mall* (1991), in which Allen stars, both deflates *Scenes from a Marriage* for comic purposes and echoes it for serious ones.

For additional reading, see Bergman's autobiographies, *The Magic Lantern* (1988), which Allen reviewed, and *Images: My Life in Film* (1994).

Bogart, Humphrey. A film actor who starred in tough-guy roles in 1940s gangster and *film noir* movies. Among his best-known characters are Sam Spade in *The Maltese Falcon* (1941), Roy Earle in *High Sierra* (1941), Rick Blaine in *Casablanca* (1942), Harry Morgan in *To Have and Have Not* (1944), Philip Marlowe in *The Big Sleep* (1946), and Frank McCloud in *Key Largo* (1948). Bogart died of cancer in 1957 at age fifty-eight.

Bogart's cynical, self-assured, hard-drinking, fist-fighting persona is the antithesis of Allen's intimidated, insecure, incompetent little man. (See **Little-Man Humor**.) For several of Allen's comic personas, Bogart represents a true "man's man"—a worldly, self-possessed ideal to aspire to. But Allen's self-deprecating humor also exposes and somewhat deflates the Bogart character, as well as his own. Allen clearly enjoys the Bogart persona, but it would be wrong to conclude that, like his character Allan Felix from *Play It Again, Sam*, Allen would wish to emulate it in real life. In fact, much of the humor from *Play It Again, Sam* is derived from the inappropriateness of Bogart's behavior to Felix's middle-class, professional world.

The differences between Allen's comic and Bogart's tough guy personas are most evident in the way they relate to women. Allen's characters are mush around the opposite sex—clumsy, bashful, and inarticulate; and the women who attract him frequently reject him. By contrast, Bogart's characters are confident, aloof, and always in demand. A "love 'em and leave 'em" sort, Bogart "never met [a dame] that didn't understand a slap in the mouth or a slug from a .45" (*Play It Again, Sam*). But Bogart's characters typically also have a noble and sentimental side buried beneath their tough veneer, and Allen also exploits that aspect of Bogart in his work.

Allen's most significant use of the Bogart persona appears in *Play It Again, Sam*, in which Bogart appears to Felix and advises him on his love life. Moreover, the ending is based on *Casablanca*, as Allen speaks Bogart's lines and his character becomes fully identified with Bogart's. But Allen invokes Bogart elsewhere too. Kaiser Lupowitz, the hard-boiled detective and narrator of "Mr. Big" in *Getting Even* and of "The Whore of Mensa" in *Without Feathers*, is based on Sam Spade; "Mr. Big," in particular, parodies *The Maltese Falcon*. Finally, Allen published a light-hearted article, "How

Bogart Made Me the Superb Lover I Am Today," in the March 1969 issue of *Life* magazine. This was ostensibly about the debut of the play version of *Play It Again, Sam*.

See also **Getting Even**; **Play It Again, Sam**; **Without Feathers**.

Brickman, Marshall. A writer, producer, and director who collaborated with Allen on the screenplays for *Sleeper*, *Annie Hall*, *Manhattan*, and *Manhattan Murder Mystery*. Brickman also made an uncredited contribution to the screenplay of Howard Morris's *Don't Drink the Water* (1969), which was based on Allen's stage play. (Allen did not participate in the film.)

Born in Brazil in 1941, Brickman attended the University of Wisconsin and wrote for the popular television shows *Candid Camera* and *The Tonight Show* before beginning his association with Allen. He and Allen won an Academy Award for best screenplay for *Annie Hall* and were nominated for *Manhattan*. Brickman received an additional nomination for writing *Simon* (1980), a cynical comedy that he wrote and directed about corrupt scientists who brainwash a psychology professor. In addition, Brickman wrote and directed *Lovesick* (1983); wrote, directed, and produced *The Manhattan Project* (1986); and acted in *Funny* (1988) and *That's Adequate* (1989).

Allen met Brickman in the mid-1960s when Allen was a stand-up comedian, performing in a Greenwich Village coffeehouse as the opening act for Brickman's folk group, the Tarriers. Brickman played banjo and guitar and entertained audiences with humorous banter as he and the other musicians tuned their instruments. Like Allen, the Tarriers were represented by Jack Rollins and Charles Joffe, who suggested that Allen and Brickman get together. Rollins and Joffe turned down their first collaboration, a screenplay for a never-made movie, *The Film Maker*, but they approved of *Sleeper*, which United Artists released in 1973.

In the first two films that he directed, *Take the Money and Run* and *Bananas*, Allen had collaborated on the scripts with a high school friend, Mickey Rose. But Allen changed his work habits when he and Brickman wrote *Sleeper*. Whereas Allen and Rose remained in the same room together, going line by line through the script as they wrote it, he and Brickman would discuss their ideas and agree on a general plan. Then Allen would write the first draft on his own and present it to Brickman for commentary, suggestions, and revision. Allen, not Brickman, wrote the draft because it was Allen who would be speaking the part, and they felt it would be easier and more natural for him to write the lines. Allen also made the final decisions and produced the final draft, but he credits Brickman for making an equal contribution to the plot and dialogue in their collaborations and for casting Paul Simon in *Annie Hall*.

Woody Allen and Mia Farrow in *Broadway Danny Rose*. Photo by Brian Hamill. Courtesy of Photofest.

Brickman has suggested that he contributed detailed structure to help fill in the gaps created by Allen's wild, inspired leaps of imagination. "I would try to go from A to B to C to D. . . . [But] what were important for him were the individual moments and the leaps, which really are his special and unique talent" (Lax 251–252). Allen has described Brickman as a good, funny writer and a friend with whom writing has been a pleasant experience.

Broadway Danny Rose. A 1984 film directed by, written by, and starring Allen, who plays personal manager Danny Rose. It costars Mia Farrow (Tina Vitale), Nick Apollo Forte (Lou Canova), Olga Barbato (Angelina the spiritualist), Edwin Bordo (Johnny Rispoli), Gina DeAngelis (Johnny's mother), Gerald Schoefield (Sid Bacharach), Herb Reynolds (Barney Dunn), Gloria Parker (water glass virtuoso), Herbie Jayson (bird act), Alba Ballard (lady who dresses parrots), Mark Hardwick (blind xylophonist), Bob and Etta Rollins (balloon act), Sandy Baron (comedian narrator), Corbett Monica (comedian at deli), Jackie Gayle (comedian at deli), Morty Gunty (comedian at deli), Will Jordan (comedian at deli), Howard Storm (comedian at deli), Jack Rollins (comedian at deli), Leo Steiner (deli owner), John Doumanian (Wardolf manager), and Howard Cosell, Joe Franklin, Sammy Davis, Jr.,

and Milton Berle as themselves. Robert Greenhut was the producer, Gordon
Willis director of photography, Dick Hyman music director, Mel Bourne production designer, Jeffrey Kurland costume designer, and Susan E. Morse the
editor. The music features "Agita" and "My Bambina" performed by Nick
Apollo Forte. Orion Pictures was the North American distributor.

Based on what Allen calls "a little idea" (Lax 276), *Broadway Danny
Rose* has a smaller scope and more modest artistic intention than many of
his other films. But it was well received, if not widely viewed. Allen considers it entertaining and well executed, an opinion widely shared by most reviewers. Pauline Kael of the *New Yorker* complained that Allen was writing
down for his audience, trying to write "a crowd pleaser" and omitting "the
hostility that made him famous," but most other commentators praised the
film. *Time Magazine*'s reviewer called it "appetizing as a pastrami-on-wry
sandwich," and Vincent Canby of the *New York Times* described it as "a love
letter not only to American comedy stars and to all those pushy hopefuls
who never quite made it to the top of show business, but also to the kind of
comedy that nourished the particular genius of Woody Allen." The film was
appreciated in Europe, and Allen received Academy Award nominations
for best director and best original screenplay. Despite its warm reception,
Broadway Danny Rose earned little more than the $8 million it cost to pro-
duce. It grossed only $5.5 million in U.S. and Canadian rentals (not includ-
ing later video and television revenues) but recouped the difference in
Britain and Europe.

The character of Danny Rose is loosely based on Allen's own big-
hearted agent, Jack Rollins, who had acquired a reputation for being abandoned by performers he had nurtured and developed. Nancy Pogel also
points out similarities to *Meet Danny Wilson* (1951), in which Frank Sinatra
(Farrow's former husband) plays a singer who betrays his agent. Candidates
for the role of Danny's ungrateful client, singer Lou Canova, included
Danny Aiello, Sylvester Stallone, and Robert De Niro, but Allen selected
Nick Apollo Forte, a Connecticut cocktail pianist and ex-fisherman who
had never acted before or even seen a Woody Allen movie. According to Allen, "I had looked at a million singers, famous ones and not so famous ones,
without finding the right person for the part. . . . Then Juliet Taylor went to a
record store and bought as many records as she could. And she saw this picture of Nick Apollo Forte. . . . I tested him. . . . and he was the best one"
(*Woody Allen on Woody Allen* 147).

In search of a role that would allow Farrow to play a brassy character, Allen was inspired by their visits to a favorite Italian restaurant whose owner
wore sunglasses even at night and sported a high bouffant hair style. Farrow
imitated the voice of a secretary at Orion Pictures and wore foam pads be-

neath her costume to make her appear more curvaceous (Fox 153). Because she feared her eyes were too soft for the tough image she wanted to project, Farrow wore sunglasses throughout the entire movie, except for one scene where she looks at herself in the mirror. Allen notes, "That was a very, very brave thing for her to do, because she had to act the whole picture without ever using her eyes, and that's really hard to do" (*Woody Allen on Woody Allen* 147).

The performers who sit at the deli table telling stories were actual comedians who worked the Borscht belt and other such venues in the 1950s and 1960s. Leo Steiner plays himself as owner of the Carnegie Deli on Seventh Avenue in New York City. Allen knew them all personally to varying degrees, and the initial scene of them congregating to schmooze is drawn on Allen's own experiences as a stand-up comic in the early 1960s. Jack Rollins, who regularly met to talk shop with Allen and other performers, has a minor speaking role as one of the group. Allen similarly honors Milton Berle, Sammy Davis, Jr., Howard Cosell, and Joe Franklin with cameo appearances. Elsewhere, Allen acknowledges the comedians he admired as a child and emulated as a young man when Danny declares, "If it's old-fashioned to like Mr. Danny Kaye, Mr. Bob Hope, or Mr. Milton Berle, then I'm old-fashioned!" A reference to Weinstein's Majestic Bungalow Colony in the Catskills pays tribute to the venue where Allen first publicly performed magic tricks, at age sixteen.

Shot in black and white in order to give the film a rough-looking appearance, *Broadway Danny Rose* employs the structure of a frame-tale, a story within a story. This device distances the audience from Danny and thereby slightly softens the happy ending. It also provides a lens through which we first see Danny. The outer frame presents the comedians at the deli. As their conversation turns to Danny, we acquire an impression of the protagonist before we actually encounter him. We learn that Danny handles with great dedication such improbable acts as a blind xylophonist and a one-legged tap dancer, but that several clients whom he developed have abandoned him upon becoming successful. We see in flashbacks how Danny not only represents his artists but helps them refine their acts and, most important, get their lives in order.

A dedicated believer in the power of positive thinking, Danny teaches his clients to believe in themselves, even inspiring balloon folders to picture themselves performing before larger, more enthusiastic audiences than they can currently imagine. As in *Manhattan*, where Ike observes that Mary's self-esteem is a notch below Kafka's, and in *Interiors* and *Hannah and Her Sisters*, where the middle sisters in particular suffer from poor self-esteem, in *Broadway Danny Rose* Allen insists on the importance of self-acceptance and shows its connection to proper action. The homilies that Danny lives by and passes on to his protegés, such as the three S's: star—smile—strong, may appear simplistic to the cosmopolitan audience that Allen typically attracts, but they can be effective vehicles for inspiring self-confidence in people with little experience of success. The outer frame thus characterizes Danny as a supportive, nurturing, overly optimistic loser with a good heart who gets trampled on by others—an endearing "little man" who, like Charlie Chaplin's Little Tramp, prevails because he does not see himself as a loser.

The inside story is set in 1969, several years before the outside frame (a reference to the recent moon landing establishes the year). One of Danny's projects, Lou Canova, is an over-the-hill Italian singer of limited talent who enjoyed some small fame in the 1950s and whom Danny reclaimed when Lou's career and personal life were in shambles. A wave of nostalgia has created an opportunity for Lou's comeback, and Danny convinces Milton Berle to see Lou's act. If he is good, Berle will hire Lou for a television performance and opening act at Caesar's Palace. But Lou, a married man, insists he cannot perform unless his girlfriend, Tina, is there. Although Danny disapproves of Lou's infidelity, he reluctantly agrees to play the "beard"—to pretend to be Tina's date so Lou's wife does not become suspicious. Most of the action revolves around Danny's efforts to get Tina to the performance, first despite her own initial angry refusal and then in spite of efforts by mafia hit men to kill Danny because they believe Danny stole Tina from their brother, Johnny Rispoli.

As in *Crimes and Misdemeanors* and *Bullets over Broadway*, Allen contrasts the gangsters' amoral sensibilities to those of an essentially decent, law-abiding citizen. Tina, the young widow of an assassinated mobster, articulates the criminals' point of view. Like the philosopher Thomas Hobbes, who insisted that the life of man in a state of nature is "nasty, brutish, and short," Tina projects a view of human society predicated solely on the struggle for personal survival. She believes life is a jungle and people should grab for whatever they can get while they can: "Do it to the other guy first, because if you don't, he'll do it to you." Elsewhere she states, "I never feel guilty. You gotta do what you gotta do, you know? Life's short. You don't get any medals for being a boy scout."

By contrast, Danny feels betrayed when performers he has developed abandon him, and he bemoans their lack of integrity: "I find them, I discover them, I breathe life into them, and then they go. And, and, no guilt, I mean they don't feel guilty or anything. I mean they just split." Tina counters, "Guilty? What the hell is that? They see something better and they grab it." But Danny insists on the value of appropriate guilt, something Allen develops at length in *Crimes and Misdemeanors* and *Bullets over Broadway*. "It's important to feel guilty; otherwise, you know, you're capable of terrible things." (Elsewhere, in such films as *Alice* and *Celebrity*, Allen points out the harmful effects of inappropriate guilt.)

Later, Danny accurately observes that Tina lacks confidence, and he imagines the success she can enjoy as a decorator if she would only believe in herself. When he quotes his Uncle Morris, "If you hate yourself, then you'll hate your work," Tina reiterates her cynical philosophy: "It's over quick so have a good time. You see what you want? Go for it. Don't pay any attention to anyone else." Danny replies, "No wonder you don't like yourself," and he quotes his Uncle Sidney's motto, "Acceptance, forgiveness, love."

The contrast in their values serves as the central issue in the movie, and the plot resolves when Tina feels guilt for encouraging Lou to leave Danny. Initially Tina refuses to accept any responsibility for her role or even to acknowledge that Lou is behaving improperly by firing Danny, although she has just witnessed Danny risk his life for Lou's career. Instead, she reiterates her earlier sentiments, "You gotta do what you've got to do," adding that "Danny's a big boy."

But like Lady Macbeth, who lived by a similarly cynical and selfish creed, Tina's happiness is undermined by a guilty conscience she does not know she has—one that takes her some time even to recognize. She becomes moody, jumpy, and unable to enjoy herself with Lou or, after he leaves her, with her new boyfriend. She tells Angelina, her spiritualist, about bad dreams and being haunted by what she did to Danny. She wants to find herself, rest easy again, and forget about Danny, but she cannot. She dreams of looking at herself in a mirror, a vision Angelina shares, but for both of them the image is unclear. Metaphorically Tina has lost self-respect; she can no longer look at herself in the mirror. At last, the Macy's Thanksgiving Day parade reminds Tina of their "adventure," as she describes it, when she and Danny escaped from the murderous gangsters. She goes to Danny's apartment to apologize, quoting his Uncle Sidney's mantra, "Acceptance, forgiveness, love." Initially Danny remains too embittered to forgive her, but then he reverses himself and runs off to embrace her.

Of all of his homilies, "Acceptance, forgiveness, love" most enables Danny to transcend his basic little-man status and ultimately achieve happiness and a modicum of success. Although he must scrape along, living like "a loser," repeatedly betrayed by his clients and abandoned by his fiancée, Danny's ability to adhere to his credo allows him to remain positive, upbeat, and committed to life. It enables him to imagine a better, happier life and thereby precludes him from seeing himself as a little man, even if others perceive him this way. Moreover, Tina's intuitive quest for Danny's forgiveness and Danny's ability to accept the past and forgive her make possible the love implied by the final shot of them together. His fellow comedians finally salute him, even as they laugh at Danny's absurdity, and Danny receives the ultimate tribute within their community when he has a deli sandwich named after him.

In spite of the film's celebration of the power of optimism and imagination, much of its humor stems from Allen's view that people are fundamentally irrational and everyday life is often surreal. For instance, when the thugs capture Danny and Tina and threaten to kill whoever stole her from their brother, Danny tries to discuss the situation reasonably with them, accurately pointing out, "What's important here is the girl's feelings," and "The fact is, she doesn't love him." In a rational universe populated by fundamentally rational people, Danny's appeal might have been successful, but under the circumstances, it is ludicrous. In similar ways throughout the film Allen generates humor as he heightens our awareness that humans are not fundamentally rational. Moreover, the consequences of human action do not always square with their causes, as we are reminded when Danny complains, "I don't deserve this!" Throughout his life Danny has done everything in his power to stay out of trouble and avoid incurring the wrath of others; yet suddenly he finds himself pursued by vengeful killers because he is doing a favor for a friend.

Some scenes are funny due to their Fellini-like surrealism, such as when Tina and Danny encounter a caped, superman-like hero among otherwise deserted marshes. Allen mixes in black humor as Tina offhandedly remembers the spot as the place where her husband's friends disposed of bodies. The disparity between her casual manner and the implications of her words sparks humor as it reminds that evil and unjust acts abound in our world. Another comically surreal scene takes place in a warehouse filled with huge, cartoon-inspired floats for the Macy's Thanksgiving Day parade. When a bullet pierces a container of helium, all of the characters speak in high, squeaky, cartoon-like voices that are incongruous to the dangerous situation. Angelina adds an element of supernatural insight similar to that of Dr. Yang in *Alice*, Treva in *Oedipus Wrecks*, and the spiritualist who counsels Robin in *Celebrity*, as well as to some of Fellini's characters, such as the spiritualist in *8½*.

In the irrational world of *Broadway Danny Rose*, even well-intended actions can have disastrous results. Captured by thugs who threaten to chop off his legs if he will not identify Tina's real boyfriend, Danny has two unpleasant alternatives: be killed for something he has had no part in or rat on Lou. Hoping to avoid such unsavory alternatives, he instead names Barney Dunn, an inept ventriloquist who Danny believes is safely out of the country. But unbeknown to Danny, Barney's plans have changed, and Barney is

savagely beaten by the thugs. Thus, the clean-living Danny suddenly finds himself at least somewhat culpable, despite his lifelong efforts to avoid harming others. Critics divide on the degree of Danny's responsibility and whether his naming Barney is an act of cowardice. But however one evaluates this, Danny at least tries to do the right thing thereafter by visiting Barney, covering his hospital bills, and otherwise assisting him. Nonetheless, the Barney Dunn episode illustrates how even the virtuous and well intended can acquire guilt, and this serves to underscore Danny's point that it is important to be able to feel guilty, even if Allen also exaggerates the point for comic effect. The episode also demonstrates why even fundamentally moral people require acceptance, forgiveness, and love.

Broadway Danny Rose anticipates the grander, more disturbing, more thorough exploration of morality that Allen provided five years later in *Crimes and Misdemeanors*. Like the latter film, *Broadway Danny Rose* presents a universe in which good actions and a good heart do not necessarily translate into happiness or success, a universe where people who ignore the moral teachings of Judaism and Christianity often thrive. However, unlike *Crimes and Misdemeanors*, *Broadway Danny Rose* concludes happily. Indeed, it is the happy ending that diminishes the film's scope, even as it pleases the audience. Ultimately the conclusion depicts how Allen would like reality to be more than it describes how he believes it is.

At the same time, the film affirms the power of imagination and a positive attitude. It suggests that despite repeated setbacks, a well-intended, optimistic person who believes in himself and others is better equipped in the long run to negotiate an uncertain, amoral universe than a purely self-interested cynic.

Bullets over Broadway. A 1994 film directed and cowritten by Allen. It stars John Cusack (David Shayne), Dianne Wiest (Helen Sinclair), Jack Warden (Julian Marx), Chazz Palminteri (Cheech), Joe Vitrelli (Jack Valenti), Jennifer Tilly (Olive Neal), Tracy Ullman (Eden Brent), Jim Broadbent (Warner Purcell), Rob Reiner (Sheldon Flender), Mary-Louise Parker (Ellen), and Harvey Fierstein (Sid Loomis). Robert Greenhut was the producer, Carlo Di Palma director of photography, Santo Loquasto production designer, Jeffrey Kurland costume designer, and Susan E. Morse editor. Doug McGrath coauthored the screenplay with Allen, and Graciela Daniele choreographed the dance scenes. The music features Al Jolson, Duke Ellington, Bix Beiderbecke, Red Nichols and His Five Pennies, Roger Wolfe Kahn and His Orchestra, the New Leviathan Oriental Fox Trot Orchestra, George Olden, Irving Aaronson and His Commanders, and Dick Hyman and the Three Deuces Musicians and Chorus. Miramax was the North American distributor.

Bullets over Broadway was Allen's first film made by Sweetland Films, an independent company that his longtime friend Jean Doumanian formed in 1992. Tri-Star released Allen from the last film in a three-film contract to allow him to accept a more lucrative contract with Sweetland, which offered a higher director's fee and a $20 million production budget. *Bullets over Broadway* was Allen's first movie made by an independent studio. It was released worldwide by Miramax, an independent distribution company that Bob and Harvey Weinstein formed to issue such meritorious films as *The Crying Game* (1992) and *The Piano* (1993). *Bullets over Broadway* ultimately cost $20 million to produce but grossed only $13.5 million in U.S. and Canadian rentals (not including later video rentals and television revenues). However, it was a great hit in Europe, especially in Britain and France, and it eventually earned $37.6 million in worldwide distribution.

Allen's second film since his highly publicized breakup with Mia Farrow and the charges of child abuse that followed, *Bullets over Broadway* served as an indicator of whether the public would spurn Allen after two courts declared him an unfit parent unworthy of having custody of the three children he shared with Farrow. But perhaps because the criminal charges of child abuse were dropped following an investigation by a Yale–New Haven medical team, the scandal did not greatly undermine the film's reception in the United States, where critics were largely amused by its upbeat tempo and its re-creation of the art deco era in Manhattan. In Europe the scandal had virtually no impact all, and the response was even more enthusiastic. One British commentator described *Bullets over Broadway* as "*Radio Days* meets *Some Like It Hot.*" Dianne Wiest received an Academy Award for best supporting actress. Jennifer Tilly was also nominated for best supporting actress and Chazz Palminteri for best supporting actor. Allen was nominated for best director and, along with Doug McGrath, for best original screenplay. *Bullets over Broadway* also received nominations for art direction (Santo Loquasto and Susan Bode) and costume design (Jeffrey Kurland).

Bullets over Broadway continues the dialogue over adultery, murder, and morality that Allen presents in *Hannah and Her Sisters* and *Crimes and Misdemeanors*. But whereas Elliot gets away with adultery in *Hannah and Her Sisters* and Judah gets away with murder in *Crimes and Misdemeanors*, the more comedic *Bullets over Broadway* repudiates both murder and betrayal. Moreover, it exposes the inherent flaw in the existentialist notion that each individual can create his or her own moral universe. By ridiculing artists who take themselves too seriously, Allen reveals the thin lines separating existentialism from sophistry, narcissism, and sociopathology. Indeed, the film concludes by endorsing conventional, bourgeois values that, regardless of their limitations, are at least capable of making firm distinctions between blatant right and wrong.

Early in the movie, playwright David Shayne and his fellow artists and their girlfriends abstractly debate the relative value of art and human life. If during a raging fire one could save either an "anonymous human being" or the last remaining copy of Shakespeare's plays, which should we choose? Sheldon Flender, whom David considers a genius because "both common people and intellectuals find your work completely incoherent," insists that we should choose Shakespeare because "it's not an inanimate object. It's art. Art is life! It lives!"

The story line puts Flender's position to the test and finds it woefully lacking. The plot centers on David's efforts to have his play produced on Broadway during the 1920s. David has made considerable sacrifices for his career, and he takes himself very seriously as an artist. Believing that his earlier plays were butchered in performance, he insists on directing his newest work, *God of Our Fathers*. (We infer that the play has considerable intellectual content but lacks passion and that the female characters are not well drawn.) When David allows Olive, a gangster's moll, to play a secondary role in order to obtain financial backing to produce his drama, David re of integrity bygards himself as a sell-out, "a whore." But he attempts to regain some sense filling the leading role with Helen Sinclair, an over-the-hill, overly dramatic, self-important, alcoholic prima donna who is a Broadway legend. Equally self-important and self-indulgent actors comprise the remainder of the cast, and their interplay spawns considerable humor.

The plot turns, however, when Cheech, Olive's bodyguard and a hit man, begins criticizing David's dialogue as unnatural and suggests changes. David initially resists input from the poorly educated gangster, but to his credit, he acknowledges that Cheech has an innate gift for dialogue and plot construction. He publicly apologizes to Cheech and secretly begins to solicit the gangster's assistance in revising the script. Although initially indifferent to the play, Cheech eventually comes to see himself as its author, and, like Flender, he refuses to abide any diminution of his art. Therefore, when it becomes evident that Olive's inept performance is preventing the play from becoming as great as it truly can be, Cheech executes her and disposes of her body at the waterfront, where he dumps his other gangland victims. Cheech's action indeed saves the play, which becomes an opening-night sensation.

Like Flannery O'Connor's story "Good Country People" (1955), in which a corrupt Bible salesman demonstrates the cruel and exploitative possibilities of existentialist philosophies based on nothingness, *Bullets*

John Cusack (left) and Chazz Palminteri (right) in *Bullets over Broadway*. Photo by Richard Cartwright. Courtesy of Photofest.

over Broadway employs black humor to reveal how easily existentialism can degenerate into total narcissism and cynical disregard for the well-being of others. As Sander H. Lee notes, "Cheech resides in a moral universe of his own making in which he views virtually everyone else as a grotesque inferior" (Lee 349). The same can be said of all the actors and artists in the film: they look down on the public and each other. In Allen's eyes, this is what unites gangsters and other self-important people, and this is why Allen so consistently ridicules intellectual pretension.

Cheech essentially makes the choice that Flender recommends in the artists' initial debate: he elects to sacrifice the human to save the work of art. But David is appalled that Cheech has coldly killed another person simply to see his play performed properly. David renounces the self-righteous life of the artist, which he now recognizes as simply self-indulgent. He sees the self-aggrandizement of the art world as dangerous and potentially horrifying, and so he returns home to beg forgiveness from his girlfriend, whom he has betrayed in pursuit of fame and artistic success. The film ends happily as David renounces his life as an artist and offers to marry Ellen, leave the big city, have children, and take up a quiet career as a teacher.

Despite its underlying moral questioning, *Bullets over Broadway* remains a comedy that derives humor by spoofing gangster films and backstage comedy thrillers. Julian Fox notes its particular indebtedness to Philip

Dunning and George Abbott's *Broadway* (1927), Al Jolson's *Go into Your Dance* (1935), and Joseph Mankiewicz's *All About Eve* (1950). *Sunset Boulevard* (1950) would seem to be another influence. However, because all of the characters in *Bullets over Broadway* are exaggerations of the types they parody, we find them funny but do not take them too seriously. Wiest, for instance, exaggerates the theatrical mannerisms of the grandes dames of the theater, whom she parodies in the character of Helen Sinclair. Her dramatic delivery of the words, "Don't speak!" is the most quoted line in the film, and it sets up a comic punch line at the end. Cheech, Olive, and Nick Valenti are easily recognizable as gangster types;[1] Flender is an exaggeration of the pure art-for-art's-sake artist; even John Cusack's wide-eyed David exaggerates the earnest, innocent, uncompromising, struggling artist type. (Allen acknowledges that the character is based in part on himself as a young man.) In contrast to the richly developed characters in *Crimes and Misdemeanors*, the broad, stereotypical characters in *Bullets over Broadway* distance the audience from the murders and make them seem unreal, as though they happened to cartoon characters. Moreover, unlike in *Crimes and Misdemeanors*, the murderer-artist does not get away with his crime. These considerations enable Allen to provoke laughs even as he continues his serious investigation of morality and proper action that he initiated with *Hannah and Her Sisters*, *Crimes and Misdemeanors*, and *Shadows and Fog*.

In addition to telling an entertaining story, the film is visually rich. The production crew re-created expressive art deco interior designs, and rich colors characterize Di Palma's photography. Outdoor scenes in Central Park, shot on cloudy days to enhance the color photography, are especially stunning. These contrast with the darker shots of gangsters executing their victims, which offer more of a *film noir* sensibility. The musical hits from the period and the nightclub song-and-dance numbers contribute to the film's energy and entertainment as they unite the world of gangsters with the world of art.

Though not as profound as some of Allen's other films, *Bullets over Broadway* reveals the dangers of taking ourselves too seriously, even as it spawns more humor than the films immediately preceding it. By applying the lofty sentiments of existentialism to gangsters, Allen both reveals the dangers of relying on each individual to create his or her own moral universe and ridicules the tendency of some artists to consider themselves inherently superior because of their talent and their commitment to art. Even in an absurd universe, *Bullets over Broadway* insists on the desirability of maintaining at least a modicum of humility and showing respect for the life and well-being of others.

NOTE

1. Chazz Palminteri, who plays Cheech, is himself someone with gangster associations who became a successful playwright. Palminteri starred in the 1993 film version of his largely autobiographical play, *A Bronx Life*, about a boy who has witnessed a gangland slaying and is mentored by a gangster.

Allen also intermingled fact and fiction when he cast a childhood schoolmate in one of the minor gangster roles. "He was the neighbourhood gangster where I grew up in Brooklyn—a gun-toting gangster at sixteen who then went off to prison." Allen adds, "And oddly enough [gangsters are] graceful with dialogue and can speak and be believable. Sometimes they're more graceful than actors who have studied for twenty years" (Fox 248).

According to Jennifer Tilly, who played Olive, Allen thought of Olive as someone "in her own little world and it just revolves around her and she just talks and talks and talks" (Fox 248).

C

Casino Royale. A 1967 film costarring Allen, who plays Jimmy Bond. It was codirected by John Huston, Kenneth Hughes, Val Guest, Robert Parrish, Joseph McGrath, Richard Talmadge, and Anthony Squire. Costars include Peter Sellers (Evelyn Tremble), Ursula Andress (Vesper Lynd), David Niven (Sir James Bond), Orson Welles (Le Chiffre), Joanna Pettet (Mata Bond), Daliah Lavi (the Detainer), Deborah Kerr (Widow McTarry), William Holden (Ransome), Charles Boyer (Le Grand), John Huston (M), Kurt Kasznar (Smernov), George Raft (himself), Jean-Paul Belmondo (French Legionnaire), Terence Cooper (Cooper), Barbara Bouchet (Moneypenny), and Jacqueline Bisset (Miss Goodthighs). Charles K. Feldman and Jerry Bresler were the producers; Wolf Mankowitz, John Law, and Michael Sayers wrote the script, which is loosely based on the novel by Ian Fleming. (Allen, Huston, Guest, Sellers, Welles, Terry Southern, Billy Wilder, Joseph Heller, Ben Hecht, Frank Buxton, and Dore Schary made uncredited contributions.) Jack Hildyard was director of photography (Nicholas Roeg and John Wilcox were additional directors of photography), Bill Lenny was the editor, and Burt Bacharach and Herb Alpert wrote the music. United Artists was the North American distributor.

A critical failure but a box office success, *Casino Royale* tried to cash in on the success of Feldman's earlier hit comedy, *What's New, Pussycat?* (1965), and on the sexy James Bond action-adventure movies that were popular in the early 1960s: *Dr. No* (1962), *From Russia with Love* (1963), *Goldfinger* (1964), and *Thunderball* (1965). Ursula Andress, Peter Sellers, and Allen had costarred in *Pussycat*, and Andress starred with Sean Connery in *Dr. No*. Although the U.S. and Canadian revenues ($10.2 million, not including later video rentals and television revenues) failed to equal the cost of production (approximately $12 million), the British-made movie was the third largest moneymaker of 1967 in the United States and a hit in Europe, where it recovered the financial losses.

Like *Pussycat, Casino Royale* was a star vehicle with a weak script. Allen had signed a three-picture contract with Feldman when he agreed to do *Pussycat*, and his manager encouraged him to perform in *Casino Royale* because the money was very good and the film would provide useful exposure in a major movie and help establish Allen in cinema. Allen flew to London to work on it, but the script was not ready. He collected his salary, lived well on an expense account, and amused himself for months by playing high-stakes poker, collecting jazz albums unavailable at home, visiting museums, appearing on television shows, and buying works of art. While in London, he wrote his play *Don't Drink the Water.* Along with Andress and Raquel Welch, Allen was introduced to Queen Elizabeth, of whom he asked, "Are you enjoying your power?" (Lax 221). Finally, after six months, they filmed his scenes and Allen returned home.

David Niven plays Sir James Bond (retired), who is the *real* James Bond, a man of great accomplishment and refined character who disdains the womanizing associated with Sean Connery's character, who is said to be an impostor. Indeed, to confuse the enemy, Her Majesty's Secret Service has promulgated a number of false Bonds. Although the producers purchased the rights to Ian Fleming's original novel, the only scene retained in the film is a baccarat challenge between Bond (this one played by Sellers) and the villainous Le Ciffre (Welles).

Allen plays the role of Sir James's inept, sexually frustrated nephew Jimmy, another manifestation of the little-man persona that Allen was developing throughout the 1960s and 1970s. Jimmy proves to be the evil mastermind behind an insidious plot to replace all of the world leaders with look-alike robots that he controls and to release an airborne bacillus that will make all women beautiful and eliminate all men taller than four-foot-six. This will leave him the tallest man in a world populated by gorgeous females—a world in which "a man no matter how short can score with a top broad." As his uncle tells him, "All this trouble to make up for your feelings of sexual inadequacy. I'm beginning to think you may be a little bit neurotic."

Allen appears only briefly in the beginning and at the end, when his identity as the evil mastermind appears as a surprise. When we first see him, he is standing against a wall facing a firing squad. In the daring tradition of his uncle, Jimmy leaps over the wall, only to face another firing squad on the other side. When we last see him, he is behind an enormous magnifying glass that exaggerates his size until the real James Bond shatters it.

Val Guest directed all of Allen's scenes, which he and Allen wrote together. According to Guest, Allen was very professional and easy to work with, but, as was the case on the set of *Pussycat*, he became extremely frustrated by Feldman's tampering with the script. "Feldman was the one person Woody hated because he had a terrible habit of making changes. . . . He'd go through all our stuff . . . cut out all the gags but leave in the build-up! He had no *idea*. So Woody spent his time moaning to me, 'This murderer! This murderer!' So I said, 'Don' worry about it, we'll put it back, on the floor.' Which we did" (Fox 36–37).

Overall, Allen enjoyed London and made good money from the endeavor, but he considered the movie "an unredeemingly moronic enterprise" (Spignesi 130). Nonetheless, the experience of filming *Casino Royale* may have served as a negative example from which he learned. "The set was a chaotic madhouse. I knew then that the only way to make a film is to control it completely" (Fox 39).

Celebrity. A 1998 film directed and written by Allen. It stars Kenneth Branagh (Lee Simon), Judy Davis (Robin Simon), Leonardo DiCaprio (Brandon Darrow), Winona Ryder (Nola), Joe Mantegna (Tony Gardella), Melanie Griffith (Nicole), Charlize Theron (unnamed blond supermodel), Famke Janssen (Bonnie), Bebe Neuwirth (prostitute), Isaac Mizrahi (artist Bruce Bishop), Anthony Mason (basketball star), Gretchen Mol, Michael Lerner, Greg Mottoloa, Irina Pantaeva, and Jeffrey Wright. Jean Doumanian was the producer, Sven Nykvist cinematographer, Santo Loquasto production designer, Jeffrey Kurland costumer, and Susan E. Morse editor. Miramax was the North American distributor.

Shot in black and white, *Celebrity* was released with an unusually large amount of publicity for an Allen movie. The scope of the film is far greater than his previous efforts, containing 242 speaking parts and 5,128 extras. In addition, *Celebrity* features at least five major movie stars and several prominent celebrities from other fields, including writer Erica Jong, fashion designer Isaac Mizrahi, and investor Donald Trump, who expresses a desire to raze St. Patrick's Cathedral and replace it with a large, modern skyscraper. On its opening weekend, *Celebrity* ranked number ten at the box office, grossing $1.6 million, but the number of viewers quickly declined after that. The reviews were mixed but generally positive. The film was widely regarded as Allen's personal assessment of an American culture that idolizes celebrities not for the achievements that occasion their fame but for the fame itself. Kenneth Branagh was alternately praised for imitating Allen's own gestures and mannerisms and criticized for acting in Allen's style, while Leonardo DiCaprio was routinely applauded for his depiction of a spoiled young movie star. *Time* called *Celebrity* "the first fully serious (and seriously funny) movie about the issue that touches, and ultimately subsumes, everything we feel about fame and the discontents it breeds."

Like Federico Fellini's *La Dolce Vita* (1960), *Celebrity* focuses on a writer who becomes caught up in the decadent world of the rich and famous. *Celebrity* also replays many of the themes found in Allen's earlier films. In Allen's eyes it is simply a fact that wide-eyed, sexy, vivacious young women are sometimes more physically attractive to middle-aged men than are middle-aged women. Some critics have accused him of misogyny for representing this phenomenon, but Allen merely acknowledges it rather than celebrates it. He reveals the attraction to be visceral, not cognitive. And like writers dating back to Chaucer and Shakespeare, he shows that people who allow themselves to be ruled by their passions lose control of their lives and become subject to mishaps and misery.

Protagonist Lee Simon's propensity for turning his back on responsible, mature women who love him in favor of seemingly more exciting, self-centered women who abuse him echoes *Annie Hall*, *Manhattan*, *Stardust Memories*, and *Husbands and Wives*. For instance, in *Manhattan* Ike Davis leaves Tracy and makes himself miserable by pursuing Mary. Moreover, Yale, Ike's self-destructive, self-indulgent friend, ruins his marriage by pursuing the same unstable woman. Allen alludes to these relationships in *Ce-*

Melanie Griffith with Kenneth Branagh in *Celebrity*. Photo by John Clifford. Courtesy of Photofest.

lebrity by having Lee wear a Yale University T-shirt when he breaks up with Bonnie, a book editor who encourages his literary gift and otherwise offers a healthy, loving relationship. In fact, by reminding us of Yale from *Manhattan*, Allen foreshadows the early demise of Lee's new affair with Nola, a young actress who warns that she has never been faithful to any man and whom Lee recognizes as "such trouble for somebody" when they first meet. (The black and white photography, prominent bridge shot, and suggestions that Nola is lesbian or bisexual also evoke associations to *Manhattan*, as does the blonde supermodel's labeling of her artistic friends as "genius." Her admission that she is "polymorphously perverse" recalls *Annie Hall*.)

As Allen suggests in *Everyone Says I Love You*, romances predicated exclusively on sexual attraction may be acceptable, even appropriate, for adolescents. But mature adults who have satisfied the urge for purely physical relationships find greater fulfillment by pursuing more balanced romances that include the pleasures of the mind and soul, as well as those of the body. However, when young men grow up without experiencing sexual fulfillment, they sometimes have difficulty evolving to the next level of maturity.

Lee married Robin, his ex-wife, when they were very young. She is sexually inhibited (she thinks about the crucifixion during oral sex), and during his twentieth high school reunion Lee realizes that he has never enjoyed a rich physical relationship with a sexy young woman. He compares himself to T. S. Eliot's character J. Alfred Prufrock, who is too fearful to embrace life, and Lee tells himself that he does not want to die without ever knowing what it would be like to sleep with a beautiful model. Therefore, like Skylar and Von in *Everyone Says I Love You*, Lee destroys a stable, loving relationship in order to pursue his unrealized adolescent fantasies. But unlike the earlier musical comedy, Lee cannot return to his abandoned lovers after his flings fizzle. He could have achieved deep satisfaction in a relationship with Bonnie, a successful book editor who nurtures his literary talents, but instead he is reduced to a pathetic, lonely figure because he succumbs to Nola's sexual appeal.

Like an adolescent, Lee prizes the spark of sexual excitement over everything else, a choice that proves self-destructive. The final images of the movie underscore how lost and out of control he has become, as Allen cuts from an on-screen, sky-written plea for HELP to a close-up of Lee alone at the screening of the movie whose filming begins *Celebrity*. Even the coaching for the skywriting scene given to the star, Nicole, now pertains to Lee: "Everything has gone wrong, and you can't believe it. You thought you had everything figured out. Convey despair."

Lee's problems stem from poor self-esteem. Like Groucho Marx and *Annie Hall*'s Alvy Singer, Lee would not belong to any club—or stay in any romantic relationship—that would admit someone like him. This is another reason why he abandons his two seemingly successful relationships and pursues hopeless ones with self-absorbed celebrities who repeatedly string him along and then abandon him. The young supermodel and the young movie star Brandon Darrow are especially adroit at showing Lee just enough interest to keep him around and hopeful, without ever giving him what he wants. His complete surrender to the model is foreshadowed from the start, when Lee immediately hands her the keys to his sports car, without even being asked. He literally makes her the driver in their brief relationship, and she remains completely in control. When he does try to take the wheel, he crashes—both literally and figuratively. Likewise, there is no indignity to which Lee will not stoop as he accompanies Brandon to Atlantic City in hopes of interesting the star in his screenplay. Desperate to break into the world of the movies, Lee even tries to promote his script while Brandon is deep in the act of sexual intercourse, but all Lee acquires is a $6,000 gambling debt and disillusionment.

Bad reviews of his first two novels have rendered Lee too insecure to write any more serious fiction. (He passes out at a cocktail party when a reviewer recalls the books and trashes them anew.) But his sobering experience with Brandon convinces him to abandon his screenplay, and Bonnie encourages him to resume writing fiction, the one activity he is truly passionate about. Therefore, when Lee leaves Bonnie, he loses not only his muse but also his newest manuscript, which she vindictively throws sheet by sheet into the Hudson River. Without Bonnie to encourage him, Lee quits writing rather than try to reconstruct the novel or start another. He thus becomes further detached from what Joseph Campbell would call "his bliss"—the activity that most animates him and makes his spirit sing. Instead, Lee unhappily pursues celebrities in order to acquire a sense of self-importance through association.

Robin replays the title character of *Alice*, an insecure, middle-aged woman who must overcome the repression of her Catholic upbringing. (Robin's Catholic inhibitions are the subject of a humorous scene in which Robin takes lessons in fellatio from a prostitute who chokes on a banana.) Robin also suffers from poor self-esteem and proves almost as self-destructive as Lee, but she is lucky. As she later tells Lee—and as Allen has asserted in interviews—successful romances are primarily a matter of luck. Through Robin, Allen underscores how irrational fears can undermine us and prevent us from accepting happiness when it appears. But Robin is fortunate to stumble on a gypsy fortune-teller who helps her recognize and overcome her self-destructive insecurities. Afraid that the man she loves is too good to be true, Robin abandons him at the wedding altar in order to escape being hurt when "the other foot falls" and Tony reveals his dark side. But the fortune-teller stops her as she passes by and points out how Robin has made the other foot fall herself. She advises Robin to seek psychological counseling and predicts that if Tony really loves her, he will take her back.

Thus Robin is redeemed by accepting the love of a good man. Tony represents a human ideal. He knows himself and lives accordingly. He recognizes what truly matters to him and arranges his life so he can spend most of his time pursuing those interests. A producer of celebrity-oriented television shows, Tony lives in the world of the rich and famous. But this is the by-product of his desire to build a successful business, not a goal in itself. Doing nice things for the people he loves appears to be one of Tony's greatest sources of satisfaction, and he appreciates his celebrity because it enables him to do this. He gladly uses his influence to get his grandfather into a desirable nursing home, secure reservations at a fashionable restaurant for his cousins, and obtain sports tickets for his nephew. But he does not expect excessive displays of gratitude, flattery, or other forms of ego enhancement. He is clear about his values and priorities, placing his love and lust for Robin above the demands of his business.

Tony's faith in Robin ultimately proves stronger than her own feelings of inadequacy. His acceptance of her even after she stands him up at the wedding demonstrates the depth of his love for her, as well as his own high level of self-esteem. Though he is undoubtedly hurt and embarrassed, he is sufficiently strong and self-assured to interpret her action correctly as what it is—an expression of her own insecurity—and not as an attack on him. Because his priorities and values remain clear to him, Tony remains focused on his love for Robin rather than on the hurt, and after she comes to terms with her fears and acquires greater self-acceptance, he marries her.

A former English teacher, Robin becomes much happier and more fulfilled after she leaves teaching and becomes a media celebrity who interviews famous but inconsequential people. As a teacher, Robin felt that her work—nurturing young people and exploring with them the greatest works of Western literature—was important. She deplored the superficiality and pretension of the media. In her second career Robin recognizes that she has become the kind of woman she used to hate and that her current work is nowhere as important or meaningful as teaching. But she is also honest enough with herself to admit that she loves her new life and finds it more rewarding than when she taught children.

Would that it were otherwise, Allen seems to say, but even as it is true that older men are physically attracted to younger women, it is also true that as a species, humans tend to bask in fame and glory. Moreover, most of us derive greater pleasure from the ego enhancement that celebrity provides than from the satisfaction derived by more meaningful but anonymous activities, such as teaching. Because humans are this way, the film suggests, humanity is doomed to perpetual superficiality. This is part of Allen's essentially pessimistic view of the human condition.

For Allen, a related aspect of the human condition is that virtue is not always rewarded and moral lapses are not always punished. Therefore, someone who chooses to live a virtuous life must do so for the inherent rewards of virtuous living and not for external reasons, such as recognition or remuneration. Allen had developed this theme more fully in *Crimes and Misdemeanors*, but Robin's recognition that she is happier being a superficial celebrity represents her acceptance of her flawed humanity and the human condition. In turn, her acceptance of this more superficial side of herself indicates growth in self-esteem, since her earlier religious upbringing presumably taught her that it is wrong to be dedicated to insignificant things and that enjoying fame demonstrates improper pride. Just as Lee seemingly needs to experience purely sexual relationships so he can mature and move beyond them, Robin needs to indulge the euphoria of fame and superficiality, something she apparently rarely experienced as a child. Eventually, perhaps, she will become sated and move on to something more substantial.

Allen thus suggests an inverse relationship between self-esteem and attraction to fame: the more self-accepting people are, the less they are enchanted by celebrity, and conversely when they suffer from poor self-esteem, they are more strongly attracted to fame. This is not to say that all celebrities have poor self-esteem, only those who become celebrities primarily because they aspire to be famous and not because they want to achieve something extraordinary.

Celebrity gives little insight into the celebrities themselves, except that they function in their own surreal worlds. Like the very rich whom F. Scott Fitzgerald describes, the very famous are different from you and me. They are often self-absorbed and tend to take themselves very seriously, sometimes ironically so, such as when Brandon Barry complains that most scripts he receives have "no fucking integrity," and when celebrity artist Bruce Bishop declares theatrically that no one should buy his paintings just to be "in."

Celebrities get away with things that ordinary citizens are punished for, and they enjoy opportunities unavailable to most others. Brandon can beat his girlfriend nearly to death, trash his hotel rooms, and resist arrest without consequence; Nicole is coddled and takes calls from the President while on the set; supermodels forever have men fawning over them; television priests are hounded for their autographs; even natural enemies bond around the common experience of media exposure, as when the black ACLU representative and the Ku Klux Klansmen act like old friends because they have appeared on so many TV shows together, and the rabbi complains good-naturedly that the skinheads have eaten all the bagels.

However, the celebrities ultimately reveal more about our society than about themselves. As Robin observes, "You can learn a lot about a culture by who it chooses as its celebrities. We did a whole show on Sonny Von Bulow, and she was in a coma. She just lay there, but she was a celebrity." Anyone with an instantly recognizable face, even inaccurate weathermen, becomes a celebrity. This point is underscored when a little boy tells his grandmother about a media hero who visited his school. When she learns the man is famous for having been taken hostage, the grandmother objects, "What's he famous for, for being captured? That doesn't make him a hero." But her complaint falls on deaf ears.

In *This Simian World* (1920) humorist Clarence Day attributes our lust for fame to the fact that humans evolved from monkeys, a species innately attracted to glitter and sensation. Had we evolved from cows, he suggests, we would be able to ponder a single idea for days, and had we sprung from cats, we would be indifferent to glory. In *Celebrity* Allen exposes the superficiality of a culture that treasures fame more than meritorious achievement, but he also accepts this phenomenon as part of the human condition. At the same time, Allen shows that is possible to resist becoming distorted by the attraction of fame, but this requires self-knowledge, self-discipline, and self-acceptance.

Central Park West. A 1995 play written by Allen. Between March 6 and December 31, 1995, it was performed off-Broadway at the Variety Arts Theater as part of a trilogy of one-act plays, *Death Defying Acts*; it is published under that title as well (Samuel French, Inc., 1996). Directed by Michael Blakemore, the production had 343 performances. Julian Schlossberg and Jean Doumanian produced; Meyer Ackerman and Letty Aronson, Allen's sister, were associate producers. Robin Wagner designed the set, and Jane Greenwood designed the costumes. The cast included Debra Monk (Phyllis), Linda Lavin (Carol), Gerry Becker (Howard), Paul Guilfoyle (Sam), and Tari T. Signor (Juliet). The play went on tour in 1996.

Widely appreciated for its humor, *Central Park West* was generally well received. Most reviewers found it to be the strongest play of the trilogy, though some viewers were made uncomfortable by its apparent connections to Allen's very public breakup with Mia Farrow.

In an Internet review, Christopher Winsor, who praises Allen as "a master of the situation comedy," describes the play as "Neil Simon meets Edward Albee, but the characters are Allen's own." Julian Fox likens it to an

"X-rated revamp of Noel Coward's *Fallen Angels*" (Fox 132). Edward Albee's *Who's Afraid of Virginia Woolf?* (1962) and Jean-Paul Sartre's *No Exit* (1945) also resonate in this story of two couples who torture each other with their betrayals and infidelities.

The title refers to an upscale section of New York City. But within the play Allen also uses it to suggest a kind of decadent self-absorption. This becomes most apparent in the exchange where one character complains, "We're alone in the cosmos!" and another replies, "This is not the cosmos—this is Central Park West." The play unveils layer after layer of betrayal, as Phyllis, a middle-aged, foul-mouthed, hard-drinking, highly successful psychoanalyst accuses her friend Carol of having an affair with her husband, Sam, a virile, high-powered attorney. Carol finally confesses but explains that they never intended to hurt anyone and that the love and passion had already gone from Phyllis's marriage anyway. Trying to put an optimistic face on it, she declares, "Look, we all clearly need new lives. . . . I say we look at tonight as a beginning. . . . I know—it sounds easy for me to say because Sam and I have each other—but I say we can be civilized and help one another get through this." But when Sam reveals he has betrayed Carol too, she loses her rational, mature perspective. Ultimately Sam, too, is betrayed, as Carol's husband, Howard, convinces Juliet, Sam's twenty-one-year-old girlfriend and Phyllis's former patient, to leave Sam for him.

Though funny, the play is also unusually caustic for Allen; only *Deconstructing Harry*, which he released two years later, possesses the harshness of *Central Park West*. None of the characters is appealing; each is either a victim or a victimizer. As in *No Exit* and *Who's Afraid of Virginia Woolf?*, the characters seem to exist to torture one another by publicly exposing their respective weaknesses and moments of shame. In so doing, they create and cling to their own living hell. Ultimately only Howard seems capable of walking away from this masochistic situation.

Phyllis, Carol, and Howard are the most fully developed characters. Phyllis is bright, accomplished, and witty, but she is also self-absorbed, and her narcissism blinds her to the realities of her own personal life. Everyone, even the busboys at the restaurant who do not speak English, knows Sam has affairs before Phyllis does. Like Hannah from *Hannah and Her Sisters*, Phyllis is "penalized by everyone because I'm a success. My sister, my friends, my husband." Howard affirms the point: "People never hate you for your weaknesses—they hate you for your strengths." But there is a dark side of Phyllis as well, as Howard points out when he asks, "What kind of woman are you, Phyllis, that all these seemingly close people willingly betray you?" In his only published novel, Howard has portrayed Phyllis as "the center of attention wherever they go . . . who never realizes he's [her husband] weak and she is inadvertently emasculating the poor bastard, so all he lives for is illicit sex."

By contrast, Carol is a weak person who emulates role models rather than develop her own personality. According to Howard, "Carol's always had an identity problem. She doesn't know who she is. Or rather she knows who she is and she's desperately trying to find someone else to be—and who can blame her." When she was a college student Carol conceived a baby because her favorite female professor, whose wardrobe, hairstyle, mannerisms, and tastes she also copied, had a small child. In Howard's harsh retelling, "In nine months she would be just like Professor Kanin . . . art major, mother, the works—she wouldn't have to go on being the unenviable character Carol." But in her eighth month of pregnancy, "reality set in" and Carol realized she did not want to be a mother, so she gave up the child for adoption despite Howard's immediate bonding with the infant. Carol's friendship with Phyllis is also based on hero worship. As Carol imitated the art professor by appropriating her lifestyle, she has tried to absorb Phyllis's identity, first by appropriating her friends and then her husband.

Only manic-depressive Howard emerges from the situation a winner. In addition to leaving with Juliet, the normally submissive Howard gains new self-respect and empowerment. Initially, knowledge that his wife has been unfaithful not only with Sam but with his writing partner and dentist too ("Think of it as an extra filling") sends him into a bout of despair that triggers a failed suicide attempt. Nonetheless, Howard immediately recognizes and accepts that his marriage has failed, telling Carol that she no longer has clout over him. Letting go of Carol enables Howard to act more honestly, according to his own desires. As a newly detached observer, he enjoys the irony of Carol's distress when Sam informs her of his new girlfriend. He implicitly concurs with Phyllis, who vindictively observes, "Sometimes there's God so quickly."

Indeed, the development transforms Howard's depression into an uplifting manic state, and in that expansive, self-confident, self-loving frame of mind, the former wimp and failed novelist now projects himself as a great film writer-producer and thereby wins Juliet from Sam. Howard may be self-delusional at this point, though he is probably just assuming a persona to impress Juliet. In either case, he responds in the best way possible, by walking away like a winner from his unloving wife and uncaring friends.

See also *Death Defying Acts*.

Crimes and Misdemeanors. A 1989 film directed by, written by, and starring Allen, who plays documentary filmmaker Cliff Stern. It costars Mia Farrow (Halley Reed), Martin Landau (Judah Rosenthal), Angelica Huston

(Delores Paley), Alan Alda (Lester), Sam Waterston (Ben, the rabbi), Claire Bloom (Miriam Rosenthal), Martin Bergmann (Professor Louis Levy), Joanna Gleason (Wendy Stern), Caroline Aaron (Cliff's sister, Barbara), Jenny Nichols (Cliff's niece, Jenny), and Jerry Orbach (Jack Rosenthal). Robert Greenhut was the producer, Sven Nykvist director of photography, Santo Loquasto production designer, Jeffrey Kurland costumer, and Susan E. Morse editor. The music features classical sections from Johann Sebastian Bach and Franz Schubert, along with jazz by Cole Porter, Richard Rogers, Irving Berlin, Frank Loesser, Xavier Cugat, Sammy Fain, and others. Orion Pictures was the North American distributor.

Crimes and Misdemeanors was Allen's first financial and critical success since *Hannah and Her Sisters*, five films and three years earlier. Allen's most ambitious artistic effort to date, it tries to achieve the profundity and moral complexity of a Russian novel or a Shakespearean tragedy. *Crimes and Misdemeanors* received Allen's best reviews ever, and its impact on the public was strong enough to engender discussions about ethical responsibility in numerous forums, including the *New York Times*, where three theologians exchanged ideas about the moral issues raised by the film. The film, which cost $13 million to produce, remained on the box office charts for nineteen weeks. Released in October, it grossed $17.6 million in 1989 and an additional $2 million in 1990, but netted only $8.5 million. However, the earnings were substantially supplemented by the film's success in Europe. Allen received Academy Award nominations for best director and best original screenplay, and Martin Landau was nominated for best supporting actor.

Throughout his cinematic career Allen has addressed the problem of living a meaningful, fulfilling, morally responsible life in an indifferent universe in which God either does not exist or exists but chooses not to intervene or reveal himself. This is essentially the absurd universe that Fydor Dostoyevsky describes in his novels, Ingmar Bergman portrays in *The Seventh Seal* (1956), and Shakespeare presents in *King Lear* (circa 1605). It is also shared by the naturalist writers from the turn of the century, such as Emile Zola and Stephen Crane; by such modern poets as William Butler Yeats, T. S. Eliot, and W. H. Auden; by such modern novelists as Virginia Woolf, James Joyce, William Faulkner, and Ernest Hemingway, by Jean-Paul Sartre, Albert Camus, and other French existentialists; and by such contemporary writers as John Barth, Robert Coover, and Thomas Pynchon. In short, the problem of deciding what constitutes proper action in a relativistic, atheistic environment is one of the dominating issues in twentieth-century literature. Allen has maintained that "existential subjects to me are still the only subjects worth dealing with. Any time one deals with other subjects one is not aiming for the highest goal. . . . I don't think that one can aim more deeply than at the so-called existential themes, the spiritual themes" (*Woody Allen on Woody Allen* 211).

As Shakespeare does in *King Lear*, Allen concludes that in an absurd universe, virtue must be its own reward, since the universe will not otherwise reward it. Nor will it necessarily punish evil. As in *Lear*, Allen's most virtuous characters suffer while the malefactors prevail, at least in the short run.

Yet like *Lear*, *Crimes and Misdemeanors* shows that virtue can indeed be its own reward. Specifically, being attuned to and living in harmony with a set of a core values confers a strong sense of identity—a sense of who we are and what we stand for. Those who do not know themselves well enough to recognize what they value, and those who recognize their values but betray them anyway, fall into conflict with themselves—a recipe for discontentment. But those who live in harmony with their values enjoy direction in life. We would not have *Lear*'s Cordelia corrupt her beliefs in order to win her father's approval or appease her sisters, even though she suffers for it. She dies prematurely, but she has lived fully and meaningfully, acting according to her beliefs, free from the inner turmoil or the jealousy, spite, and greed that infect her more prosperous sisters and make them miserable.

Similarly, Ben, the blind rabbi in *Crimes and Misdemeanors*, who is described by his sister as "a saint," retains a strong sense of what he stands for despite his affliction. Because he can still "see" who he is, his identity remains intact, while those who have drifted from their core values suffer loss of identity, even when they otherwise prosper. Ben embodies the point made during the Passover seder: that even if the nihilists prove accurate, a person will have a happier, more fulfilling life by living as if there is an inherent morality in the universe, a morality that approves of compassionate action and rejects the notion of "might makes right." Allen underscores this point by concluding the film with a lingering shot of Ben dancing happily with his daughter at her wedding.[1]

If Ben is a saint, then Judah is perhaps a fallen angel. A good but flawed man, he functions like a classic tragic hero who, through blindness to his own shortcomings, falls because of them. Though an atheist, he was raised in a religious family and inherited the basic Jewish ethical values articulated by the Ten Commandments. Outwardly, Judah embodies Allen's notion of the ideal cosmopolitan man. He has presumably worked hard and accomplished much, establishing himself as a healer, a successful ophthalmologist, a prosperous family man, an honored community leader, a connoisseur, an international bon vivant, and a man of great culture, refinement, discernment, and taste.

But Judah's tragic flaw is that when he deviates from what he believes in, he proves too weak to accept responsibility for his actions. He arrogantly asserts his own well-being over his basic moral convictions. Consequently, Judah's character and integrity deteriorate, even if he outwardly continues to prosper. The film thus raises the question whether, in an absurd universe, deterioration of character is sufficient reason for a person to refrain from committing what he himself regards as improper action.

Claiming that the passion has gone from his marriage, Judah initiates an affair with Delores, an airline stewardess he met on a business trip. After two years, the emotionally needy Delores threatens to expose the affair, as well as an illegal transfer of charitable funds that Judah had secretly committed but later rectified, with interest. Fearing that Delores will end his marriage, ruin his reputation in the community, and otherwise destroy everything he has dedicated his life to creating—essentially the same reasons that he embezzled the funds from the charities—Judah tells his gangster brother Jack that she is "killing me." He therefore reluctantly concludes that he has no better alternative, and he orders her murder.

Like Shakespeare's Lady Macbeth and Raskolnikov from Dostoyevsky's *Crime and Punishment*, Judah commits murder and escapes punishment, but becomes wracked by pangs of conscience. Like the sleep-walking Lady Macbeth, who initially believes that water will easily wash the stain of

Angelica Huston and Martin Landau in a scene from *Crimes and Misdemeanors*. Courtesy of Photofest.

blood from her murderous hands but later discovers that "not all the perfumes of Araby" can remove the scent of guilt, Judah says before ordering the killing, "I push one button, and I can sleep again at night." But in fact, just the opposite occurs. When Jack informs him that the murder has been committed and that he can now "go back" to his life, Judah's first physical response is to wash his hands and face. But like Lady Macbeth, he is unable to return to his life because he is consumed by a guilty conscience. Like her, his life begins to dissipate: he takes to drinking, has difficulty sleeping, and alienates his spouse.

Like Raskolnikov, Judah becomes consumed by a need to confess. Raskolnikov finally confesses in order to free himself from the self-inflicted torture of his own guilty conscience, and Dostoyevsky presents his confession as a triumph of free will in an atheistic universe. In effect, Dostoyevsky shows that if everyone so chooses, we can create a moral universe that rewards good and punishes evil, even if the universe is not inherently moral. Cliff suggests exactly such a course of action to Judah during the final wedding scene, claiming that surrender and confession will give Judah's story tragic dimension: "In the absence of a God or something, he is forced to assume that responsibility himself. Then you have tragedy." But Judah dismisses the idea as mere fiction. "That's movies. . . . I'm talking about reality. I mean, if you want a happy ending, you should see a Hollywood movie."

Pointedly distinguishing his film from a Hollywood movie, Allen presents an alternative ending to *Crime and Punishment*—one in which the criminal exercises his free will differently and eventually commutes his sentence of self-punishment. Unlike Raskolnikov or the classic tragic hero, Judah recovers from his fall from fortune when his conscience eases up on him. He ceases to torture himself and resumes his life as an honored community leader and successful family man—a life that he can once again enjoy now that he has unconsciously absolved himself of his guilt. On the one hand, in sheer existential terms Judah has prevailed; he has gotten away with murder and not been punished for it, apart from three or four disturbing months. In the absurd universe, the guilty are not necessarily punished unless they punish themselves, and eventually Judah chooses not to.

On the other hand, as Danny points out in *Broadway Danny Rose*, "It's important to feel guilty. Otherwise you're capable of terrible things." By accepting his crimes but refusing to feel remorse or do penance for them, Judah transforms from a righteous citizen into a sociopath—someone who knows right from wrong but violates the laws of society anyway and feels no remorse for his actions. Though it may be true that the sociopath feels no pain, few of us envy or aspire to the sociopath's psychological condition.

By acknowledging his misdeeds—his affair with Delores, his financial impropriety, and the murder of Delores—but refusing to accept any consequences for his acts, Judah undermines his own identity, particularly his identity as a Jew. Hitherto, Judah, a deservedly respected member of the community, has presumably been a law-abiding *mensch*. His affair with Delores appears to be his first, and he has otherwise seemingly adhered to the Ten Commandments. Judah, an atheist, could thus claim at least an ethical connection to his Jewish heritage, if not a spiritual one.

But as Judah himself notes, his violations of the Ten Commandments feed on each other: adultery leads to lying and ultimately to murder. To accept his acts of adultery and murder without accepting consequences for them necessarily implies rejection of the law: both secular law and the Torah, the first five books of the Old Testament that stand at the heart of Judaism. By rejecting the Torah, whose name means *law*, Judah disconnects from his Jewish identity, and by rejecting secular law he transforms what was once a truly upright citizen into a posturing hypocrite. In short, just as he had feared Delores would do by exposing him, he destroys everything he had built in life: his service to humanity, his integrity, and everything else on which his self-respect rested. In the eyes of his peers Judah remains virtuous, and the eyes of God appear to be closed. But in his own eyes, Judah can never be the same person he was without deliberately blinding himself to himself. In an absurd, postmodern universe, appearances may in fact count as much as underlying realities, and feeling good may be the only thing that finally matters. If this is the case, then Judah prevails. But the cost of his euphoria is a deliberately cultivated blindness about himself, and in the long run such blindness usually proves treacherous.

If Judah is guilty of the crimes alluded to by the title, Cliff commits the misdemeanors. (The title quotes from the U.S. Constitution, which states that a president should be removed from office if convicted of "high crimes and misdemeanors.") Another one of Allen's little-man characters, Cliff is a basically well-intended loser. An obscure documentary filmmaker, his marriage has failed, and he and his wife no longer have sex but, according to him, neither has the energy to break up. (They do finally separate after *she* finds another man.) His hopes of making the movie of his dreams are dashed when the film's subject, an inspiring, life-affirming concentration camp survivor, commits suicide. Cliff finally meets Halley, a woman with whom he shares common interests and values, but she leaves New York to pursue a job opportunity, and when she returns, she is engaged to Lester, Cliff's egotistical brother-in-law, a happy, successful producer of television documentaries whom Cliff detests because he considers Lester a self-important, money-hustling sellout.

But Lester proves to be not really as bad as Cliff portrays him, and Cliff eventually confesses his envy. Cliff projects himself as uncompromisingly principled, but in reality he is inflexible and vindictive. Although his envy and spite produce one of the film's funniest moments—a documentary of Lester that likens him to Mussolini—Cliff seems more pathetic than comic. The metaphor of blindness that permeates the film extends as well to Cliff, who refuses to see that Halley has consistently rejected his romantic overtures and that she finds Lester attractive. Cliff does achieve a modicum of insight when he acknowledges his envy of Lester, but the film concludes with him alone at the party and alone in life, despite his basic decency and fundamentally good values: he is committed to his widowed sister and her daughter, to humanistic causes, and to making films that have real substance and lasting value.

Cliff's despair, and that of his sister, Barbara, a lonely single mother, demonstrate another aspect of Allen's absurd universe: goodness and decency are not rewarded any more than evil is punished. For instance, an ostensibly sympathetic character, Barbara suffers deep, gratuitous humiliation when a date ties her to her bed for passionate sex but then defecates upon her instead, presumably leaving her to wallow in his excrement until somebody—perhaps her daughter—discovers her. Certainly Barbara has done nothing to deserve this treatment, but she receives it nonetheless. As Shakespeare does with Cordelia, Allen uses Barbara's story to demonstrate that in an absurd universe, acting virtuously does not ensure good treatment from others or from fate. Or, as a contemporary bumper sticker states, "Shit happens." The trick is to endure.

Professor Levy, the subject of Cliff's life-affirming documentary and a Holocaust survivor who endured the loss of his entire family, maintains, "We need love to persuade us to stay in life. . . . Under certain conditions we feel it isn't worth it any more." For Levy, every day requires an active choice to keep on living. Cliff is impressed that Levy has kept saying yes to life, even under the most horrifying conditions in the concentration camp, and Cliff hopes his documentary film will enable others to benefit from Levy's strength and wisdom.

Allen shows existentialist philosophies like Professor Levy's to be attractive, but not guaranteed to overcome despair, as one day Levy kills himself for no apparent reason. Unable to comprehend his mentor's death, Cliff remarks, "He's seen the worst side of life his whole life. He always . . . said, 'Yes' to life. 'Yes. Yes.' Now, today he said, 'No.' " Halley seems to express Allen's own thoughts when she replies, "No matter how elaborate a philosophic system you work out, in the end it's got to be incomplete." As Richard A. Blake states, "Halley thus voices Allen's realization that the intellect

alone cannot impose order on a universe that contains inexplicable mysteries, like the self-inflicted death of a good man or the Holocaust" (Blake 183).

The need for love and the difficulty of acquiring it thus resonate throughout the film. Several characters are desperately lonely, and Allen points out
that finding a proper mate requires good fortune, apart from anything else.
Until their luck changes or they find a way to change it, the sympathetic
characters will remain alone. Cliff and Barbara persist stoically, but Professor Levy eventually surrenders to despair.

But even love cannot always overcome poor self-esteem, and not all love
proves to be healthy. When used to compensate for deeper problems of
self-acceptance, love can turn vindictive and destructive. Delores's desperate love for Judah is jealous, possessive, and ultimately harmful. Judah was
seeking to regain passion in his life, enjoy the pleasure of initiating a young
disciple into the delights of the arts, and bask in her adoration and gratitude.
But in addition, Judah finds that he has become an emotional crutch for an
insecure, love-starved, emotionally needy person who is increasingly dependent on him.

Evocative of Alex Forrest, Glenn Close's character in *Fatal Attraction*
(1987), Delores initially appears to Judah as an attractive, younger woman
who shows interest in him. Like many other pairings of older men and
younger women in Allen's films, Judah has assumed a fatherly role, offering security and introducing Delores to high culture. We learn that her life
was at a low point before they met and that he "turned everything around."
But when Judah refuses to leave his wife and commit more fully to her, Delores becomes so desperate for love that she inflicts emotional anguish on
him in order to bind him to her. She threatens that without his love, she will
jump from the window—which is exactly how Professor Levy dies. But instead Delores tries to use their affair and her knowledge of Judah's financial
impropriety to blackmail him into committing to her. "You're going to hold
on to me with threats?" Judah retorts. Thus, in the long run Delores's desperate, possessive love transforms Judah into a murderer and herself into
the ultimate victim, which is how she has seen herself all along.[2]

The movie does feature some successful love relationships too, and a
problematic one. The film concludes with one wedding of young people
and the promise of two more: Judah's daughter to her fiancé and Lester to
Halley. Richard A. Blake observers, "The wedding functions as a sign of a
new family, new life, the continuation of the species. To underline the
theme, the camera lingers on unidentified children amusing themselves"
(Blake 186).

Although it is the realization of Cliff's worst fears, the union between
Lester and Halley promises to be happy. Lester values Halley for her intelli-

gence and wit, as well as for her looks. Moreover, she finds him resistible and thus represents a challenge to his considerable ego. Halley appears to bring out a good side of Lester, who quotes Emily Dickinson for her with some feeling and appreciation (as opposed to Cliff, who merely shows off his awareness of the poem's irony). It is at least possible that in order to impress her, Lester may attempt deeper, more substantial projects and become a deeper, more substantial person. Halley too stands to benefit from the relationship. Cynics like Cliff may conclude that Halley is marrying Lester primarily for the professional opportunities that will come to her because of his influence. But Lester is probably one of the few single men she has met who is capable of challenging her intellectually. She enjoys their witty exchanges, and he enjoys her ability to put him down cleverly—something not all men would take so well. Finally, Lester offers optimism, confidence, and good spirits—all qualities that Cliff lacks. In choosing Lester over Cliff, Halley has elected meaningful happiness over self-righteous suffering.[3]

But Cliff is not altogether unlovable. He enjoys the love of his niece, Jenny, and the warmest scenes in the film occur as he shares his passion for old movies with her. (Allen uses film clips from Alfred Hitchcock's *Mr. and Mrs. Smith* [1941] and *Happy Go Lucky* [1943] to punctuate Judah's story and create transitions to the Cliff subplot.) Around Jenny, Cliff seems natural, relaxed, and less morbid, though never truly optimistic. He also feels wise and respected. The pleasure he takes from introducing Jenny to cinematic gems parallels the pleasure Judah gleans from teaching Delores about classical music, but it is more innocent; it lacks the sexual spark in Judah's mentoring and in the mentoring relationships in Allen's other films. Cliff's close relationship to Jenny presumably feeds enough love into Cliff's life to enable him to continue saying yes to existence, even during his moments of deep despair.

The one problematic relationship is Judah's marriage to his wife, Miriam. If a concluded love affair can be covered up and allowed to evaporate into a distant memory, as Elliot's affair with Lee does in *Hannah and Her Sisters*, can a murder similarly recede and leave no lasting impact? The concluding scene suggests that it can. Judah's tale of the murderer whose remorse one day vanishes expresses the triumph of nihilism. Outwardly Judah and Miriam have regained the comfortable, mutually accepting life they had before the affair. And in the postmodern, absurdist universe, outward appearances count for a lot, because we can never be sure anything exists beneath the surface.

Nonetheless, the difference is that Miriam is now married to a sociopath, when before she was not. She is now married to a man who must every moment commit an act of Orwellian double-think in which he simultaneously acknowledges that he has committed murder and nonetheless believes he is still a fundamentally good and moral person. It is conceivable that Miriam might not notice the difference and experience her marriage in more or less the same manner as she would have otherwise. But the continual practice of double-think has to make some difference on a person's life. Even though Judah has "gotten away with murder" by escaping both society's punishment and that of his own conscience, his acceptance of behavior he had hitherto found repugnant has made Judah into a different person—a sociopath. We must expect this difference eventually to be felt in the marriage.

Cinematically, *Crimes and Misdemeanors* is notable for interior shots that concentrate our visual attention on a restricted portion of the screen and thereby isolate the characters and the action. This underscores the loneliness that permeates the film, as the characters appear cut off even from their environment. Sam Girgus describes the technique as "a form of interior camera. . . . [Allen's] technique involves a systematic use and interconnection of close-ups and flashbacks to explore and chart this interior geography" (Girgus, *The Films of Woody Allen* 118).

The photography in the Passover flashback is shot identically to the flashback scene in Ingmar Bergman's *Wild Strawberries* (1957), when Professor Borg visits his childhood home and recalls significant scenes from his youth. (Allen's cameraman, Sven Nykvist, filmed many of Bergman's movies, but not *Wild Strawberries*.) In contrast to the other camera work that isolates the characters, here the wide-angle shots take in the entire table, emphasizing the collective community of the family, even as the adults argue about the existence of God and the inherent morality of the universe.

One of the most memorable scenes in the film, the seder debate shows how such central questions as the existence and nature of God go to the heart of both religious identity and personal identity. But the debate is, by its very nature, metaphysical and hence unresolvable by any empirical method. Logical positivists like Leopold from *A Midsummer Night's Sex Comedy* and the doctor from *Shadows and Fog* would therefore call it meaningless, but the French existentialists would regard it as self-defining. Allen has often expressed his own personal refusal to surrender to his desire for a God and a moral universe, because he lacks any empirical or rational basis for adopting such a belief. Judah's aunt articulates the logical extreme that follows from a godless, meaningless universe when she cynically suggests that power is the only universal value; otherwise "nothing's handed down in stone." In taking this position, she unwittingly rejects the Ten Commandments, the moral basis of the Torah, which, according to Exodus in the Old Testament, God handed down to Moses inscribed on stone tablets.

When asked about murder, Judah's aunt argues that a person who escapes punishment gets away free. Of course, for Jews the Holocaust presents the ultimate test of faith. How can we find inherent morality in a universe in which six million people are slaughtered for no other reason than that they are Jews? How can we still affirm that God sees everything and rewards the virtuous and punishes the wicked? Judah's aunt finds no way to reconcile this apparent contradiction, and so she rejects the premise of a moral universe; she rejects the Torah. But despite the contradiction, Judah's father, Sol, clings to his faith, declaring that if he must choose between the truth and his faith in God, he will always choose his faith. Sol insists that the Nazis were punished, that they did not get away with the Holocaust, and he maintains that "whether it's the Old Testament or Shakespeare, murder will out. That which originates in a black deed will blossom in a black manner." Finally, Sol affirms that even if he proves wrong and there is no God, "I'll still have a better life than all those who doubt."

Some people, like Cliff, are incapable of making Sol's leap of faith; yet they too want a society predicated on compassion and mutual respect rather than on brute force. For them, the absurd universe gives the freedom to create the kind of world they desire by recognizing an appropriate set of values and living according to them. Because Cliff does this, because he remains true to his own basic sense of decency even in the depths of his despair, he appears superior to Judah in our eyes, regardless of whether God sees him.

NOTES

1. Allen himself regards Ben as self-delusional. "He's blind even before he goes blind. He's blind because he doesn't see the real world. But he's blessed and lucky, because he has the single most important lucky attribute anyone could have . . . genuine religious faith. It's not artificial. He genuinely believes what he's saying. And so even in the face of the worst adversity, he is OK. He goes blind. He still loves everybody and loves the world and loves life and loves his daughter. . . . The worst adversity can be surmounted with faith. But as author, *I* think that Ben is blind even before he's blind, because he doesn't see what's real in the world. But he's lucky because he has his naiveté" (*Woody Allen on Woody Allen* 223).

The theme of blindness contributes to the movie's tragic dimension by linking it with such major tragedies as *Oedipus Rex* and *King Lear*. Like those plays, *Crimes and Misdemeanors* plays off the sometimes incongruous relationship between sight and insight.

For a discussion of the eye metaphor's specific application to F. Scott Fitzgerald's *The Great Gatsby*, see Dianne L. Vipond, *"Crimes and Misdemeanors*: A Re-Take on the Eyes of Dr. Eckleburg."

2. This, of course, is not to condone the murder in any way or to suggest that Judah had no other choice than to act as he did. Indeed, Ben's advice for Judah to

admit the affair to his wife and hope for her understanding and forgiveness seems clearly to be the wise and responsible path. But Delores casts herself as a victim, claiming that dubious promises were made and opportunities sacrificed, and thus justifies her vindictive behavior to herself. Justified or not, her angry actions create a situation in which Judah feels he must choose between killing her and losing everything he cares for. And thus she unwisely makes her life dependent on his choosing to do the right thing, even though this will cost him dearly.

Disturbingly, Martin Landau has reported several instances where men in situations like Judah's have approached him and expressed their approval of Judah's decision to kill Delores (Fox 205).

3. Many commentators essentially accept Cliff's jealous view of Lester and regard him as pretentious and unworthy of Halley's affection. Even Allen himself, though acknowledging that Lester is "not a bad guy," considers him shallow and self-important (*Woody Allen on Woody Allen* 220). But Lester seems decent at the core. A good family man, he offers Cliff a job to help out his sister (Cliff's wife), even though he knows Cliff hates him, and Lester finances his niece's wedding, something he is "always doing." Even if he comes across as a knee-jerk liberal, he is at least civic-minded and apparently motivated by concern for the greater good, as well as by desire for his own fortune and fame.

Lester also proves capable of growth. In choosing Halley, for instance, he has opted for someone more substantial than the apparent bimbos he had previously sought out. He may have an excessively high an opinion of himself, but this enables him to accomplish things on a grand scale. Moreover, Halley manages his ego well, and Lester's self-aggrandizement seems preferable to Cliff's envy that typically expresses itself as judgmental self-righteousness.

D

Davis, Judy. An Australian-born actress who appears in *Alice*, *Husbands and Wives*, *Deconstructing Harry*, and *Celebrity*. Notable appearances in films by other directors include *My Brilliant Career* (1979), *A Passage to India* (1984), and *Naked Lunch* (1991).

Davis received Academy Award nominations for her role as Sally in *Husbands and Wives* and for her performance in *A Passage to India*. Allen has called her "probably the best movie actress in the world today" (*Woody Allen on Woody Allen* 247). He has also expressed a desire to make a movie pairing Davis with Dianne Wiest and Diane Keaton: "I would use the three most exciting actresses there are for the moment. And it would be so great!" (*Woody Allen on Woody Allen* 181, 247).

Death. Fear of death is a persistent theme in Allen's work. This fear keeps Allen's little men little, and his concern with the moral and existential implications of each person's inevitable death connects Allen's films and writings to the great works of Western literature, notably those of Shakespeare and Dostoyevsky. Allen has stated, "There is no other fear of significant consequence. All other fears, all other problems one can deal with. Loneliness, lack of love, lack of talent, lack of money, everything can be dealt with. . . . But perishing is what it's all about" (*Woody Allen on Woody Allen* 106).

Like *King Lear* and any number of major twentieth-century novels, plays, and poems, Ingmar Bergman's *The Seventh Seal* (1956) asks how it is possible to live an authentic, meaningful life in an absurd universe that has neither inherent meaning nor intrinsic moral structure. Its protagonist is obsessed with learning what happens to us after death, but he is never able to find the answer. According to Allen, *The Seventh Seal* is "the definitive work on the subject" (*Woody Allen on Woody Allen* 210).

Allen alludes to *The Seventh Seal* on several occasions, usually by transforming it into a joke. His play *Death Knocks* parodies the movie directly. In Bergman's film the knight forestalls Death by offering a game of chess when Death comes to claim him. In *Death Knocks* a Jewish man puts Death off by defeating him in gin rummy. *Love and Death* also parodies *The Seventh Seal*. It too poses the big existential questions, but spoofs them as it asks them. It also features Death personified, and the final shot is a comic exaggeration of the ending to *The Seventh Seal*. *Deconstructing Harry* also personifies Death, who wrongly claims a young reprobate in a case of mistaken identity. (See **Ingmar Bergman**.)

Other notable instances where Allen's characters try to come to terms with death include *Interiors*, *Hannah and Her Sisters*, *Crimes and Misdemeanors*, *Shadows and Fog*, and *Bullets over Broadway*. Of *Interiors*, Allen has stated,

What we are talking about is the tragedy of perishing. Ageing and perishing. It's such a horrible, horrible thing for humans to contemplate, that they don't contemplate it. They try to block it out in every way. But sometimes you can't block it out. And when you can't block it out, you can either go the route that Renata goes, where she tries to express certain things in poetry. But if you're not lucky, if you're someone like Joey, you don't know what to do. You can never find yourself. But even someone like Renata, who is luckier than Joey, eventually comes to another conclusion, that even though she's an artist and she has some ways of expressing these painful ideas, even the art is not going to save her. She's going to perish like everybody else. Even if her poems are read a thousand years from now. (*Woody Allen on Woody Allen* 105)

In *Hannah and Her Sisters* Allen's character Mickey becomes convinced that he is dying from a brain tumor, and this occasions an existential crisis in which he grasps for a reason to keep on living. Finally, his laughter at a Marx Brothers' movie convinces him that life is worthwhile. Echoing *King Lear*, *Macbeth*, and *Crime and Punishment*, *Crimes and Misdemeanors* explores the moral implications of an absurd universe, as a highly respected doctor struggles successfully to overcome his guilty conscience after he has his mistress murdered. Likewise, *Bullets over Broadway* reveals the downside of existentialism; it features a sociopathic hit man with writing talent who, like the existential hero, disregards social norms and asserts his own set of moral values. Like Allen's play *Death*, on which it is based, *Shadows and Fog* asks how a person can take meaningful action and live a morally responsible life in a Kafkaesque world where nothing is as it appears, no one ever knows all the facts, and death is always waiting in the wings.

Like Bergman, Allen is unable to offer any solutions to the problem of coming to terms with death; he can only explore the implications of an uncertain, incompletely knowable universe. Ultimately Allen asserts his final position on death in his joke: "I'm not interested in living on in the hearts of my countrymen. I'd rather live on in my apartment!" (*Woody Allen on Woody Allen* 105).

Death: A Play. A play by Allen. He wrote it in fall 1972, and it first appeared in his collection *Without Feathers* (1975). According to Allen, who calls the play a "German expressionist comedy," *Death* has been performed, but he has never seen it. In 1985 and 1986, BBC Radio 3 aired a radio production. *Death* was the basis for Allen's 1992 movie, *Shadows and Fog*.

The story centers on Kleinman, a hapless clerk who is awakened in the middle of the night by vigilantes intent on capturing a killer on the loose. Roused from his bed, accused first of playing ignorant and then of being naive, berated for trying to find a rational pattern behind the killings, and then accused of being the killer because he has black hair like a strand found at the crime scene, Kleinman is coerced into joining the group. However, no one tells him what his role is in the vigilantes' plan, and when he finishes dressing and goes outside to join them, all but one of the vigilantes have left. The remaining one knows nothing of Kleinman's assignment, and he soon departs after admonishing that lives are depending on what he does. Kleinman is thus left alone on an empty street in the middle of the night while a homicidal maniac is on the prowl.

Throughout the evening, Kleinman tries both to care for his safety and ascertain his assignment. He is inclined to return to his apartment, secure the door, and go back to sleep in preparation for a busy day at the office, where he is competing for a promotion. But he also feels an obligation to those who are depending on him, even if he does not know what he is supposed to do. He drifts through the night encountering a doctor, a prostitute, the vigilantes, and finally the killer.

The doctor has joined with the vigilantes because he wants to study the killer scrupulously once they have captured the maniac. He hopes to understand the criminal mind by "dissecting him down to the last chromosome . . . until I had a one hundred percent understanding of precisely what he is in every aspect." The doctor ridicules Kleinman's inarticulate objections that no physical analysis, no matter how thorough, can enable us to know a person fully. Kleinman's inability to find language to describe the metaphysical essence of human character underscores the problematic nature of human spirituality; for whereas the doctor can command precise nouns and verbs to refer to particles of matter and energy, Kleinman has insufficient linguistic tools for describing such ambiguous, undefinable, non-physical concepts as personality characteristics, motivations, desires, levels of satisfaction, and inner spirit.

Ultimately the doctor is undermined by his own hubris when he refuses to acknowledge Kleinman's warning that his escape route into an alley is a dead-end, declaring, "Are you going to argue with me? I'm a doctor." Kleinman rejects the doctor's argument by authority in favor of common sense, and he survives while the doctor is stabbed offstage.

After parting from the doctor, Kleinman encounters Gina, a prostitute who challenges his ability to distinguish reality from illusion, up from down. She points out that the earth is floating through outer space and we cannot ascertain which way is up. Kleinman answers, "I'm a man who likes to know which way is up and which way is down and where's the bathroom." Gina goes on to question the very basis of empiricism, as she points out that the stars they are watching may not even still be there, even though he sees them with his own eyes. Kleinman complains that this scares him because if he sees something, he likes to believe it is there.

After she leaves, Kleinman meets a former soldier who had been killed in battle but restored to life on an operating table, again confusing such basic categories as dead and living. Kleinman then encounters more of the vigilantes, who by now have broken into hostile splinter groups and begun to attack each other. In other words, the vigilantes are now performing the work of the maniac. Once more, the vigilantes demand that Kleinman take sides, even though he does not know anything about the competing plans. He pleads, "How can I choose when I don't know the alternatives?" But they ignore his warning that they will kill each other while the maniac remains alive, and they insist that he choose immediately.

Kleinman's moment of decision is deferred when the police arrive claiming they have found the murderer. With them is Hans Spiro, a clairvoyant who sniffs the demurring Kleinman. When Spiro proclaims that Kleinman is the killer, everyone believes him despite the lack of evidence. The vigilantes are on the verge of hanging Kleinman when another man enters and announces the killer has been trapped behind the warehouse. Everyone then runs off after hastily apologizing to Kleinman.

Alone again, Kleinman notes this is no longer his problem and decides to go home. But he is unable to extract himself from the threat of imminent death. Having a poor sense of direction, Kleinman becomes lost and encounters the maniac. The killer looks like Kleinman, though apparently he has the knack of looking like all of his victims (as does Death in *Death Knocks*). They talk, and Kleinman tries, unsuccessfully, to understand the killer's lunacy, but he remains frustrated, unable to accept the man's fundamental irrationality. Kleinman asks him why he kills, and the maniac says he does it because he is crazy.

"But you look okay."

"You can't go by physical appearance. I'm a maniac."

Finally, the madman stabs Kleinman and runs off. As Kleinman dies, he admonishes the vigilantes to cooperate.

Although Allen develops the existential themes more fully in *Shadows and Fog*, many of the basic questions and circumstances found in that movie already exist in *Death*. In particular, Kleinman enters an uncertain world in which crucial facts remain unknown: the killer's identity, his own role in the vigilantes' original plan, the differences between each faction's plan, the existence of God, and the distinction between life and death. As Gina points out in her cosmological speculations, he cannot even be sure which way is up or whether the stars he sees with his own eyes are actually there. Nonetheless, Kleinman is repeatedly urged to act decisively. For Allen, the need to act responsibly in an unknowable world is part of the modern human condition, and Kleinman's inability to take effective action leads to his death. By contrast, he behaves more assertively in the Irmy subplot that Allen added in *Shadows and Fog*, and in the movie he comes to a much better end.

Allen seems to reject the doctor's unyielding empiricism as unnecessarily cold and sterile, and to ridicule the arrogance of this man of science. But he is reluctant to stray too far from the realm of the physical senses in his quest for truth. When Gina points out that the stars might no longer exist and asks who knows what is real, Kleinman is forced to adopt the doctor's empirical position: "What's real is what you can touch with your hands." Moreover, if the doctor's scientific empiricism feels sterile and is unable to account for the special magic of life, Spiro's clairvoyance, which presumably comes from his connection to the spiritual world, proves to be an unreliable sham, and the vigilantes' preference for simple, fear-based solutions seems less desirable than Kleinman's more logical approach, which, among other things, insists on physical evidence before convicting a suspect.

The problem of coming to terms with death is certainly not unique to Allen, though it is one that especially interests him. He often uses black humor in conjunction with death, such as when Kleinman says as he is expiring that he is not afraid to die; he simply does not want to be there when it happens. Elsewhere, Allen has maintained that Ingmar Bergman "made the definitive work on the subject [of death] with *The Seventh Seal*" (*Woody Allen on Woody Allen* 210). Like *The Seventh Seal* (1956), which presents an array of responses to the absurd and unknowable human condition, Allen's *Death* presents several answers, but none is definitive. Kleinman's dying admonition to cooperate may represent part of Allen's credo. In the face of a hostile, uncertain universe, it is better to cooperate than to let fear turn us into maniacs who turn against each other.

This response requires that human reason overrule emotions, and in this respect Allen shares the values of such major literary figures as Plutarch, Cicero, Chaucer, Shakespeare, Alexander Pope, and Jonathan Swift. On the other hand, taken to the extreme, the classical preference for reason over passion can devolve into the lifeless logical positivism articulated by the doctor. To avoid such a passionless worldview and to remind us that reality is often irrational as well as rational, Allen interjects humor in the face of existential horror. Thus the humor itself becomes one of Allen's most effective responses to the modern condition, as it animates and elevates our spirits, even as it reveals the unsettling nature of our circumstances.

See also **Death**; **Little-Man Humor**; **Modernist Worldview**; *Shadows and Fog*.

Death Defying Acts. A trilogy of one-act plays: Allen's *Central Park West* (1995), David Mamet's *An Interview* (1995), and Elaine May's *Hotline*. Michael Blakemore directed the off-Broadway production that had 343 performances between March 6 and December 31, 1995, at the Variety Arts Theater. Julian Schlossberg and Jean Doumanian were the producers; Meyer Ackerman and Letty Aronson, Allen's sister, were associate producers. The cast included Debra Monk, Linda Lavin, Gerry Becker, Paul Guilfoyle, and Tari T. Signor.

The title of the production, *Death Defying Acts*, is a pun that simultaneously evokes the seriousness of true heroism, or at least an existential leap of faith, and the hype and theatricality of the circus. The comic seriousness of the title aptly applies to the theme and tone of the individual works. *An Interview* features an encounter between a lawyer and a bureaucratic St. Peter at the entrance to heaven. *Hotline* presents a neurotic's first night working at the suicide prevention clinic, and *Central Park West* shows two couples confronting one another with their betrayals and infidelities.

See also *Central Park West*.

Deconstructing Harry. A 1997 film directed by, written by, and starring Allen as writer Harry Block. It costars Richard Benjamin (Ken), Julia Louis-Dreyfus (Linda), Judy Davis (Lucy), Kirstie Alley (Joan), Demi Moore (Helen), Stanley Tucci (Paul), Elisabeth Shue (Fay), Mariel Hemingway (Beth Kramer), Amy Irving (Jane), Billy Crystal (Larry), Robin Williams (Mel, an out-of-focus actor), Julie Kavner (Mel's wife), Hazelle Goodman (Cookie), and Caroline Aaron (Doris). Jean Doumanian was the producer; Carlo Di Palma director of photography, Santo Loquasto production designer, Jeffrey Kurland costumer, and Susan E. Morse editor. Fine-Line Features was the North American distributor.

Deconstructing Harry is widely regarded as Allen's reply to critics of his personal life. In fact, at one point, Allen's character, a successful author named Harry, states that he is working on a story about the devil, and "since it's Hell, I am, as you can imagine, able to settle a lot of old scores." Harry admits that he identifies completely with the protagonist, so much so it is no longer worth disguising. In the very next scene he consigns his ene-mies—all of whom are apparently Allen's as well—to various levels of the Inferno. The entire seventh level, reserved exclusively for the media, is al-ready filled to capacity. Though not a great box office success, the film was well reviewed, and Allen received an Academy Award nomination for the screenplay.

Perhaps alluding to "The Book of Grotesques" in Sherwood Anderson's *Winseburg, Ohio* (1919), Harry concludes that "all people know the same truth; our lives consist of how we choose to distort it." This observation serves as the intellectual basis for the film, as Allen flaunts a grotesque dis-tortion of himself before his detractors and defies them to distinguish where fiction leaves off and reality begins. He deliberately cultivates confusion not only between himself and Harry, but also between Harry and Ken, Har-ry's fictional counterpart. The result is a portrait of Harry/Allen that is dis-jointed, paradoxical, relativistic, and indeterminate—but with a defiant, in-your-face attitude.

The title invites us to consider the film in postmodern terms, since decon-struction is a postmodern form of literary criticism that flourished during the late twentieth century. Its underlying premise is that reality is inherently disjointed, relativistic, paradoxical, and indeterminate, and that any sense of cohesion or order results from mental constructs that we impose on the chaos to make it manageable. The deconstructionist reveals the workings of ideologies, cultural predispositions, gender biases, and other social con-structs that, perhaps arbitrarily, confer meaning and a system of values upon a story. The intention of the deconstruction is to point out the inherent social biases, disclose hitherto undetected distortions operating below the surface, and suggest alternative patterns that reconstruct the story from a new ideo-logical perspective.

Though sometimes criticized for diminishing the literary work under consideration and for claiming greater authority than the author, deconstructionists sometimes succeed in affirming new truths unseen even by the author. Such proves the case for Harry, as one of his characters, a fic-tional student, helps conclude the film on an upbeat note: "Your books all seem a little sad on the surface, which is why I like deconstructing them because underneath they're really happy. It's just that you don't know it." Of course, unlike Harry, Allen did not require a literary critic to tell him this. He knew this about himself and his own work all along; otherwise he could not have put it in the film. Thus he wrests the claim to ultimate authority away from the deconstructionists, whose jargon and abstraction he has long ridiculed and distrusted. (Rain's story in *Husbands and Wives*, for instance, is entitled "Oral Sex in the Age of Deconstruction.") Instead, Allen returns authority to the author/auteur.

Along with *Stardust Memories*, to which it alludes, *Deconstructing Harry* is Allen's most experimental film to date. Much more than an apology for his life and career, it is a semi-ironic postmodern rendering of his current situation as a celebrity and creative artist whose personal life has also become a narrative text of sorts, published in the tabloids and represented through the media. Harry is a caricature of the caricature of Allen the media has painted of him since his scandalous 1992 breakup with Mia Farrow: bitter, completely self-absorbed, insensitive to those who love him, sexually obsessed, and incapable of fidelity.

Like Allen, Harry bases his stories on his chaotic personal life. Harry is the quintessential art-for-art's-sake writer. Such literature often depicts the creation of fictional worlds as an inherently sane act that makes bearable the reality of an insane, unjust, irrational real world. As Harry tells his analyst, "All I have in life is my imagination." His complete absorption of himself into his work enables him to impose meaning and order on his chaotic personal life. Like an alchemist, he takes everyone's suffering and transforms it into gold—"literary gold," as one of his ex-lovers accuses. But self-absorption also leaves him incapable of deep human relations. As his much happier friend Larry points out, Harry is the better writer, but Larry is a better-suited husband for the woman they both desire. "You put your art into your work. I put it into my life. I can make her happier."

In essence, Harry and his fictional characters had become a balanced, viable, self-sustaining system that fed and regenerated itself, a functional yin and yang. But as Thomas Pynchon is fond of pointing out, closed systems become entropic, and they degenerate. And a person who cuts himself off from real intimacy with other people will dissipate too. Until the publication of his newest novel Harry had been crass, insensitive, and completely self-absorbed, but he had not acted hurtfully or vindictively that we know of. But in the novel he lashes out at the people who once loved him, ruining their flawed lives and severing himself from them. Now he develops writer's block for the first time in his life: his creative balance is lost, and the system threatens to collapse as Harry's personal life disintegrates. He is isolated, frustrated, and unloved, and he finds no comfort in empty sex or his sterile, scientific view of existence.

Harry's friend Richard observes that Harry seems to have declined since breaking up with his former student and lover, Fay, the only relatively sane woman he had ever been involved with. But Harry drove Fay away, insisting that she not fall in love with him. When Fay asks his blessings for her marriage to Larry, Harry decides he loves her and refuses to accept their romance. Later, Richard comes back from the dead and tells him, "Make peace with your demons, and your block will pass." And when Harry forgives his father, who has been consigned to hell for not loving him, and finally condones his friends' marriage and wishes them well, he instantly regains his creative inspiration.

Allen's message about the necessity of making peace with our demons is explicit: failure to let go of past hurts and frustrated desires can be ruinous. When Harry finally approves Fay and Larry's marriage, he reconnects with humanity and quickly overcomes his self-imposed block. Allen reveals that we achieve this kind of reconciliation by surrender—by simply letting go of the obsessions that are holding us back. "I give up," Harry says, raising his hands and opening his palms wide as he confers his blessing on his friends.

As in *Stardust Memories*, one of his most challenging works, Allen uses a stream-of-consciousness plot to tell Harry's story. This gives the film a modernist, fragmented, and disjointed sensibility not unlike that found in Faulkner's *The Sound and the Fury* (1929). Scenes are linked not by chronological sequence or causal necessity but by a process of unconscious associations similar to those explored in Freudian psychoanalysis. Thus, events that are years and miles apart can appear together or even become embedded within each other. This technique requires the audience to reconstruct the chronological order and logical relationships—in short, to serve as deconstructionist critics.

For instance, Harry's argumentative visit to his sister Doris's house is followed by a fight that occurred years earlier between him and his ex-wife, Joan. In his novel Harry endows Joan with his sister's extreme devotion to Judaism as a way of ridiculing Joan, something Doris deeply resents. The pairing of the two scenes emanates from Harry's unconscious linking of the two women in his mind.

The stream-of-consciousness narration requires each viewer to make the necessary associations—or not. All viewers experience a different narration, depending on how fully and in what manner they reconstruct Harry's story. As in quantum physics, where the act of observation is inseparable from the event under scrutiny, all reconstructions of the collage of Harry's life are shaped by what the viewers bring to the story and how they connect the pieces in their minds. Thus each viewer is a major component of the re-constructed version he or she experiences; ultimately these reconstructions are the only experiences of the film that exist. Thus no interpreter of the film, and by extension no critic of Allen, is able to say where he or she ends and Allen and Harry begin.[1]

Allen employs other cinematic techniques to confer a postmodern sensi-bility. As in his story "The Kugelmass Episode," the play *God*, and *The Pur-ple Rose of Cairo*, he conflates the levels of reality, intermingling the worlds of actual people and those of literary characters. Allen achieves this identifi-cation of reality and fiction in several ways. The scenes alternate between Harry and his friends and the characters from Harry's newly published novel that is closely based on himself and his friends. The characters and the real people are represented by different actors, so the audience must labor to sort fiction from reality and figure out the many relationships. The result of that labor directly determines the quality of the viewer's reconstruction of reality. Even the characters in the film have difficulty separating themselves from their literary counterparts. When Lucy confronts Harry in the second scene, he inadvertently calls her by her character's name, Leslie, and she re-fers to her sister Jane by her character's name, Janet. Later, Harry's charac-ter, Ken, confronts him and gives him advice, which Harry rejects: "I'm not going to stand here and get lectured by my own creations." In fact, Ken pos-sesses greater insight into Harry's life than Harry does—but not more than Allen. Elsewhere, in mid-scene Allen substitutes Harry for Ken when re-counting how Harry met Fay in an elevator.

In addition to all of these postmodern intratextual connections among Allen (auteur), Harry (character/author), and Ken (character), the film is re-plete with intertextual references to other works by Allen. Allen does this partly to create the self-consciousness and self-referentiality of postmod-ernism. But he also elicits appropriate themes and emotions evoked by his earlier work and transposes them onto characters and situations in *Decons-tructing Harry*. In this way, the references become integral parts of the nar-ration, as well as self-conscious ornaments for the appreciation of aficionados. For instance, Harry's story of the young husband whom the an-gel of Death mistakes for his dying friend connects back to Allen's absurdist play *Death Knocks*, which in turn is a comic rendering of Ingmar Bergman's *The Seventh Seal* (1956). In the same way that *Death Knocks* humorously deflates the existential angst of Bergman's knight, who obsesses over what becomes of us after death, the story of the adulterous husband transforms Lucy's serious, potentially homicidal attack on unfaithful Harry into a farce. As Harry's therapist tells him, "So, your writing saved your life." Similarly, Harry's admonition to Fay not to fall in love with him, and his subsequent desire for her, mirrors Ike's relationship with Tracy in *Manhattan*, another story of an older man and younger woman. (Mariel Hemingway, who played the teenaged Tracy, returns to play Beth Kramer, Joan's friend who tries to prevent Harry from kidnapping his son.) Harry's betrayal of his mistress, who in turn has betrayed her sister/his wife, replays *Central Park West* where Sam similarly betrays his mistress, who has betrayed her close friend/his wife. And when Fay announces her forthcoming marriage to Larry, Allen inserts the same unsettling image of clouds covering the moon and the same ominous musical passage from Mussorgsky's *A Night on Bald Mountain* that he used to introduce the episode in *Stardust Memories* where Sydney Finklestein's hostility breaks loose and terrorizes Central Park. In this case, Allen's self-conscious, postmodern reference to his earlier film communicates Harry's emotional state after hearing Fay's news because, for viewers familiar with Allen's work, it signifies that Harry's anger is as intense and out of control as Sydney Finklestein's. These references thus confer a postmodern tone on Harry's response to Fay's betrothal that is ironic, slightly humorous, and straight-faced, all at the same time.

Allen presents a cubist view of the accusations of egocentrism and insensitivity that have been leveled against him. On the one hand, he acknowledges that much about Harry is unsavory, but he balances that against the fruit of Harry's imagination and presents both as parts of a complete package that must be accepted or rejected in its entirety. Ultimately Allen acknowledges the charges of self-absorption, but rather than defend himself against them, he dismisses them by turning them into art.

For instance, in Harry's story "The Actor," Mel suddenly becomes out of focus: people looking at him see a blur. But like an alcoholic or a neurotic who makes his family conform to his illness, Mel has his wife and children wear special glasses that enable them to see him clearly but distort everything else. Harry's analyst states the obvious significance of the story: "You expect the world to adjust to the distortion you've become." Of course, in presenting this on screen, Allen points out to the world that he is not blind. He is aware of these charges but finds them useful only as fodder for his art.

By refusing to defend himself, Allen denies his critics the right to judge him. Indeed, the need to be tolerant and nonjudgmental in a world where we can rarely distinguish fact from fiction is a major theme. But it does not negate the fact that Harry's casual betrayal of his friends and lovers makes him unworthy of our full respect. Moreover, his negative qualities are self-destructive. They debilitate him, leaving him isolated, cynical, and without anything or anyone to comfort him, except his own imagination. Ultimately Harry accepts himself as he is, for better and for worse. But he also learns to recognize, accept, and reciprocate Larry and Fay's love for him, thereby gaining wisdom and insight. Harry grows as a result of his experiences, and this enables him to continue to evolve, perhaps into a better person than he was before. Presumably Allen feels the same way about himself too.

Allen rejects charges by his critics who accuse him of employing offensive Jewish stereotypes and object to his refusal to identify himself primarily as a Jew. Harry still considers himself a Jew, although he is an atheist; but being Jewish is not the dominant component of his identity; his art is. As Harry tells Doris, who accuses him of being a self-hating Jew, "I may hate myself, but not 'cause I'm Jewish." (Allen states the identical sentiment in his 1990 essay, "Random Reflections of a Second-Rate Mind," along with other positions about Judaism and religion that Harry expresses. See **"Random Reflections of a Second-Rate Mind."**)

Doris is one of his most severe judges, yet she pities and loves him too. They both cherish memories of their childhood, but since she married an Orthodox Jew, they have grown apart, as she has defined herself increasingly around her Jewish identity. On the other hand, Harry's greatest sense of identity is as an author. Like the doctor in *Shadows and Fog*, Leopold in *A Midsummer Night's Sex Comedy*, and Judah in *Crimes and Misdemeanors*, he accepts the spiritually empty view of existence promulgated by empirical science. He regards Doris's religious commitment as superstitious, and she pities him for his inability to experience an act of faith. When she reduces his life to nihilism, cynicism, sarcasm, and orgasm, Harry sarcastically replies that in France, he could run on that platform and win. The retort is clever, but it does not make his life seem more attractive. Moreover, Doris and her husband condemn Harry for rejecting a heritage that he regards as a mere accident of history: "If our parents had converted to Catholicism a month before you were born, we'd be Catholics."

In fact, Doris's Jewish identity obliterates the modernist-postmodernist uncertainty, relativity, and discontinuity that dominate Harry's experience of life. It enables her and her husband to build their lives around a clearly articulated set of indisputable values; it makes them feel as if they know their place in the universe by creating community among the living and continuity with an ancestral past. Finally, their Jewish identity makes them feel inherently worthy and self-righteous. By contrast, postmodernism exists in an ongoing present tense, rejecting the past or employing it only ironically. And it undermines all attempts to articulate a consistent, unambiguous set of values that does not ultimately contradict itself. Thus Harry, the postmodernist, lacks all of the support and coherence his sister gains from her religious affiliation.

On the other hand, Harry judges his sister and brother-in-law as morally reprehensible precisely because their absorption in Judaism distorts their vision of reality and causes them to act ethnocentrically. Because they reject a modernist, relativistic universe, they deny the validity of other views—of other reconstructions of reality apart from their own. Harry condemns them for caring more for Jews than for anyone else, a practice he finds especially objectionable since the practice of favoring one group over all others is what underlay Nazism and most other promulgators of anti-Semitism. "They're clubs. They're exclusionary, all of them [religions]. They force down the concept of the other, so you know clearly who to hate."

Harry and Doris argue over whether the Holocaust is more a Jewish tragedy or a human tragedy. For her, the message of the Holocaust is for Jews to cling more tightly to their Jewish identity, be on guard, protect themselves, and act with their communal interests foremost in mind. For Harry, the Holocaust is primarily a human tragedy; its great lesson is that we must prevent this kind of unimaginable horror from happening to anyone. Harry feels that his sister's ethnocentrism tolerates outrages against other groups. He believes we must transcend our ethnic identities and that we can prevent future Holocausts only by breaking down barriers of identity that insulate us from other groups. But he has little respect for the human species and predicts that "records are made to be broken." (See **Holocaust**.)

The differences between Harry and his sister are deep, and Allen does not propose to resolve them. Instead, he seems to counsel mutual acceptance and seeking common ground. Helen, Harry's character for Joan, softens Harry's anger by showing him how he has treated Doris with contempt and rejected her for her religious beliefs, just as he accuses her of rejecting him. Helen then transports Harry to his sister's house, and he sees her defending Harry to her husband, expressing compassion for him in his lost state and remembering him fondly.

Although when "reconstructed" *Deconstructing Harry* is affirmative and upbeat, its tone is harsher than any of Allen's other films. Profanity is used more freely, sex is depicted more explicitly and more crudely, and Allen seems to go out of his way to offend the politically correct. The opening scene features two of Harry's characters having intercourse in front of her blind grandmother. (Allen draws laughs from the grandmother's comically flawed reconstruction of what is going on when she misinterprets their groans and outcries as enthusiastic responses to her comments.) Harry also confesses to the devil that he has had sex with two women at one time and did not care that it was exploitive, and they compare notes about intercourse with disabled girls—blind girls are so appreciative.

Overall, *Deconstructing Harry* is a tour de force of postmodern filmmaking. Even while depicting reality as fragmented, disjointed, relativistic, paradoxical, and indeterminate, Allen creates a humorous story in which a protagonist grows by acquiring greater wisdom and self-knowledge. At the same time that Allen appears to answer his critics, he seems to assert their irrelevance. Instead, he insists on the primacy of the imagination and the need to "know yourself, stop kidding yourself, accept your limitations, and get on with life."

See also **Modernist Worldview**.

NOTE

1. External reality may well exist apart from the observer, but the experience of external reality occurs only within each individual's mind. Thus, although the story *Deconstructing Harry* (or any story) exists apart from its audience, no one, not even Allen himself, has direct access to it. The only thing anyone, even the author or director, has access to is the reconstruction that takes place in his or her head. In this sense, an unviewed film is like a tree falling in the forest. If no one hears or sees it, it will generate sound and light waves, but these will never become noise or image until they enter an ear or an eye and interact with the observer's physiology. The story will not acquire cohesion, coherence, or meaning until the viewer interprets it.

Di Palma, Carlo. A cinematographer who was director of photography for most of Allen's films since 1986. Born in 1925, he filmed *Hannah and Her Sisters*, *Radio Days*, *September*, *Alice*, *Shadows and Fog*, *Husbands and Wives*, *Manhattan Murder Mystery*, *Bullets over Broadway*, *Mighty Aphrodite*, *Everyone Says I Love You*, and *Deconstructing Harry*. He also filmed the made-for-television remake of *Don't Drink the Water*. His other credits include Michelangelo Antonioni's *Red Desert* (1964) and *Blow-Up* (1967) and Sidney Lumet's *The Appointment* (1969).

Allen's visual style changed after he began working with Di Palma, when his previous cinematographer, Gordon Willis, was unavailable for *Hannah and Her Sisters*. In particular, Allen moved from using more static, tightly framed, carefully composed shorter shots that Willis preferred to very long sequences that feature more camera movement. He feels especially comfortable with Di Palma's "European style" of filming in which the camera is constantly moving. Allen also praises Di Palma's ability to use lighting to create beautiful moods and to handle color deftly (Lax 329).

Dmitri. A 1989 dance-drama based on Allen's "A Guide to Some of the Lesser Ballets," which spoofs story lines of classical ballets. *Dmitri* was choreographed by Stanley Holden, a former character dancer with the Royal Ballet who set the dance to music by Giuseppe Verdi. The Los Angeles Chamber Ballet premiered it at the Japan American Theater on February 16, 1989. Sponsored by Allen's friend Paula Prentiss, *Dmitri* cost $20,000 to produce. The dance parodies classical ballet in general and *Giselle* and Igor Stravinsky's *Petrouchka* in particular.

Allen first published "A Guide to the Lesser Ballets" in the *New Yorker* in 1972 and reprinted it in 1975 in *Without Feathers*. *Dmitri*, an absurd tale of forbidden love between a woman and a puppet, is the first dance Allen describes in his guide.

See *Without Feathers*.

Don't Drink the Water. A 1966 Broadway play written by Allen, a 1969 film adapted from the play, and a 1994 television film. The original Broadway cast included Dick Libertini (Father Drobney), House Jameson (Ambassador Magee), Tony Roberts (Axel Magee), Lou Jacobi (Walter Hollander), Kay Medford (Marion Hollander), and Anita Gillette (Susan Hollander). Stanley Prager directed, and David Merrick was the producer. The film starred Jackie Gleason as Walter Hollander and costarred Dick Libertini (Father Drobney), Howard St. John (Ambassador Magee), Ted Bessell (Axel Magee), Estelle Parsons (Marion Hollander), and Joan Delaney (Susan Hollander). It was directed by Howard Morris and written by R. S. Allen and Harvey Bullock, with an uncredited contribution by Marshall Brickman. Charles Joffe was the producer, Harvey Genkins director of photography, Pat Williams music director, Robert Gundlach production designer, Gene Coffin costumer, and Ralph Rosenblum editor. Avco Embassy was the North American distributor.

Allen directed the 1994 television remake in which he played Walter Hollander. That cast included Julie Kavner (Marion Hollander), Mayim Bialik (Susan Hollander), Michael J. Fox (Axel Magee), Edwin Herman (Ambassador Magee), and Dom DeLuise (Father Drobney). Robert Greenhut was the producer, Carlo Di Palma director of photography, Santo Loquasto production designer, Suzy Benzinger costumer, and Susan E. Morse editor. The film aired on ABC on December 18, 1994.

A Cold War comedy, *Don't Drink the Water* was produced and reproduced in three very distinct historical contexts that influenced its reception. The highly successful play enjoyed 598 Broadway performances beginning November 17, 1966. It thus appeared in the aftermath of the most dangerous and intense period of the Cold War: five years after the 1961 Berlin crisis, four years after the Cuban missile crisis, three years after the Kennedy assassination, and during the second year of direct American military involvement in the Vietnam War. Allen claims he was inspired by his own experiences of living abroad and his conjectures about what would happen if his family were to travel overseas (Fox 42–43). The play also enjoyed the casting of Lou Jacobi, whom Allen had envisioned as Walter right from the beginning. (Jacobi also stars in *Everything You Always Wanted to Know About Sex*.)

By contrast, the 1969 film starred Jackie Gleason. Allen greatly admired Gleason but felt he was wrong for the part, because he was not ethnic enough for a Jewish caterer. Likewise, *I Love Lucy*'s Vivian Vance originally played Walter's wife, Marion, but she too was inappropriately cast. "It was a crass attempt at commercialism rather than correct casting. . . . David [Merrick] was trying too hard to Anglicize it. He isn't anti-Semitic but he has an aversion to anything too Jewish." Prior to the Broadway opening, Kay Medford replaced Vance, and "suddenly, the mother became a hilarious character" (Lax 234–236).

Allen declined to write the screenplay for the 1969 film version, because "I wrote it as a play and I have no desire to rework it into something else." He also turned down an offer to act in it because he wanted to concentrate on his writing. The movie premiered during a calmer part of the Cold War and did poorly, in part because it was no longer timely. Détente had already begun in Europe, and the Vietnam War was attracting more attention and concern than the larger U.S.-Soviet rivalry that spawned it. Moreover, problems with the direction diminished the movie's effectiveness. According to Charles Joffe, Allen's agent who produced the movie, Howard Morris, his fifth choice for director, "missed the whole point of the thing. It should have been in these very cramped little quarters of this foreign embassy and he blew it up, made it much too lavish . . . no one came to see it. It was a terrible failure" (Fox 44). The film cost $8 million to produce but grossed only $1.03 million in U.S. and Canadian rentals (not including later video rentals and television revenues). It was never released to a general audience in Great Britain and has rarely been shown on television.

The 1994 television movie, which appeared four years after the Cold War ended, was also criticized for being untimely. It cost $3.5 million to produce but gained only half the ratings share of that night's top show, NBC's *A Christmas Romance*. Allen claims he made the 1994 version because the role of Walter Hollander "was perfect for me . . . it's my father and mother. Then suddenly I looked up and I was twenty years older . . . just the right age to play the part" (Fox 45).

The plot centers on a Jewish caterer from New Jersey and his family, who are vacationing in Vulgaria, an Eastern European country behind the iron curtain. They take refuge in the American embassy after the vacationing caterer is mistaken for a spy because his tourist photos inadvertently feature military installations in the background. Allen derives humor by intermixing the concerns of the Cold War with those of a Jewish family whose daughter is supposed to marry in two weeks. Instead of subordinating family issues to the urgent international situation they have created, the caterer and his wife carry on about the wedding and dismiss the desperate importunities of the embassy staff. A crazy Orthodox priest who has taken refuge in the embassy for several years and mastered magic tricks during his stay also contributes to the absurd mixture of characters and special interests, as does the developing romance between the engaged daughter and the ambassador's inept son, who has been left in charge during his dad's absence. (In *Bananas* Allen again plays with the cliché of a son taking over the family business when bumbling Fielding Mellish steps in for his father, the brain surgeon, during a delicate operation.) Although most of the action occurs within the embassy, the communist officials also become targets of Allen's barbs. They appear humorless, and their ruthlessness is acknowledged but never shown. They therefore become suitable comic villains who ultimately are the biggest losers in the story.

Everyone Says I Love You. A 1996 film directed by, written by, and starring Allen, who plays writer Joe Berlin. It costars Julia Roberts (Von), Alan Alda (Bob), Goldie Hawn (Steffi), Drew Barrymore (Skylar), Natasha Lyonne (DJ), Edward Norton (Holden), Tim Roth (Charles Ferry), Lukas Haas (Scott), Gaby Hoffman (Lane), Natalie Portman (Laura), and David Ogden Stiers (Holden's father). Tracy Ullman and Liv Tyler played characters who were cut from the final version and never shown. Robert Greenhut was the producer, Carlo Di Palma director of photography, Dick Hyman musical director, Santo Loquasto production designer, Jeffrey Kurland costume designer, Graciela Daniele choreographer, and Susan E. Morse editor. Music on the soundtrack includes "Just You, Just Me," "My Baby Just Cares for Me," "I'm a Dreamer," "Makin' Whoopie," "I'm Through with Love," "All My Life," "Cuddle Up a Little Closer," "Looking at You," "If I Had You," "Enjoy Yourself," "Chiquita Banana," "Hooray for Captain Spaulding," and "Everyone Says I Love You." Miramax was the North American distributor.

Allen's only musical comedy to date, *Everyone Says I Love You* is one of his happiest, most lighthearted efforts. The energetic, if not profound, parody of the musical comedy form received mixed reviews by the critics and public; some audiences connected to this kind of humor, and others decidedly did not. Perhaps due to the influence of his much younger future wife, Soon-Yi Previn, the film features teenagers and young adults prominently, something not found in previous Allen films, apart from Tracy in *Manhattan*, who functions in an all-adult environment, and David Shayne in *Bullets over Broadway*, a young man in his twenties who also functions in a grown-up world. *Everyone Says I Love You* is also more multicultural than most of Allen's earlier films. His view of Manhattan now features not only black

Americans, whom Allen has been criticized for largely omitting, but also Sikhs, Asians, and others of non-European ancestry. (*Celebrity* is Allen's most ethnically diverse film to date.)

Narrated by DJ, a college freshman from a family of affluent Manhattan socialites, the film follows the love lives of four main characters: Joe, DJ's natural father played by Allen; Von, Joe's love interest; Skylar, DJ's older stepsister; and DJ herself. Less fully developed are the infatuations of DJ's younger half-sisters, Lane and Laura. The final narrative thread involves the conflict between DJ's liberal stepfather, Bob, and his teenaged son, Scott, who has suddenly become a political conservative. (The film satirizes both knee-jerk liberals and conservatives.) Because this is a musical comedy, Allen is able to conclude on a more upbeat note than in his more realistic efforts. All of the plotlines end happily, except for Joe's, and he at least retains his long-standing friendship with Steffi, his ultraliberal ex-wife—DJ's mother, now married to Bob.

The main plots revolve around the characters' lack of self-knowledge. In particular, neither Joe, Von, Skylar, nor DJ knows what he or she is looking for in a mate. All are unable to distinguish between unrealistic fantasies and healthy realities. Only about eighteen years old, DJ, like her younger stepsisters, is easily swept off her feet by good-looking young men with charm. But though her impulsive infatuations are potentially damaging, DJ is going through a learning process appropriate to her age. With each infatuation DJ outgrows, she gains a modicum of self-knowledge; she at least recognizes what she does not want. Her pairing with a Harpo Marx look-alike in the final scene bodes well because it suggests she has learned to see beyond a man's external appearances and appreciate him more for who he is. Of course, even here DJ is enamored of a costumed man playing a role, and presumably time will tell if the imitator possesses anything of Harpo's real spirit. But at least DJ has chosen someone who appreciates Harpo's zany lust for life, and in Allen's cosmology, the Marx Brothers' *joie de vivre* represents the closest thing there is to spiritual enlightenment.

Skylar is twenty-one, and her failure to outgrow an overly romanticized, adolescent view of love appears more immature and more threatening than DJ's. Even DJ recognizes that Skylar is too much a dreamer, and although Skylar is engaged to a seemingly sensible and devoted, if somewhat overly strait-laced young man, she longs for someone more exciting. Her fling with Charles Ferry, a hardened criminal, severs her engagement to Holden and nearly kills her. But it also satisfies her need for adventure and allows Skylar to advance beyond her adolescent picture of love. The adventure also enables her for the first time truly to appreciate Holden for who he is.

Von parallels Skylar in many ways. An art historian in her late twenties who is married to an actor with whom she shares few common interests, Von continually measures her real life against a fantasized ideal, and she is therefore continually dissatisfied. Joe becomes attracted to Von while he and DJ are vacationing in Venice, and by chance DJ recognizes Von as the patient of the mother of one of DJ's friends. The mother is a psychoanalyst, and her daughter has bored a secret hole in the wall so she and her friends can overhear the sessions. Therefore, DJ knows everything Von has confessed about her secret desires and longings. (Allen uses a similar plot device in *Another Woman*.) DJ imparts the information to Joe, who uses it to seduce Von and take her from her husband. But after her fantasies have been realized, Von, like Skylar, sees her life more clearly and returns to her real world. Having outgrown her youthful romantic fantasies, she can now move on to the next stage of her life.

Oldest of the group, Joe never seems to grow in self-knowledge or learn to choose women capable of loving him for who he is. (This is a problem shared by Alvy Singer in *Annie Hall*, Ike Davis in *Manhattan*, Sandy Bates in *Stardust Memories*, and Lee Simon in *Celebrity*.) Joe woos Von by pretending to be someone he is not, and as Allen has shown consistently throughout his career, such deception inevitably undermines any relationship. Steffi, with whom he has shared a close friendship over the years, appears to have been the ideal woman for him, but for undisclosed reasons, they fought excessively when they were married and have proven to be better friends than spouses. We may infer that, like Alvy Singer and Groucho Marx before him, Joe does not want to be a member of any club that will have him. Indeed, Steffi speculates that perhaps, deep down, Joe does not really want to be in a successful relationship, much as Tess wonders if Bea really wants one in *Radio Days*.

Everyone Says I Love You is Allen's most generous salute yet to the Marx Brothers. In *Horse Feathers* (1932) each of the brothers performs "Everyone Says I Love You" to woo the campus widow. They first used the song with different lyrics in *Animal Crackers* (1930), and Allen concludes his movie with it. The final scene shows a New Year's Eve costume party in Paris in which everyone, including Joe and Steffi, dresses as one of the Marx Brothers. The entertainment is a musical enactment of "Hooray for Captain Spaulding," Groucho's theme song that first appears in *Animal Crackers*. Moreover, Goldie Hawn, as Steffi, does a Groucho imitation, and DJ falls in love with a Harpo look-alike. (See **Marx Brothers**.)

Most of all, *Everyone Says I Love You* expresses an absurdist spirit similar to the Marx Brothers.' Incongruity is a necessary though not sufficient component for humor, especially absurdist humor, and the musical comedy format furnishes the film's primary source of incongruity. Main characters repeatedly break out into song and dance at the least likely moments, such as when tough-talking, ex-con Charles Ferry serenades Skylar with "If I Had You," Bob sings "I'm Thru with Love" when Skylar breaks her engagement to Holden, and Steffi and Joe perform an exaggerated version of a Fred Astaire–Ginger Rogers dance routine on the bank of the Seine, in which Steffi leaps perhaps ten feet in the air and gently glides another twenty yards down the riverside. Absurd humor also flows from the incongruity between the well-executed, carefully choreographed work of professional performers and the intentionally inept singing and dancing of some of the main characters. Thus, while professional performers skillfully execute an intricate dance routine in the jewelry shop, Holden bounces along atop a desk, trying to keep pace with the music. Similarly, Joe's singing efforts are funny because he so obviously cannot sing, and we find it incongruous to see him doing so.

Finally, Allen derives humor by having unexpected characters perform musical numbers: the Asian manikins that come to life in a window display; the bum who sings "Just You, Just Me" while soliciting for change on the sidewalk; the bland ring salesman at Harry Winston's; the emergency room doctor who introduces "Makin' Whoopie"; the strait-jacketed madman who dances his way down the hospital corridor along with pregnant women, cripples, and various crawling and walking wounded; and the Sikh taxi driver who sings "Cuddle Up a Little Closer" in his native language. Even Bob's dead father gives a spirited rendition of "Enjoy Yourself" at his funeral, accompanied by a host of apparitions. The song's live-for-the-day philosophy appears to express Allen's own sentiments: "It's better to have had your wish than to have wished you had."

Whether it is because Allen was putting the Mia Farrow breakup behind him and discovering renewed happiness with Soon-Yi Previn, or for some other reason, *Everyone Says I Love You* recaptures the zany pleasure of pure play found in Allen's earliest films, writing, and stand-up comedy. At the same time, his cinematic technique and visual and musical imagination are far more developed here than in his earlier work. The result is that he expresses his absurdist spirit in a particularly rich, multidimensional fashion that is capable of revealing insights about human behavior as it generates laughs.

Everything You Always Wanted to Know About Sex* *(*But Were Afraid to Ask).* A 1972 film directed by, written by, and starring Allen, who plays the court jester, Fabrizio, Victor, and a sperm. It costars John Carradine (Dr. Bernardo), Louise Lasser (Gina), Anthony Quayle (King), Lynn Redgrave

(Queen), Tony Randall (Mission Control director), Burt Reynolds (switch-board operator), Gene Wilder (Dr. Ross), Lou Jacobi (cross-dresser), Jack Barry (himself), Regis Philbin (himself), Titos Vandis (Milos), and Heather Macrae (Helen). It is ostensibly based on Dr. David Reuben's 1969 best-selling book of the same title. Charles Joffe was the producer, David M. Walsh director of photography, Mundell Lowe music director, Dale Hennesy production designer, Arnold M. Lipin costumer, and Eric Albertson editor. United Artists was the North American distributor.

Allen conceived the idea for the movie while watching a late-night television interview with Dr. Reuben. He purchased the film rights to the book from producer Jack Brodsky, who had originally obtained them to create a possible vehicle for his partner, Elliott Gould. One of the early financial successes that propelled Allen's career as a filmmaker, *Everything* cost approximately $2 million to produce and grossed $8.8 million in U.S. and Canadian distribution (not including later video rentals and television revenues). It was the tenth top moneymaker of 1972. Allen has quipped that the film's rating was "R for Rabelaisian." *Everything* was critically well received, especially in France, though Dr. Reuben complained, "It impressed me as a sexual tragedy. Every episode in the picture was a chronicle of failure, which was the converse of everything in the book." In return, Allen has replied, "this book was silly also, and if he had really cared about it, he wouldn't have sold it to the movies. It could have fallen into worse hands than mine. It was fun to make a movie with just a couple of short pieces in it. Just for amusement's sake."

Everything consists of seven sketches, each purporting to answer actual questions that Dr. Reuben seriously raises and answers in his book. Allen cut another promising segment because he was never able to conclude it to his satisfaction. "What Makes a Man a Homosexual?" was to climax with a black widow spider (Louise Lasser) eating her mate (Allen) after sex. (A widely circulated photo from the sketch was published with a September 1972 *Playboy* interview.)

In actual fact, the vignettes have little or nothing to do with the questions that introduce them. This disconnection contributes to the spirit of absurd play and irrelevancy characteristic not only of this film but of most of Allen's fiction and films from the early 1970s. Like his other work from the period, *Everything* is rich in literary and cinematic parody, as well as in whimsy. (See also **Literary Comedy**.)

More than anything, *Everything* celebrates the unfettered exercise of Allen's imagination as he conjures absurd situations and follows them to their logical conclusions. The first skit, in which he plays a court jester, gives Allen the opportunity to parody the ghost scene in *Hamlet* and explore the comic possibilities of chastity belts and other medieval anachronisms, while ostensibly answering whether aphrodisiacs work. In response to the query, "What is sodomy?" the second skit depicts the slide into the gutter of the once-successful Dr. Ross, who has fallen madly in love with a cold-hearted sheep from Armenia. Foremost among the genre of vamp movies it parodies is Marlene Dietrich's *The Blue Angel* (1930).

The third sketch, "Why Do Some Women Have Trouble Reaching Orgasm?" is also more about cinematic parody than about Dr. Reuben's book. In this case, it spoofs the stylish 1960s Italian films by such directors as Michelangelo Antonioni and Bernardo Bertolucci. Julian Fox notes how it specifically alludes to Mario Monicelli's *Casanova 70* (1965), in which suave seducer Marcello Mastroianni must place himself in dangerous situations in order to perform sexually. Here, Allen casts himself in the role of Fabrizio, a sophisticated, self-possessed, Italian husband whose wife, Gina, can reach orgasm only when they make love in public places. This sketch replaced Allen's original conception, a piece about masturbation in which Allen and Louise Lasser were to be Onan and his wife.

The fourth sketch, "Are Transvestites Homosexuals?" derives humor by showing a very unfeminine, hairy-chested man cross-dressing in the clothes

Gene Wilder in *Everything You Always Wanted to Know About Sex.* . . . Courtesy of Photofest.

of his daughter's future mother-in-law. This skit replaced the one about the black widow spider. "What Are Sex Perverts?" parodies another icon of popular culture, the 1950s television quiz show "What's My Line?" "Are the Findings of Doctors and Clinics Who Do Sexual Research and Experiments Accurate?" spoofs mad-scientist horror films like *Frankenstein* (1931), its sequels, and *The Mad Doctor of Market Street* (1942), though its ending nods more to Philip Roth's then-current novel *The Breast* (1972), as a demented reject from the Masters and Johnson research group unleashes a gigantic breast that ravages the countryside. (In *Stardust Memories* Allen invokes another countryside ravaged by a peculiar monster, when Sydney Finklestein's pent-up hostility escapes and runs amok in Central Park.)

Though not as deep in its philosophical exploration as John Barth's story "Night-Sea Journey" (1966), "What Happens During Ejaculation?" likewise ponders existence from the viewpoint of a sperm. Inspired by Dr. Reuben's analogy comparing a man's orgasm to a missile launch, Allen locates most of the action in the operations room, where the mission control director receives information on how the sexual encounter is progressing and then orders the appropriate physiological responses. Shirtless laborers toil at the ponderous machinery below decks in order to raise the penis to full erection, and Allen himself plays a sperm, whom he likens to a paratrooper preparing for an invasion. Invoking stereotypes from old-time war movies, the sperm tries to calm himself before the assault by playing a cowboy song on the harmonica. But he is haunted by contemporary worries: What if they encounter a rubber wall or if it's a homosexual encounter? Elsewhere, Allen sparks laughs while briefly raising issues of race and miscegenation, as a single black sperm wonders why he is included in this sea of white. The practice of transposing contemporary urban issues into alien and/or anachronistic environments is characteristic of Allen's early humor, and his ability to garner laughs while foregrounding pertinent aspects of his culture accounts for much of his appeal to sophisticated audiences.

F

Farrow, Mia. A film actress who stars in thirteen of Allen's films: *A Midsummer Night's Sex Comedy, Zelig, Broadway Danny Rose, The Purple Rose of Cairo, Hannah and Her Sisters, Radio Days, September, Another Woman, Oedipus Wrecks, Crimes and Misdemeanors, Alice, Shadows and Fog,* and *Husbands and Wives.* Other notable film appearances include *Rosemary's Baby* (1968), *The Great Gatsby,* (1974), *Death on the Nile* (1978), *A Wedding* (1978), *Widow's Peak* (1994), and *Miami Rhapsody* (1995). She also starred as Allison MacKinze in the television series *Peyton Place* (ABC, 1964–1969).

Allen and Farrow were romantically involved from 1980 to 1992, and Farrow is the mother of Allen's son, Satchel, and their jointly adopted children, Dylan and Moses, as well as eight other children, two of whom she had with former husband André Previn. The remaining six, from Korea, Vietnam, and the United States, are adopted. Allen and Farrow's highly publicized breakup followed her discovery of his affair with her college-aged adopted daughter, Soon-Yi Previn, who is now Allen's wife. The scandal intensified after Farrow accused Allen of sexually abusing Dylan in August 1992. An investigation found insufficient grounds for filing criminal charges against Allen, but the judge presiding over the later custody trial was highly critical of Allen and denied him custody or visitation rights to the children. At the time of their breakup, Farrow had been scheduled to star in *Manhattan Murder Mystery,* but Allen dropped her after she made the charges of child abuse. Diane Keaton replaced her in the role of Carol in a move that was widely regarded as Keaton's show of support for Allen.

Born in 1945 to Hollywood actress Maureen O'Sullivan and director John Farrow, Mia Farrow has lived an extraordinary life. A victim of polio

who suffered prolonged isolation as a young child, Farrow was later educated in a Catholic convent in England. After her father died, she moved
with her mother to New York, and as a teenager she was befriended by the
surrealist painter Salvador Dalí, whom she met in an elevator. They sustained their friendship throughout his life. At age nineteen Farrow became a
national celebrity when she starred in *Peyton Place*, the first nighttime soap
opera on television. While working on the show, she caught the attention of
Frank Sinatra, and they were married in 1966, when she was twenty-one.
They separated in 1967 over conflicts surrounding Farrow's work on Ro-
man Polanski's *Rosemary's Baby* and divorced in 1968. (Sinatra had previously been married to Ava Gardner, with whom Farrow's father had had a
notorious affair.)

After the separation Farrow traveled to India with her sister Prudence to
study at the compound of the Maharishi Mahesh Yogi, the master of transcendental meditation. An apparent favorite of the Maharishi, she befriended the famous rock-and-roll band The Beatles, who had also come to
learn meditation. Farrow subsequently married world-renowned pianist,
composer, and classical conductor André Previn, by whom she had twins
and with whom she adopted other children. The playwright Tom Stoppard
is the godfather of her second daughter. When one of her children was diag-
nosed as autistic, Farrow worked with him and through careful observation
devised strategies that enabled him to overcome the condition. In 1974, she
nearly died of complications from a misdiagnosed ruptured appendix.

After her marriage to Previn failed in 1978, Farrow returned with her
children to her home on Martha's Vineyard, where she read Kierkegaard,
Hegel, Kant, Nietzsche, Kafka, and Camus. Her reading and reflection prepared her for the stimulating intellectual exchanges with Allen that became
part of their mutual attraction. They first met in late 1979, when actor Michael Caine introduced them, and they became a couple in 1980. Until their
scandalous breakup in 1992, Farrow and Allen were widely admired as the
ideal professional couple who shared love, family, and interesting work but
maintained separate lives and separate residences on opposite sides of Central Park.

Although Farrow was already an accomplished actress before she met
Allen, she benefited from the range and depth of the roles he wrote especially for her. Allen is one of the few contemporary directors who makes
movies about the familial roles, emotional conflicts, and psychological and
spiritual growth of women, and roles like Hannah, Alice, Cecilia in *The
Purple Rose of Cairo*, and Lane in *September* enabled Farrow to explore
character development and familial relations to a far greater extent than
most Hollywood movies allow. Moreover, roles like Tina in *Broadway*

Danny Rose, Sally in *Radio Days*, and Irmy in *Shadows and Fog* permitted her to expand her range and develop character types with which she is not usually associated.

Hannah and *Alice* draw on Farrow's life. Hannah's alcoholic, adulterous parents are based on Farrow's mother and father; indeed, Maureen O'Sullivan plays Hannah's mother. Furthermore, the film was shot in Farrow's own New York apartment, and her own children play the roles of Hannah's children. Nonetheless, as when Allen introduces elements from his own life into his films, we should avoid the temptation to identify Hannah fully with Farrow. *Alice* too draws on Farrow's life, especially in that the character derives her greatest joy from her children. Like Farrow, Alice was raised in a convent, reveres Mother Teresa, idolizes her parents, and blinds herself to their shortcomings.

Allen assesses Farrow's acting as follows: "She has very good range. She can play serious roles, she can play comic roles. She's also very photogenic, very beautiful on screen. She's just a good realistic actress, as opposed to someone like Diane Keaton who is a great comedian, who has a single personality, a very strong single personality. . . . Like Katharine Hepburn. Mia is different all the time. She's got a wide range for different parts. And no matter how strange and daring it is, she does it well" (*Woody Allen on Woody Allen* 133).

For additional reading, see Farrow's autobiography, *What Falls Away* (1997).

Fellini, Federico. An Italian film director whose work influenced Allen's. Born in 1920, Fellini died in 1993. He was married to Giulietta Masina, an actress who starred in several of his films, often along with Marcello Mastroianni. Among Fellini's most notable films are *La Strada* ("The Road," 1954), *Notti di Cabiria* ("Nights of Cabiria," 1957), *La Dolce Vita* ("The Sweet Life," 1959), *8½* (1963), *Juliet of the Spirits* (1965), *Satyricon* (1969), *Fellini's Roma* (1972), *Amarcord* ("I Remember," 1974), and *City of Women* (1981).

Fellini, Jean Renoir, Akira Kurosawa, and Ingmar Bergman are the directors Allen admires most, and characters in Allen's films occasionally praise Fellini's work (*Woody Allen on Woody Allen* 123). Allen had wanted the director to play himself in the role Marshall McLuhan assumes in *Annie Hall*, berating a self-important film professor in line at the movies. However, Fellini was unwilling to make the trip to New York to shoot a single scene (Fox 93).

Although Fellini's films from the early 1950s are shot in the stark style characteristic of Italian neorealism, Fellini is best known for his later,

highly imaginative, expressionist, almost surreal comedies that both expose and celebrate the excesses of Italian culture. His absurdist spirit and
proclivity for magical effects are among his greatest affinities with Allen,
along with their mutual suspicion of religion. However, Fellini's films are
typically more political and socially attuned than Allen's.

Although Allen downplays the similarities between his movies and those
of other directors, several of Fellini's films clearly have counterparts in Allen's oeuvre. In *Stardust Memories*, *Radio Days*, *Alice*, and *Celebrity*, Allen
realizes visions analogous to Fellini's, but within a New York cultural mi-
lieu instead of a northern Italian one. *Stardust Memories* pairs with *8½*.
Both are self-reflexive, postmodern movies about the impossibility of making movies, and both employ experimental, expressionist techniques to
communicate the protagonists' inner emotional states. Moreover, each film
appears highly autobiographical, and they share a playful, absurdist spirit
that obscures the line between the real and the surreal. Like *Amarcord*, *Radio Days* provides a comically nostalgic reminiscence of the director's
childhood; even particular shots in the latter are patterned after the former.
Alice, like *Juliet of the Spirits*, uses magic to spark the sexual and spiritual
awakening of an affluent housewife. And like Mastroianni's character in *La
Dolce Vita*, Lee Simon in *Celebrity* is a journalist who becomes caught up in
and overwhelmed by the unreal world of the rich and famous.

Fellini's influence appears as early as *What's New, Pussycat?* (1965),
where Allen directly parodies the scene in *8½* where Guido is surrounded
by adoring women whom he must literally whip into shape. The scene in
Shadows and Fog featuring Spiro, the clairvoyant, is shot in Fellini's cinematic style, as are the space alien scene in *Stardust Memories* and the
church confessional booth in *Alice* that suddenly appears before Alice's
childhood home in her opium dream. The magical realism in portions of
Broadway Danny Rose also evokes Fellini, such as when Danny and Tina
encounter a superhero in the New Jersey marshlands, and when they inhale
helium during a shootout in a warehouse, causing them to speak in high,
squeaky voices as they hide among the flamboyant cartoon floats being prepared for Macy's Thanksgiving Parade. Although *Manhattan* shares little
thematically or stylistically with *Fellini's Roma*, it too establishes a major
urban center as the title character in a movie that depicts the life of a character dwarfed by his city.

Fiction. A regular contributor to the *New Yorker* and other literary maga-
zines during the 1970s, Allen has published three collections of his fiction:
Getting Even (1971), *Without Feathers* (1975), and *Side Effects* (1980).
See also **Getting Even**; **Side Effects**; **Without Feathers**.

Films. Allen wrote, directed, and/or acted in the following films: *What's New, Pussycat?* (directed by Clive Donner, 1965), *What's Up, Tiger Lily?* (1966), *Casino Royale* (directed by John Huston et al., 1967), *Take the Money and Run* (1969), *Bananas* (1971), *Play It Again, Sam* (1972), *Everything You Always Wanted to Know About Sex* (*But Were Afraid to Ask)* (1972), *Sleeper* (1973), *Love and Death* (1975), *The Front* (directed by Martin Ritt, 1976), *Annie Hall* (1977), *Interiors* (1978), *Manhattan* (1979), *Stardust Memories* (1980), *A Midsummer Night's Sex Comedy* (1982), *Zelig* (1983), *Broadway Danny Rose* (1984), *The Purple Rose of Cairo* (1985), *Hannah and Her Sisters* (1986), *Radio Days* (1987), *King Lear* (directed by Jean-Luc Godard, 1987), *September* (1987), *Another Woman* (1988), *Oedipus Wrecks* (1989), *Crimes and Misdemeanors* (1989), *Alice* (1990), *Scenes from a Mall* (directed by Paul Mazursky, 1991), *Shadows and Fog* (1992), *Husbands and Wives* (1992), *Manhattan Murder Mystery* (1993), *Bullets over Broadway* (1994), *Mighty Aphrodite* (1995), *Everyone Says I Love You* (1996), *Deconstructing Harry* (1997), *Antz* (directed by Eric Darnell and Tim Johnson, 1998), and *Celebrity* (1998).

Allen has also made three films for television. He wrote, directed, and starred in *Men in Crisis: The Harvey Wallinger Story* (1971), a political satire of the Nixon administration that was never aired. He also wrote, directed, and starred in a 1994 television remake of his play *Don't Drink the Water.* (Howard Morris directed the 1969 film adaptation, but Allen was not involved in its production.) Allen also acted in a television adaptation of Neil Simon's play *The Sunshine Boys* (directed by John Erman, 1996).

Allen is the subject of several films, including *Woody Allen: An American Comedy* (directed by Harold Mantell, 1977), *To Woody Allen, From Europe with Love* (directed by André Delvaux, 1980), *Mister Manhattan: Woody Allen* (directed by Peter Behle, 1987), *Meetin' WA* (directed by Jean-Luc Godard, 1988), and *Wild Man Blues* (directed by Barbara Kopple, 1998).

The Floating Light Bulb. A 1981 play written by Allen. Beginning April 27, 1981, the Lincoln Center Theater Company put on sixty-five performances and sixteen previews at the Beaumont Theater. It was performed by the American Conservatory Theater of San Francisco in its 1986–1987 season and in 1990 at the Nuffield Theater in Southampton, England. The original Broadway production was directed by Ulu Grosbard and produced by Richmond Crinkley. Santo Loquasto was the set and costume designer, and Robert Aberdeen was responsible for magic design. The cast included Brian Backer (Paul), Eric Gurry (Steve), Beatrice Arthur (Enid), Danny Aiello (Max), Ellen March (Betty), and Jack Weston (Jerry). Patrick Sandford directed the British production that starred Sylvia Syms, Sam Douglas, Gian Sammarco, and Lee Montagu.

Although generally appreciated for its humor and deft character development, *The Floating Light Bulb* has also been criticized for being too conventional and derivative and for lacking the formal experimentation of Allen's then-current film *Stardust Memories*. Indeed, neither Allen nor director Grosbard ever felt entirely comfortable with the script, although Allen revised it four times. Still, *The Floating Light Bulb* was designated as one of best plays of the 1981–1982 Broadway season and included in Otis Guernsey's *Best Play* series. Aiello, Arthur, and Weston were praised for their performances, and Backer received a Tony award for his. Nonetheless, the play's impact has not been enduring, and it is rarely produced. Its sixty-five Broadway performances were far fewer than Allen's earlier comedies enjoyed: *Don't Drink the Water* was performed 598 times, *Play It Again, Sam* 453, and fourteen years after *Light Bulb*, *Central Park West* had 343 performances.

The Floating Light Bulb appears to derive from Tennessee Williams's *The Glass Menagerie* (1944). Both center around dysfunctional families and study the impact of family members' neurotic behavior on a sensitive child who withdraws into a more pleasant artificial world within his or her mind. Both are set in the mid-1940s in impoverished neighborhoods, and both revolve around desperate, struggling mothers and a young adult who cannot cope with life. In each play, the mother entertains wildly inflated and totally unfounded hopes, and these hopes are dashed when reality intrudes. There are echoes too of Arthur Miller's *Death of a Salesman* (1949), especially when the adulterous husband pampers his mistress while the wife sacrifices to keep the household going.

The greatest difference between Allen's play and Williams's is that Allen's intends to be funny, though this is not always evident from simply reading the text. In performance, however, the cast was praised for bringing out the humor. It is as though Allen wondered what *The Glass Menagerie* would be like if the characters were Jewish instead of southerners. The comic possibilities would be irresistible, but the common problems of a struggling, impoverished family would remain. Unlike the absurd literary comedy characteristic of Allen's early work, the humor in *Light Bulb* is more understated, bittersweet, and mixed with pathos. According to Grosbard, Allen's strength in that play resides in his ability to realize characters convincingly and to have the humor emanate from the dramatic situation instead of from one-liners (Lax 253–254).

Indeed, the tone is much closer to *The Purple Rose of Cairo*, which Allen released four years later. Both *Purple Rose* and *Light Bulb* have their humorous moments as they portray sensitive, working-class protagonists who insulate themselves from squalor, mean-spiritedness, betrayal, and despair by withdrawing into fantasy worlds. Given the circumstances, their retreat from reality appears to be a sane act that enables them to survive in a spiritually hostile environment and allows them to experience joy at least on some level. In the long run, however, their withdrawal from the real world leaves them entirely dependent on others to furnish their basic needs. Thus, they are unable to assert their autonomy and take control of their lives: the same act that preserves their sanity also consigns them to a life of dependency and victimhood.

This destiny of eternal dependency is literally true for Cecilia in *Purple Rose*, and it is the future we are invited to project for Paul, the sixteen-year-old protagonist of *Light Bulb* who immerses himself in a world of magic tricks. He cannot bring himself to attend school because he becomes claustrophobic, overwhelmed by the crowd of people. Even Paul's mother, Enid, fears he will never be able to care for himself, and our identification of him with Laura from *Glass Menagerie* further underscores his lack of self-sufficiency. Finally, the play concludes with Paul retreating once more into his world of illusion.

Enid, like her counterpart Amanda in *Glass Menagerie*, also withdraws from time to time from reality. An apparent alcoholic, she recognizes clearly enough that her husband, Max, is having an affair, that her youngest son, Steve, is beginning to fall in with a bad group like his father did, and that Paul has emotional problems. Unable to influence the people she loves, she nags them ineffectually and then tries to express her affection by feeding them. Like Paul's magic, Enid's compulsion to nourish her family enables her to ignore the unsettling truths about her life and focus on something more satisfying. And because her proclivity for serving food plays off the stereotype of the Jewish mother, it also provides an opportunity for comic relief.

Enid's desperate desire for Paul to succeed in his audition stems at least as much from her own financial insecurity and fear that Paul will remain dependent on her indefinitely as from her good wishes for Paul. Nonetheless, she does wish Paul well, and when she insists that he perform his routine for Jerry, a small-time manager she believes might employ him, she is sincere as well as self-serving when she encourages him to overcome his stage fright and take advantage of a rare opportunity to find a job doing something he loves. By refusing to accept Paul's withdrawal from the world, encouraging him to believe in his own capabilities, and otherwise promoting his self-confidence, development, and autonomy, Enid is probably treating her emotionally damaged son in the most constructive way possible. Just as important, she seems to know when to let up on him and accept his withdrawal, despite her own desperate desire for him to perform.

Maurice Yacowar points out, "Like Amanda, Enid depends on illusion, proposing a turban for her son's costume, pouring 'the Christian Brothers into a decanter so it looks imported'—and placing excessive hopes on a gentleman caller" (Yacowar, *Loser Take All* 231). Enid soon realizes that Jerry, the gentleman caller, is another business failure who would not have been able to find work for Paul anyway. But her moment of clarity quickly yields to her desire for romance. When Jerry begins to sweet-talk her, she opens up to him. But this seems to make him nervous and he dashes her hopes, claiming he must catch a plane that evening for Arizona, allegedly to care for his mother.

For Enid, the illusion of romance is her best option available, but even that cannot be sustained. This is where she differs from Paul, who seemingly can prolong his world of illusions indefinitely. In the long run, the inability to distinguish between illusion and reality would serve only to mire Enid deeper in despair, as it threatens to do for Paul.

Certainly Max is the least attractive character, largely because he lives a life of self-delusion as he tries to convince himself and others that he is close to hitting the lottery jackpot, that his children are fundamentally all right, that he is not perpetrating emotional violence upon his wife, or that he will be able to run off to Florida or Arizona with his mistress. (Both Jerry and Max favor Arizona as a land for fantasies.)

In *The Floating Light Bulb* magic stands as an alternative to delusion. It represents hope and possibility in an otherwise hopeless situation. In that respect, it appears as a positive diversion. However, magic always eventually proves to be false—illusion if not delusion—be it Paul's floating light bulb trick or the figurative magic of Enid's romance. Ultimately her dashed expectations seem simply cruel. Nonetheless, the characters' various illusions and delusions empower them to cope in a hostile environment. The magic interjects a sense of awe and stimulates the characters' imaginations. Likewise, the humor in the play animates the audience and distracts it momentarily from the characters' problems. The play itself distracts them from their own problems: such is the power of art, imagination, and the magic of the theater. In Allen's atheistic view of an indifferent, hostile cosmos filled with horror and despair, perhaps this is the best we can hope for.

See also **Magic**.

From A to Z. A 1960 Broadway comedy revue to which Allen contributed two sketches: "Psychological Warfare" and "Hit Parade." The two-act production was Allen's Broadway debut as a playwright. It opened on April 20 at the Plymouth Theater, but received poor reviews and closed after twenty-one performances. Christopher Hewett directed. Other contributors included Hermione Gingold, Fred Ebb, Herbert Farjeon, and Mary Rodgers. The cast included Gingold, Elliott Reid, Louise Hoff, Kelly Brown, Stuart Damon, Isabelle Farrell, Michael Fesco, Virginia Vestoff, Alvin Epstein, Borach Kovach, Paula Stewart, Bob Dishy, Beryl Towbin, Larry Hovis, and Doug Spingler.

The Front. A 1976 film costarring Allen in the role of Howard Prince. It also stars Zero Mostel (Hecky Brown), Andrea Marcovicci (Florence Barrett), Herschel Bernardi (Phil Sussman), Danny Aiello (Danny La Gattuta), Michael Murphy (Alfred Miller), and Joshua Shelley (Sam). Martin Ritt directed and produced; Walter Bernstein wrote the screenplay; Michael Chapman was director of photography, Dave Gruslin music director, Charles Bailey production designer, Ruth Morley costumer, and Sidney Levin editor.

The most overtly political of Allen's films, *The Front* is a tribute to the writers, directors, and performers who were blacklisted during the 1950s' red scare. Among them were Ritt, Bernardi, Bernstein, and Mostel, who in 1951 remarked after refusing to cooperate with the House Committee of Un-American Activities (HUAC), "I am a man of many faces, all of them blacklisted." According to Julian Fox, the topic of blacklisting immediately appealed to Allen "due to his sympathy with the participants' ideals and his longtime respect for Ritt's work as a film-maker" (Fox 83). It is the first of Allen's films that is not pure comedy, and one of the few movies that Allen has acted in but did not write or direct.

The Front appeared during a period of détente in the Cold War, when tensions between the United States and Soviet Union had decreased, the Vietnam War was over, and America was preparing to put Watergate behind it by electing Jimmy Carter to replace Gerald Ford as president. During the early 1970s several works revisited the red scare, often from a liberal perspective sympathetic to the perceived victims of the witch-hunts. Among the works dealing with the red scare from this period are E. L. Doctorow's novel *The Book of Daniel* (1971), Eric Bentley's play *Are You Now or Have You Ever Been?* (1972), William Goldman's novel and the subsequent film *The Marathon Man* (1974/1976), *We Are Your Sons* (1975)—a book defending convicted atomic bomb spies Julius and Ethel Rosenberg by their children, and the documentary film *Hollywood on Trial* (1976) by Hollywood Ten member Lester Cole. *The Front* was critically acclaimed and generally well received, especially among liberal and European audiences. It cost $3.5 million to produce and grossed $5 million in U.S. and Canadian distribution (not including later video rentals and television revenues).

The Front centers on the strange and complicated situations that arise when Howard Prince, a man with little writing talent, agrees to "front" for a blacklisted television writer by submitting the writer's work under his own name. Soon Prince makes a very good living fronting for a stable of blacklisted writers. Initially the problems that arise from his deception create humorous situations, but ultimately they prove tragic. Loosely based on the life of actor Philip Loeb, Hecky Brown is a blacklisted comedian, a former communist sympathizer who wants desperately to continue with his performing career but refuses to inform against his friends. A network "clearance man" offers to help him obtain work again if he will prove his loyalty by spying on Prince, whom the clearance man regards as suspicious because he has no traceable past. The two men develop a close friendship, and the tension between Brown's desire to clear himself and his reluctance to betray a friend provides much of the film's dramatic interest.

Similarly, Prince must also sacrifice himself in order to do the right thing by his friends. As the front, he has become rich and won the affection of a beautiful, intelligent woman who otherwise would never have been interested in him, and he stands to lose all these things if he refuses to cooperate with the perpetrators of the blacklist. Like *A King in New York* (1957), Charlie Chaplin's vicious attack on HUAC that was not released in the United States until the same year as *The Front*, the film climaxes when the protagonist attacks the committee. Chaplin does it literally, with a fire hose. Allen does it verbally, with profanity.

Ritt claims he cast Allen as Prince because "I had seen Woody's films and thought he was terribly sweet in them. It was the sweetness I wanted." Allen considered the finished movie to be neither angry nor a devastating indictment of the blacklist (Fox 84–86). Allen later cast Michael Murphy, who plays Prince's blacklisted friend, as Isaac's adulterous pal in *Manhattan*. Sander H. Lee points out how Allen uses the films' common actors and common themes to connect the two works. In *The Front* Murphy's character tells Allen's, "You always think there's a middle you can dance around in, Howard. I'm telling you, this time there's no middle." While in *Manhattan* Allen's character tells Murphy's, "You cheat a little bit on Emily, and you play around the truth a little with me, and the next thing you know you're in front of a Senate committee and you're naming names, you're informing on your friends" (Lee 48).

G

Getting Even. A collection of Allen's short fiction and plays published by Random House in 1971. Some of the stories are original to this collection, but several first appeared between 1966 and 1971 in the *New Yorker, Evergreen Review, Playboy,* and the *Chicago Daily News.* A stage adaptation, also titled *Getting Even,* was performed by Afterthought Productions at the Edinburgh Festival in 1990, and several of the sketches were anthologized in John Lahr's *The Bluebird of Unhappiness,* which the Royal Exchange Theatre of Manchester, England, performed in 1987.

Getting Even is Allen's first book of humorous sketches. It was not widely reviewed; the *New York Times* described it as "*Mad Magazine* material at its best." His other two books, *Without Feathers* (1975) and *Side Effects* (1980), are largely written in the same vein. That vein, pioneered by S. J. Perelman, Robert Benchley, and other literary comedians of the 1920s and before, is characterized by an energetic wit that delights in nonsense, its own cleverness, and its ability to toy with the super-serious postures attached to the high culture of Western arts and letters. (See **Literary Comedy.**) Allen's sketches are more parody than satire. He rarely tries to make a point, political or otherwise. And although some feminists and leftist theorists of the time may have enjoyed his humor specifically because it deflated the revered masterpieces of a cultural canon dominated by white European men, Allen himself merely sports with his subjects. He never demeans the literature or the authors, though he will deflate pretentious language and arcane academic practices whenever possible. Nonetheless, his incongruities are too broad and too absurd to be pointed.

In "A Twenties Memory," a story that evolved from Allen's stand-up comedy, the narrator purports to have been part of the crowd that gathered around

Gertrude Stein and Ernest Hemingway in the 1920s. Among the memories he shares is an argument between Stein and Picasso in which Stein declared, "Art, all art, is merely an expression of something," and Picasso rejoined, "Leave me alone. I was eating."

"The Metterling Lists" spoofs scholarship that gathers documents from an artist's or writer's life and uses them to interpret his or her work. The piece takes the form of a review of the "long-awaited" first volume of *The Collected Laundry Lists of Hans Metterling*. Metterling is ostensibly a major novelist and playwright, known to his contemporaries as the "Prague Weirdo," and the reviewer enthusiastically welcomes the new insights the laundry lists shed on his life. For instance, "According to Anna Freud ('Metterling's Socks as an Expression of the Phallic Mother,' *Journal of Psychoanalysis*, Nov. 1935), his sudden shift to the more somber legwear [from blue socks to black] is related to his unhappiness over the 'Bayreuth Incident,' " when Metterling sneezed during a performance of *Tristan* and blew off the toupee of one of Wagner's patrons. And Metterling's preference for fresh linen, as evidenced by his laundry lists, is reflected in his writing when a character agrees to sleep with a man she hates if she can lie between soft sheets.

"The Schmeed Memoirs" also deflates efforts to reconstruct the past as it parodies another literary form: the memoir. In particular, it mocks the recollections of Albert Speer, a Nazi war criminal whose *Inside the Third Reich* was translated into English in 1970. An introductory note points out that Frederich Schmeed, the best-known barber in wartime Germany, cut the hair of Hitler and many other highly placed officials. His memoirs reveal the German high command to be the Nazi equivalent of the Three Stooges. Göring and Hess fight over who gets to sit on the barbershop hobbyhorse, and Hitler becomes obsessed with growing sideburns after hearing a rumor that Churchill is contemplating them. This rivalry over facial hair anticipates the gastronomical rivalry in *Love and Death*, in which Napoleon insists that he must develop his dessert before his British counterpart develops boeuf Wellington.

In "My Philosophy" Allen shows more than passing familiarity with the Western intellectual tradition, as he spoofs the abstract jargon characteristic of modern philosophy. And like Emmanuel Kant, whose *Critique of Pure Reason* inspired Allen's *Critique of Pure Dread*, Allen delves into epistemology. "What can we know?" he asks. This same question had compelled René Descartes to conclude in the seventeenth century, "I think, therefore I am," and then to go on to deduce the existence of God. In the process, Descartes articulated the Western mind-body duality in which the mind is viewed as an entity separate from the body and humans appear to exist apart from nature. Leaving from the same epistemological starting point as Descartes, Allen simply wonders if we have forgotten all that is knowable but are too embarrassed to say anything. He then adds, "Descartes . . . wrote 'My mind can never know my body, although it has become quite friendly with my legs.' "

"Notes from the Overfed" reveals the tortured soul of a former dieter. The piece, purportedly written after reading the new *Weight Watchers* magazine and a Dostoyevsky novel on the same airplane trip, begins with a confession, "I am fat. I am disgustingly fat." But like a Dostoyevsky character, the narrator uses the confessional form first to win sympathy and then to exonerate and elevate himself. A former agnostic, he attributes his fat to a dream that changed his life: "If God is everywhere, I had concluded, then He is in food. Therefore, the more I ate the godlier I would become. . . . To reduce would have been the greatest folly. Even a sin." No longer penitent, the narrator now asserts his moral superiority. He has come full circle from the remorseful suppliant who complained that fat was neither inherently good nor bad, nor in any other way value laden. "Suddenly, I am attributing to neuter flesh, values! Yes, and what of it. . . . For life is change and fat is life, and fat is also death. Don't you see? Fat is everything!" But Allen deflates the passion of his own parody by adding a final line, "Unless, of course, you're overweight."

"Mr. Big" introduces Kaiser Lupowitz, the hard-boiled detective who narrates "The Whore of Mensa" in *Without Feathers*, and it invokes the then-current public debate over the death of God. Lupowitz is based on Humphrey Bogart's Sam Spade character, to whom Allen returned a few years later in *Play It Again, Sam*. Lupowitz's client, an attractive but evasive woman who repeatedly withholds her real identity, wants him to locate God. But before the detective can find Him, the police report that God has been killed. They are sure it is the work of an existentialist. (Nietzsche, an early existentialist, declared in the mid-nineteenth century that 'God is dead.' The quotation was frequently cited during the 1960s, when such matters of theology often carried political overtones, and it was reflected in a popular piece of graffiti: "God is Dead!"—Nietzsche. "Nietzsche is Dead!" —God.")

But Lupowitz proves the cops wrong. It was not an existentialist; it was the dame, a scientist. Just as Humphrey Bogart reconstructs Mary Astor's sordid scheme in *The Maltese Falcon* before handing her to the cops, Lupowitz lays everything out for Dr. Ellen Shepherd. He points out how she took up philosophy "because that gives you a chance to eliminate certain obstacles." She then proceeded to turn the philosophers against one another to achieve her goals, using Spinoza to eliminate Descartes and Kant to off

Spinoza. Finally, he concludes, "You make mincemeat out of Leib-
nitz . . . but that's where you made your mistake because you trusted Martin
Buber. Except, sugar, he was soft. He believed in God, so you had to get rid
of God yourself." "Mr. Big" was staged by Michael Kustow at London's
National Theatre in October 1980, and it was the basis for Gerard
Krawczyk's *The Subtle Concept*, which received the 1981 grand prize for
Best Short Film at the fifth World Film Festival in Montreal. *The Bluebird
of Unhappiness* also includes the story.

"The Gossage-Vardebedian Papers" describe a chess match played by
correspondence by two players who appear to be working from different
games; "Conversations with Helmholtz" presents interviews with a supposed contemporary of Freud who is best known for proving that death is an
acquired trait; and "Viva Vargas" anticipates *Bananas* by presenting the diary of a Latin American revolutionary. "Spring Bulletin" parodies the college curriculum, describing such courses as a philosophy class that provides
confrontations with God through informal lectures and field trips, an as-
tronomy course that addresses the care and cleaning of the universe, and an
English class in which the poems of William Butler Yeats are "analyzed
against a background of proper dental care."

Finally, *Death Knocks* is a one-act play that parodies Ingmar Bergman's
The Seventh Seal (1956). It was first published in the *New Yorker* (July 27,
1968). In the Bergman movie, a medieval knight desperate to know what
awaits in the afterlife prolongs his existence by playing chess with the Angel of Death. He presses the angel for information about the hereafter, but
the angel knows nothing. In Allen's version, Death comes to Nat Ackerman,
a Jewish dress manufacturer who postpones his fate by playing gin rummy
with him. Ackerman's constant talking and his irritating questions disrupt
Death's concentration, and Ackerman prevails. The title is a pun alluding
both to the sudden appearance of Death and the practice of "knocking" in
gin rummy.

See also **Plays**; *Side Effects*; *Without Feathers*.

God: A Play. A one-act play by Allen that first appeared in 1975 in *Without Feathers*.

See *Without Feathers*.

H

Hannah and Her Sisters. A 1986 film directed by, written by, and starring Allen, who plays Hannah's ex-husband, Mickey. It costars Mia Farrow (Hannah), Michael Caine (Elliot), Barbara Hershey (Lee), Dianne Wiest (Holly), Julie Kavner (Mickey's assistant, Gail), Carrie Fisher (April), Max Von Sydow (Frederick), Maureen O'Sullivan (Hannah's mother, Norma), Lloyd Nolan (Hannah's father, Evan), Daniel Stern (Dusty), Tony Roberts (Mickey's partner, Norman), Sam Waterston (David), Joanna Gleason (Carol), Maria Chiara (Manon Lescaut), Bobby Short (himself), and the 39 Steps (rock band). Robert Greenhut was the producer, Carlo Di Palma director of photography, Stuart Wurtzel set designer, Jeffrey Kurland costumer, and Susan E. Morse editor. The music features "You Made Me Love You," "I've Heard That Song Before," "Bewitched," "I Remember You," "If I Had You," "I'm in Love Again," "I'm Old Fashioned," "The Way You Look Tonight," Puccini's *Manon Lescaut* and *Madame Butterfly*, and Bach's "Concerto for Two Violins and Orchestra," among other selections. Orion Pictures was the North American distributor.

Hannah and Her Sisters was Allen's first popular and financial success since *Manhattan* in 1979. It cost $9 million to produce and grossed $18.2 million in U.S. and Canadian distribution (not including later video rentals and television revenues). *Hannah* was a critical success as well. Rex Reed of the *New York Post* called it "Woody's greatest triumph," and Graham McCann described it as "one of the most liberating American movies since the Capra era." *New Yorker*'s Pauline Kael was more qualified in her judgment, complaining that most of the characters were "thin" and opining that "the willed sterility of his style is terrifying to think about." Nonetheless, she concluded that *Hannah* was "an agreeably skillful movie, a new canto in

[Allen's] ongoing poem to love and New York City." Allen won an Academy Award for best original screenplay, Caine for best supporting actor, and Wiest for best supporting actress. *Hannah* was nominated for best picture, and Allen, Morse, and Wurtzel received nominations for direction, editing, and set design, respectively. Carol Joffe was nominated for her work on the set design.

Unlike Allen's earlier films, which focus on one main character or one pair of characters, *Hannah* centers around five characters who equally share our interest. Allen claims that he was inspired by Tolstoy's *Anna Karenina*, "where you get a little bit of somebody's story and a little bit of somebody else's and then somebody else's and then back to the first person. . . . I like that format of ensemble, and I wanted to experiment with it" (*Woody Allen on Woody Allen* 154). Mia Farrow and her family provided general models for the characters, as did Diane Keaton and her family and other sisters whom Allen knew well. In fact, Hannah's mother is played by Farrow's actual mother, Maureen O'Sullivan; Farrow's children appear in the film, and the set for Hannah's home was Farrow's New York City apartment. And like Elliot, Hannah's husband who woos her sister with verses from e. e. cummings, Allen sent Farrow a cummings love poem early in their courtship. Nonetheless, just as it is misleading to equate Allen's characters with Allen

Mia Farrow, Barbara Hershey, and Dianne Wiest portray sisters in *Hannah and Her Sisters*. Photo by Brian Hamill. Courtesy of Photofest.

himself, despite the obvious and intentional similarities, it would be equally misguided to suggest that Hannah represents Allen's personal view of Farrow.

Hannah returns to several basic motifs Allen introduced in films from the late 1970s. As in *Annie Hall*, a younger woman outgrows her relationship with an older, mentor/lover/father figure. And as in *Manhattan*, Allen visually showcases the art and architecture of New York. However, for *Hannah* the director of photography was Carlo Di Palma, in his first collaboration with Allen, instead of Gordon Willis, who was unavailable. Allen considers them "both wonderful cameramen. Gordon has a greater technical mastery, Carlo has more of a European style, movement and mobility" (*Woody Allen on Woody Allen* 153).

Music sets the mood and announces themes in both *Manhattan* and *Hannah*. However, while *Manhattan* relies solely on the rhythms of George Gershwin, *Hannah* mixes a classical score by Bach and Puccini with show tunes and jazz by Cole Porter, Jerome Kern, Richard Rogers and Lorenz Hart, Johnny Mercer, Count Basie, and Dave Brubeck, among others. In each movie, Allen lingers on the music so we can indulge our pleasure in it. Moreover, Julian Fox notes that each character in *Hannah* has a musical motif. Holly and Lee are associated with "Bewitched, Bothered and Bewildered"; April with "The Way You Look Tonight," Mickey with jazz by Count Basie and Dave Brubeck, and the romance between Lee and Elliot by music of Bach (Fox 167). Such use of motifs accentuates the drama and provides cohesion and unity.

Hannah's strongest ties are to *Interiors*. Both movies examine relationships among three sisters from a dysfunctional family; both center on women who impose order on chaos; each features a husband who is sexually attracted to his wife's sister; and each is deeply concerned with the inevitability of death. But only *Hannah* has the Marx Brothers, and it presents a less gloomy, more optimistic vision than *Interiors*.

The main characters intersect at Hannah: sister to Lee and Holly, wife to Elliot, and ex-wife of Mickey. But although her central position might suggest that Hannah would be the most clearly defined, or even the most foregrounded of the characters, in fact she remains the most ambiguous and least fully drawn—able to absorb whatever views of her that her family and the audience project on her. In fact, even Allen and Farrow were never entirely clear in their own minds about whether Hannah is the good sister she appears to be, nurturing and well intentioned, or whether she has a "darker side" (Lax 292).

Hannah is attractive, talented, maternal, family oriented, and generous with her money and attention. She seems to know herself well. Hannah has established priorities in her life and lives by them. An accomplished actress, she has placed her children over her career and taken a long sabbatical from acting, though she has recently returned to the stage for a critically acclaimed portrayal of Nora in a revival of Ibsen's *A Doll's House*. The daughter of adulterous, alcoholic parents, Hannah does not suffer the alcoholism or drug addiction that Lee and Holly have had to overcome. Capable and confident, Hannah hosts the gatherings that bring the family together, soothes her drunken parents when they quarrel, lends money for Holly's inevitably unsuccessful enterprises, and provides sanctuary and structure for Elliot, whose life was in chaos before he met her.

Perhaps because she is the daughter of alcoholics, Hannah has become an "enabler," and her relationships with loved ones often revolve around her assuming an enabling role. If Hannah has needs of her own, she rarely shares them with others. Consequently, because her life seems so complete and so blessed, others tend to take her strength for granted—as though it comes to her effortlessly and without cost—and she falls victim to the envy and insecurity of those she loves.

For instance, Elliot feels overwhelmed by her competence and inadequate before it. A man of weak will, he has benefited greatly from Hannah's strength but comes to resent it too. Their relationship is not revealed at length, but we learn that he had been floundering until Hannah, the enabler, brought structure, coherence, and love into his life. But by the beginning of the film Elliot has become enabled, and they need to strike a new, more equal, and mutually supportive balance in their relationship. Neither Hannah nor Elliot recognizes this until Elliot accuses her of being too self-sufficient, and Hannah confesses that she has needs too. Once Hannah thus establishes herself as a worthy recipient of Elliot's nurturing impulses, their relationship begins to heal. But Hannah remains clueless as to why there was a problem or what she may have done either to create it or resolve it.

Until Hannah voices her sense of vulnerability, Elliot's impulse to nurture finds no outlet in his marriage. Consequently, he becomes attracted to Lee, the youngest daughter of Hannah's alcoholic parents. Perhaps as a residual of childhood neglect, Lee expresses a deep need to be taken care of, and her affair with Elliot develops into one of the major plotlines in the film.

A recovering alcoholic, Lee too seems weak-willed, though she demonstrates some growth over time. She initially protests that she should not become involved with her sister's husband—a position most viewers would share—but Lee readily gives in when Elliot tells her his marriage to Hannah is all but over. He enjoys giving her pleasure—sexually, intellectually, and emotionally—and she enjoys receiving it and being the focus of his attention.

Lee's earlier affair with Frederick, a nihilistic, alienated artist, also involved an older, seemingly self-possessed father figure schooling her in love, life, and the arts.[1] But even before Elliot intruded, that relationship had ceased to be sexual and was on the verge of demise, largely because their roles had reversed. Frederick had become dependent on Lee, who was now his sole source of emotional sustenance and human contact, and Lee was unhappy and unfulfilled in the role of enabler.

Lee's affair with Elliot ends when she finally overcomes her weakness by exerting the will to do what she knows is both best for herself and the proper thing to do. Once Lee takes control of her life by ending an arrangement that has diminished her self-respect and failed to fulfill her needs, she is able to develop a more satisfactory relationship with her English professor. Although he is another authority figure who has presumably accepted the role of being her teacher and caring for her, Lee's eventual husband nonetheless seems a better choice. He is more engaged in life than Frederick and able to commit himself more fully than Elliot.

Although Holly depends on Hannah for financial assistance, moral support, and help in meeting single men, having to rely on Hannah makes Holly feel inadequate. But Holly projects her negative judgment of herself onto Hannah, convincing herself that it is Hannah who secretly regards her as a failure. And then she resents Hannah for judging her so harshly. All the while, Hannah cannot comprehend what she has done to upset Holly.[2] In fact, neither we nor Holly are shown what Hannah thinks of her sister, except that she believes Holly's aspirations are often unrealistic—and they usually prove to be just that.

A former cocaine abuser, Holly seems lost and without direction in life. She admires Hannah and tries to emulate her but finds little joy or success as an imitation Hannah. Holly often sets herself up for failure, such as when she auditions for a role in a musical, even though she is not an accomplished singer. When Hannah tries to point out such obvious flaws in Holly's plans, Holly blames Hannah for being negative and unsupportive, much as Eve blames Joey in *Interiors*.

The transformation in Holly's fortunes comes partly from a limited growth in self-knowledge and self-acceptance and partly from sheer luck. At a certain point she finally acknowledges that she is not Hannah. Specifically, Holly accepts the fact that she has no future as an actress and ceases to invest her time, energy, resources, and self-esteem in trying to be something she is not.

Gains in self-knowledge often bring about changes in fortune, and though Holly's decision to become a playwright initially seems as dubious as her other projects, she demonstrates an unsuspected aptitude and becomes a success. Holly's story reminds us that there is virtue to simple perseverance: keep trying enough different things, and sooner or later something will click. Enhanced self-knowledge and self-acceptance may speed up the process, but sometimes pure luck plays a role as well.

Mickey too finally surrenders to luck. Hannah's first husband, he also appears lost at the beginning of the film: he seems largely alone, without a mate or close friends, and his job as a television producer brings only stress and no joy. A hypochondriac, Mickey endures an existential crisis when he shows symptoms common to brain tumors. (According to Julian Fox, Allen experienced similar fears when he developed a ringing in his ear while shooting *Manhattan* and was examined for cancer.) Mickey convinces himself that he is destined to die soon, and when medical tests show that he is healthy, he is initially jubilant. But he soon realizes that his good news only postpones the inevitable, and once again he falls into despair. He tries to find reassurance in religion, but while his efforts to become a Catholic and then a Hare Krishna furnish some of the funniest moments in the movie, they fail to endow meaning upon his existence. On the other hand, a more constructive consequence of his despair is that Mickey quits his job and thereby eliminates an enormous amount of stress that had been undermining his pleasure in life.

Luck finally saves Mickey from despair. Feeling suicidal and obsessed with his own moribund thoughts, Mickey wanders the streets until he absent-mindedly enters a movie theater, buys a ticket without even being aware of what is playing, and finds himself watching the Marx Brothers in *Duck Soup*. He soon becomes caught up in the film and infected by their absurd good spirits, and he departs the movie with a new attitude of acceptance.

The Marx Brothers have inspired an epiphany: even if life has no meaning beyond its immediate experience, we can at least participate in that experience and enjoy it for whatever it is worth. And if the best we can have is an outside chance that God exists and life has inherent meaning, then we should accept that chance and place our hopes on it. Mickey would prefer more certainty, but he settles for the recognition that sometimes long shots do come in and that sometimes things just work out, even when there is no apparent reason for it.

Like Holly, who had to achieve a level of self-acceptance in order to progress in life, Mickey has needed to free himself from the inordinate stress at work and come to terms with his nihilism before he can find happiness. Once he does, luck again intrudes as Mickey accidentally encounters Holly again, several years after their disastrous first date. Propitiously, she is now looking over jazz records instead of the noxious rock and roll that sickened Mickey before. This time they both are more receptive to happiness, and they hit it off when Holly reads him her play.

The film thus concludes happily on a note of acceptance, reconciliation, and according to Maurice Yacowar in *Loser Take All*, regeneration, despite Allen's original impulse to end less tidily and less happily.[3] The crisis in Hannah's marriage has passed without her ever really knowing what was wrong or how deep the crisis was. She remains blissfully ignorant of Elliot and Lee's affair, and we leave feeling that everyone, including Hannah, is better off for this. Elliot rediscovers how much he loves Hannah; Lee forms a successful relationship for the first time; Holly finds a satisfying career and a loving husband; and Mickey comes to terms with his existential anguish and finds a loving wife.

There is a strong sense that the characters had to go through everything they endured in order to arrive at the state of harmony and acceptance they achieve at the end. Allen thus suggests that life is a messy affair but that we learn and grow by coping with our messes. And in a new hint of existential optimism, he shows that sometimes, if we can just wait, luck can intrude at some unexpected moment, and we might get what we need for true fulfillment, even if there is no rational reason for it.

NOTES

1. The casting of Max Von Sydow as Frederick establishes a link to the films of Ingmar Bergman in which Von Sydow starred. He played Antonius Block, the knight in *The Seventh Seal* (1956) who, like Mickey, is desperate to find meaning in life, discover if God exists, and learn what becomes of us after death.

2. *Interiors* and *Manhattan* also present this human tendency to project our own self-judgments onto others. In *Interiors* Eve repeatedly accuses Joey of behaving and feeling toward her the way she actually behaves and feels about Joey.

When Ike and Mary walk through the planetarium in *Manhattan*, Ike begins to point out that her disappointments with Yale "are what happens when you . . ." but Mary completes his final sentence for him: "I know. When you're having an affair with a married man." Then she projects her own harsh assessment of the situation onto Ike, accusing him, "What a terrible way to put it." Allen calls attention to this projection by having Ike remind Mary that it was she, not he, who described the affair so unpleasantly: "I didn't put it that way."

3. Allen himself finds the ending too neat and upbeat: "I should have been a little less happy than I was. . . . I should have opened it up more, not resolved so much. It's a habit from my growing up and from American films—trying to find a satisfying resolution. . . . But as I've gone on I've started to resolve the films less" (*Woody Allen on Woody Allen* 156).

Allen originally concluded with Elliot still pining for Lee, even after she has married, but this "was so down for everyone that there was a huge feeling of disappointment and dissatisfaction every time I screened it . . . so I had to put a more benign ending on it and it dissatisfied me" (Fox 170).

Holocaust. *Holocaust*, which literally means "devastation by fire," is the term commonly used to refer to the extermination of six million Jews by Adolf Hitler's Nazi regime during World War II. It had been Hitler's intention to eradicate the entire Jewish race. *Crimes and Misdemeanors* asks the central question for Jews after this genocide: How is it possible to reconcile the Holocaust with the notion that God exists or that He has created a moral universe that rewards virtue and punishes evil?

Although Allen explores a range of answers in his movies, his personal response is to discard the notion of a benign God and reject claims that people are fundamentally good. In "Random Reflections of a Second-Rate Mind" he discusses his views about the Holocaust directly:

At fifteen I received as a gift a pair of cuff links with a William Steig cartoon on them. A man with a spear through his body was pictured and the accompanying caption read, "People are no damn good." A generalization, an oversimplification, and yet it was the only way I ever could get my mind around the Holocaust. Even at fifteen I used to read Anne Frank's line about people being basically good and place it on a par with Will Roger's pandering nonsense, "I never met a man I didn't like."

The questions for me were not: How could a civilized people . . . do what they did to another people. And how could the world remain silent? . . . This mystery that had confounded all my relatives since World War II was not such a puzzle if I understood that inside every heart lived the worm of self-preservation, of fear, greed, and an animal will to power. And the way I saw it, it was nondiscriminating. It abided in gentile or Jew, Black, white, Arab, European, or American. It was part of who we all were, and that the Holocaust could occur was not at all so strange. ("Random Reflections" 71–72)

Frederick from *Hannah and Her Sisters* and Harry from *Deconstructing Harry* express these sentiments directly. A television show about Auschwitz treats the Holocaust as an aberration, but Frederick, an alienated artist, declares his surprise that such outrages do not happen more often. Harry, a novelist, suggests the same in *Deconstructing Harry* when he insists that genocide even worse than the Holocaust is inevitable: "Records are made to be broken."

Harry also argues with his sister over whether the Holocaust was primarily a Jewish tragedy or a human one. For Doris, the main lesson is that Jews must look out for themselves in an ever-hostile world. But Harry, once again articulating Allen's own sentiments, believes the overriding lesson is that all forms of chauvinism, even Jewish chauvinism, are dangerous because they feed the feelings of superiority and fear that fuel the impulse to eradicate outsiders.

But Frederick and Harry are among Allen's least sympathetic characters, not only because they are bleak but also because they are arrogant and self-absorbed. Thus, by having these narcissistic, nihilistic misanthropists express his view of human nature, Allen also shows how his pessimistic philosophy breeds bitterness, contempt, and alienation, regardless of its accuracy. Unlike Harry and Frederick, Allen, a filmmaker, generates humor as he expresses his pessimism. In so doing, he also asserts the value of laughter in the face of despair. The laughter does not alter the grim facts, but it makes them less oppressive and more manageable.

The Holocaust seems never far from Allen's mind. *Shadows and Fog* recreates the anti-Semitism that led to it, and the film reminds Jews that in dangerous, uncertain times, they have traditionally been held responsible and made scapegoats, regardless of which world order they are living under. This is especially evident in the scene where the police roundup an innocent Jewish family and when Kleinman's boss calls him a "slimy vermin more suited to extermination than life on this planet." In *Zelig* the title character's craving for social acceptance and his corresponding desire to surrender his individual identity to a larger cause find their ultimate expression when he becomes a Nazi. Zelig's disruption of Hitler's rally when he sees Dr. Fletcher and comes to his senses both ridicules Hitler and culminates the love story. Alvy Singer's insistence on continually dragging Annie to see Marcel Ophuls's "four-hour documentary about Nazis," *The Sorrow and the Pity* (1969), not only characterizes Alvy as morbid and serves as a vehicle for showing the couple drift apart; it also represents one of the redeeming aspects of their relationship, as it has deepened Annie's social awareness. At the end of the movie Alvy regards it as a personal triumph when Annie takes her new boyfriend to see the documentary.

Professor Levy, a Holocaust survivor in *Crimes and Misdemeanors* who lost his entire family, also serves a plot function. Levy continued to affirm life throughout his incarceration in the concentration camp and for years afterward, and as the subject of Cliff's documentary he brings Cliff and Halley together. Then one day he inexplicably walks out a window. His suicide not only exemplifies the long-term emotional damage wrought by the Holocaust; it also provides a plot point in which Cliff, dejected over Levy's death and its ruination of his film, admits his love for Halley. Halley's rejection of Cliff in conjunction with this reminder of the Holocaust makes Allen's view of life appear particularly bleak.

Allen sometimes shows characters appropriating the Holocaust for personal advantage, often through passive-aggressive manipulation. The scene between Cliff and Halley, for instance, also reveals how Cliff, perhaps unconsciously, invokes the tragedy of the Holocaust to gain sympathy for himself. He declares his love for Halley in conjunction with a separate, implied appeal for sympathy over Levy's death—and for his suffering in the Holocaust that presumably spawned it. By conflating the two emotional appeals, Cliff creates a situation in which Halley, who finds it painful to hurt anyone, must hurt him further if she is to deny his love. The only way she can avoid the pain of feeling as if she is a hurtful person is to give him what he wants. Fortunately for Halley, she exercises the strength not to succumb or be manipulated into a relationship she does not want.

In *Manhattan Murder Mystery* Larry also inappropriately raises the Holocaust in order to get his way. Complaining that listening to so much music by Hitler's favorite composer makes him want to conquer Poland, Larry walks out on the Wagnerian opera he has promised to attend. He thus manipulates the situation so the issue is no longer his broken promise but the Holocaust. In this way, he, not Carol, becomes the victim, and she has no way to confront him.

In addition to these more central treatments of the Holocaust, passing references permeate Allen's work. The last time Cliff made love to his wife was on Hitler's birthday. In *Hannah and Her Sisters*, Mickey, wanting to know the meaning of suffering, asks his parents, "Why are there Nazis?" Instructed by Mickey's mother to tell him why, Mickey's father replies that he does not know why there are Nazis; he does not even know how the can opener works. The "Man in the Booth" episode in *Hannah*, where Mickey undergoes medical tests, alludes to Adolph Eichmann, a Nazi war criminal who was tried and executed for his role in the Holocaust. During his trial, Eichmann was isolated in a glass booth, and Eichmann's capture and trial were later the subject of Arthur Hiller's film *The Man in the Glass Booth* (1975).

The Nazi swastika is transformed into a futuristic fashion statement in *Sleeper*. Alvy Singer shows his disdain for the proliferation of awards ceremonies by asking if Hitler will receive an award for Best Fascist Dictator. In *Manhattan* Ike complains that he has never had a relationship that lasted longer than Hitler and Eva Braun's, and he suggests to liberal intellectuals at a party that they confront Nazis who plan to march in New Jersey. He wants to use bricks and bats, but they want to write biting satire instead. (Elsewhere, Allen has stated, "Fascism . . . is an illness, not a political movement." *Woody Allen on Woody Allen* 226). Sandy tells his childhood friend in *Stardust Memories* that he has been incredibly lucky: if he had been born in Poland, he would have been a lamp shade. In *Radio Days* Joe's mother and father try to comprehend why the fascists seem to want to kill everyone. Mother says that the world could be so nice if it weren't for "certain people."

Allen's writing also alludes to the Holocaust. "The Schmeed Memoirs" in *Getting Even* mocks the recollections of Albert Speer, a Nazi war criminal whose *Inside the Third Reich* was translated into English in 1970. And

"Remembering Needleman" in *Side Effects* parodies intellectual pretentiousness and abstraction as it reminds us of the six million who perished. Needleman, a composite of leftist intellectuals from the mid-twentieth century, believed that "the only thing that was real was his IOU to the bank for six million marks."

Allen's stand-up comedy alluded the Holocaust too. One of his childhood Jewish friends was so tough that his parents voted for Hitler; a blind date was arrested by Israeli agents (presumably Nazi hunters); Allen and his wife were married by a rabbi who was so reformed that he was a Nazi. Subsequently, Allen's wife would prepare dishes like Chicken Himmler. More- over, Allen surmises that a vodka company found his name on a list they discovered in Eichmann's pocket when he was arrested.

In one of the cartoons from "Inside Woody Allen," Allen uses the Holocaust to highlight the right-wing tendencies of J. Edgar Hoover's FBI: "I was once quizzed by the F.B.I. on my loyalty. They wanted to know what I thought about Adolph Eichmann. I didn't know which answer would satisfy them."

See also *Inside Woody Allen*; **"Random Reflections of a Second-Rate Mind."** For additional reading see Mashey Bernstein, *"'My Worst Fears Realized,' Woody Allen and the Holocaust."*

Husbands and Wives. A 1992 film directed by, written by, and starring Allen, who plays novelist Gabe Roth. It costars Mia Farrow (Judy Roth), Judy Davis (Sally), Sidney Pollack (Jack), Juliette Lewis (Rain), Liam Neeson (Michael), Lysette Anthony (Sam), Blythe Danner (Rain's mother), Brian McConnachie (Rain's father), Galaxy Craze (Harriet), Benno Schmidt (Judy's first husband), Cristi Conaway (Shawn Grainger), Ron Rifkin (Rain's analyst), Bruce Jay Friedman (Jack's business associate, Peter Styles), Timothy Jerome (Paul), Jerry Zaks (party guest), Nora Ephron (party guest), and John Doumanian (party guest). Robert Greenhut was the producer, Carlo Di Palma director of photography, Santo Loquasto production designer, Jeffrey Kurland costumer (and off-screen voice of the interviewer), and Susan E. Morse editor. The music includes "What Is This Thing Called Love?," "West Coast Blues," "That Old Feeling," "Top Hat, White Tails and Tie," "Makin' Whoopie," "The Song Is You," and Gustav Mahler's *Ninth Symphony*. Columbia-TriStar was the North American distributor.

Husband and Wives appeared in conjunction with Allen's notorious breakup with Mia Farrow, a fact that stirred far greater interest in the film than it otherwise would have received. As a result, it achieved a modest profit, earning $3.5 million in ticket sales during the first five days, a record for Allen. But the popularity in America of this Bergman-like study of a failed marriage quickly declined, and the movie lasted on the U.S. charts for only five weeks. It cost $12 million to produce and grossed only $10.5 million ($5 million net) in North America; it recouped its losses in Europe and grossed about $28 million worldwide. The movie fared especially well in England and France; in Paris *Husbands and Wives* remained among the top ten box office performers for nineteen weeks.

Widely interpreted in terms of the scandal, the film nonetheless was a critical success, as most reviewers praised the acting and the script. However, the unsteady motion of the hand-held camera, which Allen employed to reflect the characters' dissonant emotional state, was frequently found to be distracting. Worse, it sometimes provoked feelings of nausea. Judy Davis received an Academy Award nomination for best supporting actress, and Allen was nominated for best original screenplay. Though they failed to win Oscars, the screenplay received awards from BAFTA and the London Critics' Circle.

Uncharacteristically gritty, violent, and visually disjointed, *Husbands and Wives* has been widely interpreted in terms of the highly publicized scandal surrounding the dissolution of Allen and Farrow's decade-long relationship. During the shooting, Farrow discovered that Allen was having an affair with her twenty-one-year-old adopted daughter, Soon-Yi Previn, whom he married in 1997. Especially upon the film's release, viewers and critics were inclined to read Allen and Farrow's failed romance as a subtext within the story. In particular, Gabe and Jack's rejection of their middle-aged wives in favor of younger women echoes Allen and Farrow's real-life relationship. Moreover, lines like "You don't know what goes on between two people" and "You can't force yourself to conform to some abstract vision of love and marriage," along with Gabe's observation that men are promiscuous because they must try to fulfill the destinies of millions of sperm, while women cater to the needs of only one egg, can be construed as Allen's explanation of his actions. The *New York Times*, which posits that *Husbands and Wives* is the first movie about a scandal to be made before the scandal actually occurred (appropriately postmodern for Allen), also suggests that Farrow's own emotional state accounts for the "washed out appearance" of Farrow's character Judy and for Farrow's "somnambulant acting."

But while this explanation of Farrow's performance may be correct, it is also the case that an emotionally drained appearance accurately reflects how Judy feels after living in a marriage that no longer thrills her. Thus, although suggestive and in some ways illuminating, the biographical approach risks overshadowing the craft and artistic intention of the film. As in most of his other movies, Allen draws heavily on his own life for themes and subject matter. But despite the many strong parallels that invite us to identify him with the characters he plays, Allen in the end is not his characters, nor does he fully endorse their actions, beliefs, or attitudes. Indeed, he consistently reveals their weaknesses and shows their failings to be responsible for their unhappiness, a fact overlooked by many of his critics who identify him closely with his characters and infer that he fully endorses them. Moreover, as Gabe tells Rain in response to her criticisms of his autobiographical novel, "I'm exaggerating for comic purposes . . . deliberately distorting it, you know, cause I'm trying to show how hard it is to be married." Elsewhere, Allen insists that his movies, including *Husbands and Wives*, are not primarily autobiographical:

When I finished the script for *Husbands and Wives* it was strictly an act of imagination. I finished the script long before anything happened that you read in the newspapers. And I gave the script to Mia, and I said to her, "Which person do you want to play?" . . . She could as easily have picked the other. . . . There was nothing autobiographical in the script at all. . . . [The characters are] just dreamed up. People thought that *Annie Hall* and *Manhattan* were autobiographical, but in fact both those scripts I wrote with Marshall Brickman, and he had lots of input on them. So whose autobiographies are they? His or mine? It's just so silly. (*Woody Allen on Woody Allen* 263)

A more productive approach to the film is to view it as another of Allen's inquiries into "What Is This Thing Called Love?"—Cole Porter's song that plays over the opening and closing credits and thereby frames the movie. Allen has commented on several occasions that he considers romantic relationships to be largely a matter of luck, and *Husbands and Wives* reveals love and passion to be irrational, perplexing, chaotic, and in the long run, perhaps mutually exclusive.

In Allen's view, as in Freud's, people are fundamentally driven by irrational libidinal desires that are capable of overriding the rational beliefs that serve the superego. This can lead to behavior that is inconsistent, antisocial, irresponsible, disloyal, and sometimes self-destructive. Consequently, the likelihood seems small that anyone can form and sustain a romance that satisfies both the libido and the superego—one that remains passionate while providing the security and consistency requisite for a stable, nurturing relationship. For Allen, the apparent impossibility of reconciling passion with stability lies at the core of his tragic view of life. We need both excitement and security in order to flourish and be happy, but one appears to come at the cost of the other. Therefore, in Allen's view, passionate love is inherently a losing proposition, except in the rarest circumstances.

As in *Another Woman*, where a seemingly actualized Marion feels sorry for Hope in the beginning and Hope pities a lost Marion at the end, *Husband and Wives* plays the dissolution of the apparently solid marriage between

Gabe and his wife, Judy, against the restitution of the failed marriage of their friends Jack and Sally. As in Ingmar Bergman's *Scenes from a Marriage* (1973), to which *Husbands and Wives* is indebted, Gabe and Judy begin to recognize serious problems in their own marriage only when their closest friends shock them with news of their impending divorce.[1] Judy is especially upset to learn that her friends are splitting up, and her inordinate irritation suggests that the breakup has hit a raw nerve within herself. As Sally later tells her, she (Sally) is doing what Judy really wants to do deep down. Subsequently, we watch as Jack and Sally reconcile after unsuccessfully trying new partners. Jack's experience with Sam, a sexy, younger New Age aerobics teacher, provides the sexual passion, lightness of spirit, and uncritical acceptance he lacked with Sally. In essence, Sam nourishes Jack's long-neglected physical needs, whereas Sally, who is sexually frigid, overly critical, and emotionally cold, had satisfied his need for intellectual stimulation. But the affair with Sam makes Jack recognize how much he values Sally's deep intellect and common sense, as well as her familiarity.

Sally's episode with Michael, a sensitive, romantic lover, shows her how much she values Jack's strength, assertiveness, and determination to prevail. She mentally disassociates while having sex with Michael (as Annie Hall does while making love to Alvy Singer). She imagines him to be a hedgehog, while Jack is a fox. Perhaps for the first time, she consciously recognizes that she definitely prefers foxes to hedgehogs. She does not elaborate on what she means by this, but the pairing suggests that she admires foxes because they are predators given to direct action and self-assertion, while hedgehogs are meek prey. Jack's violent treatment of Sam and his intrusion into Sally's house when she is in bed with Michael are expressions of the fox's dominance and strength of will that Sally admires, even as she deplores Jack's trampling her right to privacy. Sally learns in bed with Michael, and then afterward when Jack bursts into her home, that she wants to be taken by someone who forcefully claims her, not romantically wooed by a sensitive, tentative lover.

Thus, their separation and new experiences teach both Jack and Sally about what they want for themselves and about what they value in each other. In the end, they reach a level of acceptance that comes at the cost of deep passion in their lives. Sexual problems remain between them, but they enjoy the security and companionship they had previously taken for granted. They observe that "love is a buffer against loneliness as well as passion and romance" and learn to live with their sexual problems. Sally concludes, "You can't conform to some abstract notion of love and marriage."

Allen seems to agree with this last statement: each relationship is unique, and it creates its own conditions for happiness and success. Moreover, the story of Jack and Sally reminds us that the process of achieving a successful relationship is often contradictory, confusing, and painful to oneself and others. Innocent people, like Sam and Michael, can get hurt in the process. Allen does not endorse the violence and harm to others, but he cannot deny them either. In his modernist, yin-yang view of reality, they are a regrettable but necessary part of process. For instance, the same jealousy that leads Jack to strike Sam, his lowest, most despicable, and indefensible action, also leads him to assert his claim on Sally. And although he had no right to make that claim under the circumstances, his forceful assertion of it appeals to Sally's preference for foxes instead of hedgehogs, and it facilitates their reconciliation.[2]

Sally regards Judy as a fox and Gabe a hedgehog, and this distinction accounts for many of the dynamics of their relationship. It also lends support to Judy's first husband's claim that she is passive-aggressive: that she appears meek and vulnerable but always ends up getting what she wants, often by setting herself up as helpless or making herself a victim.

Experiencing Jack and Sally's breakup causes Judy to acknowledge to herself that she is attracted to Michael and would like the freedom to explore a relationship with him. Once it becomes clear to her that this is what she wants, Judy hides the fact from Gabe, on the grounds that she does not want to hurt him. Instead, she consciously or subconsciously manipulates their relationship so he will appear responsible for its failure. For instance, rather than look for deeper issues within herself, Judy blames her insecurity on a remark Gabe made years earlier about her being inhibited. Indeed, Judy blames their diminishing sexual activity on Gabe, though she too has clearly lost interest. After their argument over having a baby, she suggests making love when clearly neither of them is in the mood. In so doing, she creates a situation in which if Gabe declines, he assumes greater responsibility for the lack of sexual activity. When he accepts, she scuttles the possibility of making love by taking inordinate offense at his asking if she would trick him by failing to use birth control. Here again, Judy has managed to avoid making love—what she really wants—while still appearing as the victim who wanted to have sex but was turned off by Gabe's insulting question.

In a similar ploy, Judy asks Gabe if he believes they will break up like Jack and Sally. Gabe says no and asks if she does. Judy answers that she does not know if she will want to remain together if he does not want a baby. She thus frames the issue in a way that puts the full responsibility for the success of the marriage on Gabe, although they had no expectation of having children when they married. If he declines to have a child—and she knows he does not want one—then she can blame the failure of the marriage on him. In fact, when Gabe surprises her by giving in, she immediately reverses her position and maintains that she no longer wants a baby. Then, when Gabe confesses that he does not really want one, she accuses him of insincerity, even though she then confesses that she really *does* want one.

Likewise, Judy attributes withholding her poetry from Gabe to his being overly critical instead of acknowledging that she wanted to share it with Michael because she hoped it would create a closer bond with him. In other words, she casts her breach of intimacy with her husband as his fault, not hers. She then accuses Gabe of being flirty. Although there is truth to what she says about Gabe, in the context of the situation Judy is projecting onto Gabe her condemnation of her own behavior with Michael.

Michael's confession to Judy that he loves Sally makes Judy realize more fully that she wants Michael. To be free to pursue him, she engineers her breakup with Gabe while trying to make him appear responsible. After Sally and Jack reconcile, Sally declares that Michael's real crush is on Judy; he always speaks of her in hushed tones, and he likes her poetry. Given this encouragement, Judy picks a fight that night with Gabe, who is disturbed that she has shared something as intimate as her poetry with another man instead of him. She first accuses him of being unsupportive and then claims he is bored with her, when in fact she is bored with him. She further accuses him of using sex to express every emotion except love, a statement that is at least as true of her as of him. After declaring that Gabe views change as death, whereas she believes change is what life is made of, Judy declares that their marriage is over, "and we both know it," a position that Gabe does not necessarily share. Subsequently, she admits to the interviewer that she loved Michael and wanted to be free to explore the relationship.

Judy's passive-aggressive behavior appears most clearly when she manipulates Michael into hurting her and then begging her forgiveness. Again, she casts herself as victim but manages to come out of the episode with everything she wants, just as her first husband has pointed out. Initially she assumes the role of comforting Michael after Sally has gone back to Jack. When her excessive nurturing becomes suffocating, Michael lashes out at her, and she leaves feeling hurt. Pained at the harm he has ostensibly caused her, Michael supplicates her, denying what he has said during his outburst and telling her exactly what she has wanted to hear: how much she means to him. This brings them closer together and facilitates their eventual union, even though both subsequently maintain, and genuinely believe, that it was Michael who pursued Judy.

Gabe, like Ike Davis, Sandy Bates, Lee Simon, and so many other Allen characters, suffers from attraction to "kamikaze women"—women who are passionate and exciting but irrational, self-destructive, and destructive of those close to them. (Dorrie from *Stardust Memories* comes quickly to mind.) Jack offers two theories for Gabe's propensity for fatal attractions, though these are not entirely compelling. The first is that unconsciously Gabe chooses doomed relationships in order to punish himself for some deep-seated, secret guilt. The second is that Gabe, like everyone else from his generation, grew up on movies and novels that made doomed love appear romantic.

Gabe seems finally to have arrived at a point in his life where he recognizes the unhealthy nature of this attraction and has consciously disciplined himself to resist it. He married Judy because, although she reminded him of the woman with whom he had had his most passionate love affair, Judy appeared stable and sane. But over time Judy ceases to excite him the way Harriet did, a fact that Judy perceives even though he denies it. In this respect, like Jack and Sally, experience has induced Gabe to settle for diminished passion in return for increased stability.

But Gabe nonetheless remains drawn to unhealthy relationships, and Judy correctly intuits that the pretty, bright, creative coeds he teaches exert a draw on him. In particular, Gabe takes an interest in Rain, a talented young fiction writer whose story "Oral Sex in the Age of Deconstruction" has impressed him. On the other hand, his stature as a successful novelist, as well as his intellect and verbal acuity, make Gabe attractive to her. We learn that Rain has a history of destructive relationships with older, successful men, and as Gabe finds himself tempted by her, he voices perhaps the best line in the film: "Why do I hear $50,000 worth of psychotherapy dialing 911?" Gabe assumes his share of responsibility for the dissolution of his marriage to Judy, because, even though he knew a romance with Rain would inevitably end in disaster, "My heart does not know from logic." Like Judy, at least part of him wants to be free to pursue his new infatuation.

But Gabe seems to have acquired some degree of wisdom and self-control, and, recognizing the inevitable bad end of a romance with Rain, he cuts it off before it can develop into more than a single, passionate birthday kiss. Like Ike Davis in *Manhattan*, Gabe makes a point of acting consistently within his own code of ethics. Unlike Jack (and Ike's best friend, Yale), he has always been faithful in every relationship, and he has refrained from seducing his students, although other professors do. And like Ike, Gabe remains alone at the end of the film.

In Allen's absurdist worldview, virtue must be its own reward, as it otherwise often goes unrewarded and unvalued. (Such is the lot of the hedgehog.) A year and a half later Gabe is alone, "out of the game," and mostly taking refuge in his writing. But in many ways virtue *is*, in fact, its own reward. If Ike is lonely, his decision not to pursue Rain has spared him from becoming miserable and ridiculous like her obsessed former analyst and the other men who have become infatuated by her. Moreover, Gabe's writing develops in ways that may be promising; it is less confessional and more political. In other words, he is becoming less self-absorbed and more concerned with the real problems of others, and in Allen's universe this is a good thing. (Ike, too, recharges by retreating into his creative work after his affair with Mary fails.) Neither happy nor sad, Gabe does not seem less well off than when he was married to Judy. At least he is not conflicted by his responsibilities to a passionless marriage and his infatuation with an inappropriate object of affection. Moreover, he regards his current situation as a temporary but necessary phase, and he expects eventually to seek new companionship, hopefully with someone who is neither passive-aggressive nor a kamikaze.

Ultimately, *Husbands and Wives* does not answer Cole Porter's question, "What is this thing called love?" Instead, it shows the query to be unanswerable. Different people experience it differently and desire different things from it. As Jack points out, "Unreal expectations are what kill" most relationships. Whether interpreted as a justification of his ending his relationship with Farrow or as a sincere expression of Allen's view of human nature, or both, *Husbands and Wives*, like Gabe's novel, suggests that we must choose between a life of passion that precludes close attachments and eventually leaves us "lonely beyond belief" and a stable, familiar, secure existence that contains little excitement or thrill. With Gabe, Allen invites us to wonder, "Is the notion of ever-deepening romance a myth we all grew up on, along with simultaneous orgasms?"

NOTES

1. In both *Husbands and Wives* and *Scenes from a Marriage* characters describe their lives to an off-camera interviewer and shield their poetry from their spouse but share it with a different member of the opposite sex. Other similarities include domestic violence brought about by confused passions and husbands who leave their wives for younger women. (I am indebted to my student Shirin Irani for pointing out several of the exact parallels between the films.) In *Woody Allen on Woody Allen*, interviewer Stig Björkman also notes similarities to Bergman's *From the Life of the Marionettes* (1980), and Sander H. Lee points out affinities to Jean Resnais's *Mon oncle d'Amerique* (1980).

2. The paradoxical ability of contradictory feelings to coexist simultaneously within a person appears in Freud's theories of human nature, and it is part of Allen's modernist worldview. In addition to the other things we are, human beings are animals, and we remain instinctively attracted to winners, regardless of how much our Judeo-Christian tradition would have us revere the virtuous and the meek. If Jack's masculine, territorial domination is uncivilized and politically incorrect, Allen seems to suggest, it is also part of the human condition. It is further-

more part of the human condition that some women who otherwise believe that everyone should conform to the social norms that make civilization possible are nonetheless attracted to dominating males who, like the alpha dog in a pack, trample on the rights of others to take what they want.

This is not a state of affairs that Allen necessarily celebrates, but unlike his critics who deplore him for showing people who are thus paradoxically motivated, Allen acknowledges that it is the case, just as it is the case that older men and younger women are sometimes strongly attracted to one another, regardless of whether this is intellectually or morally defensible. Allen then continues to examine the impact of these motivations on human relationships and individual happiness.

Inside Woody Allen. A comic strip featuring Allen drawn by Stuart Hample in collaboration with Allen. Hample collected a selection of the cartoons under the title, *Non-Being and Something-ness* (1978). The strip premiered in 1976 in 180 newspapers in some sixty countries; it ran for eight years.

Hample befriended Allen soon after Allen began his performing career, and when Hample suggested drawing a cartoon strip based on the Woody Allen persona, Allen and his agents endorsed the idea, figuring it would promote Allen's film career, which was then about to move into its second, more serious phase. Allen and Hample collaborated on each strip.

Inside Woody Allen develops Allen's neurotic little-man persona as it covers such standard Allen themes as the existence of God, the meaning of life, fear of death, sex, family, Jewish identity, psychiatry, and being a celebrity. Like his writings and films, the strips are highly literate, and they appeal to a well-educated audience with a large vocabulary and familiarity with cultural references. In general, each strip leads to a single punch line. For instance, a cartoon entry in Woody's private journal points out that three hundred years later, René Descartes's basic conclusion remains valid, "But unfortunately, now it reads, 'I thought therefore I was.'" Readers unfamiliar with Descartes's original declaration, "I think therefore I am," are at a clear disadvantage.

In another strip Allen inverts our typical association with faith and religion by tying it instead with atheism. The picture shows a woman dressed like Annie Hall asserting, "There's no way you can prove there isn't a God," and Woody replies, "Right. You just have to take it on faith." Another strip underscores Woody's low self-esteem. An attractive woman tells Woody he is "the handsomest, wittiest, sexiest man I've ever met," and he thinks, "This

girl is fantastic. But can I trust her judgment?" Liberal "coddling" of criminals is spoofed by a strip showing Woody being robbed at gunpoint. Woody
asks the crook if he is doing this because he came from a broken home, or
because he wants to topple society or avenge mistreatment. But the robber
rejects those excuses and accepts his own greed. "Let's not rule out the
profit motive," he replies.

Appliances and machines still trouble cartoon Woody, but at least the jolt
from his toaster provides therapeutic shock treatment. Even the I Ching rejects him because he is Jewish; right-wing political agencies still cannot be
trusted, and the Holocaust is never far from mind: "I was once quizzed by
the F.B.I. on my loyalty. They wanted to know what I thought about Adolph
Eichmann. I didn't know which answer would satisfy them." Woody's un-
fortunate childhood is also represented: his parents tried to cure him of
masochism by beating it out of him.

Non-Being and Something-ness is introduced by R. Buckminster Fuller,
designer of the geodesic dome, who theorizes that the purpose of the universe is to create Woody Allen and that the human population of the world
exists to provide an audience for him.

Interiors. A 1978 film directed and written by Allen. It stars Geraldine
Page (Eve), Diane Keaton (Renata), E. G. Marshall (Arthur), Maureen
Stapleton (Pearl), Mary Beth Hurt (Joey), Sam Waterston (Mike), Kristen
Griffith (Flyn), and Richard Jordan (Frederick). Charles Joffe was the pro-
ducer, Gordon Willis director of photography, Mel Bourne production de-
signer, Joel Schumacher costumer, and Ralph Rosenblum editor. Like
Annie Hall, the movie has no musical soundtrack. United Artists was the
North American distributor.

Allen's first film after the popular, highly acclaimed *Annie Hall*, *Interiors* surprised and disappointed many fans who were expecting another sophisticated comedy but instead received a somber, Bergman-like study of a
dysfunctional family. *Interiors*, which cost $10 million to produce, was bet-
ter received in Europe, and it ultimately earned a slight profit despite grossing only $4.6 million in U.S. and Canadian rentals (not including later video
rentals and television revenues). The film's artistic merit was acknowledged in its Academy Award nominations for best director (Allen), original
screenplay (Allen), actress (Page), supporting actress (Stapleton), and art
direction (Bourne and Daniel Robert).

Although the swerve from comedy to tragedy caught his audience by surprise, Allen received support for the project from United Artists, especially
from top executives Robert Benjamin and Arthur Krim, who later went on
to found Orion Pictures and back several more of Allen's films. Allen has

maintained that he "always wanted to make serious films—in addition to comic films—and when I got the opportunity and I felt the time was right, *Interiors* happened to be the first one that I made. . . . I simply think that I have enough ideas in my head to make a serious film now and then. I was not trying to prove anything. And when I say 'serious,' I only mean a film that is not primarily intended to make the audience laugh" (Spignesi 167). He later added, "I was not going to start off with any half-hearted measure. I was not going to do a little bit of drama or a conventional drama. And if I failed, I failed. That's OK. But what I was aiming for, if I had made it, would have been very, very significant. I'm not saying I made it, but the ambition was good, the ambition was high" (*Woody Allen on Woody Allen* 95).

Filming *Interiors* was difficult and stressful for Allen, who feared it would fail utterly. He revised the screenplay, reshot scenes, and labored in the editing room. According to editor Ralph Rosenblum, Allen was afraid the film would fail utterly, but he rescued it with his dedication and hard work (Lax 335).

Allen considers the film flawed but worthwhile. "I'm not unhappy with it, but I think after seeing it, I would have done different things. Just from a technical point of view, a structural point of view. Just out of pure writer's instinct now I would have brought Maureen Stapleton into the story earlier." He would now make the dialogue "more colloquial and less literary" and do more with the photography to build upon the feeling of coolness they were trying to create (*Woody Allen on Woody Allen* 98, 117).

Allen's models for creating a "very, very significant" family drama come primarily from Russia and Scandinavia, where there is a tradition of literature and art that explores the inner dynamics of family relationships and reveals spiritual anguish and desire. Foremost among his models are the great nineteenth-century Russian novelists Leo Tolstoy, Fydor Dostoyevsky, and Ivan Turgenev and playwright Anton Chekhov. Robert Benayoun also notes the influence of Norwegian painter Edvard Munch and German expressionist Emil Nolde. But contemporary Swedish filmmaker Ingmar Bergman exerts the greatest influence, with *Interiors* especially indebted to Bergman's *Cries and Whispers* (1972).

Both films reveal the internal relationships of a family dominated by an emotionally disturbed mother. In particular, they show how the mother's inability to project love shapes her three daughters' interactions with her, their father, and each other. Nancy Pogel notes that both films treat "the effects of emotional distance, coldness, and indifference on the quality of human life. Both . . . contrast bravery (defined as active confrontation with life and the meaning of death) with escape or the inability to deal with such fundamental issues of existence" (Pogel 99–100).

In addition to affinities of character and theme, similarities between the films abound in the details. *Cries and Whispers* and *Interiors* both conclude with the most sensitive sister writing in her journal, recalling happier childhood days with her sisters. White roses are closely associated with both mothers, who typically also dress themselves in white. In each, the older sister rebuffs a heartfelt attempt by her sibling to establish a closer bond. Moreover, much of the camera work in *Interiors* and the composition of several important shots employ Bergman's style. Like Bergman, Allen emphasizes his characters' isolation by placing them against stark backgrounds and featuring them in one-shots, cutting between individual speakers instead of showing them together within a single frame. Neither film has a soundtrack, and both employ silence to express emotional distance.

Despite these similarities, Allen rejects the notion that *Interiors* derives from *Cries and Whispers*, maintaining that his characters lack the "cold cerebral guilt" of their Swedish counterparts and pointing to American family drama as a greater influence. Indeed, Arthur Miller's *The Death of a Salesman* (1949) has a significant presence in the film.

Allen also drew from real-life experiences, especially from the family of Louise Lasser, his second wife and costar of *Bananas*. Like Eve, the mother in *Interiors*, Lasser's mother had attempted suicide, first unsuccessfully and later successfully. According to Allen, Eve's response to her husband's announcement that he wants a trial separation was inspired by a real-life incident in which, under similar circumstances, the wife simply left the table, walked into her room, and killed herself. "Now in *Interiors* I didn't want to take it that far. But I was imitating that incident" (*Woody Allen on Woody Allen* 99).

The title alludes to Eve's obsession with room interiors and metaphorically to the characters' inner emotional states. According to Stephen Spignesi, Diane Keaton suggested the title, which had originally been *Windows*. (Shots of windows permeate the film.) However, Maurice Yacowar suggests that Allen may have been inspired by a passage in Ernst Becker's *The Denial of Death*, a book that Allen admires and that Alvy Singer recommends in *Annie Hall*. Becker describes the sense of bitterness and betrayal that results when a loved one fails to live up to expectations: "We feel diminished by their human shortcomings. Our interiors feel empty or anguished, our lives valueless, when we see the inevitable pettiness of the world expressed through the human beings in it" (Yacowar, *Loser Take All* 190).

Like other modernist and postmodernist storytellers, Allen does not judge his characters; he simply reveals their psychological states and their impact on others. Moreover, he shows how the same action or statement, when viewed from different contexts, can change from being positive to negative, or vice versa. The audience sees all the points of view and the hidden motivations and is left to draw its own conclusions.

Basically, *Interiors* describes the impact of the dissolution of a marriage on the various members of the family. When Arthur leaves Eve, he spawns personal crises for himself, Eve, and their three grown daughters. Until Arthur's unexpected announcement, the family had lived in a seemingly perfect world of refinement and high culture, exquisitely orchestrated by Eve and insulated from the instabilities of the outside world. The names Arthur and Eve and the state of chaos into which the family is thrown when their protected world is shattered evoke Adam and Eve and the fall from Eden. For some family members their fall from grace is devastating, but for others it is a *felix culpa*, a fortunate fall that eventually effects positive change by forcing them to embrace life actively. Like the fall from Eden, Arthur and Eve's divorce brings about death—and awareness of mortality—and it introduces passion and violence into a family that had sustained its artificially harmonious world by suppressing emotion.

Eve, the central character, is the ultimate art-for-arts-sake artist who needs to impose order on every manifestation of chaos in order to survive. Yacowar notes, "All the characters suffer from Eve's attempt to impose a placid, pale, elegant, but lifeless world upon them" (Yacowar, *Loser Take All* 187). Eve represses all expressions of passion and chaos in her life, not only in her restrained behavior, carefully modulated voice, and impassive face but also in her clothing and the room interiors she creates. She even manipulates others through passive-aggressive behavior, acting the martyr so her son-in-law Mike will allow her to remove a lamp from the living room of his own house, where it is useful, to the bedroom, where it better fits into the aesthetic scheme she has imposed. As Richard A. Blake puts it, Eve "attempts a kind of ideal artistic order that is unattainable. Her search for perfection leads her to suicide, and her family to desperation. . . . Nothing, no sensation, color or sound, may intrude upon the placid, perfect world she strives to create" (Blake 72).

Eve favors her oldest daughter because Renata is artistically inclined. Renata's ability to render her feelings in poetry contributes to the sense of an ordered, controlled universe that Eve wants to create. Her second daughter, Joey, enjoys no artistic talent, and Eve rejects her, criticizing her frequently and declaring that she prefers Frederick, Renata's alcoholic husband who is jealous of his wife's success, to Joey's supportive, politically engaged lover. Eve thinks of Arthur, her husband, whom she put through law school, as her "creation," and she tries to control him with her own vulnerability and his reluctance to see her hurt. If Eve favors Renata and slights Joey, Arthur has always been closer to Joey and distant from Renata.

Both parents seem removed from Flyn, the third daughter who was still young when Eve was hospitalized following a mental breakdown, and who grew up largely isolated and ignored, never really integrated into the family or ever fully actualized as a person. Frederick contemptuously dismisses Flyn as "form without any content" but later tries to rape her. Flyn is indeed intellectually shallow—a sensuous daughter in an excessively cerebral family—but she does not merit Frederick's contempt, much less his cynical effort to rape her because, "It's been such a long time since I made love to a woman I didn't feel inferior to." In fact, Frederick *should* feel inferior to Flyn, as she at least knows how to behave decently to others, something that he has forgotten in his self-indulgent self-loathing. An actress who has moved far from home, Flyn is the least contaminated by negative family influences. Moreover, she is the most self-accepting of the sisters. And although Allen has maintained that she "dehumanized herself" (Pogel 108), Flyn enjoys an honest awareness of her own strengths and limitations. In this respect she is similar to Pearl, another sensualist. Flyn grieves more openly than her sisters, and she seems less afflicted by conflicting emotions over her mother's death than they are.

Eve's manipulation of Arthur succeeds, but only to a limited degree. We learn that Arthur took lovers while Eve was hospitalized, and ultimately he leaves her and does not reconcile, even after she attempts suicide following one of his visits. On the one hand, Arthur's rejection of Eve is a selfish repudiation of their presumed marriage vows and a betrayal of the woman whose hard work and sacrifice enabled him to attend law school and create the affluence and refinement that he enjoys. On the other hand, his walking away from Eve's claustrophobic, emotionally empty world is also an act of sanity that enables him to resurrect his own passion and love of life. Thus, in Allen's paradoxical, modernist view, Arthur's behavior is worthy of both condemnation and praise.

Much of *Interiors* is devoted to revealing the dynamics spawned by the parents' unequal treatment of their children. These relationship also seem paradoxical. Though we might logically expect the child who was most favored by a particular parent to show greater loyalty to that parent, the reverse often takes place. Renata, Eve's favorite, isolates herself from her mother, and Joey pulls away from her father, with whom she had once been close. On the other hand, Renata has always resented that Arthur distanced himself from her (perhaps because she most resembles Eve). But Renata, not Joey, is the first to support Arthur's decision to remarry, while Joey defends Eve's interests. In fact, Joey assumes primary responsibility for looking after Eve when Arthur moves out. But Eve is blind to Joey's unflagging efforts to win her mother's love. Eve projects her own negative feelings onto

Joey, accusing her daughter of being unsupportive, even willfully destructive, when in fact it is Eve who has always undermined Joey.

Joey sums up the situation in her final speech to Eve: "It's ironic, because I've cared for you so, and you've had nothing but disdain for me. And yet I feel guilty. I think you're really too perfect to live in this world. . . . Everything's so controlled. There wasn't any room for any real feelings between any of us, except Renata, who never gave you the time of day."

Other characters project their own worst feelings about themselves onto family members and then react violently against the reflected image. For instance, Frederick projects his own self-doubts onto Renata and then attacks her for lying to him when she praises him. In fact, Renata genuinely believes that Frederick has talent, though she finally accuses him of squandering it for spite. Allen complicates the dynamics of the situation by showing Renata's proclivity for telling white lies to avoid hurt feelings, in contrast to Joey and Frederick's insistence on acknowledging brutal truths. Renata's position seems motivated more by a desire to avoid unpleasant confrontations than to spare the feelings of others, but it also has the latter effect. Joey and Frederick seem more honest but also harsher. Frederick's use of the truth, in particular, is vicious, self-loathing, and destructive.

Moreover, Allen makes it impossible to sort out the valid claims of each position from other unconscious motivations that inform them. For instance, Joey's pragmatic, hard-nosed belief that they should not encourage Eve's unrealistic hopes for a reconciliation with Arthur may also be a way for her to strike back at Eve, to redirect the suppressed rage she feels over her mother's cold treatment of her. By contrast, Renata, the favored daughter who maintains that validating Eve's hopes lifts her spirits and does little harm, treats her mother more kindly, if less honestly.

The matter of who should care for Eve reveals additional complications. Shortly after Eve's attempted suicide, Joey seeks to get closer to Renata but is rebuffed. She then accuses Renata of hiding behind her work, while she has "inherited mother." When verbally attacked, Renata characteristically counterattacks; here she accuses Joey of feeling guilty about her feelings toward Eve, "You could never stand her." Joey replies. "My whole life I've only wanted to be her." And then Renata shifts the topic to her own jealousy of Joey's relationship with Arthur, suggesting that during Eve's nervous breakdown when they were children, Joey had displaced Eve in Arthur's affections: "For a while there, you were her, weren't you." Thus, when Joey later accuses Arthur of taking lovers while Eve was hospitalized, we are unsure whether her resentment is on her mother's behalf or her own.[1]

A story that deals quite literally with matters of life and death, *Interiors* addresses Allen's own fear of death and art's ultimate inability to shield us from it. The dissolution of Arthur and Eve's marriage shatters the insulated world that Eve had created and compels all of the characters to acknowledge the ultimate ending of things. This awareness leaves Eve and Renata in despair but enables Arthur and Joey to flourish. Eve commits suicide, and Renata experiences severe writer's block shortly after her parents separate. She also has a terrifying epiphany when she recognizes the predatory aspect of nature and the fact of her own inevitable demise. Significantly, the only time Frederick shows her any warmth comes when she describes her revelation and expresses her fear and vulnerability to him. This anticipates Elliot's response to Hannah in *Hannah and Her Sisters*.

Allen comments, "Some artists think that art will save them, that they will be immortalized through their art. . . . But the truth of the matter is, art doesn't save you. . . . I've made this joke before, that I'm not interested in living on in the hearts of my countrymen, I'd rather live on in my apartment!" (*Woody Allen on Woody Allen* 103–105). Allen adds, "What we're all talking about is the tragedy of perishing. Ageing and perishing. It's such a horrible, horrible thing for humans to contemplate, that they don't contemplate it. They start religions, they do all kinds of things not to contemplate it. . . . But sometimes you can't block it out. And when you can't block it out, you can either go the route that Renata goes, where she tries to express certain things in poetry. . . . But even someone like Renata [eventually concludes] . . . art is not going to save her. She's going to perish like everybody else. Even if her poems are read a thousand years from now" (*Woody Allen on Woody Allen* 105). Renata, like Eve, has tried to use her art to insulate herself from her own mortality, and she has failed. Recognition of that failure creates a crisis in her life.

Although Allen identifies most closely with Renata,[2] he offers Pearl as the person best able to deal with the inevitability of death. Pearl's intuitive solution is to embrace life. Allen calls Pearl "the breath of spring in the movie. She represents vitality and life and vibrancy" (*Woody Allen on Woody Allen* 100). She dresses in loud, happy colors, enjoys the pleasures of the body—food, sex, sunbathing, dancing—and is emotionally open. Pearl performs card tricks and parlor games; as Sander H. Lee observes, "Allen often uses magic as a metaphor for an intuitive ability to better understand the things that are truly important in the world" (Lee 81–82). At the end, Eve's suicide almost kills Joey too, but after Mike rescues his mate, Pearl resuscitates her with mouth-to-mouth artificial respiration. Thus Pearl, who had earlier answered Joey's call, "Mother," literally gives Joey the gift of life and symbolically becomes her new mother, even though Joey has resisted Pearl more than any of the sisters.

Allen believes the introduction of Pearl into her life will give Joey a new chance for living an authentic, fulfilling existence. "The others, I think, are too far gone. . . . If Joey had had a different mother, she'd been fine. What they're all lacking is some warmth. So, yes, I think she gets a new mother in the end, and this mother is going to make a difference in her life" (*Woody Allen on Woody Allen* 100).

The experience of dealing with her parents' divorce and her beloved father's remarriage to someone completely opposite to Eve prepares Joey for this transition. Throughout the movie Joey has complained that she feels the need to express something but does not know what she wants to say or how to say it. But the restructuring of the family forces her to express herself, and in the process she discovers her true feelings and gains some self-knowledge. First Joey, who typically contains her anger and resentment, confronts Renata for leaving her to take care of Eve. Then she accuses Arthur of having taken lovers and proposing to marry a "vulgarian." At the wedding celebration, she impulsively screams at Pearl for breaking one of Eve's vases. Although her responses to Arthur and Pearl are certainly rude and judgmental, they are also therapeutic, in that Joey increasingly brings to the surface the feelings she has been repressing. This is a new and liberating process for her.

Joey truly finds her voice when she confronts her mother for the last time: "I feel such rage toward you. Oh, Mother, don't you see, you're not just a sick woman. That would be too easy. The truth is there's been perverseness and willfulness of attitude in the things you've done. At the center of a sick psyche there is a sick spirit. But I love you, and we have no other choice but to forgive each other." These incisive words and her final, futile effort to save Eve bring a degree of closure to Joey's relationship with her first mother and prepare her to accept Pearl as a new mother who can show her how to enjoy life. Significantly, although Renata still suffers from writer's block, the movie ends with Joey's recording her thoughts in a diary. Throughout the movie Joey has expressed only anger, sadness, frustration, and dissatisfaction, but her diary entry hints at a new, more positive, and self-accepting attitude as it recalls fond childhood memories of her mother and sisters. Thus *Interiors*, which is rather bleak for most of its duration, concludes on a hopeful note.

NOTES

1. Allen hints at Arthur Miller's *Death of a Salesman* here, as Arthur's disappointment over Joey's failure to find herself and amount to something mirrors Willie Lowman's disappointment in his son Biff, who had become disillusioned and lost motivation in life when he discovered his father was having an affair.

2. Some critics have identified Allen with Joey, but he sees no similarities apart from her tweed jackets and gray sweaters. He has, however, expressed an affinity with Renata (*Woody Allen on Woody Allen* 100–105).

Jewish Identity. See **Holocaust**; "**Random Reflections of a Second-Rate Mind**."

K

Kavner, Julie. A film and television actress who appears in *Hannah and Her Sisters*, *Radio Days*, *Alice*, *Oedipus Wrecks*, *Shadows and Fog*, *Deconstructing Harry*, and the made-for-television remake of *Don't Drink the Water*. Allen typically casts Kavner in parts calling for an ethnic Jewish woman, such as Joe's mother, Tess, in *Radio Days* and Treva in *Oedipus Wrecks*. Kavner has also appeared in films by other directors, notably *This is My Life* (1992), *I'll Do Anything* (1994), and *Forget Paris* (1995).

Kavner has also acted in television movies, and she originated her role as an ethnic Jew in *Rhoda*, a popular television sitcom that ran on CBS from 1974 to 1978. Kavner played Brenda, Rhoda's dumpy, witty, philosophical but unfulfilled younger sister. She later acted in skits on the *Tracey Ullman Show* (Fox, 1987–1990) and is the voice of Marge Simpson on *The Simpsons*, an adult cartoon that first appeared on the *Tracey Ullman Show* and subsequently spun off as a highly successful half-hour show (Fox, 1990–present). Allen describes Kavner as "wonderful" (*Woody Allen on Woody Allen* 157).

Keaton, Diane. An actress and director who lived with Allen in 1968–1969 and appears in Allen's *Play It Again, Sam* (play and film), *Love and Death*, *Sleeper*, *Annie Hall*, *Interiors*, *Manhattan*, *Radio Days*, and *Manhattan Murder Mystery*. She also played Harvey Wallinger's cross-eyed wife in *Men in Crisis*, Allen's satire on the Nixon administration that was never broadcast. Other notable film appearances include *The Godfather* Parts I, II, and III (1972, 1974, 1990), *Lovers and Other Strangers* (1970), *I Will . . . I Will . . . for Now* (1975), *Harry and Walter Go to New York* (1976), *Looking for Mr. Goodbar* (1977), *Shoot the Moon* (1981), *The Little*

Drummer Girl (1984), *Mrs. Soffel* (1984), *Crimes of the Heart* (1986), *Baby Boom* (1987), *The Good Mother* (1988), *The Lemon Sisters* (1990), *Father of the Bride* I and II (1991, 1995), *Look Who's Talking Now* (1993, voice only), and *The First Wives' Club* (1996). Keaton won an Academy Award as best actress for her performance in *Annie Hall*, and she received an Academy Award nomination for her portrayal of feminist Louise Bryant in Warren Beatty's *Reds* (1981). She also starred in the television movie *Amelia Earhart: The Final Flight* (1994) and directed episodes of the acclaimed television shows *China Beach* and *Twin Peaks*. In 1987, Keaton directed her first full-length film, *Heaven*, a documentary. She has also directed *Unstrung Heroes* (1995), a quirky comedy about a boy whose mother is dying. An accomplished photographer, Keaton has published two volumes of photographs.

Born in Los Angeles in 1946 as Diane Hall, Keaton attended Orange Coast Junior College and Santa Ana College in California and received training in acting at the Neighborhood Playhouse in New York. Keaton first met Allen in 1968, when she auditioned for his play, *Play It Again, Sam*. One night during rehearsals, Keaton and Allen went out to dinner, and Allen found Keaton "completely hilarious. I just couldn't stop laughing." Their relationship deepened during tryouts in Washington, D.C., and she moved in with him soon after they returned to New York. They lived together for a year before their developing interests took them in different directions. According to Allen, he and Keaton "just grew apart." He observes that when they initially formed their relationship she was in her early twenties, naive, new to New York, and inexperienced. However, as she matured over time, Keaton developed her own interests in such fields as painting, photography, and the graphic arts. These did not especially engage him, and she preferred to spend time in places he did not particularly care for, such as California, Santa Fe, and the Grand Canyon. When the relationship finally dissolved, "We parted amicably" (Lax 243–244).

Indeed, Keaton and Allen continued to collaborate on films and have remained close friends ever since. Throughout his career Allen has sought Keaton's advice because he respects and admires her artistic instincts (Lax 244).

Allen specifically praises Keaton's visual perceptiveness, along with her cerebral and musical acuity. "I got to look at things through her eyes very frequently, and it really upgraded and broadened my perception." In turn, Allen believes he has been a positive influence on Keaton as well: "I was from New York, very urban. Liked the streets of New York, liked basketball, liked jazz, had read a lot. She was from California, liked visual things, photographic things, paintings, colours. She had her feelings about movies, I had mine. And over the years it was a healthy interaction." He adds, "It's always perhaps the most important screening I have of any of my movies, when she's in town and I can get to see her" (*Woody Allen on Woody Allen* 52–54).

Although most of the films in which Allen has cast Keaton are comic, notably *Play It Again, Sam, Sleeper, Love and Death*, and *Manhattan Murder Mystery*, she plays a leading role in *Interiors*, Allen's first foray into serious drama. And though Mary Wilke, Keaton's character in *Manhattan*, is ripe for ridicule—she is neurotic, insecure, opinionated, and confused about men—the script takes few jibes at her, and Keaton does not play Mary for laughs. In *Annie Hall*, the film that stands between *Love and Death* and *Interiors*, Keaton's title character begins as a comic figure who is similarly neurotic, but her neurosis and that of Allen's character, Alvy Singer, are the primary basis of the film's humor. However, as the story progresses Annie becomes psychologically healthier, more self-accepting, and more self-directed; consequently, she functions less as a humorous character and more as a serious foil to Alvy.

Annie Hall was a pivotal movie for Keaton and Allen in other ways too. It was Allen's first film to center on the female protagonist as well as the male lead, and it marked the beginning of his movement away from broad comedy to stories whose larger artistic purpose is to explore the nature of personal relationships and the human psyche. Keaton had earlier appeared in *The Godfather* and other films, but *Annie Hall* established her as a major talent. According to Allen, the part was "tailored" for her; he even chose "Hall" as Annie's last name because it had been Keaton's family name.

Moreover, Keaton's Annie Hall "look" became a major fashion trend in the late 1970s. Keaton, whom Allen describes as an "eccentric dresser," created the style herself. According to Allen, Ruth Morley, who was responsible for costuming, objected when Keaton appeared on the set wearing trousers, a button-down shirt, vest, tie, and broad-brimmed hat, but Allen insisted, "She's a genius. . . . Let her wear what she wants. If I really hate something, I'll tell her. Otherwise she can choose for herself" (*Woody Allen on Woody Allen* 52, 83–85).

Following *Annie Hall* Keaton demonstrated her versatility when she portrayed Theresa Dunn in *Looking for Mr. Goodbar*. Whereas Annie Hall projected genuine midwestern wholesomeness, Theresa Dunn is a kindergarten teacher whose wholesome image hides an anguished soul. The daughter of a repressive father and aggressively passive mother, Theresa leads a promiscuous life in singles bars until she is murdered. The following year, 1978, Keaton appeared in Allen's *Interiors* and portrayed

Renata, a daughter in another dysfunctional family and a talented poet whose husband and sister resent her success.

Between 1982 (*A Midsummer Night's Sex Comedy*) and 1992 (*Husbands and Wives*) Mia Farrow, who entered into a long-term love relationship with Allen, played the leading female roles in virtually all of Allen's films. Keaton did not perform in any of his films during that decade, except for a cameo appearance in 1987 as a club singer in *Radio Days*. However, in 1993, when Allen and Farrow broke up over Allen's involvement with Farrow's adopted daughter, Soon-Yi Previn, Allen asked Keaton to assume Farrow's role in *Manhattan Murder Mystery*. Allen had written the role specifically for Farrow and was unable to revise it substantially for Keaton "because it's a murder mystery, and it's very tight plotted, so it's very hard to make big changes." Instead, he essentially switched roles with her, making himself the straight man and Keaton the more flighty and daring partner. Allen claims Keaton "made this part funnier than I wrote it" (*Woody Allen on Woody Allen* 257).

Overall, Allen's assessment of Keaton is that she is "equal to the greatest screen comediennes we've ever had. . . . The two best female comedians would be Diane Keaton and Judy Holliday. It's always fun to work with Diane. She's a good friend of mine, and she brings out the best in everybody. She has the kind of personality that lights up the whole project. She's such a positive personality" (*Woody Allen on Woody Allen* 257).

For additional reading, see Jonathan Moor, *Diane Keaton*.

King Lear. A 1987 film directed, written, and edited by Jean-Luc Godard, who plays the Professor. Allen plays the film editor. It costars Burgess Meredith (Don Learo), Peter Sellars (William Shakespeare Jr., V), Molly Ringwald (Cordelia), Leos Carax (Edgar), and Kate and Norman Mailer as themselves. Menahem and Yoram Golan were the producers, Sophie Maintigneux director of photography, and François Musy production designer. Cannon distributed the movie.

Very loosely based on Shakespeare's masterpiece, Godard's *King Lear* is highly experimental and largely incoherent—perhaps in imitation of Lear's delirium. It is Godard's first English-language film. Apart from showings at the Cannes, Montreal, and London film festivals, and on college campuses, *King Lear* has rarely been screened, and it received poor reviews. David Robinson of the *New York Times* describes it as "a casual assembly of disconnected and mostly nonsensical scenes in which Shakespearean lines occasionally surface without point" (Fox 172).

Set in modern times and centered around Don Learo, a mafia godfather, *King Lear* experiments with sound, image, and plot. Replete with postmodern self-references, it opens with the director and producers discussing the film; images of famous deceased directors appear; periodically, and occasionally actors speak lines from Shakespeare's *King Lear*. William Shakespeare Jr. V assiduously records these.

Allen was originally cast as the Fool, but Godard subsequently appropriated that role for himself; in the modern setting the Fool is now the Professor. Instead, Allen appears briefly at the end of the film as the enigmatic editor who splices the film and then sews the celluloid back together with needle and thread. Allen considered the project "silly" but agreed to participate because of his respect for Godard as a provocative experimenter in the film medium. Godard, in turn, has long admired Allen's work.

"The Kugelmass Episode." A short story by Allen that first appeared in the May 2, 1977 issue of the *New Yorker* and was republished in Allen's collection *Side Effects*. Winner of the 1977 O. Henry Award, the story was adapted for stage in a series of platform performances directed by Michael Kustow in 1980 at London's National Theater and in John Lahr's *The Bluebird of Unhappiness*, which was performed in 1987 at the Royal Exchange Theatre in Manchester, England.

The absurdist story describes the travails of a middle-aged, Jewish literature professor who is transported by a magician into the world of *Madame Bovary*. Kugelmass has a love affair with the heroine and brings Emma back to modern New York with him. There, she becomes first Kugelmass's loving mistress and then a demanding shrew. In the meantime, readers of the novel are left baffled and frustrated as first a strange Jewish man appears in the story and then Emma disappears from it.

The pleasure of the story comes from Allen's sustained development of the absurd premise and the refinement of the details, instead of from the nonsequiturs and implausible juxtapositions characteristic of his earlier literary comedy. For instance, when Kugelmass first appears in the fictional bedroom of Emma's house at Yonville, Allen draws the scene for almost two paragraphs without striving for a laugh. Even Kugelmass's observation that she speaks in the same fine English as a paperback translation works as a bona-fide supporting detail and not just as a wise crack by a smart-aleck literary comedian. Similarly, Emma's gushing that "I love what you have on . . . I've never seen anything like it around here," helps flesh out the improbable scene, even as it sets up the punch line: "It's called a leisure suit." In turn, the punch line not only makes fun of leisure suits; it also characterizes Kugelmass by showing him to be the kind of person who would wear one. Finally, the exchange encourages us to imagine how a young woman from provincial France in the mid-nineteenth century might regard today's fashions. Just as *Annie Hall*, which appeared the same year, retains humor at its core but features more fully realized scenes, more complex characters, and a more highly developed plot than *Love and Death*, "The Kugelmass Episode" finds pleasure from developing more or less realistic characters and scenes.

See also *Side Effects*.

L

Lasser, Louise. A film and television actress who was married to Allen between 1966 and 1969. She appears in *What's New, Pussycat? What's Up, Tiger Lily? Take the Money and Run, Bananas, Everything You Ever Wanted to Know About Sex*, and *Stardust Memories*. Other film appearances include *Such Good Friends* (1971) and *Coffee, Tea, or Me?* (1973). Lasser starred on the television sitcoms *Mary Hartman, Mary Hartman* (syndicated, 1976–1977) and *It's a Living* (syndicated, 1981–1982). She also acted in *Men in Crisis: The Harvey Wallinger Story* (1971), Allen's made-for-television satire of the Nixon administration that was never aired.

Allen and Lasser met in 1960, while Allen was still married to his first wife, Harlene Rosen. Allen and Rosen separated in 1961 and divorced in 1962. That year Allen conceived and wrote a television pilot entitled *The Laughmakers* starring Lasser, Alan Alda, and Paul Hampton, but ABC declined to pick it up because the sophisticated humor appealed to too limited an audience. Allen and Lasser were dating while he was writing the screenplay for *What's New, Pussycat?* and he secured a role for her as the Nutcracker who massages Peter Sellers's back in the sauna scene. They married on Groundhog Day in 1966, while working together on *What's Up, Tiger Lily?* Eve, the mentally ill mother in *Interiors*, is patterned in part on Lasser's mother, who also made a failed suicide attempt, followed by a successful one. Lasser herself partly inspired the role of Dorrie in *Stardust Memories*. In that film, she has an uncredited role as Allen's incompetent secretary. Allen considers Lasser a friend for whom he and his family retain warm feelings. He maintains that he "became a human being with Louise" and that she made an enduring contribution to his life. She assisted his transition from writer to comedian and helped him appreciate living in New

York City. Nonetheless, Allen states, living with her became impossible
because "she was crazy as a loon." According to Allen, she would have two
good weeks a month, followed by two bad weeks, "but the two weeks are so
worth it." But then the two good weeks diminished to two good days. "It
was like [Arthur Miller's] *After the Fall*. When I read some of the dialogue
of that, I swear I thought to myself, 'God, I've heard Louise say these lines.'
. . . I think I used some of this in Charlotte Rampling's character [Dorrie] in
Stardust Memories" (Lax 169–170).

Literary Comedy. An absurd kind of humor that relies primarily on word
play, fast-paced wit, nonsense, and deflation of high culture. In America,
literary comedy emerged as a popular form in the mid-nineteenth century,
flourished in the 1920s, and continued throughout the twentieth century.
Many of Allen's films and published writings from the 1960s and early 1970s
fall into this tradition, which is well suited for the stand-up comedy that Allen performed early in his career and for the flippant sketches he published
in the *New Yorker* and in his three books, *Getting Even*, *Without Feathers*,
and *Side Effects*. Allen's early films are also indebted to this tradition.

Examples of literary comedy in American humor extend at least as far
back as the California gold rush, when George Horatio Derby, an officer in
the Army Corps of Engineers, published under the name of John Phoenix.
Derby was a prankster who once agreed to manage a mining town newspaper for a few days while the editor left town. In his friend's absence, Derby
reversed all of the paper's editorial positions. His 1854 review of a symphony concert anticipates Allen's practice of mocking pretentious intellectuals. In particular, Derby uses the language of civil engineering to spoof
inflated artistic commentary.

The symphonie opens upon the wide and boundless plains, in longitude 115 degrees West, latitude 35 degrees, 21 minutes, 3 seconds North and about sixty miles
from the west bank of the Pitt River. These data are beautifully and clearly expressed by a long (topographically) drawn note from an E flat clarinet.

Elsewhere Derby remarks that "so vivid and lifelike was the representation
[of a pioneer campfire] that a lady sitting near us, involuntarily exclaimed
aloud, at a certain passage, *'Thar, that pork's burning!'* " Compare this to
Allen's "A Guide to Some of the Lesser Ballets" from *Without Feathers*:

The overture begins with the brass in a joyous mood, while underneath the double
basses seem to be warning us, "Don't listen to the brass. What the hell does the
brass know?"

Allen may or may not have read Derby or turn-of-the-century nonsense
magazines like Gilette Burgess's *The Lark*, but he certainly was familiar

with their exuberant and absurd style. Nonsense writing enjoyed a renaissance in the 1920s, as Don Marquis spoofed pretentious artists in *Archie and Mehitabel*, letters describing the friendship between a free verse-poet who has been reincarnated as a cockroach and an alley cat who claims to have been Cleopatra in a previous life. Dorothy Parker, Alexander Woolcott, Franklin Pierce Adams, and the other Algonquin wits flourished at this time, as did writers who were more direct influences on Allen: *New Yorker* authors S. J. Perelman, Robert Benchley, and James Thurber and movie star Groucho Marx. All of these comedians share with Allen the joys of turning language into a playground, where the greater pleasure comes not from making sense but from bouncing sounds, rhythms, images, and meanings off one another and provoking the imagination with absurd and amusing possibilities.

Allen's literary comedy developed during the late 1960s and early 1970s as the Vietnam War was progressing, acid rock was developing, and hallucinogens were becoming popular within a growing counterculture. Thus Allen's spoofs on high culture and his propensity for the wacky and surreal were well suited for audiences of antiwar, antiestablishment college students and young professionals who were seeking experiences that were "far out." Magical realism, which shares the energy and surrealism of literary comedy, also flourished in America during the Vietnam War era. But except for *Stardust Memories* and *Oedipus Wrecks*, Allen does not appear as greatly influenced by magical realism as by literary comedy. Magical realism typically understates its surreal moments, accepting them as natural and as commonplace as everything else. Literary comedy, on the other hand, accentuates the incongruities.

Literary comedy derives its appeal from the pleasure it takes in its own cleverness. The more clever and multifaceted the joke, the more highly it is valued. The humor is fast-paced and does not invite prolonged analysis, which would typically deflate it. The literary comedian seeks to entertain through a series of quick laughs instead of building slowly to a central climax. Typically characters are quickly sketched and identified by one or two outstanding traits; they are not developed at length. Relationships among people or events may be unexpected and absurdly funny, but they are rarely deep or difficult to follow.

Literary comedians often rely on pairings that are so completely unrelated that their disconnection becomes funny, such as when Benchley, in "More Songs for Meller," describes a bullfight in Madrid in which the bull's place in the royal box has been taken by the algebra teacher of a girl who has come to town to sell her father. Another common technique is the comic equation, in which something trivial or unrelated is inserted into an otherwise serious list. For instance, in "But Soft . . . Real Soft," Allen presents a list of candidates for authorship of Shakespeare's plays: "Sir Francis Bacon, Ben Jonson, Queen Elizabeth and possibly even the Homestead Act." All the possibilities are credible but the last, which is absurd and deflates the entire list. Literary comedy also employs sustained conceits, such as when Derby lampoons at length the lofty language of music reviews. In "The Whore of Mensa" Allen sustains the metaphor of sexual prostitution as he applies it to a ring of college women who exchange mental stimulation and emotional fulfillment for money.

In many ways, literary comedy approaches the absurdism of Marcel Duchamp and the surrealism of René Magritte or Salvador Dalí, who also flourished in the 1920s. After all, the train coming through Magritte's fireplace is not so far removed from Benchley's algebra teacher in the bull's royal box, or the underwear in the shape of the kaiser on roller skates that Allen imagines in "Selections from the Allen Notebooks." However, the American literary comedians lack the political edge and anticapitalist agenda found in the anti-art of the Europeans. Whereas Duchamp and the dadaists attacked the aristocratic and bourgeois-capitalist cultures that produced the "high culture" of Western arts and letters and sought ways to demonstrate how language and image inevitably corrupt meaning and truth, the American literary comedians simply want to get a laugh.

For additional reading, see Marc S. Reisch, "Woody Allen: American Prose Humorist," and Walter Blair and Hamlin Hill, *America's Humor.*

Little-Man Humor. A uniquely twentieth-century form of American humor that underscores the ineffectualness of modern men in the face of unsympathetic government bureaucracies, callous business procedures, demanding social institutions, out-of-control technology, and domineering women. The little-man's counterpart in Jewish humor is the longer-standing tradition of the schlemiel—the ne'er-do-well whose every aspiration, even the most modest ones, is dashed. Allen, whose diminutive physical stature literally makes him a little man, drew heavily on both traditions in his early career, when he developed his comic persona as a scrawny, incompetent, socially inept loser. He employed his little-man persona in his stand-up comedy routines, his fiction, and his films, notably *Take the Money and Run*, *Bananas, Play It Again, Sam*, and *Annie Hall*. Later films, including *Zelig*, *Hannah and Her Sisters*, *Crimes and Misdemeanors*, and *Shadows and Fog*, employ other variations on the little-man type, and other films, such as *Manhattan* and *Stardust Memories*, feature elements of it.

Little-man humor flourished in the 1920s and 1930s, as *New Yorker* publisher Harold W. Ross nurtured such writers as Robert Benchley and James

Dorothy Leon and Woody Allen in a scene from *Stardust Memories*. Courtesy of Photofest.

Thurber and cartoonists Peter Arno and William Steig. At the same time, Buster Keaton and Charlie Chaplin popularized the little man in movies. Indeed, Chaplin's Little Tramp character was known throughout the globe, and Chaplin himself became one of the most beloved people on earth between the world wars. Little-man humor accommodates a wide range of tones, from Chaplin's eternal optimism in the face of repeated setbacks to Thurber's despair. But all of the little men are underdogs who are ill equipped to survive in a modern, mechanized, urban world of heavy industry, bullying police, and liberated women. Whereas their predecessors in American humor, the boastful frontiersmen, exaggerated their deeds and overstated their prowess, little men are notable for their inability to cope with even routine tasks. Their frustrations often come from dealing with mechanical things, like starting a car or closing a zipper. And they are easily frightened by figures of authority and assertive women. (T. S. Eliot's poem "The Love Song of J. Alfred Prufrock [1915] anticipates the type: Prufrock does not even "dare to eat a peach," and he is indecisive and intimidated by the women he is attracted to.)

Thurber's title character from "The Secret Life of Walter Mitty" (1939) stands out as the epitome of little-man humor. Intimidated even by parking lot attendants and, most of all, his wife, Mitty retreats into a fantasy world in which he is suave, masterful, and accomplished—a professional of many talents. But his reveries are inevitably interrupted when his wife reappears to criticize him anew for his personal failings, and in his final fantasy he imagines his own execution.

Nancy Pogel suggests, "The little man permits us to identify with the source of our own desire for fulfillment, precisely because he is so bereft of satisfaction for his own desire. . . . His emptiness and alienation remind us of our own, while his helplessness mediates between our needs and the promise inherent in his being on the screen. . . . Yet at the same time that he invites empathy, the little man does not make the audience so vulnerable as to make the identification dangerous; initially, he also evokes from the spectator a comforting adult superiority, for even in our alienated lives, we arrogantly think ourselves far more at one with our worlds than he" (Pogel 10).

Although Allen's little men are basically decent people who seek love, intimacy, and sexual fulfillment, the overriding force that drives them is fear. They feel threatened and disempowered by a hostile and unpredictable world; consequently their innate fear typically overwhelms their desire to take control of their lives and create their own happiness. They always remain cognizant of the possibilities for imminent horror and death, and several are particularly aware of the Holocaust. For them, happiness is a luxury they cannot afford, since it must always be subordinated to the demands of survival. The result is the strain of underlying hopelessness and despair characteristic of Allen's work. His little-man characters are so obsessed with survival that they cannot even imagine themselves happy and secure.

Allen's little men secretly aspire to greatness and sometimes even fool themselves into believing they are exceptionally sexy or accomplished (or both). In fact, they are not only physically small; they are also typically weak in character, commitment, and self-confidence. That weakness also derives from believing themselves to be disempowered.

This condition leaves ample room for character development, and in some of Allen's films, the little men grow as a result of their experiences. For instance, at the end of *Bananas*, Fielding Mellish assumes responsibility for the success of the revolution he has inadvertently become part of. At the beginning of the film, Fielding would not have been able even to imagine himself capable of such a task. Moreover, he overcomes the fear of physical harm that in the past had made him steer clear of politics and anything else potentially confrontational. According to Pogel, Fielding represents the beginning of "a developing self-awareness and concern for personal integrity in Allen's little-man characters" (Pogel 45).

As satisfying as it is to root for the underdog, Allen's little men do not always seem entirely worthy of success in the way that Chaplin's Little Tramp always seems worthy. Virgil Starkwell has no compunctions about his life of crime; Fielding Mellish cheerfully directs a driver into the car behind him; Ivan from *Love and Death* has no exceptional merits. According to Pogel, "For all his importance as a searcher . . . the little man of Allen's films is also at times a ludicrous anachronism, a foolish character—even a corrupted one. While he invokes our sympathy and our conscience, while he represents our hopes for renewal, he is also part of a larger joke that mocks his (and our) innocence, his (and our) search for integrity, his (and our) longing for authenticity." Pogel goes on to quote Mikhail Bakhtin as she implicitly notes the similarity between Allen's humor and Rabelais's: "Allen's attitude toward his little man is ambivalent: the laughter he creates is 'gay,' triumphant and at the same time mocking, deriding'" (Pogel 11).

Allen remains strongly identified with his little-man persona, even though films from his middle and later period do not draw as directly on it. In many of his stand-up routines, writings, and films, Allen's characters appear as inept bumblers at the mercy of larger forces. For instance, in one of his Vietnam War–era routines Allen claims that his draft status is 4-H: in case of war, he is to be a hostage. Another routine depicts him as unable even to cheat in school; he was caught looking into the soul of the boy next to him during his metaphysics exam. In *Take the Money and Run*, Virgil Starkwell's poor penmanship foils his attempt to rob a bank, and a sudden downpour melts the fake gun he had carved from a bar of soap to break out from jail. *Bananas* pays homage to Chaplin's *Modern Times* (1936), when Fielding Mellish, a professional product tester, demonstrates an executive exercise machine that goes berserk and attacks him. In both films, the little man is completely at the mercy of technology that has gone out of control, a theme that often reappears in Allen's work. Elsewhere in *Bananas*, Fielding appears as an inept revolutionary, inept president, inept criminal defendant, and inept bridegroom on his honeymoon night. Phonographs and other appliances turn against Allan Felix in *Play It Again, Sam*, and Miles Monroe is reduced to slapstick in *Sleeper* as he deals with futuristic machines. In *Annie Hall*, Alvy Singer becomes completely flustered in the presence of an escaped lobster, a scene that is first comic and then later recalled nostalgically as evidence of the truly good times that Alvy and Annie shared. Even in a later, more serious film like *Hannah and Her Sisters*, Mickey Sachs accidentally fires a gun while contemplating suicide, and Joe in *Everyone Says I Love You* nearly suffers heart failure when he goes out jogging to meet and impress Von. Although not every Allen character shares this little-man ineptitude—Gabe Roth in *Husbands and Wives* and Lenny in *Mighty Aphrodite* are exceptions—many do.

The various neuroses that Allen's early characters typically display—sexual insecurity, paranoia, obsessive-compulsive behavior, and occasional self-delusion—contribute to their little-man identity, because the neuroses render them ineffectual in the modern world. In fact, one of Allen's greatest accomplishments as a cinematic artist is his ability to explore seriously these neurotic characteristics and their consequences, even as he uses them for comic purposes.

Thus, in *Play It Again, Sam* Allan's sexual insecurity, coupled with his opposite tendency to project himself as a grand seducer and lover of women, reduces him to a figure of comic ridicule. In typical little-man fashion, he is so clueless that he must seek advice from the long-deceased Humphrey Bogart, whose tough-guy characters Allan would like to emulate. Unable to compete in the real world, like Walter Mitty he retreats into the more pleasant world of his imagination.

Neuroses motivate other Allen little men too. Zelig is so insecure that he becomes a human chameleon, changing identity with each new group of people he joins. Alvy Singer is incapable of functioning outside comfortable and familiar New York City, and he is reduced to a buffoonish hypochondriac when he travels to California. Moreover, his obsessive need to control the circumstances of his life leads him to behave in ways that unduly restrain Annie and lead to the dissolution of their relationship. By exaggerating his characters' neurotic behavior, Allen generates humor, such as when Alvy's paranoia over anti-Semitism causes him to picture Grammy Hall imagining him as a long-haired, bearded Hasidic Jew dressed in traditional garb, or when he interprets another man's innocent utterance, "D'jou?" (a slurred form of "Did you?") as an accusation, "Jew!"

In later films Allen's characters often retain elements of the little man but are not always treated comically. For instance, Kleinman, Allen's character in *Shadows and Fog*, is suddenly blamed for not fulfilling his duty, although no one will tell him what his duty is. Allen's artistic intention seems more to create a Kafka-like sensibility of isolation and disorientation than to generate humor. In *Crimes and Misdemeanors* Cliff Stern is a loser who possesses some admirable qualities but masks his envy and insecurity by claiming to be highly principled. Although his envy and spite produce one of the film's funniest moments—a documentary of Lester that likens Cliff's brother-in-law to Mussolini and a braying ass—Cliff, the little man in *Crimes and Misdemeanors*, seems more pathetic than comic.

Whether used comically or seriously, the little man figures prominently in most of Allen's films and much of his fiction, and it serves as one of the primary vehicles for Allen's exploration of neurosis and modern society.

For additional reading, see Blair and Hill, *America's Humor* and Maurice Yacowar, *Loser Take All: The Comic Art of Woody Allen.*

Love and Death. A 1975 film directed by, written by, and starring Allen, who plays Boris. It costars Diane Keaton (Sonia), Brian Coburn (Dmitri), Henri Coutet (Minskov the Herring Merchant), Henry Czarniak (Ivan), Harold Gould (Count Anton), Olga Georges-Picot (Countess Alexandrovna), Lloyd Battista (Don Francisco), Denise Peron (Don Francisco's sister), James Tolkan (Napoleon), and Alfred Lutter III (Young Boris). Charles Joffe was the producer, Ghislain Cloquet director of photography, Wily Holt production designer, Gladys De Segonzac costumer, and Ralph Rosenblum editor. The music was taken primarily from Sergei Prokofiev's *Lieutenant Kije Suite* and his score for Sergei Eisenstein's *Alexander Nevsky* (1938), though it also features Prokofiev's *The Love of Three Oranges* (1921) and Peter Ilyich Tchaikovsky's *The Sleeping Beauty* (1890). United Artists was the North American distributor.

Love and Death is both a homage to and spoof of the great Russian novels by Leo Tolstoy and Fydor Dostoyevsky; two Ingmar Bergman's films, *The Seventh Seal* (1956) and *Persona* (1966); and Eisenstein's *Battleship Potemkin* (1925). It was only marginally successful in the United States, though it was popular in Europe. *Love and Death* was filmed in Paris and Budapest, cost about $8.5 million to produce, but generated only $7.4 million in U.S. and Canadian rentals (not including later video rentals and television revenues). The production involved actors and crew members from numerous European nations—many of whom shared no common language with Allen—and extras from the Soviet Red Army then occupying Hungary. Plagued by mishaps and bad weather, it ran a million dollars over budget. Nonetheless, the film was generally well received by critics, and Allen received the Silver Bear award at the 1975 Berlin Film Festival for "creating a new style of comedy."

As is typical of Allen's early films, the plotline is thin. Set during Napoleon's invasion of Russia, the story centers on Boris, one of Allen's little-man characters who tries to avoid fighting for his country but inadvertently becomes a war hero. Subsequently, he marries his cousin Sonia, whom he has always loved, and is convinced by her to try to assassinate Napoleon. When the plot fails, Boris is executed.

Allen manages to cram this loose story line with literary and cinematic allusions, most notably to Tolstoy's *War and Peace* (1869) and Dostoyevsky's

Brothers Karamazov (1880). As Sander H. Lee points out, Allen raises existential questions that permeate his work, though he treats them primarily as matters of parody and not serious study. The questions Lee identifies are "(1) Is it possible to create a deeply satisfying romantic relationship with just one person? (2) Is there one set of absolutely true moral principles, or is ethics simply a matter of opinion? (3) Is there a God? (4) What will happen to me when I die?" (Lee 46).

Released two years after the U.S. military exit from Vietnam, the film conveys a mild antiwar sentiment. The war between Russia and France appears pointless to Boris, who wonders what difference there would be living under Napoleon instead of the czar, except that the czar is taller. Elsewhere, Boris's officers justify the war, saying it is necessary in order to spare the Russian people from an overly rich diet of heavy French creams and sauces. (Indeed, food plays a substantial role throughout, as a vendor hawks snacks to the troops during the battle scene and Napoleon becomes obsessed with developing his new pastry before the Duke of Wellington issues his new culinary creation, Boeuf Wellington.) The cowardly Boris emerges a hero after he hides in a cannon and is shot into a tent containing several French generals, who immediately surrender. The battle scene contains a close-up of one soldier's shattered eyeglasses, a passing reference to *Battleship Potemkin*, whose famous sequence of rising lion statues Allen parodies elsewhere. The comic nature of the battle scene undercuts the horror of the carnage; nonetheless, the fact that Boris emerges as one of only fourteen survivors suggests the futility of the action, and Boris ridicules another survivor who expresses his thanks that God was on their side. The absurdity of battle is also apparent in Allen's parody of the famous scene from *War and Peace* in which Tolstoy shifts the point of view from the soldiers on the field to the generals overlooking the action. In Allen's treatment, the generals literally see a field of sheep running across the plain. (This also suggests the opening sequence of Charlie Chaplin's *Modern Times* [1936], in which a flock of sheep replaces a horde of workers crowding into a factory.) Allen's liberal viewpoint becomes further apparent in Boris's remark that the serfs instead of the aristocrats should run the country, since the serfs are the only ones who know how to fix things and make the society work.

But although Allen's liberal, antiwar politics are occasionally embedded in the humor, it would be wrong to regard the film as a political statement. More than anything else, Allen uses the tradition of Western literature, cinema, and philosophy as a vast playground in which he can at once acknowledge the relevance and importance of the profound existential and moral issues raised by the great writers of the past and simultaneously make fun of them. Thus, the abstract and obtuse language of philosophy becomes an easy target for Allen's humor, as Boris and Sonia debate the merits of high-minded relative absolutes and then yield to their basest physical passions. Likewise, Allen parodies the famous dueling scene in *Brothers Karamazov*, in which Zossima experiences a life-changing epiphany when his opponent fires and misses, and Zossima, then an army officer, refuses to fire back. In a moment of euphoria, Zossima begs the man's forgiveness and subsequently resigns his military commission to become a monk. In Allen's treatment, Boris gains a similar advantage over his rival. Count Anton, a crack shot, fires first but succeeds only in slightly wounding Boris. Instead of firing back, Boris renounces killing and discharges his pistol up into the air, only to be wounded again by the falling bullet. Unexpectedly spared by Boris's gesture, Anton becomes euphoric and experiences a life-changing epiphany, but instead of dedicating himself to religion, he maintains he will devote himself to singing. Upon hearing the count's voice, Boris declares he should have shot him.

After the duel, Boris marries Sonia, and they retire to the country, where they feast on snow and Boris spends his days writing poetry. At one point he writes that he should have been "a pair of ragged claws" crawling across the ocean floor, but Boris then rejects the line as "too sentimental." In fact, the verse comes from T. S. Eliot's bleak poem "The Love Song of J. Alfred Prufrock" (1915).

The lovers' idyllic life in the country is disrupted by the advance of the French troops, and despite Boris's little-man inclination to flee, Sonia convinces him that they must assassinate Napoleon. The assassination sequence mixes slapstick comedy, in the tradition of the Marx Brothers, with philosophical parody—as Sonia and Boris stand poised to murder the emperor, who lies unconscious beneath them, they break out into an abstract disputation that echoes the moral musings from Dostoyevsky's *Crime and Punishment* (1866). When their plot fails, Boris is arrested, but Sonia escapes. Sentenced to be executed, Boris is visited in jail by his father, and they work into their conversation a string of one-liners that allude specifically to the works of Dostoyevsky: "Remember that nice boy next door, Raskolnikov. . . . He killed two ladies. . . . Bobok told it to me. He heard it from one of the Karamazov Brothers. He must have been Possessed. . . . He was an Idiot."

Despite a dream in which an angel promises him a last-minute reprieve, Boris is executed the following morning. (Nancy Pogel points out the ironic references to the final salvation in *War and Peace*, *Brothers Karamazov*, and *Crime and Punishment*.) He is then taken away by the angel of death, a figure whom Boris had seen earlier as a child and who echoes the Death character in Bergman's *The Seventh Seal* (1956), except that Allen's Death appears more like a Halloween ghost in a white sheet that covers his face and body, while Bergman's is dressed in a black robe and has a pale white face. As in the ending of *The Seventh Seal*, Boris exits following the angel and dancing the Dance of Death, though his steps are more lively and high-spirited than those of the knight and his attendants in the Bergman movie. In the final scene the dead Boris passes by Sonia's window, interrupting a soliloquy that parodies one from Bergman's *Persona*. When Sonia, like the knight from *The Seventh Seal*, asks what death is like, Boris simply replies, "It's worse than the chicken" at their lousy local restaurant. Thus, like Bergman, Allen leaves unanswered the fundamental question that has haunted humanity throughout the ages, what happens after death? However, Allen's comic treatment of our state of existential uncertainty renders it less profound but far more tolerable.

See also **Death**; **Literary Comedy**; **Little-Man Humor**.

For additional reading see Ronald D. LeBlanc, "*Love and Death* and Food: Wood Allen's Comic Use of Gastronomy."

M

Magic. Allen studied magic as a child and performed in amateur shows as a teenager. He reflects this background in *Stardust Memories*, where Sandy Bates sees himself as a child dressed as a magician performing tricks before an audience, and in *The Floating Light Bulb* where Paul, the sixteen-year-old protagonist, immerses himself in a world of magic tricks.

Allen's predilection for magic is one of his affinities with Federico Fellini, who also used otherworldly effects to create an atmosphere of magical realism. In Allen's "The Kugelmass Episode," a story in *Side Effects*, a magician interjects a humanities professor from City College into *Madame Bovary*. Magical and other-worldly effects also play prominent roles in *Don't Drink the Water, Stardust Memories, A Midsummer Night's Sex Comedy, The Purple Rose of Cairo, Zelig, Shadows and Fog, Oedipus Wrecks,* and *Alice*. Several critics have commented on the role of magic in Allen's work. Maurice Yacowar maintains, "For Allen, magic is a metaphor for our attempts to overcome our helplessness in nature and society" (Yacowar, *Loser Take All* 228). And Sander H. Lee observes that "for Allen, those with magical abilities may intuit the motivations behind people's actions. They are able to understand and appreciate the important things in life without engaging in endless abstractions and powerless symbols of organized religion. . . . The symbols of organized religion rarely exhibit the intuitive powers of magic for Allen. Indeed, they usually imply self-absorption and a lack of true reflective ability" (Lee 82).

Manhattan. A 1979 film directed by, written by, and starring Allen, who plays Isaac Davis. It costars Diane Keaton (Mary Wilke), Michael Murphy (Yale), Mariel Hemingway (Tracy), Meryl Streep (Jill), Anne Byrne

(Emily), Karen Ludwig (Connie), Wallace Shawn (Jeremiah), Michael
O'Donohue (Dennis), Gary Weis (TV director), Kenny Vance (TV producer), Damion Sheller (Willie, Isaac's son), Bella Abzug (herself), Tisa
Farrow (party guest), Victor Truro (party guest), and Helen Hanft (party
guest). Charles Joffe was the producer, Robert Greenhut executive producer, Gordon Willis director of photography, Mel Bourne production designer, Albert Wolsky and Ralph Lauren costumers, and Susan E. Morse
editor. Marshall Brickman collaborated with Allen on the screenplay, and
Tom Pierson adapted and arranged original music by George Gershwin.
United Artists was the North American distributor.

A critically acclaimed box office hit, *Manhattan* remains a favorite
Woody Allen film of many aficionados, especially New Yorkers, who admire the romantic view of the city projected by the movie's exquisite black-
and-white photography. Although it won no Academy Awards, *Manhattan*
was nominated for best original screenplay (Allen and Brickman) and best
supporting actress (Hemingway), and it received numerous additional honors throughout the world. The movie cost approximately $8 million to pro-
duce but grossed $17.6 million in U.S. and Canadian distribution (not
including later video rentals and television revenues). It received an R rating
instead of PG primarily because it concerns a sexual relationship between
an older man and a teenaged girl.

Manhattan is one of the most visually sophisticated and visually striking
movies Allen has made. Camera work and music combine to project New
York City as a character apart from the humans whose stories we follow. In
fact, Allen has referred to it as "sort of one of the characters" (*Woody Allen
on Woody Allen* 108). He uses the characterization of the city both to celebrate New York and underscore the pettiness of the human characters who
appear tiny on screen in comparison to Manhattan's enormous skyscrapers
and expansive bridges. If the human characters are mostly neurotic little
men and women, New York is splendid: powerful, grand, almost majestic.
The wide-angle Scope-screen highlights the elegance of the city's dominating skyline and expressive architecture. Gershwin's vibrant music infuses
Allen's picture of Manhattan with energy and vitality, and fireworks ex-
ploding to the rhythms of "Rhapsody in Blue" in the opening sequence
make the city seem heroic and victorious. Scenes set by the 59th Street
Bridge, in the Hayden Planetarium, and in and around Central Park reveal
New York to be a place for falling in love.

Allen claims *Manhattan* "evolved from the music. I was listening to a
record album of overtures from famous George Gershwin shows, and I
thought, 'This would be a beautiful thing to make a movie in black-
and-white, you know, and make a romantic movie'" (Fox 109).[1] "I had a real urge

to show New York as a wonderland, and I completely exorcized that feeling in *Manhattan*" (Lax 276). Many of the opening shots were taken from Allen's own apartment on Fifth Avenue. Allen had not originally planned the spectacular fireworks display that dramatically concludes the overture of New York landmarks, skylines, and street scenes, but when he learned that there were to be fireworks in Central Park, he arranged to film them from a nearby apartment.

The human characters are dwarfed by the city's grandeur, both visually and metaphorically. Moreover, it literally intrudes on their lives and sometimes subsumes them, such as when the noise from street traffic threatens to drown out dialogue or when Ike meets Tracy at her school and the camera shows them in long shots only; they are almost impossible to discern from the crowd.

In contrast to the city's forthright assertiveness, all of the major characters, except for teenaged Tracy, are confused, indecisive, and, most of all, self-absorbed. As a result, they suffer from lapses in integrity. Maurice Yacowar maintains that *Manhattan* centers around our "need for personal integrity in a decaying culture" (Yacowar, *Loser Take All* 198). But profound lack of self-knowledge and narrow vision underlie the characters' inability to sustain high levels of personal integrity, and they are undermined by underlying feelings of unworthiness that lead them to commit self-destructive acts.

Although Allen's character, Ike, knows who he is and what he stands for better than his friends Yale and Mary know themselves, he nonetheless also falls victim to self-delusion. The clearing of that delusion becomes the main action of the story. Ike, who calls himself the "winner of the August Strindberg award" for failed relationships, has never had a romance that lasted longer than Hitler and Eva Braun's. His first wife was a kindergarten teacher with a proclivity for drugs and cults; his second left him for another woman. He is attracted to seemingly strong, erudite, accomplished women who prove to be insensitive to him, insecure, and incapable of loving him. The movie climaxes when Ike realizes that he does not want a mate who is, by her own admission, "trouble." Instead, he wants to be loved, valued, and appreciated.

Mary provides the tough lesson that finally teaches Ike he really wants happiness instead of trouble. In the abstract, Mary represents Allen's ideal woman: she is cultured, intelligent, good looking, and articulate. Moreover, the forcefulness with which Mary pronounces her opinions suggests that she has a firm sense of self; she knows who she is and what she stands for. Ike is attracted to all of these things. Ike's second wife, Jill, shares these admirable qualities, but like Eve in *Interiors*, another highly refined, highly accomplished woman, both are cold and self-absorbed. Unlike Tracy, Ike's seventeen-year-old girlfriend, neither is affectionate, and neither concerns herself much with Ike's interests and well-being.

Mary Wilke (Diane Keaton) and Isaac Davis (Woody Allen) are silhouetted in the shadow of the Queensborough Bridge as they chat on a Sutton Place bench in *Manhattan*. Courtesy of Photofest.

Mary enters her romance with Ike apparently strong and self-possessed, but she quickly proves weak, emotionally needy, and unsure about what she wants. Ike becomes her willing rescuer, but as soon as he assures her that he is committed to their relationship, Mary begins to regain interest in Yale, Ike's best friend with whom Mary previously had had an affair. Allen visually foreshadows Mary's emotional isolation from Ike when Yale phones her as she is at home with Ike. Ike sits in the well-lit living room reading a paper while Mary works off-camera; a wall partitions the frame into separate sections, and the entrance to her study is totally dark. Visually, Mary has already left him; a black void is in her place.[2] Moreover, the fact that she lies to Ike about the caller's identity signals to the audience that their relationship is in danger.

Their propensity for creating doomed relationships and committing other self-destructive acts suggests that at some fundamental level, Ike and Mary suffer from poor self-esteem—that they continually undermine themselves because unconsciously they do not believe themselves worthy of happiness or success. In fact, Ike tells Mary that her level of self-esteem is "a notch below Kafka's," but he is unable to recognize his own shortcomings in that regard. However, although Ike and Mary mirror each other in many ways, Ike's experiences painfully compel him to recognize his own self-worth and assert it forcefully. Once he does, he becomes able to appreciate Tracy's love for him and seek a happier life. Mary, on the other hand, remains blind and seems destined to commit the same mistakes over and over.

Ike initially cannot express anger. He tells Mary that he is the type who internalizes his rage and develops cancer instead. But as their breakup scene develops, he becomes more outspoken about his feelings, and in the following scene he interrupts Yale in the middle of a class in order to confront him. As was true for Joey in *Interiors*, Ike's expressions of anger at Mary and Yale prove therapeutic because they declare to himself and the world that he deserves better treatment from the people he loves. After making that declaration, he stops seeking abusive relationships and immerses himself in constructive activities—writing and playing with his son.

Ike's experiences have prepared him for the critical recognition that there are "people in Manhattan who are constantly creating these real unnecessary neurotic problems for themselves because it keeps them from dealing with more unsolvable, terrifying problems about the universe." Having thus recognized himself, as well as his friends, he acknowledges that what he really wants is affection and joy. Instead of dwelling on his fears and misfortunes, he begins enumerating people and things that make life worth living— an intuitive self-therapy for combating his neurotic pessimism. When his free associations lead him to Tracy's face, Ike has his final realization and, in a sequence that both emulates and parodies *The Graduate* (1967), he runs through Manhattan to find her. Thus, Mary's mistreatment of Ike has initiated a sequence of revelations that facilitates his growth in self-knowledge.

Ike grows professionally too, while Mary stagnates. Both are talented writers who make good money writing material they do not respect. Like Allen himself, who was a highly paid television writer before quitting to develop himself as a stand-up comedian, Ike has been a successful but unfulfilled writer of television comedy. But Ike finally quits in disgust in order to write something of value, even though he suffers economically and must move to a less comfortable apartment. In so doing, he exercises courage, a quality he had praised at the beginning of the film but had rarely practiced in his own life. (The test of courage he describes requires us to dive from a bridge to save a drowning person, but Ike exempts himself because he cannot swim.) Although he is afraid of the uncertain situation he has created, he manages to deal with his fears and write a good book, with the promise that he might make an acceptable living writing about things that matter to him. Initially one of Allen's little-man characters, Ike chooses to do what truly fulfills him, despite his overwhelming fears. By refusing to give in to his insecurities, he ceases to be a little man.

Mary, on the other hand, despite all of her erudition, never creates anything of value to herself or society. Although Ike encourages her to develop
her fiction, for which she has an aptitude, Mary squanders her considerable
talent writing empty novelizations of movies—work that pays well but results in nothing she can respect. And although she can intellectually appreciate art and high culture, Mary never integrates their passion and wisdom
into her life. An intellectual snob, she uses her cultural knowledge mostly to
appear superior. She adopts the critical jargon that excludes all but the cultural elite, and she passes cynical, derisive judgments on artists and writers
whom Ike (and Allen) admire, including such renowned figures as Gustav
Mahler, Vincent Van Gogh, and Ingmar Bergman, whom Ike passionately
defends. The only art that animates her is abstract and conceptual, without
moral implications or human passion. Apparently her expansive familiarity
with Western culture has failed to give her much insight into her own life,
nor has she used its wisdom to construct a set of values to live by.

Yale, an English professor, is another highly educated person who ostensibly centers his life around literary explorations of feeling but in fact never
pushes himself to realize his own potential. Fundamentally lazy and self-
indulgent, he knows himself poorly, vacillating between his wife and mistress while he tries to figure out what he really wants. Professionally he says
he aspires to finish a book on Eugene O'Neill and publish a literary magazine, but he squanders his time and money on more frivolous things. Moreover, as Sander H. Lee observes, "Throughout the film, Yale manipulates
everyone he supposedly cares for in order to satisfy his own yearnings, no
matter what the consequences. Yale rationalizes his choices by mocking legitimate moral concerns while pretending to himself that humans, being in-
escapably flawed, are not really responsible for their acts" (Lee 88–89).
Like Mary, Yale has failed to use his extensive education and immersion in
high culture to give insight or direction to his life or to inspire a code of ethics to live by.

Allen also ridicules other intellectuals who use jargon to insulate themselves from the rest of society and appear superior to it. He suggests that
such people live in an unreal world of abstractions and that their narrow vision blinds them to genuine physical threats from the outside. At a cocktail
party Ike is flabbergasted when he encounters a young woman who claims
to have "the wrong kind of orgasm." (The woman is played by Tisa Farrow,
Mia's sister.) And when Ike suggests to other party-goers that they take
bricks and bats to confront a band of neo-Nazis planning to march in New
Jersey, the intellectuals suggest publishing biting satire instead. Their belief
that satire would have any impact at all on Nazis underscores how danger-
ously narrow and removed their world is.

By contrast, Tracy wants to enjoy both art and life as more than cerebral abstraction. She has fun with the camera Ike has given her, and she gives him a harmonica so he can explore his musical side. Whereas watching old movies with Mary is a stimulating cerebral activity for Ike, with Tracy it becomes an occasion to tease and play with each other. Tracy represents both innocence and hope for the future. Too young yet to be cynical, she is nonetheless self-possessed and attuned to her own values. She is strong enough to go to London, despite Ike's last-minute request for her to stay, yet she expresses optimism about the future.

In some ways, Tracy seems too good to be true: young, attractive, willing, intelligent, attentive, affectionate, totally devoted but never demanding. Tracy's idealized character undercuts some of the film's realism and contributes to the sense that the movie is fundamentally a romance, as Allen says he conceived it. At the same time, Ike remains the central character, and Tracy's exaggerated goodness facilitates the story of Ike's growth in self-knowledge and self-acceptance. Mariel Hemingway plays the role credibly, but, as Nancy Pogel observes, "So young, so unformed, so uncorrupted is Tracy that even while we are asked to believe in her, we are forced to admit that she may be more romantic fantasy or elusive ideal than obtainable reality" (Pogel 122). Pogel compares Tracy to the girl next door in musical comedies or the "good girls" in film noir movies, and she notes that, according to Janey Place, the good girls in these films, "offer the possibility of integration for the alienated, lost man. . . . She gives love, understanding . . . asks very little in return . . . and is generally visually passive and static" (Pogel 123).

Indeed, Tracy's role in the movie is to redeem alienated Ike, and Ike's realization that he has wanted Tracy all along provides the movie's climax. To arrive at that recognition, he learns to see Tracy not as an abstraction—a teenaged school girl—but as the individual she is: a loving, artistic, beautiful, sexy, perceptive, insightful, optimistic, curious, fun-loving person who likes to laugh. And although he must wait six months for her return from London, the film ends on a hopeful note, as Tracy tells him that he must acquire some faith in people.

The fact that Tracy is seventeen years old at the start of the movie (and eighteen and "legal" at the end) troubles some critics, who find her too young for an adult, sexual relationship with a man in his forties. But as Natalie Gittelson observes, "*Manhattan* testifies with eloquence and candor that Allen may have a soft spot in his heart for young, young women. But there is little of Humbert (*Lolita*) Humbert here. Although sex is by no means devalued, the real attraction lies between kindred spirits. The older Allen grows the more he seems to value innocence in women—not sexual innocence, but that shiningness of soul that age so often tarnishes" (quoted in Pogel 122).

Julian Fox notes that the Ike-Tracy relationship parallels a two-year relationship Allen had with Stacey Nelkin that began when the actress was seventeen. Fox also points to Allen's thirteen year-old-pen pal, Nancy Jo Sales, whom Allen met in person only once, in the presence of her stepmother and another adult. According to Sales, Allen would write to her with questions about her life and interests that might serve as raw material for the movie (Fox 111).[3] In retrospect, Allen's love affair with twenty-one-year-old Soon-Yi Previn when he was in his mid-fifties also casts a new perspective on the film, suggesting that life sometimes does imitate art. The apparent success of their relationship, now a marriage, demonstrates that at least in some instances May-December romances can be meaningful and endure. Certainly, *Manhattan* suggests they can be mutually rewarding.

NOTES

1. Executives at United Artists were concerned that the black-and-white photography would alienate viewers, but Allen was not bothered. He figured that he would be better off without viewers who could not handle something as broad as black and white cinema, since his other, more subtle efforts would be lost upon them anyway (Lax 330).

2. For an in-depth analysis of the camera work in *Manhattan*, see Sam B. Girgus, *The Films of Woody Allen*. Girgus argues that the wide-angle Scope-screen "decenters, displaces, dislocates, and distorts" in order to communicate "the psychological, social, and moral separation and isolation of the characters"(48).

3. Allen's relationship with Sales recalls Mark Twain's correspondence in his old age with little girls he called his "Angelfish." Both suggest an unusual intimacy between an adult man and a little girl, but neither relationship was physical. (See Hamlin Hill, *Mark Twain: God's Fool.*)

Manhattan Murder Mystery. A 1993 film directed by, written by, and starring Allen, who plays book publisher Larry Lipton. It costars Diane Keaton (Larry's wife, Carol), Alan Alda (Ted), Anjelica Huston (Marcia Fox), Jerry Adler (Paul House), Lynn Cohen (Lillian House), Melanie Morris (Helen Moss), Ron Rifkin (Sy), Joy Behar (Marilyn), and William Addy (Jack, the building superintendent). Robert Greenhut was the producer, Carlo Di Palma director of photography, Santo Loquasto production designer, Jeffrey Kurland costumer, and Susan E. Morse editor. Marshall Brickman collaborated with Allen on the screenplay. The music includes "I Happen to Like New York," "The Best Things in Life Are Free," "The Hallway," "Take Five," "I'm in the Mood for Love," "The Big Noise from Winnetka," "Out of Nowhere," "Have You Met Miss Jones?" "Sing, Sing, Sing,"

"Misty," "Overture to *Guys and Dolls,*" and Richard Wagner's *The Flying Dutchman*. Columbia-TriStar was the North American distributor.

Apart from Diane Keaton's cameo singing appearance in *Radio Days, Manhattan Murder Mystery* reunited Allen with Keaton on screen for their first time since *Annie Hall*, fourteen years earlier. Keaton was a late replacement for Mia Farrow, whom Allen had originally cast as Carol Lipton but dropped after Farrow accused him of sexually abusing their adopted daughter, Dylan. Since it was too late to rewrite the part specifically for Keaton, he essentially swapped roles with her, making himself the staid straight man and Keaton the exuberant amateur detective (Fox 237–238).

The movie was popular among critics and viewers, who welcomed the reunion of Keaton and Allen and applauded Allen's return to a lighter form of comedy. Initially it performed well at the box office, earning over $3 million during its first week. But like other Allen films of the era, interest waned in North America but flamed in Europe. *Manhattan Murder Mystery* cost $13.5 million to produce but grossed only $11.3 million in U.S. and Canadian distribution (not including later video rentals and television revenues). But it more than recouped its losses in France, Italy, and Great Britain, where it was enthusiastically greeted. In Rome and Great Britain, it reached the number one spot during the week of its release.

Allen maintains that he had always wanted to make a murder mystery; in fact, the original drafts of *Annie Hall* were, like *Manhattan Murder Mystery*, about a married couple who suspect foul play next door. Throughout his career Allen has shied away from the genre because, although murder stories are sometimes entertaining, he finds them typically shallow unless, like *Crime and Punishment, Macbeth*, or his own *Crimes and Misdemeanors*, "the murder is only a vehicle upon which the author is able to explore very deep and philosophical ideas" (*Woody Allen on Woody Allen* 256). And even though *Manhattan Murder Mystery* is indebted to Alfred Hitchcock's *Rear Window* (1954), as well as to Billy Wilder's *Double Indemnity* (1944), Allen disagrees with critics like François Truffaut who find deep meaning in Hitchcock's films. He thinks some are "quite wonderful," but Allen finally regards Hitchcock's movies as "delightful, but completely insignificant" (*Woody Allen on Woody Allen* 256). Nor does he exclude *Manhattan Murder Mystery* from his overall assessment of the genre. He calls the film an "unambitious undertaking . . . a trivial picture" that was "fun for me . . . a little personal reward . . . an indulgence." Nonetheless, he believes that it "does realize its modest ambitions" (*Woody Allen on Woody Allen* 255).

Those ambitions are primarily comedic. By contrast to its immediate predecessors, *Crimes and Misdemeanors, Alice, Shadows and Fog*, and *Husbands and Wives*, the film does little to explore character, human relations, or personal values. Instead, it strives to generate laughs by showing how a middle-aged New York couple foils what seems to be the perfect murder. Most of the comedy derives from clever lines and acting.

The problem of sustaining passion in a romantic relationship drives several of Allen's films from the period, notably *Husbands and Wives* and *Mighty Aphrodite*, and in *Manhattan Murder Mystery* Larry and Carol are drifting apart because the thrill is ebbing from their marriage. Like Annie Hall, Carol seeks out new people, experiences, and adventures, while Larry, like Alvy Singer, resists change, preferring to watch sports and old movies on TV. Instead of enjoying each other's company, they are motivated by obligation. Following the opening shot, an impressive aerial nighttime pan of New York City, we first see the couple at a hockey game that excites him and bores her. We learn that her attendance is in exchange for his accompanying her to an opera that does not interest him.

Later, Carol feels angry and betrayed when Larry breaks his end of the bargain by leaving the opera early. "I can't listen to that much Wagner," he complains. "You know, I start getting the urge to conquer Poland." A funny line that demonstrates Larry's wit, the remark also reveals Larry's passive-aggressive manipulation. He uses Hitler's love of Wagner's music to make himself out as victim and thereby create an excuse to leave the performance early, which is what Larry wants to do all along. Moreover, he has created the situation so that Carol cannot object; if she does, she finds herself arguing against the horror of the Holocaust. Carol has no alternative but to go along, and Larry gets his way.

Having given up a career in an ad agency to raise a now-grown son, Carol seeks greater independence and new personal challenges. A good cook, she wants to open a restaurant. Her friend Ted, who has a crush on her, enthusiastically supports the plan, while Larry simply foresees the endless headaches entailed in running an eatery. Established early in the story, these differences over the restaurant characterize Carol as confident, creative, and optimistic, if somewhat impetuous and impractical. By contrast, Larry appears cautious, pessimistic, and pragmatic, with limited imagination but a sharp wit. The disagreement also exposes the growing rift in the Liptons' marriage.

The contrast in personality types provides the comic tension that fuels the story. When Lillian and Paul House, an elderly couple who recently moved next door, invite them in for coffee, Carol accepts over Larry's silent objections, which he communicates with exaggerated facial expressions that are funny to us, if not to them. During the visit Carol is charmed by the old lady, while Larry is stupefied by her stamp-collecting husband. A few days later they return to find that Lillian has died of a sudden heart attack. But when they encounter Paul soon afterward, he appears in surprisingly good spirits. After Carol notices factual discrepancies between what the Houses said during their first visit and what Paul mentions now, she suspects foul play and becomes increasingly obsessed with investigating the supposed crime. (In this respect she anticipates Lenny Winerib in *Mighty Aphrodite*, who also retreats from a troubled marriage by immersing himself in a mystery.) Ted shares her enthusiasm, and solving the murder mystery becomes an exciting, creative activity they share. But Larry excludes himself because he thinks the premise is implausible, and he believes they are violating Paul's right to privacy.

The contrast between Carol's boldness and Larry's caution becomes even more highly exaggerated when Carol sneaks into Paul's apartment and rummages through his papers in search of evidence. The break-in serves several plot and thematic purposes. First, it takes Carol's obsession to a new level. Virtually without evidence and motivated by the thrill of possibly thwarting evil, she breaks the law. But in becoming a criminal, Carol introduces the necessary excitement into her life that she has been missing, and her bond to Ted becomes stronger as they become more deeply engrossed in the mystery. Her break-in also causes Larry to become involved, as he nervously returns with her to confront Paul and recover the reading glasses that Carol accidentally left behind. But Paul has already discovered the spectacles in his bedroom, and although he does not challenge Carol's implausible explanation that she must have accidentally kicked them into the other room when they recently visited, the glasses signal to him that she has been snooping. A second intrusion involves Larry more deeply. He reluctantly accompanies Carol back into Paul's apartment when she insists on returning, despite his nonstop objections. With comic clumsiness evocative of Keaton and Allen's earlier pairings, Larry and Carol rummage through Paul's belongings in search of additional clues.

At this point, convention suggests that Allen would develop Carol's growing interest in Ted and Larry's admiration for Marcia Fox, a confident, attractive, worldly, intelligent, and accomplished writer whose work he is publishing. Instead, Allen suppresses those aspects of the story by having Carol politely turn down Ted's advance and by showing that Larry is completely unaware of, and unable to imagine, Marcia's interest in him. Nonetheless, Ted and Marcia serve a purpose by provoking jealousy in Larry and Carol. Moreover, when Larry tells Marcia of his concern that Carol is becoming attracted to Ted, Marcia off-handedly observes that he should show more interest in the mystery Ted and Carol share. Larry's eagerness to grasp at a possible solution for keeping Carol renders him oblivious to Marcia's subsequent proposition that Larry and she get together. The scene thus demonstrates the depth of Larry's feelings for Carol and his commitment to her, as it motivates him to take the uncharacteristic step of becoming more involved in solving the imagined crime.

Similarly, the scene where Carol refuses Ted evolves into another plot point, as she inadvertently glimpses the woman thought to be dead riding in a passing bus, very much alive. Carol initially goes to Ted with the new revelation but later convinces a somewhat more willing Larry to help her watch for Lillian. When Larry sees her too, he becomes an active, if not altogether enthusiastic, participant.

Working together as a couple for this first time on a creative, exciting project, Larry and Carol rediscover their passion for one another. They track down Lillian in a run-down hotel, only to find her dead in her room. After a chain of eerie, dangerous, and bewildering developments, they follow Paul and watch as he incinerates the corpse. But since Lillian is already officially dead and no body remains, they cannot accuse Paul of a crime. Instead, they enlist Ted and Marcia and try to trick Paul into exposing his guilt by blackmailing him. The plan backfires when Paul abducts Carol and threatens to kill her unless Lenny produces Lillian's nonexistent corpse. Only Lenny's bold action and the intervention of Paul's spurned secretary save Carol, as Paul dies backstage in a shootout patterned after the one from *Double Indemnity*, while *Double Indemnity* plays on the opposite side of the screen. Subsequently, Marcia explains to Ted (and the audience) how Paul had double-crossed Lillian and his secretary and planned to run off with a young actress instead. Ted is enchanted by Marcia's cleverness, and they appear destined to unite as a couple at the end.

Sander H. Lee appropriately questions whether the adventure is sufficient to rescue the Liptons' marriage. He believes neither character has fundamentally changed, and a return to their previous life will still deny Carol the excitement she craves. Lee adds that "where Jeffries [from *Rear Window*] has authentically worked through many of his anxieties about romantic commitment, there is no suggestion either that Carol and Larry have endured a similar catharsis, or that such an experience is even available to them" (Lee 346).

Lee's reservations are based on the assumption that the Liptons' relationship will revert to what it had been before their adventure. But there are reasons to believe that both Larry and Carol will change in positive ways that can enable them to reinvigorate their marriage. First, Larry has demonstrated the depth of his love for Carol, to both her and himself. At the beginning of the film, the extent of his devotion was not evident to either of them. Furthermore, he has experienced his passion for her with an intensity he has probably never previously known. His jealousy of Ted has also made him newly aware of how much he cares for Carol. Given this newly heightened awareness, it is likely that Larry will no longer take his wife for granted. Nor will he as readily allow himself to drift from her. Larry has also demonstrated his innate courage and capacity for action. So he may become more open to new experiences and other, perhaps less risky adventures. He might even now be willing to support Carol's restaurant idea or some other enterprise that carries risk but offers a challenge and allows Carol to develop her interests more fully.

For her part, Carol begins the postmystery phase of their relationship feeling satisfied and accomplished instead of frustrated and bored. Her jealousy of Marcia and her ability to turn down Ted so readily have made her more aware of her love for Larry. And having risked his life to save her, Larry is presumably more attractive to her, and she is presumably more confident of his love. Assuming that Carol comes out of the experience feeling more empowered and that Larry is now able to support and appreciate her empowerment, there is hope that their marriage will strengthen.

If these alterations in their relationship prove only temporary, and Larry and Carol revert to their previous existence, then Lee's prediction of an unhappy or failed marriage will probably be correct. But the final shot shows the couple laughing together, something they had not previously done throughout the film. Moreover, the fact that Carol makes the joke at Larry's expense suggests her growing sense of empowerment, the lack of which had been the core of their marital crisis. Consequently—although in Allen's uncertain, irrational universe nothing is for sure—the prospects for an improved, more loving, and more passionate marriage appear good.

Marx Brothers. A vaudeville comedy group that made zany film comedies during the Great Depression. Their most notable films include *The Cocoanuts* (1929), *Animal Crackers* (1930), *Monkey Business* (1931), *Horse Feathers* (1932), *Duck Soup* (1933), *A Night at the Opera* (1935), *A Day at the Races* (1937), and *Go West* (1940). In addition, Groucho starred as host of *You Bet Your Life*, a humorous game show that began on radio in 1947 and aired on television from 1950 to 1961.

Allen greatly admires the Marx Brothers, especially Groucho, whom he met and with whom he corresponded toward the end of Groucho's life. (Allen described Groucho as being like one of his Jewish uncles, and Groucho paid Allen the compliment of calling him "a funny man." [Lax 171].) Famous for his cigars and bushy eyebrows and mustache, Groucho specialized in verbal humor that Allen emulated in some of his early fiction and films. During the making of *What's New, Pussycat?* Allen had lobbied for Groucho to be cast as Michael's sexually frustrated psychologist, Fritz Fassbender, but Charles K. Feldman, the producer, chose another comic actor Allen admired, Peter Sellers.

The other Marx brothers were Chico, who played a fast-talking, quick-witted Italian immigrant; Harpo, a curly-haired, satyr-like mute with expressive hands, eyes, face, and body; Zeppo, who played the romantic lead in some of the early films; and Gummo, who performed on stage but made no films. Harpo played the harp, Chico the piano, Groucho the guitar, and Zeppo sang. Their music was featured in most of their films. (*Duck Soup* was the one film to omit the otherwise obligatory love story that also occasioned many of the musical performances.)

Allen celebrates the Marx Brothers' high spirits, fun-loving absurdity, and overriding playfulness. In several films he alludes directly to them in order to make an important point or express a character's state of mind. Alvy Singer introduces *Annie Hall* by repeating Groucho's joke that he would not belong to any club that would admit someone like him, and Allen uses the joke as the basic explanation for why Alvy is unable to sustain a successful romantic relationship. In *Hannah and Her Sisters* suicidal Mickey discovers that life is worth living after he views *Duck Soup*, and in *Manhattan* Groucho heads Ike's list of things that make life worth living. Lenny Winerib suggests naming his adopted child Groucho or Harpo in *Mighty Aphrodite*, but his wife vetoes the idea. Groucho's smiling face covers the wall of Sandy's apartment when Sandy is happily in love in *Stardust Memories*, and Allen's musical comedy, *Everyone Says I Love You*, culminates at a Parisian gala in which all the guests come dressed as one of the Marx Brothers. The film's fickle teenaged narrator finally finds true love with a Harpo look-alike. (The Marx Brothers first sang "Everyone Says I Love You" in *Animal Crackers*; using different lyrics, they each separately serenade the campus widow with it in *Horse Feathers*.) Allen mocks arcane academic research in *Stardust Memories* when a scholar tells Sandy she is doing a study of Gummo because he is the one brother who made no films.

In addition to these direct references, Allen has made numerous indirect allusions to the brothers in his films. The slapstick scene from *Love and Death* in which Boris introduces Sonja to Don Francisco imitates the one from *A Night at the Opera* in which Groucho introduces Mrs. Claypool and Mr. Gottlieb. Boris's word play about the seconds in the dueling scene also reflects a strong Groucho influence. *Bananas* makes passing reference to *Duck Soup*. A futuristic mirror scene in *Sleeper* also plays off *Duck Soup*, and Miles tries to impress Luna by dancing like Groucho. When Luna and Miles prepare to operate on the Leader's nose, their slapstick antics emulate *A Day at the Races*, where the Marx Brothers prepare to give Margaret Dumont a medical exam. And when Luna maneuvers Miles while he dangles from a large magnetic computer tape, she evokes the scene in *A Night at the Opera* where Harpo is dunked into the ocean while clinging to the ship's rigging.

Masturbation. Several of Allen's film characters sing the praises of self-gratification. In *Love and Death*, when asked how he became such a wonderful lover, Boris tells the Countess he practices a lot when he is alone. While pretending to be a psychiatrist, Zelig claims to teach a course in advanced masturbation at the Psychiatric Institute: "If I'm not there, they start without me." In *Manhattan* Ike describes autoeroticism as sex with someone he loves. In *Stardust Memories* Sandy's mother tells the world he used to masturbate as a child; she even holds up the girlie magazine she found in his room. Perhaps Sandy articulates the central attraction that masturbation holds for Allen when he tells Isobel that masturbation and art are two things he has control over.

Men in Crisis: The Harvey Wallinger Story. A 1971 made-for-television film directed by, written by, and starring Allen, who plays Harvey Wallinger. The twenty-five-minute satire of the Nixon administration was never released. Originally entitled *The Woody Allen Comedy Special* and then *The Politics of Woody Allen*, *Men in Crisis* was filmed at Columbia University in ten days while Allen was between other projects. He offered it without charge to the public television station in New York City, WNET, which scheduled the film for broadcast in February 1972. The timing coincided with the beginning of President Nixon's campaign for reelection, a fact that no doubt influenced both Allen's decision to make the satire and public television's decision not to air it after all. Allen, whose politics are liberal, opposed Nixon, and the satire lampoons the Republican president. Fearful that broadcasting an attack on Nixon at this time might jeopardize its future funding, PBS asked Allen to cut scenes that might be particularly offensive, such as when former Vice President Hubert Humphrey gives his boss, President Lyndon Johnson, the finger; when a nun gushes that Wallinger is "an unbelievable swinger, a freak"; and when Mrs. Nixon suggests she is eager to have an affair with Wallinger while her husband is away.

Allen refused to make the cuts, and PBS took steps that indirectly ensured *Men in Crisis* would not be shown. It notified member stations that although PBS would not distribute the movie, they were free to air it on their own. But it warned that showing the film might raise legal problems that could endanger the stations' broadcast licenses, including demands for equal time from other candidates and lawsuits from people who were targets of the satire.

In a subsequent interview, Allen called the cancellation an honest dis-agreement. He acknowledges that the material in question was in bad taste, though he adds that "It's hard to say anything about that administration that wouldn't be in bad taste." Allen considers the piece amusing, but without any particular depth or political insight. He believes that Nixon's opponents would have enjoyed it, and Nixon's supporters would have dismissed him as "a crackpot. It was all so silly. It wasn't Jonathan Swift" (Lax 119).

Made about half a year before the Watergate break-in that ultimately brought down the Nixon presidency, *Men in Crisis* centers on Harvey Wall-inger, a Nixon aide based loosely on national security adviser Henry Kiss-inger, who proves to be the power behind the president. Like other early Allen films, the movie uses a loose, sketchlike format that shows the influ-ence of Allen's careers as a stand-up comedian and a television comedy writer. Allen relies on quick laughs and one-liners, such as when the narra-tor declares that in 1968, the Republicans chose as their candidate "a man of force and magnitude—of personal charisma and a profound grasp of major issues—but that man refuses the nomination and they settle for Richard Nixon." Elsewhere, the narrator states that Attorney General John Mitchell "has many ideas for strengthening the country's law enforcement methods and is hampered only by lack of funds and the Constitution." The mock docu-mentary form both draws from *Take the Money and Run* (1969) and antici-pates *Zelig* (1983). Shots of Wallinger and Nixon lookalike, Richard M. Dixon, are interspersed with real footage that catches actual politicians in embarrassing moments, such as when Hubert Humphrey, dressed in academic regalia, trips on stage as the narrator declares that the Democrats have chosen as their candidate "a man of style and grace," or when Vice President Spiro Agnew serves into the back of his tennis partner during a match.

Like Kissinger, Wallinger has gained notoriety as a ladies' man. But in fashion typical of the early Allen films, his success with women proves largely illusory. Louise Lasser appears as a former girlfriend who found him unsatisfying sexually, and Diane Keaton plays his cross-eyed wife who studied at Vassar to become a blacksmith.

For additional reading, see Caryn James, "Pointing the Way to *Annie Hall* and Beyond," Eric Lax, *Woody Allen* (118–120), and Barbara Stewart, "Showering Shtick on the White House."

Metafiction. *Metafiction* is a term coined by Robert Scholes to refer to fic-tion that is about literature instead of being directly about life. It is charac-teristic of postmodern literature and film, and Allen frequently employs the form. Notable among his metafictions are his play *God*; "The Kugelmass Episode," a story in *Side Effects*; and his films *What's Up, Tiger Lily? Play It*

Again, Sam, *Stardust Memories*, *The Purple Rose of Cairo*, and *Deconstructing Harry*.

Allen's first film *What's Up, Tiger Lily?* illustrates the self-awareness characteristic of metafictions. Phil Moskowitz remarks that he was almost killed before the opening credits. He notes, "Don't look now, Baby, but this is the obligatory scene where the director has to walk by with his wife." Moskowitz, whose gun is empty, later seeks help from the audience: "If all you in the audience who believe in fairies will clap your hands, then my gun will be filled with bullets"—a reference to another movie, Disney's *Peter Pan* (1953). *Stardust Memories* and *Deconstructing Harry*, and *God* present Allen's most sophisticated uses of the form as they intermingle different layers of fiction and reality.

For additional reading, see Robert Scholes's *Fabulation and Metafiction*.

A Midsummer Night's Sex Comedy. A 1982 film directed by, written by, and starring Allen, who plays Andrew Hobbes, an investment counselor and amateur inventor. It costars Mia Farrow (Ariel Weymouth), Tony Roberts (Dr. Maxwell Jordan), Mary Steenburgen (Adrian Hobbes), José Ferrer (Professor Leopold Sturgis), and Julie Hagerty (Dulcy Ford). Robert Greenhut was the producer, Gordon Willis director of photography, Mel Bourne production designer, Santo Loquasto costumer, and Susan E. Morse editor. The music is by Felix Mendelssohn, primarily from his "Overture to *A Midsummer Night's Dream*" but also from his 3rd (Scottish) Symphony and other pieces. Kurtz & Friends and Zander's Animation Parlour provided the animation, and Orion Pictures was the North American distributor.

Allen's first movie with Mia Farrow, *A Midsummer Night's Sex Comedy*, along with *Stardust Memories*, began a pattern of films that fared better critically and financially in Europe than in the United States. With the notable exception of *Hannah and Her Sisters*, this pattern continued throughout Allen's collaboration with Farrow during the 1980s and early 1990s. American commentators typically regarded the film as lightweight and "trivial." Indeed, Allen himself has called it "a light . . . small intermezzo with a few laughs. . . . I wanted it to be a bonbon, a little dessert or something" (*Woody Allen on Woody Allen* 132). European critics and audiences were more attuned to his efforts to render the ambience of an enchanted midsummer night. They also better appreciated his celebration of the countryside, and *Sex Comedy* spent seven weeks among the top ten films in London. The first movie Allen made under his new contract with Orion Pictures, *Sex Comedy* cost $7 million to produce but yielded only $4.5 million in North American rentals. However, its European earnings enabled it to exceed breaking even slightly.

The film's stunning visuals stand out among its most memorable features. Just as Allen had glamorized the city in *Manhattan*, here he wanted to show nature "in all its beauty." He shot the film at the 400-acre Rockefeller estate near Pocantico Hills in Westchester County, New York, and he had his production crew build a rustic country house based on one featured in a magazine. (The house was later sold. The buyer moved it, brought it up to code, and inhabited it.)

As in *Manhattan*, cinematographer Gordon Willis played a major role in the filmmaking. According to Allen, "We talked a lot about the colouring. We wanted to film on the most beautiful days in the country that you could think of. We just made it as lovely as we could. And everything was subsumed into that" (*Woody Allen on Woody Allen* 132). Several shots mimic masterpieces by the impressionist painters, notably Édouard Manet's *Le Déjeuner sur L'Herbe* ("Luncheon on the Grass") and Auguste Renoir's lush pictures of colorfully dressed young men and women picnicking along the river.

Although Allen characteristically maintains that no resemblance exists between *Sex Comedy* and Ingmar Bergman's *Smiles of a Summer Night* (1955; Lax 314), the latter is clearly another significant influence, both visually and in terms of plot and theme. Both films are period pieces set near the turn of the century (*Sex Comedy* is set around 1910), and both contrast the past to the present and future.[1] Both films prominently feature jealous lovers, an outdoor dining scene, and a pistol accident; both revolve around re-pairing of couples who have been improperly paired, and both trace back to Shakespeare's *A Midsummer Night's Dream*, another comedy about re-coupling in enchanted woods on a summer evening. Julian Fox notes additional similarities to *Smiles of a Summer Night*, as well as to Max Ophuls's *La Ronde* (1950) and Jean Renoir's *Une Partie de Campagne* (1936) and *La Règle du Jeu* (1939). Nancy Pogel also draws comparisons to Renoir's *Picnic on the Grass* (1960).

Several commentators have observed that *Sex Comedy* reflects the euphoria Allen felt during his early romance with Farrow, whom he had then been dating for about a year. Whether it was due to their nascent love or to some other factor, *Sex Comedy* is among Allen's most optimistic movies. In fact, its central theme is about the eternal presence of hope.

Maxwell, Andrew's playboy doctor-friend, repeatedly declares that "marriage is the death of hope," and the film questions the possibility of finding the appropriate mate and sustaining a satisfying marriage. It also addresses the larger existential questions that fascinate Allen: Is there more to existence than we experience with our senses? What happens after death? Do we possess spirits or souls?

In each case, the comedy initially presents pessimistic views on these matters but then ultimately reverses them. In fact, their reversal defines the happy ending and brings the plot to a satisfactory close. On the other hand, by telling the story in the format of a romantic comedy, Allen qualifies his new-found optimism: the genre makes no pretensions to being truthful or realistic. Allen can dismiss *Sex Comedy* as a mere bonbon and disassociate from the optimism it projects.

Our first views of romantic coupling are not hopeful. Andrew's wife, Adrian, no longer responds sexually to him, and Adrian's beautiful, intelligent, and sexually liberated cousin Ariel is marrying a pompous, overly cerebral humanities professor, not because she loves Leopold but because he will confer stability on her chaotic life and offer long-term security. As she confides to Andrew, "For a woman the years slip away quickly." Coincidentally, Ariel and Andrew had dated years earlier, and both secretly regret not having acted on the powerful lust they had felt for one another one magical summer night by the brook. But when they try again that weekend, they are no longer the same people; the time is no longer right, and the experience is dismal.

The pairings become further complicated when Maxwell, Andrew's best friend, inhales Ariel's scent upon first meeting her and falls instantly in love. She too instantly recognizes his fragrance and is drawn to him. Leopold's cultivated life of the mind contrasts Maxwell's animal magnetism, and Maxwell's determination to act on his physical and emotional feelings, regardless of their social acceptability or propriety, contrasts Andrew's respectful reticence and self-restraint. In short, the pairings among the couples pit the mind against the body, the superego against the id. And as we might expect from a "sex comedy," the id prevails.

If Maxwell is a creature of the body, Leopold is all mind. Leopold takes empiricism to its logical extreme. He denies the existence of any unseen or unsensed forces, smugly insisting, "Apart from this world there are no realities." He thinks that people who believe in God or the spirit world are too weak to face the disquieting truth that there is nothing more to life than what we experience with our senses, and he considers himself superior because he rejects the comforting self-delusions offered by metaphysics.[2]

In this portrayal of Leopold, along with his representation of other empiricists and harsh realists, such as the doctor in *Shadows and Fog* and Monk in *The Purple Rose of Cairo*, Allen suggests a link between absolute empiricism and emotional disconnection. Although he remains skeptical about metaphysics, Allen recognizes that it is an act of despair to surrender all hope that existence may entail more than we comprehend. The empiricists have become harsh and insensitive because they have convinced themselves that no possibility exists of an afterlife where their own good actions can be rewarded or their suffering can become meaningful. They have, in effect, denied themselves any hope of judgment, redemption, or, in less Christian terms, cosmic purpose. Moreover, radical empiricists who dismiss all unseen, immeasurable forces necessarily reject passion and emotion, which give life its color, intensity, and meaning.[3]

Leopold embraces the life of the mind and rejects his body and feelings. While the other guests practice archery, Leopold, a pacifist who spurns physical contests, prefers to vent his violent impulses on a chess board. For Leopold, even great art is to be appreciated intellectually, not felt, as indicated by his remark that he "explained to Ariel exactly why Michelangelo's [Sistine] ceiling was indeed great." Contemptuous of our Neanderthal ancestors who were driven by lust and lived by brute force, he extols refined civilization, whose highest product he considers to be well-educated men such as himself. "Am I to be overpraised merely for being a civilized human?" he asks his adoring university colleagues in a gesture of false humility. In turn, they fawn over his many intellectual accomplishments and assure him that Ariel will be "the final jewel in your crown." That Leopold is a poor choice for Ariel is first indicated by this suggestion that she will become his ornament.

Though Leopold considers himself above such petty emotions, he is clearly driven by pride, both intellectual and sexual. His intellectual pride becomes apparent when he "consents" to give lectures, belittles other art historians, and denounces Maxwell's book on nature upon first meeting him. Ironically, Leopold's knowledge of botany proves inferior to Maxwell's, but Leopold's certainty that he is correct enables Maxwell to steal his first kiss from Ariel.

It is Leopold's sexual pride, less glaring than his intellectual pride, that transforms him and the plot. The story can reach a successful conclusion only when Leopold acknowledges and embraces his long-repressed animalistic nature, and his male vanity brings this about. His singing the song of the cuckoo upon arriving in the country foreshadows his subsequent cuckolding. And when Leopold discovers that Andrew has made love to Ariel, he falls into a jealous rage. In his fury Leopold literally hunts down his enemy, a primitive act he had earlier disparaged. Aiming for Andrew, he shoots Maxwell in the chest with an arrow. But Leopold has already recognized Maxwell as a rival for Ariel, and instead of remorse he feels satisfaction, followed by lust. Returning to the house, he ravishes Maxwell's date, the compliant nurse Dulcy, who had earlier roused his animal instincts. Leopold dies at the height of his passion, but as the film closes, his spirit reassures his friends that he now leads an enchanted existence among those other blessed souls who expired while making love. In short, by opening himself to the animal passions he had so long denied, Leopold experiences not only deep sexual fulfillment but also real joy. Most of all, he recognizes and achieves full identification with his spiritual essence.

Ironically, the same act that stirs Leopold's blood lust also casts him as Cupid for Maxwell and Ariel; he unites the couple when he shoots Maxwell in the heart. Both sensualists who recognized each other's scent at first meeting, they have at long last found their proper mate by trusting their basic animal attraction.

More provocative is the reinvigoration of Andrew and Adrian's marriage. Thinking that he is dying after being struck by Leopold's arrow, Maxwell confesses to Andrew that he and Adrian had had an affair about six months earlier. "The moment was perfect. I seized it. You only live once." Feeling betrayed, infuriated, and confused, Andrew leaves Maxwell languishing and looks instead for his pistol; he intends to commit suicide. When Adrian interrupts, Andrew confronts her, and she admits to the affair. She blames Andrew for not paying attention to her. But her confession lifts her guilt and liberates her libido. Ignoring his angry protests, she ravishes Andrew on the spot. The experience is so gratifying that Andrew instantly forgives her and Maxwell, and the plot draws to a neat conclusion.

Andrew's forgiveness of his friend makes moot the remaining, unresolved conflict between the id and the superego. Though not as cerebral as Leopold, Andrew nonetheless also essentially identifies with the superego, as he adheres to basic social conventions. These conventions, which serve the superego by helping to maintain social order, are mostly expressions of respect and commitment and typically require passivity and restraint instead of action. For instance, years earlier Andrew declined to seduce Ariel out of respect for her chastity, an act he later regretted, especially when he subsequently discovered that she had been sleeping with virtually everyone he knew. Andrew also essentially respects his marriage vows. Though attracted to Ariel all weekend, he does not pursue her until after he becomes convinced that his marriage has failed and her betrothal to Leopold is untenable. Because he respects and expects loyalty from his wife and friends, he feels especially betrayed by Adrian and Maxwell. (In this regard Andrew and Maxwell mirror Ike and Yale from *Manhattan*.)

Maxwell, on the other hand, is more impulsive and action oriented. He believes in seizing the moment, regardless of the consequences, even if this means betraying his best friend and possibly ruining his marriage. By conventional standards, Maxwell's behavior is morally reprehensible. Yet at the same time his complete surrender to his instincts becomes the driving force that eventually creates positive change. It shatters the tranquil but unsatisfactory status quo and sets in motion the process of recoupling that ultimately causes Leopold to discover his animal being, reinvigorates the marriage of Andrew and Adrian, and pairs Maxwell with Adrian. In this respect, an Eastern-like paradox underlies Allen's philosophy: sometimes suppressing instincts to act in a morally responsible way can lead to undesirable consequences, and sometimes morally reprehensible, impulsive behavior can produce positive results. Elsewhere, in such films as *Crimes and Misdemeanors*, Allen takes up the problem of surrendering too fully to the libido. But *Sex Comedy* exists to celebrate nature, both as it blossoms in the landscape around us and as it resides just as resplendently within each individual.

NOTES

1. In addition to the transitions in the characters' personal lives, *Sex Comedy* presents a world in flux. For instance, Andrew invokes such early twentieth-century discoveries as ectoplasm and cosmic rays to challenge Leopold's empirical rejection of an unseen world, and Ariel and Dulcy's sexual liberation contrasts Adrian's more conventional notions of womanhood. A shot of all three women smoking together also reminds us of the period's nascent women's rights movement. Nancy Pogel observes, "The film sits on the brink of modernism, looking backward toward innocence and authenticity and forward toward a sophisticated, fragmented world where personal integrity and a sense of place within the natural order are less available" (Pogel 168-169).

2. Sander H. Lee suggests that Leopold is loosely based on Bertrand Russell, the pacifist-mathematician-philosopher who flourished around the turn of the century. Leopold's intellectual roots further extend to Ludwig Wittgenstein and A. J. Ayer, leader of the Vienna school of logical positivism. Ayer, like Leopold, insists that the only meaningful assertions are tautologies and propositions that are empirically verifiable. Leopold's self-satisfied declaration, "I did not create the cosmos; I merely explain it," evokes Pierre LaPlace, an early nineteenth-century astronomer-mathematician who, when asked where God fit into his view of the universe, proclaimed, "I have no need of that hypothesis."

3. So strong is this impulse to surrender hope that it even leads these super-rationalists to commit bad logic. Logically an empiricist can say only that he or she has no reason to believe in metaphysics, based on current evidence. But good science requires withholding final judgment until all the facts are in, something very different from outright disbelief. The good logical positivist would recognize that the propositions "there is a spirit world" and "there is no spirit world" are equally meaningless because both are unverifiable. The only logically tenable position for the empiricist is to act skeptically but reserve final judgment. But skepticism is different from outright rejection; a true skeptic remains willing to be convinced at some future time.

Mighty Aphrodite. A 1995 film directed by, written by, and starring Allen, who plays sportswriter Lenny Winerib. It costars Mira Sorvino (prostitute Linda Ash), Helena Bonham Carter (Lenny's wife, Amanda), Claire Bloom (Amanda's mother), Michael Rapaport (Kevin), Peter Weller (Jerry Bender), Dan Moran (Ricky, the pimp), Jack Warden (Tiresias), Olympia Dukakis (Jocasta), F. Murray Abraham (chorus leader), Jeffrey Kurland (Oedipus), David Ogden Stiers (Laius), Danielle Ferland (Cassandra), and the Dick Hyman Chorus (chorus). Robert Greenhut was the producer, Carlo Di Palma director of photography, Santo Loquasto production designer, Jeffrey Kurland costumer, and Susan E. Morse editor. Graciela Daniele choreographed the Greek chorus, and Dick Hyman arranged and performed the music, which features "Manhattan," "The In Crowd," and "You Do Something to Me," among other selections. Miramax was the North American distributor.

Following the financial success of *Bullets over Broadway, Mighty Aphrodite* was also anticipated to do well. Its world premiere at the Venice International Film Festival was a great success, as were subsequent screenings at the Toronto and Chicago festivals. However, after a strong opening in New York, American interest in the film waned, and *Mighty Aphrodite*, which cost approximately $15 million to produce, grossed only slightly over $5 million in U.S. and Canadian distribution (not including later video rentals and television revenues). Like many other Allen films, it fared much better in Europe and recouped the North American losses. Moreover, the film benefited from publicity surrounding Allen's European musical tour that coincided with the movie's release. (That tour is documented in Barbara Kopple's *Wild Man Blues*, 1998.) In France *Mighty Aphrodite* earned more on opening day than any previous Allen film, and its interest in England was enhanced by Allen's jazz performance in London's Royal Festival Hall and by rare media promotions in which Allen himself appeared.

The critics mirrored the box office. European commentators were enthusiastic, but American critical reaction was mixed. The film received praise for its lighthearted fantasy, visual effects, and acting—Sorvino won both a Golden Globe and Academy Award as best supporting actress and Allen received an Academy Award nomination for the screenplay. But some critics viewed the movie as a self-serving attempt to show Allen as a loving parent in order to regain the good graces of the public after Mia Farrow accused him of sexually abusing their adopted daughter. (Maureen Dowd called *Mighty Aphrodite* "a campaign film.") Other critics reiterated a growing feminist complaint against Allen's practice of casting himself as a romantic lead paired with much younger women.

Mighty Aphrodite parodies classical Greek tragedy in order to present both the dangers and virtue of acquiring knowledge. It thus sparks humor as it shows the importance of personal growth and acceptance. The story centers around Lenny Winerib, a New York sportswriter who, like King Oedipus, becomes obsessed with discovering information he was never supposed to learn. Oedipus discovers that he has killed his father and fornicated with his mother; Lenny learns that his bright and talented adopted son is actually the child of prostitute Linda Ash and an unknown father who was one of her tricks. (Sorvino maintains that her only instruction from Allen was, "I don't want a glimmer of intelligence to show through because not only is she dumb, she's stupid" (Fox 254). The discovery unsettles Lenny, who imagined that his son was the product of refined, genius parents, but when he sees that Linda loved the child and regrets giving him up, Lenny disregards the warning of the Greek chorus and, assuming that he knows what is better for her than she does, tries to change her life. This intrusion represents an arrogance, or hubris, that mimics Oedipus's tragic flaw. As with Oedipus, Lenny's efforts lead him to unexpected recognitions that make him miserable. Specifically, he learns that his marriage is falling apart, and his wife, Amanda, is becoming involved with another man. With that knowledge comes the additional realization of how much he loves her. Fortunately for Lenny, he is a character in a comedy, not a tragedy, and a couple of unexpected plot reversals bring about closure and a happy ending for all concerned.

The problems in Lenny and Amanda's marriage are evident from the beginning. The first scene features the open-air Greek theater in Taormina, Sicily, where the chorus introduces the story by placing Lenny in the company of Achilles and Oedipus. The second scene shows the couple arguing over Amanda's desire to adopt a child. If they are to have a child, he wants to father it—"pride of ownership," he explains. But Amanda hopes to avoid the disruption to her career that childbirth would necessarily entail. An art curator with ambitions of opening her own gallery, Amanda gets her way in this matter and in most others. They adopt a little boy they name Max, after discarding Groucho, Harpo, and other suggestions by Lenny; they change apartments in spite of Lenny's desire to remain where they currently reside; and they spend more and more time with Amanda's professional associates: wealthy, refined patrons of the arts whom the sports-oriented Lenny finds boring and pretentious.

As Amanda becomes increasingly absorbed by her new friends and her professional ambitions, she and Lenny grow apart. Much of the child-rearing responsibilities fall on him because she is too busy to attend to Max. Fortunately, Lenny adores his son and does not resent the added work. Amanda frequently cancels their plans in order to pursue investors for the

(Left to right) Jimmy McQuaid, Woody Allen, and Helena Bonham Carter in *Mighty Aphrodite*. Photo by Brian Hamill. Courtesy of Photofest.

Amanda Sloane Gallery (her maiden name), not, as Lenny notes, the Amanda Winerib Gallery. In other words, he perceives her to be disassociating from him and their marriage. Finally, Lenny is forced to admit that their relationship is no longer fun.

Within this context of frustration and fractured love, Lenny, like Oedipus, becomes obsessed with solving a mystery. Oedipus disregards warnings not to discover who murdered his predecessor, only to learn that he himself is the murderer. Lenny's life too is altered in profound and unexpected ways by his pursuit of forbidden knowledge. Telling him to "let sleeping dogs lie," the chorus warns Lenny that obsession is the most dangerous human weakness, and the silliest. But he ignores the admonitions, declaring that he is a man of action. In contrast to the chorus, tragic heros are all men of action. Indeed, while the fate of the chorus typically remains static, the heroes' misguided actions lead both to their fall from fortune and their acquisition of tragic insight. Thus, when Lenny spurns the chorus and commits himself to discovering Max's parentage, he initiates a process that will result in both loss and gain.

The revelation that Max's natural mother is a prostitute and his father was one of her anonymous clients delivers a blow to Lenny's faith in a rational world. A great believer in the power of genetics—he boasts earlier about his

own genes—Lenny is stunned to discover that the mother of his preco-
cious son is stupid and does not even realize that her profession is degrad-
ing. In a rational universe, intelligent children would not come from such
backgrounds, but in Allen's irrational universe, such non sequiturs occur
routinely, and we are all challenged to accept them and come to terms with
them.

Linda humbles Lenny through her high degree of self-acceptance. She
enjoys her work, considers herself fairly bright with good taste, and is frank
and open about sexual matters. Linda shows some real perception when she
tells Lenny that he is a loser. And when Lenny first tries to get her to change
her career, she rejects his judgment of her and kicks him out of her apartment. Later, when Lenny presumes to select someone he believes would be
a proper husband for her, Linda is clearly disturbed by Lenny's admonition
that she must lie about her past in order not to turn him off. And when the
blossoming relationship explodes after Kevin inadvertently sees one of Linda's pornographic movies, Linda's practice of honesty and self-acceptance
appears preferable to Lenny's denial of a past that he considers shameful but
she does not.

On the other hand, Lenny's concerns for Linda's well-being are well
founded. He gets her to admit that she misses her child and shares such conventional, middle-class aspirations as love, family, and career. Lenny is correct when he points out that her life as a prostitute and porn star do nothing
to bring her closer to achieving these goals. If he is guarded and passive because he fears loss, she is unrealistic and self-destructive when she rests her
fate on improbable long shots. The contrast between them becomes especially apparent when they go to a horse race, and Linda is crest-fallen when
her sixty-to-one bet yields nothing. Lenny, on the other hand, picks a sure
thing to place and wins a pittance.

In the end, each emerges as stronger and happier by acquiring some of
the other's attributes. Linda recognizes the value of redirecting her life toward what she really wants, and when a handsome, open-minded helicopter
pilot falls unexpectedly from the sky into her life, she is prepared to take advantage of the opportunity to create a loving, secure life.

Like other of Allen's little-man characters dating back to *Bananas* and
Sleeper and extending through *Manhattan Murder Mystery*, Lenny becomes
stronger and more attractive to the woman he loves after events compel him
to act courageously. When Linda tells him that Ricky, her pimp, plans to kill
them both if she quits prostitution, Lenny rises to the occasion. Instead of
playing it safe by scuttling his attempt to rescue her from a dead-end life,
Lenny uncharacteristically risks his safety by standing up for Linda. Although Ricky threatens and intimidates him, Lenny persists in making his

case for her freedom. He becomes more self-assured when the conversation turns to basketball, and he begins to converse with Ricky as an equal instead of as a potential victim. Once he thus regains his self-confidence, he is able to forge an acceptable resolution to the problem. Noting Ricky's desire for difficult-to-acquire Knicks tickets, he trades prime seats for Linda's release. Thus, by combining Linda's self-acceptance with his own intelligence, quick-wittedness, and creativity, Lenny fills the role of mythic hero by freeing Linda from her pimp and enabling her to create a more fulfilling life for herself.

In deference to his marriage vows, Lenny had hitherto resisted all possibilities for sex with Linda. But after Amanda tells him she wants to separate, he comes to Linda for solace. She has just been beaten by Kevin, who has learned about her and Lenny's deception, and they comfort one another by making love. But if Linda later benefits from a literal *deus ex machina* when her helicopter pilot, a "god from the machine," drops from the sky, accepts her for who she is, and changes her life, Lenny enjoys an equally miraculous development when Amanda, on the verge of being seduced by her benefactor, suddenly realizes that she really loves Lenny. They reconcile, and Lenny never returns to see Linda, who, unbeknown to him, is pregnant with his child.

The film thus concludes happily but with irony appropriate to Greek tragedy. Much later Lenny encounters Linda in a toy store where they have come to shop for their children. Both are happily married, and each admires the other's child. Linda never learns that she is Max's mother, nor does Lenny discover that he is the father of Linda's baby. Presumably both go on to live happily ever after.

But the *deus ex machina* ending, a plot device deplored by Aristotle because it is improbable, undermines the credibility of the cheerful conclusion. At the same time, it reasserts the irrational nature of an absurd universe. The story's incredible resolution also contributes to the film's uplifting comic energy, even as it underscores the dearth of truly compelling evidence that love and passion can be sustained for an extended time. The absence of such evidence, Allen suggests, is a fundamental human tragedy.

Thus Allen gives us a happy ending but snatches away any rational basis we might have for believing it. However, just as intelligent children can sometimes spring from stupid parents, unlikely turns of good fortune can arise at unpredictable times. Precisely because the absurd universe is irrational, the opportunity for genuine *deus ex machina* endings and the possibility of lasting love always remain.

Modernist Worldview. Throughout his career Allen has expressed a view of reality that is shared by modernist and postmodernist writers, artists, and even scientists. The modernist vision is most readily apparent in his films *Stardust Memories* and *Deconstructing Harry*, his one-act play *God*, and his fiction. Nonetheless, his belief that human desire and behavior are paradoxical and irrational, experience is relative, and the universe is absurd and incompletely knowable informs virtually all of his work. For Allen and many other modernist writers and artists, the paramount problem thus becomes discovering how any person can live a meaningful, fulfilling, vigorous, ethical existence predicated on some notion of proper action in such an atheistic, unknowable, relativistic, irrational world.

As opposed to the Newtonian-influenced worldview embodied by the literary realism of the late eighteenth and nineteenth centuries, the modernist worldview perceives reality with a greater sense of ambiguity, paradox, and uncertainty and a reduced sense of causation and reason. It is concerned with both external, material reality and internal, psychological reality, which is paradoxical, nonlinear, and nonchronological, and works through associations rather than causation. The modernist outlook replaces the single, objective point of view found in both classical tragedy and the realist's omniscient narrator, employing a relativistic viewpoint in its stead.

Modernist literature thus frequently employs multiple narrators; modern art superimposes different perspectives of the same subject onto one another; modern physics orients itself around a theory of relativity that rejects absolute frames of reference other than the speed of light. In these examples, the nature of reality depends upon the perspective of the viewer; therefore, reality is necessarily subjective to some degree. Moreover, whereas in classical tragedy and literary realism objective facts exist and they are almost always ultimately knowable, in the modernist vision this is not so. To the modernist there exist limits to what we can know with certainty, and even the existence of simple facts is problematic. In the modernist outlook, facts do not exist independent of the observer or the person who communicates them. Ontology and epistemology intermingle and become finally indistinguishable.

In the twentieth century, for the first time since the Renaissance, Western thought acknowledges that empiricism has real boundaries and that limits on human knowledge exist. In the modernist gestalt, empiricism, causation, and logic are restricted not only in the "softer" disciplines—the humanities and social sciences, but even in the "hardest" of disciplines—physics and mathematics. The modernist view yields quantum mechanics and relativity theories along with chaos theory. Here space and time are discontiguous, fragmented, and warped; parallel lines intersect; order systematically degenerates into chaos; and chaos conversely regenerates into order. Modernist science and mathematics are important to the study of Allen because they inform his absurd view of life and root that view in physical reality.[1]

By definition, we cannot become any more concrete or any less abstract than when we describe physical reality. Thus, when Allen and other modernist writers and artists depict reality as paradoxical, relativistic, inconsistent, incompletely knowable, fragmented, and dependent on the observer for its completion, they are not acting arbitrarily or capriciously. Quite the opposite, they embody a vision that applies to the most objective aspect of reality that we can identify: the physical world.

In the modernist vision, the Enlightenment promise of a rational, predictable, coherent universe gives way to a less rational, if not altogether irrational, vision of reality in which logic ultimately turns on itself, creating paradoxes and contractions. By the time quantum mechanics was completed in the 1920s, Freud had already declared that humans are fundamentally irrational beings subject to powerful primal, often contradictory impulses from the unconscious, including simultaneous impulses toward creation and destruction and the ability to love and hate simultaneously. Thus, in the modernist worldview dualistic, either-or propositions give way to understandings about how reality can be both-and-neither at the same time.[2]

The modernist vision has informed much of the twentieth century's music, visual art, and other disciplines, in addition to the narrative arts: literature, theater, and film. By superimposing several views of the model, Picasso paints his subject through a cubist vision that simultaneously acknowledges all of the possible perspectives by which the model can be seen. Even the painter's individual viewpoint loses absolute authority. In *Nude Descending a Staircase* (1911), Marcel Duchamp "unfreezes" his subject in time, showing multiple images of the naked woman walking down the stairs. From his perspective, people, objects, and events occur in space-time, not simply in space. Thus, the multiple nudes incorporate time into the fabric of the space-bound canvas and complete his vision of the subject. This viewpoint deliberately contradicts the one John Keats expresses in "Ode on a Grecian Urn" (1819), where the poet praises art for being static, unchanging, outside of time, and insulated from temporal events. And as in quantum physics, where the nature of the observation determines whether subatomic particles will appear as matter or energy, conceptual art and interactive art since the 1960s require the viewers to complete the artwork in each individual's mind or to participate physically in the process of its creation. Here again, the observer becomes inseparable from the event. In a very literal sense, Picasso, Duchamp, and others who rendered the modernist vision in artistic representations are the realists of our century, even as Rembrandt was a consummate realist of the late Renaissance. Each artist embodies the paradigm of his time.

Likewise, in "Pierre Menard, The Man Who Wrote the *Quixote*," (1941) Jorge Luis Borges examines how language and literature exists in space-time. Borges's character, Menard, is a nineteenth-century French symbolist who creates, through acts of original imagination, passages that are word-for-word identical to Cervantes's *Don Quixote*. However, according to Borges's narrator, Menard's novel is superior because, when read as products of a late nineteenth-century mind, the identical words acquire new and richer meanings. Thus, for example, when Cervantes calls history "the Mother of Truth," he offers mere rhetorical praise, but when Menard writes these same words, "The idea is astounding. Menard a contemporary of William James, does not define history as an inquiry into reality but as its origin. Historical truth, for him, is not what has happened; it is what we judge to have happened" (Borges 43). Part of the effect of Borges's story is to show that language also exists in space-time, that words and sentences are affected by time.

In modernist music, traditional ideas of harmony and tonality lose their authority, giving rise not only to new musical forms, but to new understandings of what music is. Like Georg Cantor investigating the foundations of mathematics, physicists concerned with the characteristics of subatomic particles, and artists concerned with color, texture, and basic geometric shapes, many twentieth-century composers have turned to the fundamental components of their art form, exploring basic properties of sound and silence instead of, or in conjunction with, writing melodies or developing harmonies and themes.

In similar ways many modernist writers explore fundamental properties of language itself, sometimes at the expense of plot, character development, and even denotative meaning. Thus, for example, James Joyce dismantles and reassembles language in his most dada-like work, *Finnegan's Wake*; Virginia Woolf seeks to recreate the rhythm of the waves in *The Waves*; and Faulkner layers his sentences over each other like a painter applying *impasto* in *Absalom, Absalom!* Though not as extreme as the World War I–era dadaists, who subordinated concepts and meaning to language's more visceral properties of sound and rhythm, these writers nonetheless explored the basic properties of language and brought them to the forefront of their work.

Sigmund Freud, working during roughly the same period that Cantor, Einstein, Paul Cézanne, Picasso, Duchamp, and Arnold Schoenberg were active, recognized that the human unconscious works associatively instead of logically and that our various neuroses shape our experience of reality. Consistent with the modernist viewpoint, Freud's work implies that all human experiences of reality are interpreted; no one experiences reality in a totally objective fashion. It also shows that as observers, we complete the event, at least in our own experience of it. Freud's work also treats time non-linearly, showing that long-forgotten events from the past can impinge directly on present events: thus in a very real sense, the past and present paradoxically coexist within the present. The past does not cease to be real once it has lapsed in time.

T. S. Eliot expresses the same sentiment in "Burnt Norton" (1934), where he speculates that the present and past coexist within the future, and that the past already contains the future. Eliot finally concludes that time becomes "unredeemable" if it exists solely in an eternal, ongoing present (such as it appears to exist in the consciousness of animals and in the "postmodern" treatment of time).

When turned on narrative fiction, the modernist lens provides the perspective shared by Joyce, Woolf, Faulkner, John Dos Passos, Ralph Ellison, Thomas Pynchon, and John Barth, to name a few. These writers abandon traditional cause-effect plot structures. They experiment with point of view, frequently eliminating the authoritative third person and objective and/or omniscient narrator (a privileged viewpoint that does not exist in the world of relativity theory); they blur the distinctions between facts and fictions, creating worlds where characters and readers alike operate in a state of uncertainty; they require readers to piece things together for themselves, or to make no connections at all, thereby making the reader, like all other observers, an integral part of the event. These writers frequently violate traditional narrative conventions because those conventions are inadequate for presenting a modernist vision. We should recognize that many of the violated conventions are products of the outmoded objectivist paradigm, and they embody objectivist assumptions about reality, such as a causally motivated plot structure or an omniscient, third-person narrator.

The modernist authors, and such modernist filmmakers as Orson Welles, Federico Fellini, Jean-Luc Godard, Quentin Tarantino, and Allen are describing the world they see through a modernist lens, which refracts space, time, causation, knowledge, and communication differently than the objectivist lens. Unlike their realist predecessors, the modernists recognize that everyone perceives existence through lenses of some kind and that all lenses refract. They know, therefore, that a purely objective and direct experience of external events is unavailable to human beings, if such an experience can even be said to exist at all.

Finally, in the modernist worldview if God exists, He (or She) remains aloof from human affairs and hidden from sight. Consequently, no code of ethics is "God given," and all notions of morality are necessary human constructs that are inherently subjective, inconsistent, and paradoxical.

In his 1967 essay "The Literature of Exhaustion," John Barth claims that today's writers must find new ways to address this modernist worldview and the unique problems it engenders—the "felt ultimacies" of our time. Foremost among these problems is the despair that accompanies the belief that nothing we humans do has any meaning.

Barth argues that today's storytellers must create new literary forms that are not only appropriate to our culture and our experience of reality, but that also communicate something of real worth and feeling; they must be more than detached, formal abstraction. As Barth's Scheherazade maintains elsewhere, "Heartfelt ineptitude has its appeal . . . so does heartless skill. But what you want is passionate virtuosity" (*Chimera* 24). Or as Barth's narrator declares in "Title," as he struggles to find a subject for his story:

> The fact is that people still lead lives, mean and bleak and brief as they are, briefer than you think, and people have characters and motives that we divine more or less inaccurately from their appearance, speech, behavior, and the rest. . . . People still fall in love, and out, yes, in and out, and out and in . . . and what goes on between them is still not only the most interesting but the most important thing in the bloody murderous world. . . . And that my dear is what writers have got to find ways to write about. (*Lost in the Funhouse* 113)

NOTES

1. Allen's awareness of the implications of modern science is directly apparent in *A Midsummer Night's Sex Comedy*, a turn-of-the-century period piece in which Andrew challenges Leopold's claim that there is no unseen world by citing the then newly discovered cosmic rays (radium). And in *Shadows and Fog* and the play *Death*, on which the film is based, Kleinman becomes unsettled when a prostitute he encounters undermines his ability to distinguish reality from illusion, up from down. She points out that the earth is floating through outer space and we cannot "tell which way is up" and that the stars he is watching may not even still be there, even though he sees them with his own eyes. Kleinman complains, "That's very scary, because if I see something with my own eyes, I like to think it's there."

2. The Doppler effect provides a common experience of contradictory but co-existing truths. A person standing on the sidewalk, listening to a car blaring its horn, will hear the sound wail. The horn's pitch will rise as the car approaches. The pitch will then lower as the car passes by. Measurements taken at the sidewalk would confirm that the frequency of the sound waves increased as the car approached and diminished as it drove away. But measurements taken inside the car would show no variation in the frequency. The horn would blare at a steady pitch for the driver and would not wail. This is because, relative to the driver, the horn is stationary, and so all of the sound waves propagate at the same frequency. But relative to the pedestrian, the horn is moving, and the velocity of that motion increases the frequency of the waves as the car approaches and lessens the fre-

quency as the car leaves. Thus we can see that even a question of basic, physical, measurable fact—did the horn wail or not?—depends on the circumstances of the observation.

My Favorite Comedian. A 1979 film directed by Allen. Allen compiled the sixty-two-minute selection of scenes from Bob Hope movies for a fund raiser for the Lincoln Center's Film Society, which was honoring Hope. *My Favorite Comedian* was also shown at the New York Film Festival that fall. Allen reviewed Hope's work extensively for the project and later commented, "I had more pleasure looking at Hope's films than making any film I've ever made" (Fox 116).

Allen's admiration for Hope appears in his other films too. In *Broadway Danny Rose*, Danny declares, "If it's old-fashioned to like Mr. Danny Kaye, Mr. Bob Hope, or Mr. Milton Berle, then I'm old-fashioned!" And in *Manhattan Murder Mystery* Allen pays additional tribute to Hope by showing Larry's keen desire to catch a Bob Hope movie on television.

N

New York Stories. A 1989 trilogy of short films: Martin Scorsese's *Life Class*, Francis Ford Coppola's *Life Without Zoe*, and Allen's *Oedipus Wrecks*. All are set in New York. Allen suggested the anthology as a venue for short story ideas he did not wish to expand into full-length movies. He admired similar compilations from earlier cinema and wanted to revive the format. He originally favored sharing the screen with European directors, but producer Robert Greenhut convinced him to make the trilogy with other Americans, who were more commercially viable. Scorsese and Steven Spielberg were the initial choices, but Coppola was added after scheduling conflicts with *Who Killed Roger Rabbit?* forced Spielberg to drop out.

Despite the high-profile directors, the film was a financial failure. It cost approximately $19 million to produce (of which *Oedipus Wrecks* cost $6 million) but grossed only $10.8 million in U.S. and Canadian distribution and netted only $4.7 million. *New York Stories* fared better critically. *Oedipus Wrecks* won the greatest praise of all, and it received some of Allen's best reviews ever.

See also *Oedipus Wrecks*.

Nykvist, Sven. A Swedish cinematographer who was director of photography for *Another Woman*, *Oedipus Wrecks*, *Crimes and Misdemeanors*, and *Celebrity*. Born in 1922, Nykvist is also known for his work with Ingmar Bergman, for whom he filmed *Sawdust and Tinsel* (1953), *The Virgin Spring* (1959), *Winter Light* (1962), *The Silence* (1963), *Persona* (1966), *The Hour of the Wolf* (1967), *The Shame* (1968), *Cries and Whispers* (1972), *Scenes from a Marriage* (1974), and *Fanny and Alexander* (1982).

Allen has expressed great admiration for all three major cinematographers he has worked with. Whereas Gordon Willis, Allen's first major director of photographer, is primarily concerned with framing each shot, Nykvist is more concerned with the actors. According to Eric Lax, he likes to frame the actors tightly and illuminate their faces close together in a style the cinematographer calls "two faces in a teacup" (Lax 328). According to Allen, he likes to keep the camera in motion but not as much as Carlo Di Palma (Lax 329).

O

Oedipus Wrecks. A 1989 short film directed by, written by, and starring Allen, who plays Sheldon Mills, a lawyer. It appears as part of a trilogy entitled *New York Stories*, which also features short films by Martin Scorsese and Francis Ford Coppola. *Oedipus Wrecks* costars Mia Farrow (Lisa), Julie Kavner (Treva), Mae Questel (Sheldon's mother, Sadie Millstein), George Schindler (Shandu the Magician), Marvin Chatnover (psychiatrist), Paul Herman (Detective Flynn), Andrew MacMillan (newscaster), Ira Wheeler (Mr. Bates), Molly Regan (Sheldon's secretary), Jessie Keosian (Aunt Ceil), Bridget Ryan (Rita), and Mayor Ed Koch as himself. Robert Greenhut was the producer, Sven Nykvist director of photography, Santo Loquasto production designer, Jeffrey Kurland costumer, and Susan E. Morse editor. Touchstone-Buena Vista was the North American distributor.

Oedipus Wrecks, which runs forty-one minutes, is the final tale in *New York Stories*; the other two are Scorsese's *Life Class* and Coppola's *Life Without Zoe*. *New York Stories* met with some critical success, and *Oedipus Wrecks* was especially singled out for high praise; it received some of Allen's best reviews ever. Allen found the technical problems troublesome while he was filming it, but he was "quite happy" with how his segment came out. "But then forty minutes is a very *controllable* length" (Fox 199; Allen's emphasis). While filming *Oedipus Wrecks*, Allen predicted it would resonate and become "the *Gone With the Wind* of Israel" (Lax 249). Nonetheless, the trilogy was a significant money loser. It cost $19 million to produce (of which *Oedipus Wrecks* cost $6 million) but grossed only $10.8 million in U.S. and Canadian distribution and netted only $4.7 million. (See *New York Stories.*)

Allen claims that the idea for *Oedipus Wrecks* originated while he was staring out into the sky, listening to a record by the late jazz artist Sidney Bechet. "I thought to myself, 'Gee, I miss him so much. It would be so dramatic and so fantastic, if I could see a huge figure of him playing up there. . . . ' That image stuck with me. And I thought, 'Wouldn't it be funny, if it was my mother, and she would be such a nag' " (*Woody Allen on Woody Allen* 203). In the original version, Sadie was going to intrude in everyone's lives, and New Yorkers would turn on her and finally appreciate the daily torment her son, Sheldon, endures. But Allen preferred his revised plot in which she meddles only in Sheldon's life.

Allen denies that Sadie is based on his own mother or on any other specific person, not even necessarily on Jewish mothers. He notes that many other ethnic groups also feature aggressive, overbearing mothers, whose behavior he believes is "motivated from genuine affection—a deep love really" (Fox 199). Sadie is played by Mae Questel, who also sings in *Zelig*. Decades earlier, she provided the voice for such animated characters as Betty Boop and Popeye's Olive. "The second I saw her, the second she read, she was right on the nose. She couldn't be better. She even looks like my mother" (*Woody Allen on Woody Allen* 205). During the shooting Allen encouraged Questel to supplement his script with improvised nagging of her own (Fox 199). Jesse Keosian, who plays Aunt Ceil, had been Allen's high school biology teacher. She was cast after answering an advertisement calling for older women to act in small movie parts.

The plot centers around Sheldon Mills, a successful fifty-year-old lawyer whose mother still controls his life. Demanding, overbearing, and completely insensitive to the humiliation she routinely causes her son, Sadie Millstein continually points out his past and present shortcomings and criticizes his choices. Sadie's behavior smothers Sheldon, who wishes her no harm but would like to see her disappear from his life. When she does in fact vanish without a trace during a magic show act, Sheldon is first distressed. But after about a week he begins to flourish. He is at peace for the first time; even his fiancée, Lisa, finds his lovemaking more relaxed and uninhibited.

However, Sheldon's new-found tranquility is short-lived, as Sadie's image suddenly dominates the sky over New York City, where she remains for weeks. Looking down from above, she comments publicly on every aspect of Sheldon's life, telling the whole world how he wet his bed as a child, criticizing him for changing his surname to one less Jewish sounding, and expressing her disapproval of his plan to marry Lisa, a Christian. As Maurice Yacowar notes, "Mrs. Millstein's apparition over the Chrysler Building embodies the guilt of the assimilated" (Yacowar, *Loser Take All* 273).

Introduced by the song "I Want a Girl Just Like the Girl Who Married Dear Old Dad," *Oedipus Wrecks* validates the Oedipus myth even as it spoofs it. Unbeknown even to himself, Sheldon adores his mother and desires a mate just like her. *Oedipus Wrecks* is the story of this realization. Like Oedipus, Sheldon deliberately starts out on a path that will lead him away from his parents: he changes his name, joins a gentile law firm, and dates Christian women. But like Oedipus, Sheldon discovers that there is no escaping his heritage and that he will be better off embracing it.

Like Sophocles' *Oedipus Rex*, which it parodies, *Oedipus Wrecks* relies on a central plot reversal, and it climaxes when the protagonist experiences a sudden insight about himself. But whereas Oedipus's fortune seems promising before it suddenly collapses, Sheldon's initially appears dismal until a piece of boiled chicken dripping with congealed fat sparks the necessary recognition, and his cruel fate reverses.

Specifically, Sheldon recognizes that he values Jewish culture (and cooking) and that deep down he really wants a wife who is like his mother. In the process of arriving at these insights, he learns to accept himself more fully. And it is Sadie who furnishes the lesson by taking to the sky. By making herself larger than life and then broadcasting her son's most embarrassing moments to the world, Sadie forces Sheldon to claim her and the other things he is ashamed of. He can no longer pretend not to be her son or not to be Jewish, as he had by changing his name and disassociating himself from his ethnic background. Eventually Sheldon learns to live with his embarrassments, and this enables him finally to accept them; they are simply too public for him to do otherwise. As Sander H. Lee observes, "The primary conflict between Sheldon and Sadie is her contention that Sheldon is turning back on his heritage. All of her complaints are attempts to force Sheldon to face up to the facts about himself, to accept the role he's inherited by virtue of his background and ethnicity" (Lee 250). Lee further observes that Treva too becomes fully realized only when she abandons all of her false guises and accepts herself as the Jewish woman she is (Lee 252).

Thus, if Sadie's projection into the sky manifests Sheldon's worst nightmare, as she announces every intimate detail about him to the world, it also sets in motion the chain of events that eventually brings Sheldon greater happiness through greater self-acceptance. His public humiliation frees Sheldon from a relationship with a woman who is somewhat self-centered and not fully committed to him. Moreover, Sadie's apparition leads Sheldon to Treva, a carbon copy of his mother who adores Sheldon and wants to nurture him. Treva's first words to Sadie are, "I love your son." Thus, as in Greek tragedy, Sheldon's path to self-knowledge passes through self-deception, and his humiliation facilitates growth.

In the end Sheldon both accepts his Jewish heritage and opens himself to receiving love as he learns to accept himself. Like the protagonists in *Manhattan* and *Stardust Memories*, he finds happiness when he finally seeks out a woman who will shower love on him.

P

Play It Again, Sam. A 1969 play written by and starring Allen and a 1972 film written by and starring Allen. Joseph Hardy directed the original Broadway production, and David Merrick produced it. The cast included Allen (Allan Felix), Dianne Keaton (Linda), Tony Roberts (Dick), Jerry Lacy (Bogart), and Sheila Sullivan (Nancy). Dudley Moore played the role of Allan Felix in the London production. In the film adaptation, Allen, Keaton, Roberts, and Lacy revived their roles from Broadway, and Susan Anspach played Nancy. Herbert Ross directed; Arthur P. Jacobs was the producer; Owen Roizman director of photography, Ed Wittstein production designer, Anna Hill Johnstone costumer, and Marion Rothman editor. Paramount was the North American distributor.

Play It Again, Sam played an important role in Allen's career in several ways. His second successful Broadway play as a writer—it enjoyed 453 performances between February 12, 1969, and March 14, 1970—*Play It Again, Sam* enabled Allen to develop his acting skills before a live audience. It was also another sizable financial success for Allen as a movie writer-actor. The film cost approximately $1.3 million to produce and grossed $5.8 million in U.S. and Canadian distribution (not including later video rentals and television revenues). It went on to be a hit overseas as well. But *Play It Again, Sam* had an even greater impact on Allen's career than the new opportunities that resulted from his financial and artistic achievements. The Broadway production brought Allen together with Diane Keaton, who became not only his lover for a year, but also his collaborator, inspiration, and confidant throughout much of his career. (See also **Diane Keaton**.)

Like much of Allen's work, *Play It Again, Sam* conflates fiction and reality. The story centers around the efforts of film reviewer Allan Felix to recover from his recent divorce, meet new women, and establish a new relationship. His married friends Dick and Linda try to assist him. But Felix also takes advice from his fantasy world in which Humphrey Bogart appears to him and tells him how to handle women: "I never met one that didn't understand a slap in the mouth or a slug from a .45." Bogart is everything Felix is not: cynical, self-possessed, hard-drinking, worldly, and a love-them-and-leave-them ladies' man. Felix, on the other hand, is fundamentally incompetent and insecure.

The physical, emotional, and other personal disparities between the men become the basis for much of the humor, since whenever Felix tries to act in Bogart's self-assured manner, he fails utterly and looks ridiculous in the process. As Sam Girgus points out in *The Films of Woody Allen*, the film's opening sequence draws Felix into Bogart's world and causes us to identify him with Bogart by cutting among Felix, Bogart, and Ingrid Bergman as Felix sits in the theater watching the ending of *Casablanca*. (The play begins with Felix watching the end of *The Maltese Falcon*.)

Bogart's film persona was famous for being paradoxically double-sided: cynical but noble, jaded but romantic. The story's basic premise and its basic system of values stem from the fact that Felix admires and tries to emulate Bogart's animus—his tough, controlling side—when Felix's innate character is actually like Bogart's caring, self-sacrificing anima. The story thus climaxes when Felix accepts his own altruistic side and acts on it. As Bogart tells him, "When you weren't coming on phony, you got a pretty good dame to fall for you."

In the final scene, Felix's identification with Bogart, which had been comically ludicrous at the beginning of story, becomes legitimate and complete. Allen merges the two characters by having Felix deliver verbatim Bogart's speech from *Casablanca* when Rick sends the woman he loves off with her husband. As he says the lines, Felix is simultaneously both straight and ironic. He means every word of it seriously, they express his true sentiments exactly. At the same time, he realizes he is quoting Bogart, and he loves it. "I waited my whole life to say it." But the identification is real because Felix copies Bogart's actions as well as his words. As Bogart tells him, "You're passing up a real tomato because you didn't want to hurt a guy." In the course of events, Felix has learned, "There's other things in life beside dames, and one of them is to know you did the right thing for a pal."

Cinematically, *Play It Again, Sam* demonstrates Allen's growth as a filmmaker. Although he did not participate significantly in the movie's direction, his script provided its basic vision, and that vision is more expressionistic than anything he had done previously as a movie writer or a director. In particular, Allen reveals Felix's imaginary world as well as his real one. The intermingling of these levels of reality is another primary source of humor—one that Allen comes back to in several of his films. Not only are Felix's imaginary conversations with Bogart and with his ex-wife, Nancy, depicted on screen, so too are the several scenarios Felix conjures when he anticipates telling Dick that he's had an affair with Linda or telling Linda that Dick needs her and she must go back to him. Each fantasy derives humor by interjecting Felix into a film cliché from the 1940s or thereabouts.

Thus Allen pays homage to the films he grew up with and admired as a child; at the same time he reveals the extent to which Felix's imagination and his perceptions of reality suffer from those early movies. Ultimately Felix must recognize that cinema and reality are different, and that the ideals and codes of conduct the movies present may in fact be inappropriate in a nonfictional context. And though *Play It Again, Sam* has been criticized for its superficial treatment of women, most of whom are purely sex objects, it nonetheless finally rejects Bogart's dominating, insensitive treatment of "dames." The "real" Bogart proves to be the noble, caring, sentimental one. And Felix experiences his finest moment and his greatest personal growth when he becomes attuned to his feminine side, his anima, and acts in a nurturing, self-sacrificing fashion.

See also **Humphrey Bogart**; **Little-Man Humor.**

Plays. Allen's work first appeared on Broadway as part of an unsuccessful two-act revue entitled *From A to Z* (1960). He contributed two sketches, "Hit Parade" and "Psychological Warfare." Since then, he has written four plays that have been performed successfully on Broadway: *Don't Drink the Water* (1966), *Play It Again, Sam* (1969), *The Floating Light Bulb* (1981), and *Central Park West* (1995). He has published five additional one-act plays.

Central Park West is a one-act play that appears in *Death Defying Acts*, a trilogy by Allen, Elaine May, and David Mamet. Allen's other one-act plays are *Death Knocks* (1968), *Death: A Play* (1975), *God: A Play* (1975), *The Query* (1976), and *My Apology* (1980). *Death Knocks* was first published in the *New Yorker* (July 27, 1968) and reprinted in *Getting Even*. *The Query* first appeared in the *New Republic* (September 18, 1976) and was reprinted in *Side Effects*, where *My Apology* was first published. *God* and *Death* first appeared in *Without Feathers*; *God* was subsequently performed by the National Radio Theater of Chicago, featuring Tony Roberts and Allen's voice. BBC Radio 3 later presented both plays as radio dramas. Allen claims to have written a sixth one-act play, entitled *Sex*, as part of a trilogy with *Death* and *God*; however, it has never been published (*Woody Allen on Woody Allen* 234).

John Lahr's *The Bluebird of Unhappiness* (1987) dramatizes *Death Knocks*, *My Apology*, and Allen's short stories "Mr. Big," which appears in *Without Feathers*, and "The Kugelmass Episode," which appears in *Side Effects*. In 1990, Afterthought Productions presented an adaptation of *Getting Even* at the Edinburgh Festival.

See also **Central Park West**; **Don't Drink the Water**; **The Floating Light Bulb**; **From A to Z**; **Getting Even**; **Play It Again, Sam**; **Side Effects**; **Without Feathers**.

The Politics of Woody Allen. See **Men in Crisis: The Harvey Wallinger Story.**

The Purple Rose of Cairo. A 1985 film directed and written by Allen. It stars Mia Farrow (Cecilia), Jeff Daniels (Tom Baxter, Gil Shepherd), Danny Aiello (Monk), Dianne Wiest (Emma), Zoe Caldwell (countess), Irving Metzman (theater manager), Van Johnson (Larry), Deborah Rush (Rita), John Wood (Jason), Karen Akers (Kitty Haynes), Milo O'Shea (Father Donnelly), Alexander Cohen (Raoul Hirsch), Eugene Anthony (Arturo, the maître d'), Stephanie Farrow (Cecilia's sister), and Michael Tucker (Gil's agent). Michael Keaton was originally cast in the Gil Shepherd/Tom Baxter role, but he was replaced after Allen found him "too contemporary" for the part. Robert Greenhut was the producer, Gordon Willis director of photography, Stuart Wurtzel production designer, Jeffrey Kurland costume designer, and Susan Morse editor. Music director Dick Hyman wrote original music; also included are "Cheek to Cheek," "I Love My Baby, My Baby Loves Me," and "Alabamy Bound." Orion Pictures was the North American distributor.

One of Allen's personal favorites, *The Purple Rose of Cairo* received strong critical endorsements from Vincent Canby, Rex Reed, and Pauline Kael. Nonetheless, it was Allen's first significant financial failure as writer-director. It cost $13 million to produce and grossed $5.1 million in U.S. and Canadian revenues (not including later video rentals and television revenues). The film fared better financially in Europe, especially Great Britain and France. Allen received a Golden Globe award and an Academy Award nomination for the screenplay, and *Purple Rose* won the BAFTA Award for Best Film and Screenplay. The London's Critics' Circle named it Best Foreign Film, and in France, where it also won major awards, the movie created a sensation at the Cannes Film Festival.

Allen has attributed the film's lack of success in North America, along with that of *Zelig* and *Radio Days* from the same era, to its failure to fit easily into a marketing strategy; it is neither an art film nor a commercial movie. Julian Fox suggests that the film's bleak sensibility, muted colors, and unhappy ending also contributed to its poor financial showing, as did Allen's absence on screen (Fox 155). When asked if he also filmed a happy ending, Allen replied that this *is* the happy ending (Spignesi 191). Nonetheless, for Allen *The Purple Rose of Cairo* was "the closest I've come to a feeling of satisfaction. After that film I thought, 'Yes, this time I think I got it right where I wanted to get it'" (*Woody Allen on Woody Allen* 116).

Set during the Great Depression in a small New Jersey town, *The Purple Rose of Cairo* is Allen's most fully developed metafiction—a story about a story. The plot centers on Cecilia, a waitress married to an abusive, unemployed factory worker, and on Tom Baxter, a character in a black-and-white 1930s movie about high society entitled *The Purple Rose of Cairo*. Obsessed with Hollywood, Cecilia escapes from her unhappy and impoverished existence by going to the cinema whenever possible. When, after catching her husband with another woman, Cecilia retreats into the theater for multiple screenings of *The Purple Rose*, she is noticed by the on-screen romantic character, Tom Baxter. Whether, as Stephen Spignesi suggests, it is because Cecilia has willed him into her life, or whether his immense desire for freedom and his strong emotional attraction to her also empower him, Tom succeeds in stepping down from the silver screen and into the theater, the real world where he now exists in color. He approaches Cecilia and convinces her to run away with him. She does, and they fall in love.

The plot turns when Gil Shepard, the actor who played Tom, comes to town to convince Tom to return to the screen. Gil meets and woos Cecilia, who must choose between the real-life actor and his fictional character. Whereas Tom is literally incapable of deception or insincerity, Gil romances Cecilia solely to send Tom back to the movie. Thus, the film concludes sadly when Cecilia chooses life in the real world over Tom's perfect, elegant movie world—and Gil immediately betrays her.

Although Cecilia's experiences are extraordinary, she does not change much because of them, and her life emphatically stays the same as it was at the beginning. The film ends after Gil abandons Cecilia, and she takes solace once more by going to the movies. Though initially heartbroken, by the final shot she is completely absorbed in the romance on screen as she watches Fred Astaire court Ginger Rogers by singing and dancing "Cheek to Cheek." In short, Cecilia copes in the same way she always has—not by seriously confronting her problems and figuring out a viable strategy for improving her situation, but by retreating into a fantasy world.

Certainly the constraints of the Depression and the fact that Cecilia is a woman with no apparent skills limit her opportunities for creating a better life. But Cecilia's despair and low self-esteem are even more limiting. Before she meets Tom, she has surrendered to despair. She perceives herself as powerless and thus literally cannot imagine herself taking control of her life. Cecilia tolerates her husband's abuse, and she appears sincere when she tells Tom that she is "nothing."

Rather than think about how to free herself from an untenable life, Cecilia creates an existence built around escapism. By focusing all of her imaginative efforts on Hollywood instead of herself, she chooses to defer her problems rather than resolve them. Thus, although her escapism comforts her in the short run, in the long run it condemns her to remain in her miserable existence.

However, because life is never entirely predictable, the possibility of radical, unimaginable change always exists, however remote. When Tom exceeds Cecilia's imagination and leaves the screen to enter her life, he makes her feel loved and important. In turn, Cecilia's increased self-esteem energizes her imagination and leads her to stand up for herself. For the first time she entertains the possibility of a better life, and she tries to realize it by embracing love when she finds it. Exercising strength of character we have not seen before, Cecilia remains with Tom after Monk beats him, and she openly defies Monk by running away with Gil. These acts require courage and self-confidence, and they enable Cecilia to try to seize control of her life. She tells Monk as she leaves him, "I got a chance to change my life . . . [because] out of the blue, for the first time in my life, someone's in love with me."

But Cecilia's efforts are doomed by her idealized and unrealistic view of Hollywood and movie stars. Gil's love proves to be a Hollywood-inspired illusion, and he leaves town without her after he has promised to take her away. Cecilia possesses the determination, self-confidence, and openness to love necessary for transforming her life. But without Gil or Tom, she loses both the confidence and inner strength she needs to forge her destiny alone. The final shot of Cecilia lost in the world of Fred and Ginger suggests that she has reverted to her former despair. She is defeated, and when the movie is over, she will go back to Monk and return to life as before, where she risks going on the same way until they are "too old to even hope for something better."

Our only source of optimism for Cecilia is the unlikely but nonetheless extant possibility that some more sincere, nonfictional man will unexpectedly come along to love her and reenergize her belief in herself. After all, if Tom Baxter can step down from the screen, anything is possible.[1] If a new man does come and she has not yet become too hard and bitter, Cecilia has demonstrated her willingness and ability to embrace happiness. But like

Aunt Bea in *Radio Days*, she has not shown the capacity to take charge of her life in the absence of love.

If Cecilia suffers from a limited imagination, Allen does not. Following a tradition of metafiction dating back at least to Luigi Pirandello's *Six Characters in Search of an Author* (1921), *The Purple Rose of Cairo* presents reality as layered. Allen generates humor and raises some philosophical questions by having those layers intersect and intermingle. He uses this technique to similar effect in his 1975 play, *God*, in which a female audience member—a fictional character in *God* but an "outside," "real" person in respect to the play within the play—goes onstage and interacts with the characters from the play within the play but without assuming a role. The character who plays the writer wants to sleep with her, but the character who plays the actor complains that their levels of reality are incompatible: "You idiot, you're fictional, she's Jewish—you know what the children will be like."

Tom's intrusion into Cecilia's real world and, later, Cecilia's intrusion into his movie world create complications that are both entertaining and thought provoking. The audience members are outraged because instead of the story they paid for, they must watch the remaining characters sit around without a script and talk aimlessly on-screen. "There's no story," complains a man accompanying an elderly woman. "Mrs. Lupas likes a story." Another woman feels cheated because she has been denied the consistency she expects from art and cinema. "I want what happened in the movie last week to happen this week. Otherwise, what's life about anyway?" Others speculate that communists or anarchists are somehow behind Tom's action. One man suggests turning off the projector, but another fears this will leave Tom stranded out in the real world, with no way of getting back inside the movie. "You don't want an extra guy running around." The lawyers seek a quick resolution, lest hundreds of Tom Baxters wander loose throughout the country, each a slew of potential lawsuits. The producer advocates destroying all copies of the film, as well as the original print and negative: a final solution that will not only destroy the miscreant Tom Baxter but also wipe out his kind and their entire universe.

The on-screen characters also react strongly to their new circumstances. One character suggests changing the definitions, so their world is the real world and the outside world is illusory. Another character wants to join Tom, but most prefer their lives to those of the viewers. The countess confronts and insults the audience members. But not everyone prefers a life without change. If the countess and her millionaire friends are content, the working-class characters are not. One tries to convert the others to communism. And when Tom returns with Cecilia and tells the others that it's "every man for himself," Arturo the maître d' becomes ecstatic. No longer compelled to seat customers showing after showing, he realizes his dream by tap dancing across the stage at the Copacabana.

The metafiction also casts new light on the existential and ontological questions that preoccupy Allen. For instance, Tom knows without a doubt that God exists; in fact he acknowledges two creators: Irving Sachs and R. H. Levine, the screenwriters of his *Purple Rose of Cairo*. Tom desperately seeks freedom to explore the world and himself (he identifies himself as an adventurer and explorer), but his behavior is restricted by how his writers have defined his character—an authorial version of DNA. For instance, though he finds the thought appealing and has no moral objections to the proposition, Tom turns down an offer for free sex from a bevy of prostitutes because the true-blue loyalty that has been written into his character renders him incapable of betraying Cecilia. (In this respect he directly contrasts her real-life love interests, Monk and Gil.)

Even death takes on new dimensions in the metafiction. For the characters inside the movie, death is merely the interval between screenings. Because they exist only when the film is being shown, they argue passionately against turning off the projector. When the projector is switched off, their world goes suddenly dark and silent, and they essentially die, until they are resurrected in the next showing.

The metafiction operates in an Einsteinian reality in which, as in relativity theory, any point is capable of being regarded as the center of the universe. The movie characters show that we are all the central character in our own lives—the center of our own universes. Each character believes he is the main character around whom the story revolves and that the others are minor or supporting parts. And by withholding the main plot of their movie from us, Allen deliberately declines to resolve the dispute. From what we know, each could plausibly be the inner film's central figure.

The characters' narcissism is paralleled by that of the Hollywood actors and producers, who also take themselves very seriously. Allen exploits this for a laugh when both Tom and Gil are surprised and offended by the suggestion that Tom is not the protagonist. Their comic narcissism reverberates more brutally in Monk, who resides unambiguously in the real world. His self-absorption reduces Cecilia to a minor character in his life and leads her to feel like a secondary character in her own existence as well. Because Monk is the person most removed from fiction, his narcissism proves the most destructive. Moreover, he, Cecilia's boss, and other "realists" are the least imaginative figures in the film. It seems no coincidence that these characters who insist on restricting their thoughts and imagination to what is probable and already known are also the harshest figures. (In this respect

Monk parallels Leopold in *A Midsummer Night's Sex Comedy* and the doctor in *Shadows and Fog*.)

Finally, the metafiction explores the age-old issue of fate versus free will,
a literary problem that dates back at least to the fifth century B.C., when
Sophocles wrote *Oedipus Rex*. The issue reappears in the writings of such
disparate groups as the Puritans and the existentialists. Allen contrasts the
determined world of the inside film to the uncertain nature of Cecilia's (and
our) external reality. Whereas the determined world of the fiction is secure
but entirely confining, the real world offers freedom but no security. The
world of fiction is controlled; at best reality is only manageable.

The fictional characters act predictably and consistently. Moreover, they
are largely content; most prefer the security of their predetermined, scripted
world. However, some characters like Tom and the maître d' feel con-
strained by their inability to realize their deepest passions, and they desire
the possibilities inherent in the unpredictable real world. On the other hand,
some real people want to sacrifice their freedom for the comfort and reas-
suring predictability of the scripted world. As the producer groans, "The
real ones want their lives fiction, and the fictional ones want their lives real."

For Allen, this choice between predictable fiction and uncertain reality is
the crux of his movie. But there are no easy answers. True to his essentially
pessimistic worldview, he shows that neither reality nor fiction ultimately
offers a satisfying alternative:

A woman's dream man comes off the screen and she's in love with him, and then the
real actor appears and she's forced to choose between reality and fantasy. And of
course one can't choose fantasy, because that can lead to madness, so one has to
choose reality. And when you choose reality, you get hurt. As simple as that.
(*Woody Allen on Woody Allen* 148)

See also **Metafiction**.

NOTE

1. Flannery O'Connor and Isaac Bashevis Singer validate their religious beliefs by showing how the inherent uncertainty of reality necessarily offers hope
for salvation and/or divine purpose. Allen further addresses the possibility of unlikely twists of fate in "Random Reflections of a Second-Rate Mind," as he considers a Holocaust victim in 1990 dining in an elegant New York restaurant. "I
wondered, if an angel had come to him . . . when he was scheming desperately not
to be among those chosen for annihilation, and told him that one day he'd be sitting . . . in a trendy Italian restaurant among lovely young women in designer
jeans . . . would he have grabbed the angel around the throat and throttled him in a
sudden fit of insanity?" See **"Random Reflections of a Second-Rate Mind."**

R

Radio Days. A 1987 film directed and written by Allen, who narrates but does not appear on screen. The cast stars Mia Farrow (Sally White), Dianne Wiest (Aunt Bea), Seth Green (Joe), Julie Kavner (Joe's mother, Tess), Michael Tucker (Joe's father), John Mostel (Uncle Abe), Julie Kurnitz (Irene), Wallace Shawn (Masked Avenger), David Warrilow (Roger), Joy Newman (Cousin Ruthie), Renee Lippin (Aunt Ceil), Tony Roberts (master of ceremonies), Danny Aiello (hit man), Jeff Daniels (Biff Baxter), Robert Joy (Fred), Kenneth Mars (Rabbi Bamuel), Diane Keaton (singer), and Kitty Carlisle (singer). It also features Tito Puente and his orchestra. Robert Greenhut was the producer, Carlo Di Palma director of photography, Dick Hyman music director, Santo Loquasto production designer, Jeffrey Kurland costumer, and Susan E. Morse editor. The music features "Dancing in the Dark," "Chinatown, My Chinatown," "Let's All Sing Like the Birdies Sing," "I Double Dare You," "South American Way," "Begin the Beguine," "Remember Pearl Harbor," "Just One of Those Things," "You'd Be So Nice To Come Home To," "Night and Day," and Rimsky-Korsakov's "The Flight of the Bumblebee," among other selections. Orion Pictures was the North American distributor.

Radio Days occasioned Allen's first collaboration with Diane Keaton since *Interiors*, nine years earlier. Annie Hall had aspired to become a professional singer, and in *Radio Days* Keaton sings "You'd Be So Nice to Come Home To" in a cameo appearance as a nightclub performer. The movie opened as a hit, number ten in its first week on the *Variety* charts, but its popularity soon diminished, and it failed to make a profit. It cost $16 million to produce and netted only $6.4 million in U.S. and Canadian distribution (not including later video rentals and television revenues). The film fared better in Europe—especially in Sweden and Italy, and *Radio Days* held the number one spot in Rome for ten weeks. Critical opinion was also mixed. Some were enthusiastic about Allen's ability to recreate the ambience of an earlier time and place; others, like Pauline Kael, criticized the direction as confused and complained that the film failed to add up to much. Allen himself has professed disappointment in *Radio Days*, claiming that he had intended it to be grander, funnier, and more moving, but that it "fell short in every important way" (Fox 183). Nonetheless, Eric Lax maintains that it is one of Allen's favorites (Lax 277).

Federico Fellini's *Amarcord* (1974), whose title translates as "I Remember," appears to be the dominant cinematic influence, even though Allen denies it (*Woody Allen on Woody Allen* 164). Both films present affectionate childhood recollections of the late 1930s and early 1940s (one in Italy, one in New York). In fact, Allen admits a closer identification with his childhood character Joe than he does with most of his other characters, and we have the sense that these vignettes approximate his actual memories. Like Joe, Allen grew up in an extended family in a Jewish, working-class neighborhood in New York, and his parents constantly quarreled. For a while he lived by the ocean, and he and his friends would watch for German subma-

(Front, left to right) William Magerman, Seth Green, Leah Carrey and (rear, left to right) Michael Tucker, Julie Kavner, Dianne Wiest, Joy Newman, Renee Lippin, and Josh Mostel as they appear in *Radio Days*. Photo by Brian Hamill. Courtesy of Photofest.

rines. He destroyed his mother's fur coat with dye he made from a chemistry set. Allen's uncle inundated the family with fish, and his marriage-minded aunt was unable to find a husband. His family shared a telephone party line and listened in on their neighbors' conversations; another neighboring family were communists (*Woody Allen on Woody Allen* 158).

Amarcord and *Radio Days* show structural similarities as well. Both present a series of associated vignettes centered around the director's family and his community. Both contrast the worlds of the wealthy elite and the working poor. *Amarcord* progresses chronologically, following the family and the townspeople through a calendar year. *Radio Days* also progresses chronologically, from 1938 to January 1, 1944. Both draw humor from eccentric characters and extreme behavior. Both derive humor from memories of school experiences and childish pranks, though Fellini accentuates how bizarre the teachers seem, how seriously they take themselves and their subjects, and how severely they react to the students, while Allen shows more of the children's sense of excitement and discovery.

Even specific shots in *Radio Days* are indebted to *Amarcord*. For instance, the panning shot of the girls' backsides as they swivel on the drugstore counter stools evokes the shot from *Amarcord* of the boys watching the girls on bicycle seats as they pedal into market. Though less directly connected, the scene where little Joe sees a German submarine silently surface and submerge projects an otherworldly sense of awe and wonder similar to that in *Amarcord* where the little boy looks up through a thick, white fog and suddenly sees a white ox that lingers momentarily, then disappears back into the mist. (Both recall the moment in Faulkner's *Go Down, Moses* [1942] where Sam Fathers salutes a great stag that stands briefly and then walks off.) And just as Gradisca's infatuation with movies and her search for love provide a counterpoint for Titta's family in *Amarcord*, Sally's obsession with appearing on radio and her search for love offset the domestic scenes in *Radio Days*.

Radio Days most significantly departs from *Amarcord* in its use of music as a dominant presence in each scene and as a structuring device, and perhaps this is why Allen does not emphasize the movies' similarities: "The inspiration was that I wanted to make a memory for each important song from my childhood. . . . And when I started to write the memories of the songs, I got inspiration for other scenes and sequences which could strengthen and support these memories. If I had done *Radio Days* faithfully, I would have done about 25 different songs and described what comes into my mind when I hear them." Allen adds, "I think of *Radio Days* as a cartoon. And I picked out the actors for their cartoon quality. If you look at my Uncle Abe, my mother, my schoolteacher, my grandparents, they were supposed to be cartoon exaggerations of what my real-life people were like" (*Woody Allen on Woody Allen* 162, 164).

Unlike more traditional stories, *Radio Days* presents a cinematic snapshot of a particular time and place rather than follow a single character through the resolution of a problem or nest of problems. Therefore, Allen had to devise other means for sustaining his viewers' interest. "When you don't have a 'What happens next?' story, when you're working with anecdotal material, the trick, I feel, is that you have to sustain each thing on its own brilliance, on its own rhythm, on its own style. . . . It's a difficult kind of film to do, a non-plot, non-conventional plot film" (*Woody Allen on Woody Allen* 160).

Allen's solution to his narrative problem was to use radio broadcasts to interweave scenes featuring a broad array of characters. His own voice-over narration also gives the movie coherence by effecting transitions between scenes, making connections between characters and events, and providing a constant authorial voice that contributes to the impression that someone is in control of the story. Furthermore, Sally's ambition to become a radio personality and Aunt Bea's desire to find a husband serve as constants throughout the entire film. Though told in fragments, these plotlines sustain viewers' curiosity in the manner of traditional, character-driven stories.

Sally's plotline even achieves resolution, though Bea's remains open ended. Significantly, Sally is the only character to grow during the five years spanned by the film—the only character to take constructive steps to improve her life. All the others seem to accept the status quo and strive to do their best within it, but the "voice of God" tells Sally to take diction lessons, and after several months of conscientious practice she overcomes her gutter accent that had been the greatest obstacle to success. By the movie's end Sally returns as a patron to the club where she used to work as a cigarette girl, and she triumphantly leads a group of her new, high-society friends to the top of the roof, the scene of earlier embarrassment.

Aunt Bea, on the other hand, continues to search for a mate, but she never seems to grow or otherwise transform as a result of her experience; she only becomes more lonely and more dependent on the family, finally spending New Year's Eve without a date. Bea seems like a good, caring person, but apart from her ambition to get married and her fondness for music, we know little of what she wants from life. It is likely that she does not know what she wants either; certainly she never tries to achieve it. Bea is too consumed by her quest for a husband to develop other interests or aptitudes, and she is so eager to be what her date wants her to be that she represses her own personality.

Allen hints that Bea may be unconsciously undermining herself, but he does not explore the possibility deeply. Nonetheless, Joe's mother observes that Bea has a talent for choosing losers, and she sometimes wonders if Bea really wants to get married; Bea is so picky. When Bea answers that she rejected one suitor because his clothes did not match, Tess points out that this is not an adequate reason. But Bea does not pay attention. Certainly the wartime shortage of men was a genuine and substantial obstacle to Bea's quest. But she was choosing losers even before the war, such as the date who abandoned her in 1938, when he thought the Martians had landed during the famous Orson Welles broadcast. Her apparent lack of introspection and inability to project a strong, independent personality presumably contribute to her failure. In this respect, her contrast to Sally is striking.

Little Joe, Allen's young alter ego, is the third major recurring character. He is always listening to the radio, or it is on in the background, and the scenes devoted to Joe reveal how much the radio influences his life. His parents fear that it distracts him and teaches him bad habits, and that the advertisements create unrealistic desires, much as parents of Joe's generation were later to complain about television. For instance, Joe's yearning for a Masked Avenger ring with a secret compartment leads him to steal money he collected for Israel, and Joe outrages the rabbi when he calls him "my faithful Indian companion," a phrase he learned from the Lone Ranger.

But for Joe, the radio opens a rich world in his imagination in which the Masked Avenger hunts down evildoers everywhere, while Biff Baxter routes out fascist spies. And it permeates and often motivates almost every aspect of his life. Because he and his friends are following Biff Baxter's instructions, they go to the rooftop where they see their future substitute teacher dance naked before a mirror. (Joe's blond schoolmate is played by Fletcher Previn, Mia Farrow's son.) The radio occasions a magical evening with Aunt Bea and her boyfriend when they see a live radio performance and Bea wins an on-air contest, and it even enables Joe finally to learn what his father does for a living, when he inadvertently flags down his dad's taxi after trying to carry a heavy radio set home. The radio also leads Joe to witness effects of the social stigma against homosexuality and to put a particular face on the abstract concept of a homosexual. Awakened by music on the radio late at night, Joe hears Bea's date reveal that he is gay. Joe sees the depth of the man's suffering for his lost lover and Bea's bewildered but compassionate response to his confession. Finally, the radio sometimes makes Joe feel especially connected to his family and community. When Joe ruins his mother's coat, the special radio coverage of Polly Phelps, who had fallen down a well in Pennsylvania, dispels his parents' anger, brings the family closer together, and establishes a common bond of concern and goodwill with Americans everywhere.

Other constants that unify the film include the bickering between Joe's parents, which is accompanied by underlying affection, and Uncle Abe's snide remarks to Aunt Ceil. Abe's underlying affection is less evident. Joe's father's get-rich schemes and Abe's obsession with fish also recur, as do Roger and Irene and the Masked Avenger. But Sally remains the only character who changes over time. At least in adult Joe's memories, all of these others remain essentially the same, and the different vignettes serve to flesh out their portraits more fully rather than reveal character development.

Like *Amarcord*, *Radio Days* contrasts an ethnic, extended family of modest means with more affluent members of their community. Both groups are aware of the class differences and respect them. The only time the two worlds intersect comes when Joe's family meets one of the radio whiz kids at the zoo. When the whiz kid reacts condescendingly, Joe's parents, instead of being insulted, are impressed by his poise. Abe has been convinced by his communist neighbors that capitalists are oppressors, and he points out that a fancy Manhattan club excludes blacks and Jews. However, although he recognizes the injustice, he does not become upset by it. Instead, he seems to accept it as the way things are and does not appear greatly offended by his exclusion from high society. Joe's family fantasizes about wealth and glamour, but they largely accept their lives as they are, without resentment or excessive envy. Only Sally rises from the lower class to the upper, and her success seems to derive from determination, persistence, hard work, and good luck, which comes in the form of the sudden inspiration to improve her speech. Significantly, once she eliminates the vocal qualities that readily identify her as lower class, she is able to achieve her dream.

Allen does not romanticize his family's working-class circumstances, but he does not demean them either. The extended family provides emotional and financial support, and the neighborhood affords a sense of community. Of course, family and neighborhood differences also create conflict. But if not altogether happy, most characters have achieved a level of acceptance. For this reason, they do not experience significant development.

The radio personalities project elegance, but their sophistication runs only surface deep. They appeal to us and to the working-class characters because of their glamorous lifestyles, not because of who they are or how they conduct their lives. They own beautiful things, enjoy sensual delights, and act with self-assurance, but we do not receive any glimpses of deep feelings or substantial accomplishment. The ideal marriage that Roger and Irene project on the radio is peppered with infidelities on both sides; the radio game show host played by Tony Roberts tries to be clever and witty but proves lame; and the self-righteous announcer who tells stories about miraculous personal successes, such as the baseball player who loses his limbs, appears ridiculous instead of inspirational. The fact that someone as ignorant as Sally, who wonders who Pearl Harbor is, could thrive among the celebrities once she changed her look and her voice also illustrates the fundamental shallowness of high society as represented in this film. Allen's presentation of these shortcomings is matter-of-fact, not judgmental. Nonetheless, the working class ultimately seems more authentic, less self-absorbed, and better attuned to themselves and their community.

In addition to the dominance of the radio and the details of the characters' lives, the film's music and photography contribute to Allen's evocation of the era. We learn that Aunt Bea listens almost exclusively to music, and she is responsible for Joe's acquaintance with the wonderful tunes that were current during the last years of the Depression and the beginning of World War II. The music is drawn primarily from Big Band swing, Latin American rhythms, and early jazz, though it also contains show tunes by Cole Porter and popular songs sung by Bing Crosby. Other notable performers include Glenn Miller, Tommy Dorsey, Artie Shaw, Richard Himber, Duke Ellington, Guy Lombardo, Sammy Kaye, and Xavier Cugat and His Waldorf-Astoria Orchestra.

Against this backdrop of lively, passionate, and generally upbeat music is Carlo Di Palma's rich photography. The family scenes in particular are often illuminated by warm lighting and rich tones that communicate a sense of warmth, much as Rembrandt used light to create a similar effect. The anniversary scene where Joe's father gives his mother a fur coat—their sole outward display of affection—is shot in this fashion. On the other hand, drugstore scenes from the Polly Phelps episode evoke the isolation of Edward Hopper paintings. In several instances Di Palma uses long shots to keep us at arm's length from the characters, perhaps to suggest the dimness of the memory that inspired the scene.

Radio Days ends on a note of fading memories as the narrator acknowledges that with each passing New Year, the characters, place, and time seem more removed. The film itself thus resuscitates and gives these memories new life, while at the same time underscoring how distant they have become.

For additional reading, see Navacelle, *Woody Allen on Location: A Day-to-Day Account of the Making of* Radio Days.

"Random Reflections of a Second-Rate Mind." A 1990 nonfiction essay by Allen that was first published in *Tikkun* and reprinted in *The Best American Essays, 1990*, edited by Joyce Carol Oates.

As the title suggests, the essay's organization is stream-of-consciousness, but Allen answers some of his critics about how he perceives himself as a

Jew, and he presents his view of human nature and the Holocaust. He also comments briefly on his childhood career as a dreidel hustler and declares, "I have always preferred women to men. This goes back to the Old Testament where the ladies have it all over their cowering, pious counterparts. Eve knew the consequences when she ate the apple. Adam would have been content to just follow orders and live on like a mindless sybarite. But Eve knew it was better to acquire knowledge even if it meant grasping her mortality with all its accompanying anxiety." Allen also admires Lot's wife for deliberately defying God, and he singles out Job's wife as "my favorite woman in all of literature" because "she was too much of her own person to let herself be shamelessly abused by some vain and sadistic Holy Spirit." In particular, he praises her final words, "Curse God and die."

In general Allen regards his world from a broader human perspective than a strictly Jewish one. He takes *Tikkun* to task for its subtitle, *A Bimonthly Jewish Critique of Politics, Culture and Society*, because its emphasis on a Jewish point of view "subtly helps promulgate phony and harmful differences." "But why a Jewish critique?" he asks. "Or a gentile critique? Or any limiting perspective? Why not a magazine with articles written by human beings for other humans to read? . . . After all, what if other magazines felt the need to employ their own religious perspectives? You might have *Field and Stream: A Catholic Critique of Fishing and Hunting*. This month: 'Angling for Salmon as You Baptize.' "

Allen generally supports Israel; he even endorsed a pro-Israeli political action committee (PAC) despite his basic opposition to PACs. But he publicly denounced Israeli human rights abuses during the Palestinian uprising of the late 1980s and early 1990s known as the intifada. Allen complains that in their deep concern to protect Israel, intellectuals and other Jews attacked him for advocating what he believes is a very reasonable position: "The central point seemed to me inescapable: Israel was not responding correctly to this new problem":

I was amazed at how many intellectuals took issue with me over a piece I wrote a while back for the *New York Times* saying I was against the practice of Israeli soldiers going door-to-door and randomly breaking the hands of Palestinians as a method of combating the intifada. I said also I was against the too-quick use of real bullets. . . . I was for a more flexible attitude on negotiating land for peace.

For Allen the main point is, "Do you want the soldiers going door-to-door and breaking hands?" And he expresses frustration with critics who likewise reject the brutality but nonetheless attack him for publicly voicing his objections. From their perspective, Allen's statements weaken Israel and put its survival at risk, and in their opinion, the threat to Israel outweighs the human rights considerations. From Allen's perspective, Israel's commitment to democracy, human rights, and rule by law, not the mere fact that it is a Jewish state, makes it special. Therefore, he believes that indiscriminate brutality undermines Israel's moral authority and weakens it. He feels his own position is "not only more in keeping with Israel's high moral stature but also in its own best interest."

Allen answers critics who call him a self-hating Jew: "While it's true I am Jewish and I don't like myself, it's not because of my persuasion." He adds, "The most outlandish cut of all was from the Jewish Defense League, which voted me Pig of the Month. . . . If only they knew how close some of my inner rages have been to theirs. (In my movie *Manhattan*, for example, I suggested breaking up a Nazi rally not with anything the ACLU would approve, but with baseball bats.)"

But although he acknowledges the real threat posed by anti-Semitism—"one day I may have to fight because I'm a Jew, or even die because of it, and no amount of professed apathy to religion will save me"—Allen rejects all religions, including Judaism, because they are "exclusive clubs that serve no good purpose; they exist only to form barriers, trade commercially on human misery, and provide additional differences amongst people so they can further rationalize their natural distrust and aggression." (Harry expresses identical sentiments in *Deconstructing Harry*.)

Allen's personal response to the Holocaust is to discard the notion of a benign God and reject claims that people are fundamentally good:

At fifteen I received as a gift a pair of cuff links with a William Steig cartoon on them. A man with a spear through his body was pictured and the accompanying caption read, "People are no damn good." A generalization, an oversimplification, and yet it was the only way I ever could get my mind around the Holocaust. Even at fifteen I used to read Anne Frank's line about people being basically good and place it on a par with Will Rogers' pandering nonsense, "I never met a man I didn't like."

The questions for me were not: How could a civilized people . . . do what they did to another people. And how could the world remain silent? . . . This mystery that had confounded all my relatives since World War II was not such a puzzle if I understood that inside every heart lived the worm of self-preservation, of fear, greed, and an animal will to power. And the way I saw it, it was nondiscriminating. It abided in gentile or Jew, Black, white, Arab, European, or American. It was part of who we all were, and that the Holocaust could occur was not at all so strange. . . .

The real mystery that got me through my teen years was that every once in a while one found an act of astonishing decency and sacrifice. One heard of people who risked their lives and their family's lives to save lives of people they didn't even know. But these were rare exceptions and in the end there were not enough humane acts to keep six million from being murdered.

See also **Holocaust.**

Roberts, Tony. A film and stage actor who appears in *Play It Again, Sam, Annie Hall, Stardust Memories, A Midsummer Night's Sex Comedy, Hannah and Her Sisters*, and *Radio Days*. Roberts also costarred in the Broadway productions of *Don't Drink the Water* and *Play It Again, Sam*, and he acted in the National Radio Theater of Chicago's production of *God*. He also appears in *Serpico* (1973), directed by Sidney Lumet.

Roberts plays the role of Allen's best friend and/or business partner in all the films except for *Radio Days*, in which Allen does not act. His character is typically sensual, self-assured, and hedonistic, in contrast to Allen's more cerebral, indecisive, and inhibited roles. However, despite the differences in ethnic background and personality type, their relationship is usually warm and caring, and Roberts's character often looks after Allen's. For instance, Dick tries to fix up the despondent Allan Felix after Allan's wife leaves him in *Play It Again, Sam*, and Rob bails out Alvy Singer after Alvy is arrested for bad driving in *Annie Hall*.

The friendships also manifest through clever, playful put-downs, such as when Rob calls Alvy "Max" because it seems like a good name for him, or when Andrew (Allen) claims in *A Midsummer Night's Sex Comedy* that Maxwell (Roberts) has to believe in the spirit world because all of his medical patients go there.

Roberts and Allen's characters become sexually involved with the same woman in several of the films, usually with significant consequences. Allan falls in love with and has a single sexual encounter with Dick's wife in *Play It Again, Sam*. His decision to give her up after both he and Linda recognize that Dick needs her defines the happy ending, as it elevates Allan to Bogart-like stature when he sacrifices for a friend. In *A Midsummer Night's Sex Comedy* Maxwell has slept with Andrew's wife, Adrian, prior to the opening scene, a fact that has created serious problems in Andrew's marriage; later both men compete for Ariel, though they seem to reconcile at the end. Finally, in *Hannah and Her Sisters*, Norman (Roberts) fathers Hannah's child through artificial insemination when Mickey (Allen) is believed to be infertile, an act that ultimately contributes to Hannah and Mickey's divorce.

Allen claims that "Tony Roberts . . . has always been a friend. I like to work with friends and with people I like, because one spends so much time with them" (*Woody Allen on Woody Allen* 128).

Scenes from a Mall. A 1991 film starring Allen as Nick Fifer, an affluent sports lawyer. It was directed by Paul Mazursky and costarred Bette Midler (Deborah Fifer), Bill Irwin (mime), Daren Firestone (Sam), Rebecca Nickels (Jennifer) and Paul Mazursky (Dr. Hans Clava). Mazursky and Roger L. Simon wrote the screenplay; Pato Guzman and Patrick McCormick were coproducers, Fred Murphy director of photography, Marc Shaiman music director, Pato Guzman production designer, Albert Wolsky costumer, and Stuart Pappé editor. Touchstone-Buena Vista was the North American distributer.

Scenes from a Mall was the first film since Martin Ritt's *The Front* (1976) in which Allen acted but did not write or direct. Inspired by Mazursky's notion that suburban shopping malls have replaced city streets and town squares as the locus of public and private life, the movie received some praise for the quality of the dialogue. But overall it was a critical and financial failure. The film cost $34 million to produce but grossed only $9.3 million and netted only $4.2 million in North American distribution. It fared somewhat better in Europe. In Paris, where female readers of *Elle* magazine voted Allen their third "most potent fantasy lover," the movie led all other films in box office revenues when it opened. Nonetheless, *Scenes from a Mall* was a big money loser for its backer, Disney, as critics expressed their disappointment that Allen had not directed or written the script.

Allen's role is the antithesis of those he normally plays. A fashionable dresser who wears tortoiseshell glasses, designer jackets, and a "dork knob" pony tail, Nick Fifer embraces the material values of American consumerism and bashes New York while boosting Los Angeles.

The story centers around Nick and his wife, Deborah, a middle-aged Los Angeles couple who are celebrating their sixteenth wedding anniversary and the fact that their children have gone on vacation and left them alone for the first time in years. A trip to the shopping mall to buy sushi for their party becomes the unexpected venue for a series of revelations about Nick and Deborah's inner thoughts and secret lives. Both express hidden resentments and suspicions, and both, it turns out, have been having affairs. Thus, like Ingmar Bergman's *Scenes from a Marriage* (1974), which the title both deflates for comic purposes and echoes for serious ones, *Scenes from a Mall* unveils the tumultuous, unstable inner reality that lurks beneath the surface of this seemingly tranquil and ideal bourgeois family. Allen returned to this same theme the following year as writer, director, and actor in *Husbands and Wives*.

September. A 1987 film directed and written by Allen. It stars Mia Farrow (Lane), Sam Waterston (Peter), Elaine Stritch (Diane), Dianne Wiest (Stephanie), Denholm Elliott (Howard), Jack Warden (Lloyd), Ira Wheeler (Mr. Raines), Jane Cecile (Mrs. Raines), and Rosemary Murphy (Mrs. Mason). Allen shot the film twice with different casts. The cast in the original, discarded version included Mia Farrow (Lane), Christopher Walken (Peter), Maureen O'Sullivan (Diane), Dianne Wiest (Stephanie), Charles Durning (Howard), and Denholm Elliott (Lloyd). Sam Shepard replaced Walken as Peter a few weeks into the shooting, when Walken amicably departed over artistic differences. Robert Greenhut was the producer, Carlo Di Palma director of photography, Roy S. Yokelson music director, Santo Loquasto production designer, Jeffrey Kurland costumer, and Susan E. Morse editor. The music includes "On a Slow Boat to China," "Out of Nowhere," "Just One More Chance," "My Ideal," "What'll I Do?" "Who," "I'm Confessin' (That I Love You)," "Moonglow," "When Day Is Done," and "Night and Day." Orion Pictures was the North American distributor.

Allen accurately anticipated that *September,* a playlike film with a small cast, single setting, and Chekhovian sensibility, would not fare well at the box office. He decided to do it anyway because this was the project he wanted to work on (Lax 347). In fact, the film was not screened in most U.S. cities and had short runs in the few theaters and college campuses where it did appear. And unlike other Allen movies that lost money in the United States but nonetheless broke even or garnered a profit in Europe, *September* did not fare well overseas either. Overall, it cost $10 million to produce and grossed only $486,000 in U.S. and Canadian rentals (not including later video rentals and television revenues).

The initial idea was to make a film in Farrow's rustic, New England country house, which Allen had always considered a terrific movie location. Farrow and her children would be able to enjoy the woods, while Allen, who is notorious for disliking the country, would content himself making the movie. Allen proceeded with the plan, but by the time he was ready to film, he had missed the late-summer effect he desired; so his production crew built an interior set instead. According to Allen, "Just like in *Interiors*, the house is a character. The house was the initial inspiration for the script, so it was important." He adds, "It was very important . . . to provide the house with a lot of perspectives that were interesting. I wanted to be able to see deep all the time. . . . And I wanted a warm colour for the house. . . . But the key thing was that I wanted Santo to provide me with sufficient angles, so that you wouldn't get bored with the house, or claustrophobic" (*Woody Allen on Woody Allen* 174).

But the house's warmth and intimacy deliberately contradict the human characters' loneliness, isolation, and despair. Allen describes the movie as "a group of middle-aged people in a country house with unfulfilled dreams and unfulfilled passions and sad futures" (*Woody Allen on Woody Allen* 179). Crippled by deep and enduring emotional wounds, most are unable to establish close personal bonds. But some handle their plight better than others, and the film examines their diverse responses to an empty life of pain. It then extrapolates to the absurd condition of all of humanity, as it reiterates Allen's bleak view of a hostile, impermanent, meaningless universe.

The story parallels the real-life drama of actress Lana Turner, whose abusive lover, Johnny Stompanato, Jr., was stabbed to death in 1957 by her thirteen-year-old daughter, Cheryl Crane. Allen acknowledges familiarity with the incident but denies that it was a primary inspiration. Instead, he maintains, "I'd always wanted to make a play, a movie, about a very flamboyant mother who had been involved with a gangster and who killed him, but the daughter took the blame for it. So the story just formed" (*Woody Allen on Woody Allen* 170).

Allen elaborates on the mother-daughter relationship: "I wanted the mother . . . [to be] shallow and selfish, egotistical. But even at her age, she dresses and thinks of herself as beautiful and feminine and sexy. And the annoying thing to her daughter is that she attracts men of substance. . . . So these mothers [Diane from *September* and Eve from *Interiors*], they are talented and beautiful but they have a wrecking effect on their daughters. The daughters lose on every front. The mothers get good men, they get attention and yet they are still cruel and cold and without generosity" (*Woody Allen on Woody Allen* 180).

Like Anton Chekhov's *Seagull* (1898), *September* tells a story wherein almost everyone loves someone who loves someone else. Lane, the resentful, emotionally crippled daughter of a former movie star, has spent the summer recovering in her family's Vermont home from her failed relationship with a married lover. Howard, a much older widower, has fallen in love with Lane in a fatherly, protective kind of way. But though Lane appreciates his sentiments, she can neither return nor accept them.

Instead, Lane has fallen in love with Peter, an earnest advertising agent who has taken time off to write a novel based on his father, a victim of the red scare, whom Peter admires as a survivor. Though Lane and Peter slept together earlier in the summer and he still solicits her support for his writing, Peter has quietly fallen for Stephanie, Lane's best friend, who has a husband and children in Philadelphia. Stephanie admits to trying to attract Peter throughout the summer, mostly to prove to herself that she still could. Moreover, Peter's sensitivity and imagination remind her of a young artist she once loved. These qualities are apparently missing in her husband, a radiologist, and Stephanie feels an emptiness in her life. But she will not talk to her spouse about it, because she fears it would hurt him too greatly. Instead, she speaks curtly to him on the phone, cuts him off abruptly, and sleeps with Peter. In the end, Stephanie returns to her family in body but not in spirit.

Diane lives for the moment. She is shallow, egocentric, and insensitive to Lane and others, but her high spirits and animated personality make her the most attractive character of the bunch. Unlike Lane, who clings to past hurts and defines herself around them, Diane prefers to forget the past and concentrate on having a good time now. She too has suffered, but she has clung to life emphatically and done whatever was required to endure. Like Peter's father, she is a survivor.

An animated person, Diane energizes others. Although she is morally flawed, Diane not only enjoys her life but also comforts her husband, Lloyd, a quantum physicist who suffers from existential angst. Moreover, even casual acquaintances benefit from the excitement Diane generates. Through Diane, Allen seems to concur with the John Barth character who declares "A certain kind of *spiritedness* was absolutely good, no matter what a person's other Answers are" (Barth, *Giles Goat-Boy* 691).

September investigates how we should respond to our own moral lapses and those of others. Most of the characters have committed some act of betrayal. Lane and Stephanie each violate a marriage, Peter exploits Lane for the sexual and emotional comfort she offers, and Stephanie lures Peter away from Lane. These actions diminish the characters in our eyes. But they appear weak and flawed, not evil.

Diane's betrayal of Lane is the most injurious and the most vulnerable to moral judgment, even though it took place far in the past. In essence, Diane, the survivor, sacrificed her daughter's emotional well-being for her own freedom. Years earlier, Diane killed her abusive boyfriend and escaped jail by having Lane confess to firing the pistol. A child at the time, Lane never subsequently revealed the truth, but she suffered severe emotional trauma from the affair. Shallow and narcissistic, Diane has consistently refused to acknowledge the connection between the cover-up and Lane's emotional devastation. When Lane finally does accuse Diane of firing the lethal bullet, Diane's expression and behavior give her away, even though she denies the shooting. Characteristically, Diane avoids the issue rather than relive it and resolve it through a process that might be painful for her but cathartic and therapeutic for Lane. Instead, Diane abruptly ends their quarrel by granting Lane's claim to ownership of the house. Then she make plans to depart as quickly as possible.

Significantly, by conceding the house, Diane purchases Lane's silence but not her forgiveness. Although Diane would like a better relationship with her daughter, she is not interested in obtaining Lane's absolution, only her continued complicity. Otherwise, as far as Diane is concerned, the past is buried and forgotten, and absolution is unnecessary. For her part, Lane is willing to exchange her silence for the house, but she is unwilling to forgive Diane. Lane values the wrong done to her too highly to sell it off, but she will swap her silence for financial security.

Ironically, it is precisely Diane's lack of introspection or deep self-scrutiny that enables her to thrive in a hostile world. Because she can let go of her own past pain and brush aside harm she has inflicted on others, Diane enjoys her life. Because the others remain preoccupied with hurts from the past and anxieties about the future, they cannot.

Perhaps because Lane was so severely damaged by her trauma, she does not share Diane's affirmation of life. Her inability to do so may be understandable, but it is also lamentable, for the impulse to affirm life regardless of the circumstances enables survivors to survive.

Although Lane wins some sympathy for her childhood experience, her emotional disability leaves her depressed and in despair. She may be more sympathetic than Diane, but she is far less appealing. Unlike Diane, Lane seems to drain more energy than she gives out. Emotionally frail, she requires more encouragement and reassurance from others than she offers to them. Moreover, Lane manipulates through passive-aggressive behavior, such as when she agrees to the plan to see the movie another night but then points out in a deliberately indifferent tone that tonight's is the only performance. Thus, though Lane may be morally superior to Diane, she is less attractive, not only to Peter but to viewers as well.

Through Diane and Lane, Allen suggests that ignorance may indeed be bliss, and insensitivity may prove the greatest blessing of all. That shallowness may lead to a happier life than sensitivity contradicts the underlying core of Western thought and religious practice, as well as the Western tendency to trust rational consciousness over the irrational subconscious. Whereas Socrates preached self-scrutiny as a means to deeper, more profound happiness, and Judaism and Christianity maintain that God rewards righteousness and punishes wrong action, Allen suggests that in an absurd, atheistic universe these positions do not necessarily hold. In some instances, shallowness may insulate us from pain better than insight, and wrongdoers are at least as likely to flourish as their more virtuous counterparts.[1]

The absence of fundamental logic and fairness in the universe may be regrettable, Allen maintains, but it is the case, and we must face up to its implications. Lloyd's science has revealed the universe to be arbitrary, random, and meaningless—"haphazard and unimaginably violent." Profoundly shaken by scientific truths he cannot deny, he is thankful that Diane's merriment sometimes insulates from "the knowledge that it doesn't matter one way or the other."

In this paradoxical, absurdist view of the world, people who have done terrible things may also commit acts of kindness, and our moral assessment of anyone must be based on a full composite of their deeds. There is no ultimate judge who assesses a person's life, decides which acts outweigh the others, and convicts or acquits. Finally, each individual viewer is left to decide how much Diane's energy and enthusiasm offset the damage she has inflicted. By refusing finally to absolve or condemn Diane, Allen compels us to experience the condition of the absurd universe: There is no ultimate judge—for her or for us. Each viewer renders his own judgment of Diane, the other characters, and his fellow humans, or he declines to render any judgment at all. Individual judgments may contradict one another, and no supreme arbitrator exists to resolve the disputes.

NOTE

1. In this respect Diane is like Robin in *Celebrity*, who flourishes after giving up a meaningful job teaching Western literature in favor of a frivolous career in television. Both women recall the attractive couple on the sidewalk in *Annie Hall* who attribute the success of their relationship to the fact that each partner is fundamentally shallow.

Shadows and Fog. A 1992 film directed by, written by, and starring Allen, who plays Kleinman, a clerk. It costars Mia Farrow (Irmy, the sword swallower), Kathy Bates (prostitute), John Cusack (student), Jodie Foster (prostitute), Julie Kavner (Kleinman's ex-girlfriend, Alma), Madonna (Marie, a circus vamp), John Malkovich (Irmy's boyfriend, the clown), Kenneth Mars (Omstead, the magician), Kate Nelligan (prostitute), Wallace Shawn (Simon Carr), and Lily Tomlin (brothel madam). Robert Greenhut was the producer, Carlo Di Palma director of photography, Santo Loquasto production designer, Jeffrey Kurland costumer, and Susan E. Morse editor. The music is from Kurt Weill's *Threepenny Opera*. Columbia Tri-Star was the North American distributor.

Based on Allen's early play *Death*, which first appeared in *Without Feathers* (1975), *Shadows and Fog* failed at the box office. It cost approximately $14 million to produce but grossed only $1.2 million in U.S. and Canadian distribution (not including later video rentals and television revenues). The film opened in Paris in order to capitalize on Allen's growing popularity in Europe. It was initially well received in France, and in Italy it won the David Di Donatello Award for the year's best foreign film. But *Shadows and Fog* did not do well in England or Germany, and it was not enthusiastically received in the United States. Though some reviewers liked it, many regarded the film as little more than homage to the early German expressionist filmmakers like Fritz Lang, F. W. Murnau, Robert Wiene, and even Alfred Hitchcock, who spent part of his early career making films in Germany. They felt *Shadows and Fog* contributed little new to the genre. Allen has stated he was trying to make a comedy with a "serious or tragic dimension." "And this is not easy for me. . . . Because it's very hard to strike a balance in a story so that it's amusing and also . . . tragic or pathetic" (*Woody Allen on Woody Allen*, 235).

The title evokes the Allegory of the Cave from Plato's *Republic* in which the philosopher suggests that humans are like cave dwellers who have never seen light and mistake shadows for reality. Shot in a shadowy manner evocative of such murder mysteries as Wiene's *The Cabinet of Dr. Caligari* (1920), Hitchcock's *The Lodger* (1926), Murnau's *Sunrise* (1927), and Lang's *M* (1931), *Shadows and Fog* presents a Kafkaesque world in which the protagonist, Kleinman, perpetually struggles to ascertain what is going on. Kleinman is both literally and figuratively in a fog about what is happening around him and what is expected of him. At the same time, various forms of authority—the police, his boss, and the leaders of vigilante groups—all hold him accountable for his actions and failures to act.

Allen thus raises one of the central questions in twentieth-century arts and letters: How can we behave morally, ethically, and in ways that promote our own well-being in a fundamentally irrational, emotionally driven world in which we can never, with absolute certainty, know basic facts and confidently distinguish illusion from reality? As Irmy points out, even the stars that we see in the sky may not actually still be there. Kleinman, who in *Death* declares he "likes to know which way is up and which way is down, and where's the bathroom," is reluctant to commit himself without knowing all of the pertinent facts; nevertheless, he is compelled to act anyway. Thus Allen, like so many other twentieth-century literary figures, presents the modern condition: we are accountable for our behavior, even though our knowledge of all relevant facts and circumstances is inevitably incomplete.

Many modernist and postmodernist writers set their stories in analogous uncertain and unknowable environments, though the tone and overall sensibility of *Shadows and Fog* most closely parallel Franz Kafka's *The Trial* (1925). Like Kafka's protagonist, K, who is never informed of the crime he is accused of having committed, Kleinman remains metaphorically in the dark throughout the film. Ironically, when we first see him, he is turning on a light over his bed as a group of vigilantes wakens him in the middle of the night. The harsh overhead lighting sets the scene for an interrogation, and the vigilantes immediately begin accusing Kleinman in general but not specific terms, so he cannot defend himself. This sense of Kleinman's being deemed guilty in the abstract but not in the particular establishes a major theme for the entire film.

As events progress, Kleinman remains unable to ascertain his assignment, even while he is repeatedly reminded that lives are at stake and people are counting on him. Meanwhile, his community turns increasingly against him. Despite warnings to the contrary, he goes to the police station to defend the character of a family being unfairly arrested. But his good deed is interpreted as interference, and Kleinman himself becomes an object of suspicion. Later he discovers that the police chief and the priest have placed his name on a list whose secret purpose is ominous but unknown. And when circumstantial evidence links Kleinman to the killer, he must flee to the circus outside town to escape an angry mob that is quick to condemn him. After saving Irmy, the sympathetic runaway sword swallower whom he had met earlier in the evening, and then teaming with Omstead the magician to capture the killer, Kleinman realizes that his former associates distrust and dislike him and that his old life offers nothing of value to him. So he joins the circus as the magician's assistant in order to indulge his love of the art of illusion.

Like German expressionist films, *Shadows and Fog* is shot in black and white. The lighting is typically dim, and many exterior shots are distant and obscure. Allen backlit the fog in order to create an unrealistic and poetic sensibility. The circus scenes often employ sets and frame compositions evocative of *The Cabinet of Dr. Caligari*, which also confuses fact and fantasy, sanity and insanity. In the scene in which Spiro, the clairvoyant, investigates Kleinman, Allen employs the cinematic style of Federico Fellini, another modern director who presents the world as irrational, absurd, and a little magical. Moreover, in *Shadows and Fog* both time and place are indeterminate. There is an Old World sensibility to the stone city streets, but the costumes, sets, and other props are free of anything that would allow us to distinguish either the country or the decade in which the story takes place, except that the electric lights indicate that the action occurs sometime after the 1880s, and the currency is dollars, though the bills do not look American. This inability to fix time and place contributes to the Kafkaesque, dreamlike nature of the film and to our sense that Kleinman is lost in an undefinable world that has few, if any, points of reference.

Unlike *Death* and *The Trial*, which end in horror and despair, *Shadows and Fog* concludes on a note of affirmation. Kleinman's name derives from the Yiddish expression for "little man," and through much of the film Kleinman acts like the helpless schlemiel of Jewish humor who is impotent before the forces that assail him. In the past, Kleinman had acted as a person of small moral stature too: a sycophant at work, he had humiliated his first fiancée, abandoning her at the altar while making love to her little sister in a closet. However, in the shadows and fog of his uncertain predicament, and despite his fear and overwhelming sense of vulnerability, Kleinman repeatedly acts virtuously: going to the police station to speak up on behalf of the Minsk family and returning to the priest for a refund of the donated money so Irmy can help a destitute mother, an act that Kleinman knows will cause his name to be restored to the secret list. Finally, he risks his life to save Irmy when the killer accosts her.

In the uncertainty of his predicament, Kleinman allows himself to be guided by an open heart and a basic sense of decency. In so doing, he emerges a better person for his experience. As in Shakespeare's *King Lear*, Kleinman's universe is one that does not necessarily reward virtuous action. But as in *Lear*, in *Shadows and Fog* virtuous action is indeed its own reward, because it is the vehicle that transforms Kleinman from a schlemiel into a person of substance.

Kleinman comes to several crucial recognitions in the process of his transformation, notably that his fiancée, Eve, is "a cold fish" and that his boss, before whom he has always groveled in hopes of receiving preferment, considers him a "slimy vermin more suited to extermination than life on this planet." He now also knows that the police and the local church view him suspiciously and that his fellow citizens distrust him. Armed with that knowledge, he puts aside "the gray hat of compromise"—the attempt to live a safe, secure, insulated, rationally directed life that had hitherto rendered him a little man. Instead he agrees to indulge his greatest passion by studying magic as Omstead's assistant, irrespective of the very low pay and other inconveniences. Whether he will win Irmy, or whether she will remain with her boyfriend the clown, who is now smitten by the baby they have rescued, is problematic. But in either case, the Kleinman who will soon depart with the circus is a better person than the one who was roused from his bed the night before, and he stands to become a more confident, self-assured, and self-satisfied person because of his experiences and his choices.

Thus Allen seems to give an existentialist response to the question of belief in God. Although Kleinman is incapable of making "the leap of faith necessary to believe in my own existence," much less a leap of faith in God, he ultimately chooses virtuous action determined by a basic, commonsense notion of human decency and goodwill. In addition, he chooses a new line of work calculated to bring joy to his heart. In this way, he confers meaning on his existence, regardless of the confusing and indeterminate circumstances that envelop him.

The question of acting properly in a confusing, uncertain world is well developed in *Death*, where Allen originated the Kleinman plot. In fact, he was able to retain much of the original dialogue from *Death*. On the other hand, he added the Irmy subplot and the circus element and developed the role of the prostitutes in the movie. The prostitutes in particular contribute to the film's humor, as well as to its philosophical speculation.

Among the characters Allen retains from *Death* is the doctor who looks forward to discovering the exact nature of the criminal mind by "dissecting him down to the last chromosome . . . until I had a one hundred percent understanding of precisely what he is in every aspect." Secure in his empirical, purely materialistic view of reality, the doctor ridicules Kleinman's hope for the possibility of a soul or a God. But the doctor, who wonders where insanity stops and evil begins, never realizes his ambition of studying every aspect of the killer's physical being, because the killer murders him first. Here, as in *A Midsummer Night's Sex Comedy*, where he also parodies logical positivism, Allen pits magic and illusion against scientific empiricism, and empiricism comes up lacking. After all, it is the magician, not the scientist, who ultimately foils the murderer. Moreover, the doctor's spiritually empty view of life and humanity seems especially harsh, sterile, and unproductive. Certainly the coldly rational doctor is no better able to fight off the irrational forces of destruction than are the maniac's other victims. Although Kleinman remains an agnostic, having denied his ability to believe in God three times before the cock crowed, his basic decency and respect for other humans suggest something more than the doctor's severe, mechanistic vision of a universe composed solely of indifferent particles of matter and energy.

In addition to raising these existential questions—or perhaps as a way of adding substance, immediacy, and depth to them—*Shadows and Fog* raises the problem of anti-Semitism more forcefully than any other Woody Allen movie. The title evokes *Night and Fog* (1956), Alain Resnais's half-hour black-and-white documentary about Auschwitz that repeatedly asks, "Who is responsible?" As Mashey Bernstein points out, "Hovering under this plot lurks the theme of the Holocaust. In their attempt to capture the murderer, the townspeople reveal all the fear and greed of people looking for a scapegoat. They are characters out of every Jew's nightmare, incipient anti-Semites and Nazis, every one of them. . . . Innocent people with Jewish names are rounded up under false pretenses and allusions are made to the familiar canards against Jews, including the poisoning of wells." Bernstein also notes how Allen shows the Catholic church to be in collusion with the anti-Semites, and how Kleinman's boss has described him as being "only fit for extermination" (Bernstein, 224, 225). Even the echoes of Kafka and German expressionism evoke the climate of terror and paranoia in which anti-Semitism thrives. Made as the balance of power was just entering a post–Cold War "new world order," *Shadows and Fog* reminds viewers of the dangers of responding to unknown circumstances with anger, fear, and violence. More specifically, Allen reminds Jews that in dangerous, uncertain times, they have traditionally been held responsible and made scapegoats, regardless of which world order they are living under. In addition, the echoes of the Holocaust give substance and immediate relevance to Allen's hypothetical questioning of the nature and value of ethical action in a dangerous, irrational, and uncertain world.

See also *Death: A Play*; **Holocaust**; **Little-Man Humor.** For additional reading, see Mashey Bernstein, "*'My Worst Fears Realized,' Woody Allen and the Holocaust.*"

Side Effects. A best-selling collection of Allen's short fiction and plays published by Random House in 1980. The play *My Apology* is original to this collection; everything else first appeared between 1975 and 1980 in *New Yorker*, *New Republic*, *New York Times*, and *Kenyon Review.* The last of Allen's three books, *Side Effects* follows *Getting Even* (1971) and *Without Feathers* (1975).

Taken as a whole, the collection reflects Allen's transformation between 1975 and 1980 from a comedian into a serious artist who explores human nature, relationships, and proper action. During the same period Allen released his last pure comedy, *Love and Death* (1975); acted in his first truly political film, *The Front* (1976); made *Annie Hall* (1977), the pivotal movie that effected his transition from humorist to artist; filmed his first serious drama, the Bergman-inspired *Interiors* (1978); celebrated New York City in the visually stunning *Manhattan* (1979); and released the Fellini-like *Stardust Memories* (1980), perhaps Allen's most experimental film. The stories in *Side Effects* likewise range from the broad literary comedy characteristic of his earlier writings to more fully developed stories that strive for more than just a laugh.

Among the more purely comic sketches are "Remembering Needleman," "The Condemned," "By Destiny Denied," "The UFO Menace," and "Fabrizio's: Criticism and Response." These were written earlier than the other stories; all but "Fabrizio's" (1979) first appeared between 1975 and 1977. "The Query," a play, was first published in the *New Republic* (September 18, 1976). It, too, is an absurdist comedy, a sort of shaggy dog story about Abe Lincoln and a bad joke. Though not published until 1980, the other play, "My Apology," is also just for laughs. In it, Allen directs the one-liners at himself, not at any outside targets, as he imagines himself condemned to death in Socrates' place.

Like the fiction from his earlier books, "Remembering Needleman" parodies intellectual pretentiousness and abstraction. Needleman, a composite of leftist intellectuals from the mid-twentieth century, wrote such tomes as *Non-Existence: What to Do If It Suddenly Strikes You*. As Maurice Yacowar points out, Needleman's belief that "the only thing that was real was his IOU to the bank for six million marks" alludes to the six million Jews killed in the Holocaust, thereby interjecting Allen's notion that "academic study cannot be detached from real political consequences" (Yacowar, *Loser Take All*, 90). "Fabrizio's" also spoofs intellectuals by presenting a restaurant review and responses to it as though they are a scholarly debate in an academic journal. "The Condemned" makes fun of existentialism and the literary formula of the would-be assassin plagued by moral doubts, such as those that also afflict Dostoyevsky's characters and Boris and Sonja in *Love and Death*:

A feeling of nausea swept over him as he contemplated the implications of his action. This was existential nausea, caused by his intense awareness of the contingency of life, and could not be relieved with an ordinary Alka-Seltzer. What was required was an Existential Alka-Seltzer—a product sold in many Left Bank drugstores.

The protagonist's name alludes to cinematographer Ghislain Cloquet, who was director of photography for *Night and Fog* (1956), Alain Resnais's documentary about Auschwitz, and for *Love and Death*.

"By Destiny Denied" pretends to be notes for an eight-hundred-page book, and "The UFO Menace" describes UFO sightings by such famous historical figures as Goethe, who screamed at the fiery red balls that were chasing him that he was a genius and consequently unable to run fast. A more contemporary account mentions the "strange tongue" of the aliens that "sounded like when you back your car over a fat person."

By contrast, "The Kugelmass Episode," "The Diet," "The Lunatic's Tale," "Nefarious Times We Live In," "Retribution," and "The Shallowest Man" introduce different kinds of storytelling that are less absurd, less concerned with garnering laughs, more nuanced, and more fully developed. Apart from "Nefarious Times" (1975), they all first appeared between 1977 and 1980. These stories do not continually undermine their own seriousness, as Allen's earlier ones do. Instead, they build to a dramatic conclusion or even to a deliberate anticlimax. Some even make a point.

Like the literary comedies, "Nefarious Times We Live In" derives its humor from one-liners and absurdities. But Allen satirizes several subjects in order to reveal them as inherently ridiculous. This practice represents a radical departure from his self-parody and nonsense. In the earlier work, it is Allen himself who comes across as absurd; in "Nefarious Times" the objects of his satire appear insane. The story was written the same year that would-be assassins made two attempts on President Gerald Ford's life. One of the assailants, Lynette "Squeaky" Fromme, was a member of the Charles Manson cult that had murdered actress Sharon Tate and her friends. That year, the U.S. Senate's Church Committee reported abuses by the FBI, CIA, and other national security agencies. "Nefarious Times" satirizes both the government and charismatic cults.

It is narrated by a third would-be assassin, a former cult member who maintains the army had used him to test the effects of LSD—one of the practices revealed by the Church Committee. "Cumulative side effects took their toll on my perception and when I could no longer tell the difference between my brother Morris and two soft-boiled eggs, I was discharged." The equation of his brother with soft-boiled eggs suggests the dada-like absurdism of Allen's earlier work. But here Allen is describing not an outlandishly fictitious image from his own imagination, but an actual government practice that had been widely reported in the press, and this gives a new bite and relevancy to Allen's writing.

It also dates the story. Other topical targets of his satire are the Moonies, EST therapy, secret CIA tests on the citizens of New York, and government infiltration of protest groups. The narrator takes up residence in San Francisco and sustains himself by agitating at Berkeley and then informing for the FBI.

"The Kugelmass Episode," winner of the 1977 O. Henry Award for best short story, first appeared in the *New Yorker*. It was subsequently adapted for stage. Like *Annie Hall*, which also appeared in 1977, "The Kugelmass Episode" reflects Allen's transition from comedian to artist. He still plays with the Western literary canon and retains the absurdity of his earlier stories, but he abandons their loose plot structures and instead employs a more conventional story line in which a magician transports a humanities professor from City College into the world of *Madame Bovary*. Allen develops individual scenes more fully than in his previous books, as Sidney Kugelmass enters Emma Bovary's home—much to the consternation of readers of the novel who are confused by the sudden appearance of a bald Jewish man. Eventually Kugelmass returns with Emma to modern-day New York, removing her from the novel. There, she becomes Kugelmass's loving mistress and then a demanding shrew. "I cannot get my mind around this," a frustrated reader declares. "First a strange character named Kugelmass, and now she's gone from the book. Well, I guess the mark of a classic is that you can reread it a thousand times and always find something new." (See **"The Kugelmass Episode."**)

"The Diet" also sustains more fully developed scenes as it parodies Kafka's "Metamorphoses," while "The Lunatic's Tale" comes closer to a conventional story than anything Allen had previously written. First published in 1977, it is a first-person narration by a successful doctor who has been driven to despair. On one lightning-filled night he merged the mind of his wife, a brilliant woman he loved, with the sexy body of an ignorant woman he lusted for. Much of the story is devoted to describing the unsettling deceptions that conducting an affair entails, thereby establishing the desire and need for the secret operation, and the plot leads to a climax, followed by an anticlimax—he then grows dissatisfied and develops a crush on an unexceptional, plain-looking stewardess instead. But the comic deflation at the end makes a real point: a formerly successful surgeon has been reduced to a homeless lunatic because of his inability to remain satisfied with any woman who will have him. (Allen later returned to this premise in *Stardust Memories*, where a mad scientist performs a similar operation but falls in love with the ugly, stupid "reject." And he invokes the theme in *Annie Hall*, citing Groucho Marx's remark that he would not join any club that would accept someone like him.)

"Retribution" deals with the same theme. Published in 1980 in *Kenyon Review*, a prominent literary magazine, it develops relationships among the characters far more complex than in Allen's earlier fiction, and the major source of the pleasure comes from revealing those complexities. Except for the final line, the story is not intended to be humorous. Instead, Allen conveys the dilemma experienced by a young Jewish man who falls in love with a sexy, attractive WASP (white, Anglo-Saxon Protestant) woman from

Connecticut, but then becomes even more attracted to her mother. Allen, like Philip Roth, presents the allure that alien, upper-class WASP culture holds for a middle-class Jewish boy. Harold Cohen's girlfriend, Connie, is tall, self-possessed, intelligent, attractive, and accomplished; her brilliant little sister, Lindsay, is flirtatious, and their mother, Emily, has a wide, warm smile, "a ravishing pioneer face" and a "chesty, big laugh." She oozes warmth and seductiveness.

But over time Harold becomes aware of a twisted side to this wholesome WASP culture that he so deeply longs to join. As he develops a close friendship with Emily, Connie refuses to have sex with him, because Harold has become almost a son to her mother, which makes him like a brother to her— and that feels too much like incest for Connie. Then Emily's seemingly idyllic marriage proves illusory, as she and her husband suddenly divorce.

Harold's greatest moment of illumination comes when, over the objections of everyone in his family, he marries Emily. After the wedding ceremony, Connie finds him alone in the bedroom and tries to seduce him because, "You turn me on like you can't believe." When Harold reminds her that she had been turned off to him because he had become a brother symbol, Connie replies, "It's a whole new ball game. . . . Marrying Mom has made you my father."

As his relationships with Connie and Emily evolve, Harold distances himself from his family and assimilates more fully into the WASP culture. But Connie's incestuous passion for a father figure reveals to Harold just how far apart their worlds are. His epiphany instinctively leads him to reidentify with his own family and his Jewish background for the first time in the story. At the same time, it creates a comic anticlimax.

Also published in *Kenyon Review* in 1980, "The Shallowest Man" illustrates Allen's evolving departure from comedy and his developing interest in questions of morality and proper action. Allen employs a frame tale, in which an omniscient third-person narrator tells the story of Koppelman telling how Lenny Mendel visited a dying poker pal solely to impress a pretty nurse at the hospital. Despite his insincere motives, Mendel's repeated appearances greatly cheered his friend, who, shortly before expiring, described them as "the most touching and deepest experience he had ever had with another human being." Impressed by Mendel's humanity, the nurse agreed to date him, and they had a year-long affair together.

Sitting at a delicatessen lunch table, Koppelman and his friends debate the meaning of the story and divide over whether Mendel's motives matter more than the results of his actions. Koppelman offers the story as an example of a shallow person, while Moscowitz condemns Mendel even further:

"It goes to show how some people are just no good." But Abe Trochman maintains that the point is that "a dying man becomes the beneficiary of his friend's sudden adoration of a woman," while Lupowitz retorts, "Mendel went out of obligation. He returned out of self-interest." The third-person narrator, who possesses the greatest authority in any frame tale, remains silent, and is content to let the story end with Bursky's declaration, "What's the difference? . . . It was an entertaining anecdote. Let's order."

The ending confers an element of cubism onto the narrative, in which each point of view is legitimate, even though they contradict one another. The withdrawal of the omniscient narrator echoes Allen's growing tendency in his films simply to present his characters without judging them. The different responses shed little light onto Mendel, but they do characterize the men who utter them: Lupowitz is cynical, Trochman is disposed to see the best in people, Moscowitz the worst, and Bursky accepts things as they are. In Allen's cubist reality, each man experiences the story according to the lens he views it through. Allen returned to the frame-tale device in *Broadway Danny Rose*.

Side Effects embodies the artistic transformation Allen underwent in the late 1970s. Although most of the pieces are humorous and some employ modes similar to his earliest writings, there is a general evolution toward the concerns of realism, if not toward conventional, realistic literary forms. Compared to his earlier books, *Side Effects* features more fully realized characters and scenes, greater social and political awareness, and deeper exploration of issues and relationships. After the publication of *Side Effects*, Allen largely put aside his writing in order to devote himself more fully to his movies, which similarly grew in complexity, depth, and exploration of character.

See also **Getting Even**; **Plays**; **Without Feathers**.

Sleeper. A 1973 film directed by, written by, and starring Allen as Miles Monroe. It costars Diane Keaton (Luna), John Beck (Erno), Mary Gregory (Dr. Melik), Don Keefer (Dr. Tryon), John McLiam (Dr. Agon), Bartlett Robinson (Dr. Orva), Chris Forbes (Rainer), Marya Small (Dr. Nero), Peter Hobbs (Dr. Dean), Susan Miller (Ellen), Lou Picetti (MC), Brian Avery (Gerald), Spencer Milligan (Jeb), and Spencer Ross (Sears Swiggles). Marshall Brickman collaborated on the screenplay. Jack Grossberg was the producer, David M. Walsh director of photography, Dale Hennesy production designer, Joel Schumacher costumer, and Ralph Rosenblum editor. Allen served as music director, scoring both his own original compositions and standard numbers, which he performed with his New Orleans Funeral and

Ragtime Orchestra and the Preservation Hall Jazz Band. United Artists was the North American distributor.

According to those who worked with Allen during his early career, *Sleeper* was the first movie to show his promise as a gifted filmmaker. Editor Ralph Rosenblum believes that *Sleeper* represents Allen's transition to a true cinematic professional, as the project involved more money and Allen demonstrated greater ambition in his subject matter and technique (Lax 335). The filming did not go smoothly or easily, and Allen ran behind schedule and a million dollars over budget, completing the final edit a mere two days before its scheduled opening. Ultimately, the movie cost $3.1 million to produce, but it grossed $8.3 million in U.S. and Canadian distribution (not including later video rentals and television revenues). Allen and Joffe shared about $2 million of the profits. The warmly reviewed film became the sixteenth biggest U.S. moneymaker of 1974, and it further established Allen and Keaton as a cinema couple.

Although *Sleeper* relies on numerous quick gags and one-liners, it is more visually attuned than Allen's earlier directorial efforts, *Take the Money and Run*, *Bananas*, and *Play It Again, Sam*. The humor is more physical and the plot more cohesive. Furthermore, the comedy involves a modicum of character development and articulates some of Allen's political values, something his films rarely do explicitly.

Woody Allen and Diane Keaton in *Sleeper*. Courtesy of Photofest.

Sleeper is very much a product of its time. Its projection of a future dominated by totalitarian governments is typical of Cold War–era literature, and
the movie alludes strongly to George Orwell's *Nineteen Eighty-Four* (1949)
and Aldous Huxley's *Brave New World* (1932), which were models for
much futuristic literature in that time of nuclear stalemate and superpower
confrontation. The filming on *Sleeper* began only one month after American troops completed their withdrawal from Vietnam and while the Watergate investigation was revealing serious abuses of power by the Nixon
administration. (Watergate culminated the following year with President
Nixon's resignation on August 9, 1974.) Warnings about government oppression were common during the Cold War, from both the political right,
which feared the expansion of repressive communist regimes, and the left,
which feared American imperialism, the military-industrial complex, and
corporate fascism. *Sleeper* appeals to these common projections of the future, at once confirming the audience's worst fears and simultaneously as-
suaging those fears by reducing them to burlesque.

The assumption of a totalitarian future is intrinsic to the plot. Miles Monroe is a thirty-five-year-old clarinetist and health food store owner who underwent minor surgery for an ulcer in 1973. Complications set in, and he
was cryogenically preserved in aluminum foil until members of a rebel underground discovered him exactly two hundred years later. Miles is potentially valuable to the underground because, unlike everyone else in the
future, the government does not have a file on him or a record of his finger-
prints. Claiming to be nonpolitical, Miles initially resists, but he flees when
he learns that the government will reprogram him if it catches him. His
brain, he objects, is his second favorite organ. Eventually Miles allies with
the rebels and destroys the Leader's nose, thereby precluding the possibility
that the recently perished Leader can be cloned and return to hold the government together.

In the process of escaping, Miles teams with Luna, a shallow but renowned poet who sells twenty to thirty poems a week "plus greeting cards"
and whose chief model is Rod McKuen, an overly sentimental poet who
was popular in the early 1970s. Initially Luna is a complacent citizen who
loves the Leader, a friendly-looking Big Brother figure whose image appears everywhere. She wonders innocently, "What makes people suddenly
go berserk and hate everything, anyway? . . . Why does there have to be an
underground? After all, there's the orb [a futuristic device for sexual gratifi-
cation]. There's the telescreen. There's the orgasmatron [another device for
sexual fulfillment]. What more do they want?" But after Miles kidnaps her
while fleeing security forces, she eventually falls in love with him and
learns that there is more to life than mechanical sex and the telescreen, and

she comprehends how the government has been using these forms of gratification to control and manipulate the population. Sander H. Lee notes how Luna initiates a transformation in Allen's representations of women, most of whom are largely one-dimensional in his earlier films. According to Lee, although Luna "shares many of Miles's flaws, she has a distinct personality, and her growth over the course of the film raises her to the level of Miles's equal, lifting her out of the traditionally subservient role women usually play in Allen's earlier films" (Lee 45).

Sleeper, like *Bananas*, tapped into the worldwide preoccupation with revolution against totalitarian regimes that existed in the 1960s and 1970s. Luna's character development, her growing political awareness, and her forthright desire for sexual fulfillment further appealed to viewers sympathetic to the feminism and sexual revolution of that period. *Sleeper*'s attacks on materialism and consumerism likewise found receptive audiences among the counterculture.

However, in both films, although Allen sympathizes with the fight against oppression, he ultimately rejects political solutions. *Bananas* illustrates the adage that power corrupts and absolute power corrupts absolutely, as the rebel leader, Esposito, turns into a tyrant within moments of overthrowing the repressive dictatorship that preceded him. *Sleeper* shows how followers, as well as leaders, can abuse their influence power by carelessly investing their support. Luna moves easily from being a government apologist to a committed rebel without ever gaining any deep understanding of the real political situation. As Nancy Pogel notes, "Allen suggests that a lack of personal integrity and clear identity makes one susceptible to political enthusiasms of all sorts" (Pogel 69). Ultimately Miles destroys the Leader, thereby throwing the government into chaos, but he refuses to join the underground because he knows it will be no better. "In six months we'll be stealing [its leader] Erno's nose. Political solutions don't work."

Miles rejects God and politics. And when Luna argues that science has proven that meaningful relationships between men and women cannot last, because "there's a chemical in our bodies that makes it so we all get on each other's nerves sooner or later," he calls science "an intellectual dead end" and dismisses scientists as "little guys in tweed suits cutting up frogs on foundation grants." When Luna asks what he does believe in, Miles answers, "Sex and death. Two things that come once in a lifetime. But at least after death you're not nauseous."

Miles's flippancy is a large part of Allen's answer to the meaning of life. Miles and Allen believe in laughter, because it is fun and it feels good. In this sense laughter is always a redeeming, uplifting, and energizing experience. Its truth is visceral, not cognitive, and visceral truths are ultimately deeper, more forceful, and more primal. We feel the basic truths more than we know them.

When Miles states that he believes in sex and death, he implicitly claims to believe in the libido: the unconscious force of life, the instinct for procreation that also leads to death. According to Freud, sex and death are the two basic impulses of the libido. Miles's reply is consistent with the absurdist sensibility that permeates Allen's early work. His frenetic spirit seems to embody the unfettered play of his libido, which delights not only in sex but also in its own cleverness and creativity. At the same time, his ego—his conscious self—dreads the inevitable movement toward death that the libido also embodies.

As a comedy, *Sleeper* generates laughter and high spirits—a libidinal expression of pleasure. Allen had originally planned to make a two-part film set first in the present and then in the future, but that proved too great an undertaking, so he decided to make the futuristic portion. But whereas Allen's earlier films rely primarily on verbal humor and literary and cinematic parody, *Sleeper* employs a more visual form of humor. "I wanted to make a kind of slapstick-style movie, a visual movie" (*Woody Allen on Woody Allen* 68). Elsewhere, he describes his desire for *Sleeper* to be "a great big cartoon . . . cute and funny" (Fox 70).

Visual humor in *Sleeper* ranges from slapstick gags that culminate with a pie in the face or a character slipping on an immense futuristic banana peel, to costuming that places Allen in an absurd, inflatable hydrovac suit, dresses the "male" robot-servant of a gay man in a maid's outfit, and uses the Nazi swastika as a fashion statement. Allen includes Keystone Cops-like chase scenes in which bumbling security agents pursue Miles and Luna, and he employs cartoon-like imagery when he shows the Leader's nose flattened by a steamroller. The stark white, brightly lit, futuristic set designs provide a sterile background that contrasts the visually absurd antics.

Like Allen's other early films, *Sleeper* retains the fundamentally absurd spirit that also appears in his fiction and stand-up comedy. Characteristically, he plays off earlier literature and employs word play, incongruous pairings, and other techniques of literary comedy. (See **Literary Comedy**.) For instance, when Miles and Luna sneak into the operation on the Leader's nose, he tells the security guard, "We're here to see the nose. I heard it was running." Elsewhere, Miles impersonates Miss America, who was also a satiric target in *Bananas*; machines dispense absolution in futuristic churches, and newspaper headlines proclaim that the pope has fathered twins.

Moreover, Allen pays special homage to the Marx Brothers. When Luna and Miles prepare to operate on the Leader's nose, their slapstick antics emulate the scene from *A Day at the Races* (1937) where the Marx Brothers prepare to give Margaret Dumont a medical exam. (The computer assisting them in that operation speaks in the same monotone voice as HAL, the dysfunctional computer from Stanley Kubrick's *2001*, 1968.) When Luna maneuvers Miles while he dangles from a large magnetic computer tape, she evokes the scene in *A Night at the Opera* (1935) where Harpo is dunked into the ocean while clinging to the ship's rigging. A futuristic mirror scene plays off *Duck Soup* (1933), and Miles tries to impress Luna by dancing like Groucho.

Allen makes comic references to other literature as well, even to *Bananas*. Luna composes a song for the rebels, the same song that Ernesto sings to his revolutionaries in Allen's earlier film. Allen also parodies live theater, from the ridiculous to the sublime. A futuristic robot-tailor and his robot-partner argue like Jewish tailors from vaudeville routines. The gag climaxes with a familiar punch line about a poor-fitting suit, as the Jewish-sounding robot-tailor finally consents to alterations: "So, we'll take it in."

The film's strongest literary parody makes sport of Tennessee Williams, a favorite target for Allen's burlesque. When Miles lapses into the character of Blanche from *A Streetcar Named Desire* (1947), Luna snaps him out of it by assuming the role of Stanley Kowalski, as played by Marlon Brando. The scene concludes with Miles collapsed on the ground, supported by Luna and Erno, saying in his best Blanche DuBois falsetto, "I always rely on the kindness of strangers."[1]

Allen uses the futuristic setting as a vehicle for looking back on the present from a removed comic perspective. For instance, he pokes gentle fun at fitness advocates who promote healthier diets. A former health food store owner, Miles learns that cigarette smoking is good for us, as are deep fat, steak, cream pies, and hot fudge. Orwell warns in *Nineteen Eighty-Four* that governments of the future will manipulate the population by reducing language, making it more abstract and less precise, so citizens will be incapable of formulating deep and disruptive thoughts. Allen depicts such a future by having Luna and her friends speak in the empty-headed slang of the 1950s. For instance, when Luna wants to express her great admiration for someone's art, she says, "It's keen. It's pure. No. No. It's greater than keen."

Allen makes fun of more contemporary targets when Miles is asked to explain unidentified artifacts from the 1970s. Miles learns that the nuclear war broke out when Albert Shankar, the outspoken head of the National Teachers Union, got hold of a nuclear warhead. He derides the National Rifle Association as "a group that helped criminals get guns so they could kill citizens. It was a public service." (Allen attacked the NRA again almost twenty-five years later in *Deconstructing Harry*.) Miles identifies Joseph Stalin and Chiang Kai-shek as leaders he did not like, Norman Mailer as someone famous for donating his ego to the Harvard Medical School, Charles de Gaulle as a French chef with his own television show, and television evangelist Billy Graham as someone "big in the religion business. He knew God personally—they were romantically linked for a while." Miles notes that the feminists who were burning their bras produced only small fires but complains that the *Playboy* centerfold girls did not actually exist in real life. He confirms a theory that convicted criminals had been forced to watch videotapes of abrasive sports announcer Howard Cosell. (Cosell also appears in *Bananas*, where he interviews participants in a political assassination and announces Fielding's wedding night, and he has a cameo in *Broadway Danny Rose*.) Miles further confirms that Richard Nixon had been president but committed an act so horrendous they wiped out all record of him. He adds that the Secret Service used to count the silverware whenever Nixon left the White House.

Despite these occasional satiric jibes, *Sleeper* is primarily a romantic comedy that pairs Allen and Keaton as an insecure, inept, but lovable couple. It warns of a future in which powerful governments will use technology to control their citizens, but most of all it reaffirms the values of love, individual freedom, and self-expression as it celebrates the spirit of play.

NOTE

1. Blanche also appears in Allen's one-act play *God*, and Williams's *The Glass Menagerie* (1944) is the basis for Allen's play *The Floating Light Bulb*. See **Tennessee Williams**.

Stand-up Comedy. Allen began working as a stand-up comedian after he lost interest in writing for television. One of the highest paid television writers in Hollywood, he went from earning $1,700 per week in 1960 writing for the *Garry Moore Show*, to working for free at New York coffee houses while he developed his craft. But he enjoyed the freedom to develop his own material, and what he learned about performing, delivery, and working a live audience influenced his later work as an actor and playwright.

Influenced by Mort Sahl and Lenny Bruce, Allen joined a newly emerging tradition of 1960s stand-up comedy that broke down the barrier between the comic and his audience and addressed topics that had been largely taboo in the 1950s: sexual inadequacy, sexual prodigy, psychoanalysis, religion, race relations, politics, and ethnic roots. But Allen's humor lacks Bruce's acerbic edge or Sahl's satirical thrust. Instead, he treats political issues absurdly. For instance, while Sahl might ridicule the Ku Klux Klan's bigotry and Bruce might direct his barbs at both the Klan and its liberal opponents who practice more subtle forms of racial discrimination, Allen eschews condemnation altogether and instead reduces the Klan to farce. A routine describing his abduction by Klansmen in the South, when he is dressed as a ghost en route to a costume party, first makes fun of Allen's own naiveté and lack of perception; he assumes the Grand Dragon is someone going to the party dressed as a dragon. In the end, he gives himself away as Jewish by making a pledge when they solicit a contribution, but he ends up persuading the notoriously racist and anti-Semitic Klansmen to endorse the cause of brotherhood and make a $2,000 contribution to Israel.

Much of Allen's humor is directed at his own limitations. He mocks his small, unimposing physical stature by pretending to be a great lover, and he develops other aspects of the little-man persona that characterizes his early films. For instance, the little man's ineptitude with machines appears in a routine where a talking elevator exacts revenge for an act of violence Allen committed on his television. In the end the elevator, which is better spoken than Allen, hurls anti-Semitic epithets at him.

Although Allen's initial audience was mainly young, college-educated listeners, his popularity quickly spread to mainstream America. However, his stand-up career got off to a slow start, because he needed to get over his shyness before an audience and learn to deliver his lines effectively. His agents, Charles Joffe and Jack Rollins, worked extensively with him, critiquing every performance, and soon Allen began performing at such popular cabarets as New York's Village Gate, Mister Kelly's in Chicago, and 'the hungry i' in San Francisco. (Harry Belafonte was the other big act Rollins and Joffe developed at the time.) Between fall 1963 and spring 1964, Allen's fee rose from $1,000 per week to $5,000 per week, and by the end of 1964 he was earning $10,000 per appearance and performing before sold-out audiences in Caesar's Palace in Las Vegas and Carnegie Hall in New York. He also performed on television, as a guest on the popular *Ed Sullivan Show* and on late-night shows that appealed to adult audiences, especially Johnny Carson's *Tonight Show*, which Allen frequently guest hosted.

Allen's break-through opportunity to write for the movies grew from his stand-up comedy. In 1964 actress Shirley MacLaine, who had performed some of Allen's television skits, caught his act at the Blue Angel and encouraged producer Charles K. Feldman to watch him. Convinced that Allen could reach a modern audience because he had an "unusual ability to deal with sexual yearnings and inadequacies with such charm and wit," Feldman hired him to write the screenplay of *What's New, Pussycat?* (Fox 29). *Pussycat* proved an enormous financial hit that established Allen's credibility in Hollywood. Nonetheless, Allen continued to perform before live audiences through 1972, when his career as a filmmaker took over.

Allen issued five record albums of his routines but was disappointed that they were never enormously successful. The first three have original material: *Woody Allen* (recorded live at Mr. Kelly's in Chicago, March 1964), *Woody Allen, Volume 2* (recorded live at the Shadows in Washington, D.C., April 1965), and *The Third Woody Allen Album* (recorded live at Eugene's in San Francisco, August 1968). *Woody Allen: The Nightclub Years: 1964–1968* (1976) and *Woody Allen Stand-up Comic, 1964–1968* (1978) are compilations of the previous albums. *The Nightclub Years* has been reissued as a compact disc by EMI Records.

Stardust Memories. A 1980 film directed by, written by, and starring Allen, who plays film director Sandy Bates. It costars Charlotte Rampling (Dorrie), Marie-Christine Barrault (Isobel), Tony Roberts (Tony), Jessica Harper (Daisy), John Rothman (Jack Abel), Anne De Salvo (Sandy's sister), Joan Newman (Sandy's mother), Ken Chapin (Sandy's father), and Sharon Stone (beautiful girl on the train). Robert Greenhut was the producer, Gordon Willis director of photography, Dick Hyman music director, Mel Bourne production designer, Santo Loquasto costumer, and Susan E. Morse editor. The music includes Hyman's "Hebrew School Rag" and "Just One of Those Things," "Easy to Love," "Tropical Mood Meringue," "I'll See You in My Dreams," "Three Little Words," Moonlight Serenade," "Stardust," and Mussorgsky's *A Night on Bald Mountain*, among other selections. United Artists was the North American distributor.

One of Allen's personal favorites, *Stardust Memories* was not well received in the United States, where its stream-of-consciousness plot structure and Fellini-like surrealism confused many viewers unaccustomed to these cinematic techniques. European audiences were more receptive to Allen's experimentation, and overall the film did slightly better than break even. The film cost $9 million to produce but grossed only $4.1 million in U.S. and Canadian rentals (not including later video rentals and television revenues).

In addition to difficulties with the movie's experimental style, many critics felt Allen was making a personal statement, attacking and belittling his critics and core audience. Allen emphatically denies this, despite the many obvious similarities between himself and his character. "They thought the lead character was *me*! Not a fictional character, but me, and that I was expressing hostility toward my audience. And, of course, that was in no way the point of the film. It was about a character who is obviously having a sort of a nervous breakdown and in spite of success has come to a point in his life where he is having a bad time. But the reaction was like, 'So you think critics are no good, you think the audience is no good.' . . . You know, I've never been the character I've played. And Charlie Chaplin was never the tramp or any of his characters. And Jerry Lewis is not the nutty character he impersonates in his films. There are some similar traits, but it's not me." Allen adds, "If I did think that [the audience and critics were fools], which I don't, I would be smart enough not to say it in a movie" (*Woody Allen on Woody Allen* 121–122, 128). Sander H. Lee offers a plausible interpretation that disassociates Allen from Sandy but also accounts for their obvious similarities: "Allen is presenting a portrait of a man who is intended to appear just as depraved as Allen's critics have accused him of being" (Lee 115). Allen predicted that in time viewers would disassociate him personally from the film and appreciate it on its own merits, and this seems to have become the case.

Just as Allen denies that he was overly influenced by Ingmar Bergman when making *Interiors*, he maintains that Federico Fellini did not exert an undue influence on *Stardust Memories*. Nonetheless, the parallels are strong enough for us to regard *Stardust Memories* as Allen's American version of *8½* (1963). Although neither Allen nor Fellini identifies completely with his protagonist, they share obvious affinities with their main characters, both of whom are famous filmmakers experiencing personal and professional crises. Both are beset by admiring fans and demanding producers, and both lapse easily into fantasy worlds, which we have difficulty discerning from reality. Furthermore, each film uses a stream-of-consciousness narrative technique, and each climaxes when the fictional director, after fantasizing being shot, discovers an acceptable ending for his movie. Finally, both films employ experimental, expressionist techniques to communicate characters' inner emotional states, and they share a playful, absurdist spirit that obscures the line between the real and the surreal.[1]

Bergman's *The Silence* (1963) is another cinematic influence, and Allen's ex-wife Louise Lasser inspired the character of Dorrie, a creative, clever, sexy but mentally ill woman with whom Sandy has had an affair. Lasser, whose suicidal mother inspired Eve in *Interiors*, was a wonderful person, according to Allen, but "crazy as a loon." Like Dorrie, she initially had two good weeks a month followed by two bad ones, but the happy times made the difficult ones worthwhile. However, her condition deteriorated until she would have only two good days a month (Lax 169–170).

In *Stardust Memories* Allen addresses a narrative problem that was often treated by experimental writers of the 1960s and 1970s: how to tell a story that is original, honest, affirmative, and appropriately suited for its moment in human and literary history. In *Stardust Memories* the artistic challenge for Allen is to confer some semblance of value on human existence, even while affirming the unpleasant realities that life has no inherent meaning and that no act we commit has any ultimate value.

Like Bergman's Knight in *The Seventh Seal* (1956) or the Fisher King in T. S. Eliot's "The Waste Land" (1924), Sandy Bates asks how it is possible to commit a meaningful act in a totally indifferent universe and in a world filled with overwhelming human suffering. Bates despairs over his inability to make a difference or even to create useful illusions. He is aware of the horrors and catastrophes that occur each day throughout the world, and his diverting comedies seem trivial, but nothing else he can imagine can significantly ease the pain and anguish that he empathizes with. The film's story, then, centers on how Sandy, and Allen, deal with despair and simultaneously bring their respective films to successful conclusions that enable them to retain their nihilism but provide some kind of affirmation too.

Allen turns to metafiction to achieve this paradoxical goal. Critic Robert Scholes coined the term *metafiction* to refer to stories that are about stories, as opposed to *fiction*, which refers to stories that are directly about life. (See **Metafiction**.) God's existence may remain problematic and the purpose of our lives dubious, but an author's existence is verifiable and the purpose of a story discernable, even if it proves ambiguous and subject to interpretation. We cannot know if our own lives follow predetermined destinies, but narratives typically fulfill the destiny willed on them by their authors. Hence, a narrative that is about finding a way to tell a story can assume a rational universe and provide a happy ending without contradicting the larger premise that the universe is irrational and all human struggle is absurd. Therefore, by shifting the focus of the story from the internal characters to the narrative process itself, authors attempt to do a literary "end around" the nihilistic worldview, even though they cannot contradict it outright. At the same time, since the inside story is typically a fiction about life, the storyteller can also address genuine human concerns and the "felt ultimacies" of the times. Thus an author can "actually do with his left hand what his right hand demonstrates to be impossible" (Dunne 21).

Stardust Memories, then, is the story of Sandy Bates's effort to find an ending to his film that will at once satisfy the studio heads who want a box office success and leave him feeling intellectually and artistically honest. Contained within that story is the story of Sandy's past romance with Dorrie, an unstable manic-depressive, and his current romance with Isobel, a self-possessed, affectionate mother of two boys. Superimposed on both those stories are Allen's own problems in finding a suitable narrative structure for his tale of Sandy Bates, and his own obvious personal affinities with Sandy.

Thus, as he did earlier in *Play It Again, Sam, God*, and "The Kugelmass Episode," and later in *The Purple Rose of Cairo* and *Deconstructing Harry*, Allen establishes multiple layers of fiction and reality. He then uses a stream-of-consciousness narrative technique to interweave these layers, jumping

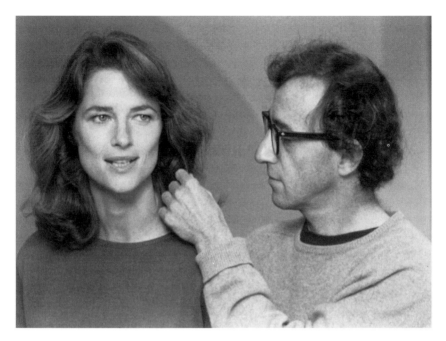

Charlotte Rampling and Woody Allen in a scene from *Stardust Memories*. Courtesy of Photofest.

among them without signaling to us where we are or where we are going. As a result, Allen casts us into a state of uncertainty that mirrors his modernist view of reality: we cannot distinguish fact from fiction, discern logical connections among the characters and scenes, or place events in a coherent chronological sequence.

As we learn through repeated viewings to reassemble the events, sort out the layers of reality, and impose a coherent narrative on the fragments we have witnessed, we share Sandy's achievement of imposing order on chaos and bringing the movie to a successful conclusion, even as we realize, like Sandy, that death arrives unexpectedly and remains inevitable, and nothing can change that fact.

As the story of a story, *Stardust Memories* begins with Sandy's first, unsuccessful effort to conclude his unnamed film. The protagonist, played by Sandy (who is played by Allen), sits in silence on a train filled with dour, severe-looking people. Across the tracks is a train filled with sexy, funloving people, and a pretty girl (Sharon Stone) throws him a kiss. He tries desperately to find the conductor, but it is too late. His train leaves the station, and he is stuck on the glum train. Subsequently, the characters from both trains appear on screen walking around a garbage heap—the ostensible point being that both trains lead to the same destination: happy people and severe people all end up dead.

Not until this point do we discover we are watching a film within a film and not the "outer" film. However, Sandy's ending to the inner film is too morbid for the studio executives, who want something more upbeat, especially since the movie will be released at Easter. But Sandy is stressed out, at odds with himself, and on the verge of a nervous breakdown; he does not feel the joy necessary to create a happy ending. He becomes enraged when the executives try to take the film from him and impose a hokey, unauthentic, upbeat conclusion, but he is unable to offer a mutually acceptable solution until he resolves the problems in his personal life. Thus, our ability to separate fiction from reality becomes further strained as the inside and outside stories become intertwined: the resolution of the outside story (Sandy's love life) becomes a prerequisite for concluding the inside story (the train travelers).

As in *Manhattan*, the challenge for Sandy is to learn to know himself and accept himself sufficiently so he can choose self-accepting, emotionally healthy, supportive women who are capable of expressing real, sustained affection for him instead of self-absorbed, emotionally needy, unstable women who are, by their own admission, "trouble." He is attracted to accomplished, intelligent, articulate, women who suffer from deep mental or emotional problems. His most passionate, exhilarating affair had been with Dorrie, a hot-tempered manic-depressive who required lithium and had only two good days a month—but those good days seemed almost worth it. Indeed, Sandy enjoyed some near-perfect moments with her, including the one for which the film is named, when Sandy and Dorrie are quietly reading the Sunday paper at home. As they listen to Louis Armstrong play "Stardust" on the stereo, they bask in each other's presence yet remain comfortable within themselves, attuned to their own unshared thoughts. They are both alone and connected.[2]

But neither Dorrie nor Sandy is able to sustain these perfect moments for very long, and they soon lose the ability to create new ones as Dorrie becomes irrationally jealous, overly sensitive, and temperamental and Sandy becomes increasingly stressed by demands on him from her and others. By the time *Stardust Memories* begins, they have already parted, and she has been hospitalized, released, and married.

At the same time, Sandy has moved on to a relationship with Isobel, a married French woman with two children. Yet he still finds himself longing for Dorrie, and the film climaxes when he finally makes a commitment to Isobel, choosing the relaxed good times she offers over the intense emotional swings characteristic of "those dark women with all their problems" who "give you a hard time," as Isobel describes them. "And you like it!"

When Sandy finally chooses a healthy, nurturing relationship over unhealthy, destructive ones, he is able to complete his film. Thus Sandy solves his artistic problem by solving his personal problem. By staging the reconciliation between Isobel and Sandy inside a train in the station, Allen merges Sandy's inner story of the passenger on the train with the outer story of Sandy's inability to find a suitable ending for that inside film. When Sandy tells Isobel that happiness and good times can alleviate the despair of an absurd universe and then kisses her, he simultaneously provides a happy ending for both movies.[3]

But in the movie's final scene, Allen undercuts the happy ending by stepping outside both films, as he shows the actors commenting on their experiences working with the director. By turning our attention to the fact that we have been watching actors delivering lines, Allen distances us from the characters and undermines the seriousness of their problems and the ultimate value of their personal victories. He thereby manages to give us the upbeat ending and undermine it at the same time. In this way he maintains his intellectual honesty by not pretending our existential predicament is better than it is and still furnishes a happy ending.

If coming to the recognition that he no longer wants relationships with troubled women with problems is the key realization at the heart of the film, then Sandy's weekend retreat at the Stardust Hotel provides the setting that provokes this insight to emerge. Thus the title has a double reference: to Sandy's epiphany while watching Dorrie and listening to "Stardust" and to the events from his stay at the Stardust Hotel. The retreat, a retrospective of Sandy's films, enables Allen to move back and forth not only between Sandy's fictional and real-life worlds but also between his personal past and present. Like Barth's genie from *Chimera*, whose project "is to learn where to go by discovering where I am by reviewing where I've been," Sandy learns to go forward by going backward during his Stardust weekend (*Chimera* 10).

The intergalactic spacemen who advise Sandy suggest another reference to stardust that raises core issues in the film. The spaceships prove to be hot-air balloons, so there never were spacemen in actuality. Consequently, Sandy's dialogue has presumably been with himself—a communication with his better self in which he tells himself what he already knows subconsciously but needs to acknowledge consciously and accept: enjoy the good times, stop worrying about the meaning of life, choose Isobel over Dorrie, and tell funnier jokes.

When Sandy ignores this advice by remaining depressed, rejecting Isobel, and offering to run off with Daisy, a Dorrie surrogate, he betrays himself by choosing the most destructive path possible.[4] The gap between what he unconsciously wants and what he consciously chooses becomes too wide, and Sandy passes out, suffering from a nervous breakdown. However, his descent into his unconscious ultimately brings about clarity and positive change.

Like many other Woody Allen characters, Sandy's fear of death and his inability to control death have created much of the anger, despair, and sense of impotence that he suffers from. But during his breakdown, Sandy experiences what seems to be his own death, and he survives it. Like the mythic hero's descent to the underworld, Sandy's death experience transforms him and leaves him stronger by enabling him to confront his worst fear. It is not that he defeats death, but that he moves past it. With death now behind him, he can move forward again and embrace life.

Sandy's death experience not only teaches him how much he cherishes his life; it also enables him to recognize what he really wants and what his true priorities are. This recognition provokes him to choose Isobel, while his liberation from fear rekindles his creativity and enables him to complete his film.

Significantly, Sandy's recollection of his perfect moment with Dorrie comes as he thinks he is dying and he tries to save himself by clinging to the best memory of his life. This effort brings about an epiphany, a vision of himself at peace, comfortably alone with his thoughts but nonetheless attuned to another person. Such moments, he perceives, are what give value to life. Paradoxically, although his recollection is of Dorrie, the harmony he experiences is more characteristic of what he shares with Isobel, with whom he feels relaxed and accepted. And even although Sandy shouts out Dorrie's name while semiconscious, he awakens with the conviction that it is Isobel he wants. Sandy's realization prompts him to follow Isobel to the train station to declare his love, thereby precipitating the resolution of both plots.

On the other hand, because Allen's modernistic, paradoxical worldview cannot sustain an unambiguously happy ending, he also includes elements to undermine the upbeat conclusion: the fact that it is Dorrie whom Sandy remembers when seeking a final memory, not Isobel; the exaggerated, almost clichéd nature of their final reconciliation,[5] and the final scene in which the actors discuss their experiences. As Michael Dunne reminds us, "The writer of metafiction requires the active complicity of the reader if he is to succeed in all this slight-of-hand." Thus Allen leaves us in a realm of uncertainty in which we can believe in the happy ending if we choose, but it requires an act of faith on our part. Those capable of making that leap of faith will enjoy the affirmation; those who cannot must accept despair.

NOTES

1. Nancy Pogel describes the similarities between the films at length.

2. Ironically, when Sandy visits Dorrie in the mental hospital she declares, "I can't be alone, but I can't be too close."

3. Allen merges the two levels by giving the actors double roles. Sandy is played by Woody Allen and his unnamed protagonist is played by Sandy, who is also Woody Allen. And on the final train scene, Isobel appears as both a character in Sandy's film and a lover in his life. Allen further intertwines the levels of reality by making it impossible to determine which level he has left us in at the film's conclusion. In the final seconds, when he walks up to his empty seat to retrieve his glasses and then looks back thoughtfully at the blank screen, we have no way of knowing if we are viewing Sandy Bates or Woody Allen, or perhaps even a third director who mediates between them.

Maurice Yacowar rejects the happy ending. "Sandy has imposed a happy ending on his fiction (1) that he fails to make in his life, and (2) that is analogous to his producers' attempt to brighten Sandy's downbeat conclusion" (Yacowar, *Loser Take All* 225). I find the ending more upbeat, though in modernist fashion it is also deliberately open-ended and subject to interpretation.

The ending parallels the conclusion of *Manhattan*, which is also ambiguously affirmative. In both movies, recollections of simple things that give life meaning inspire Allen's character to action. In *Manhattan* Ike recalls Tracy's face and runs off to find her; in *Stardust Memories* he remembers a perfect moment of tranquility with Dorrie, and he goes on to choose Isobel.

4. Sandy's affair with Dorrie presumably ended some time earlier, but Allen uses the character of Daisy to serve as Dorrie's surrogate. Sandy tells Daisy she reminds him of Dorrie, and images of Daisy frequently trigger the flashbacks that tell us the story of Sandy and Dorrie's romance. Like Dorrie, Daisy is "trouble," by her own admission unable to form close relations with men. She also seems to be in love with a woman with whom she had an earlier sexual relationship, a fact Sandy is aware of because he has overheard her on the phone. (In this regard she is like Jill in *Manhattan*, a woman to whom the Allen character is apparently attracted because of her lesbian tendencies.) Shortly after speaking to the "spacemen," Sandy rejects their advice and suggests that he and Daisy run off together. They are interrupted before they can pursue the prospect further, and he suffers his nervous breakdown shortly thereafter, imagining a fan has assassinated him.

Several commentators have noted the similarity between Sandy's hallucination and the assassination of John Lennon, which occurred just a few months after *Stardust Memories* opened. Allen himself has remarked, "So many people were outraged that I dared to suggest an ambivalent love/hate relationship between an audience and a celebrity; and then, shortly after *Stardust Memories* opened, John Lennon was shot by the very guy who had asked him for his autograph earlier in the day. . . . This is what happens with celebrities—one day people love you, the next day they want to kill you. And the celebrity also feels that way towards the audience; because, in the movie Sandy hallucinates that the guy shoots him; but in fact Sandy is the one who has the gun. So the celebrity imagines that the fan will do to him what he wants to do to the fan. But people don't want to hear this—this is an unpleasant truth to dramatize" (Jacobs 149).

   5. The reconciliation scene has echoes of the play that Alvy Singer writes at the end of *Annie Hall*. But Alvy deliberately distorted the ending of his play to compensate for the fact that in real life, the relationship between Annie and Alvy failed. The allusion to *Annie Hall* thus hints that in real life, Isobel and Sandy do not reconcile, even if the characters in Sandy's movie do.

T

Take the Money and Run. A 1969 film directed by, written by, and starring Allen as bank robber Virgil Starkwell. It costars Janet Margolin (Louise), Marcel Hillaire (Fritz), Jacqueline Hyde (Miss Blair), Lonny Chapman (Jake), Jan Merlin (Al), James Anderson (chain gang warden), Ethel Sokolow (Virgil's mother), Henry Leff (Virgil's father), Louise Lasser (Kay Lewis), and Jackson Beck (narrator). Mickey Rose collaborated on the screenplay, which was adapted from one of Allen's unproduced stage plays. Charles Joffe was the producer, Lester Shorr director of photography, Marvin Hamlisch music director, Fred Harpman production designer, Erick M. Hjemvik costumer, James T. Heckert supervising editor, and Ralph Rosenblum editorial consultant. The music features performances by Oscar Peterson and Eubie Blake. Palomar Pictures, in conjunction with Cinerama Releasing Corporation, was the North American distributor.

Although *What's Up, Tiger Lily?* (1966) was the first film made under Allen's artistic control, *Take the Money and Run* was the first movie he directed. His debut came only after Val Guest expressed prior commitments and United Artists declined to hire Jerry Lewis to direct, even after Allen met with Lewis and they agreed in principle about what the film should be. United Artists offered a budget of only $750,000, a sum producer Joffe found insufficient: "It would have killed the project" (Fox 47). Instead, they contracted with Palomar Pictures, an independent production company that had backed the stage play of *Play It Again, Sam*, and agreed to a $2 million budget for *Take the Money.* During the filming Allen achieved extraordinary efficiency by using a single-truck mobile studio that cameraman Fouad Said had developed for the television show *I Spy.* They shot the movie in San Francisco to save more money. Consequently, Allen came in at $1.53 million, $470,000 under budget and one week ahead of schedule, but still double the budget United Artists had tendered.

The film received encouraging, if not ecstatic, reviews. Influential *New York Times* critic Vincent Canby endorsed it, calling it "something very special and eccentric and funny" and declaring that "Allen and Mickey Rose . . . have illustrated in fine absurd detail the world that Allen has been talking about all these years." Pauline Kael of the *New Yorker* generally liked the film but complained about the unhappy ending and Allen's lack of attention to the supporting cast, and Stanley Kaufman of the *New Republic* bemoaned the lack of structure: "He [Allen] comes out and casts his lines a number of times, trying to catch as many laughs as possible. After a while, he quits, hoping that his average has been high."

Take the Money did a little better than break even, grossing only $2.59 million in U.S. and Canadian distribution (not including later video rentals and television revenues). Although it lost $610,000 on its first release, it eventually found its audience, especially in New York, where it sold out at the art theaters in which it premiered. *Take the Money* also achieved some popularity in Europe, notably in Greece. Moderate as it was, the film's success prompted United Artists to sign Allen to a subsequent three-film contract in which he would receive a $2 million budget per film, total artistic control once the idea was approved, and 50 percent of the net profits.

For Allen, *Take the Money* provided a significant learning process. He had no trepidations about directing because he was very clear about what he wanted to appear on screen. But he needed to learn the process of filmmaking. For one thing, he had to hire a director of photography, art director, and costume designer. (The remaining members of the production crew were provided for him.) Allen initially tried to obtain Michelangelo Antonioni's cameraman, Carlo Di Palma, and then Akira Kurosawa's cameraman, but they were unavailable. "So I had very grandiose ambitions. But when it came down to it, I hired absolute hacks. And I'm glad I did, because years later I started to work with Gordon Willis, who is a great cameraman, truly great. If I had hired him or Carlo Di Palma for my first movie. . . . I would not have known how to utilize them" (*Woody Allen on Woody Allen* 22). Allen subsequently fired his first director of photography and the costume designer, though he was pleased with the new cameraman, Lester Shorr, whom he has praised as "professional" (*Woody Allen on Woody Allen* 20).

Take the Money also taught Allen about editing. He and supervising editor James T. Heckert spent eight months on the film but were unable to fashion a coherent movie that could appeal to audiences. According to Allen, "It was like a human being without the heart. I was making all kinds of terrible mistakes. I didn't put music into many of the scenes, so they just played coldly and dryly." Finally, the producers hired Ralph Rosenblum as an editorial consultant to reshape the material. Rosenblum had recently performed similar services to rescue Mel Brooks's first movie, *The Producers* (1968), and William Friedkin's *The Night They Raided Minsky*'s (1968). According to Allen, his own version was "sure death," and he credits Rosenblum's editing for breathing life into the film (Lax 260–261). Rosenblum restored some of the footage that Allen had deleted but fortunately had not discarded. He rearranged scenes and edited the film to make the movie tighter, with a quicker tempo and a greater sense of direction. Moreover, he demonstrated how jazz could be used to animate the visuals on screen, something Allen has since become noted for. Rosenblum substituted Eubie Blake's ragtime for the somber background music Allen had chosen for Virgil's first date with Louise. According to Allen, "The whole thing came to life. I was suddenly just bouncing along. It made all the difference." Allen, who improvised extensively while filming, had shot six different endings, but these were either too violent or too sentimental. Rosenblum rejected as grotesque and offensive Allen's preference for a black humor conclusion showing Virgil gunned down in a hail of bullets, as in *Bonnie and Clyde*. After the funeral Louise Lasser, who had lingered behind, would hear him whisper from the grave, "Psst. It's me. Get me out." They finally settled on an anticlimactic conclusion that was later criticized (Lax 260–261).

Like Allen's fiction from the same period, *Take the Money* relies heavily on parody. Specifically, it parodies the European black and white, documentary-like cinéma vérité style that had been popular earlier in the 1960s. It also spoofs such American film classics as *I Am a Fugitive from a Chain Gang* (1932) and the "March of Time" newsreels (narrator Jackson Beck had been the voice for the Paramount newsreels in the 1930s and for the *Superman* radio show in the 1940s). Moreover, Allen plays off more contemporary movies like *The Defiant Ones* (1958), *West Side Story* (1961), *Cool Hand Luke* (1967), and *Bonnie and Clyde* (1967). And he spoofs American liberalism that seeks to attribute all criminal behavior to poverty, unsupportive parents, peer influence, and other environmental factors. Although Allen's own politics are generally somewhat left of center, he finds knee-jerk liberalism that denies personal accountability always ripe for satire, as it is in *Annie Hall* and *Everyone Says I Love You*.

As in his fiction and stand-up comedy, Allen continues to develop the little-man persona with which he was becoming closely identified. In this instance, he plays Virgil Starkwell, an inept bank robber who falls in love with a pretty laundress named Louise. (His name alludes to Charles Starkweather, a famous criminal of the 1950s.) Virgil tries to go straight, and he gets a legitimate job. But a coworker recognizes him and blackmails him, forcing Virgil to return to a life of crime. Louise stands by her man, even after he is captured and sent to prison, and she helps him flee when he escapes.

These clichéd, melodramatic circumstances serve as a vehicle for Allen's absurdist spirit. Virgil is a loser, and the movie is essentially a series of loosely related skits intended to produce laughs by exaggerating how great a loser he is. Virgil is such a loser that he plays the cello in his school's marching band. The gun he steals to commit a robbery proves to be a cigarette lighter when he finds himself shooting it out with the cops. His prison pals forget to tell him the breakout has been postponed, leaving him alone in the prison yard at night, and the fake gun he sculpts from a bar of soap melts when rains pours down during his escape. He is such a loser that the bank clerks cannot read his handwriting when he hands them a stick-up note. When he slides into a restaurant booth and begins to provide details of a planned robbery to the criminal behind him, he fails to notice that his cohort has left and a couple of policeman have taken his booth. When his gang finally goes to pull off the job, another gang appears at the same time, intent on robbing the same bank. The customers and employees vote overwhelmingly to be robbed by the rival gang. Though he does garner the Gangster of the Year award, Virgil never realizes his life's ambition to make the Ten Most Wanted list. "It's very unfair voting," explains his old friend Kay Lewis (Louise Lasser). "It's who you know." Kay goes on to praise Virgil's ability to fool everyone. "I actually believed he was an idiot. You never met such a nothing."

Stock situations from gangster films become settings for Allen's absurdism. As in his prose, Allen routinely garners quick laughs by inserting completely incongruous images into familiar situations. A standard shot of prisoners talking to visitors behind a glass partition reveals a prisoner with a ventriloquist's dummy who is being visited by another dummy from the outside. In order to protect their identities, Virgil's parents assume disguises when they are interviewed on camera—Groucho masks with big eyebrows and mustaches that make them look ridiculous. Another parody of the documentary-style interview appears when Virgil's analyst answers questions about Virgil while in session with another patient, whom he periodically compares unfavorably to Virgil. Virgil's first job interview is conducted like the popular television quiz show "What's My Line?" (a gag he returns to in *Everything You Always Wanted to Know About Sex*), and his wife tutors their son during a high-speed police chase.

The structural problems Allen encountered while making the film stemmed from the fact that, like the literary comedy of his stand-up routines and his early fiction, he relies on a rapid sequence of gags instead of character development, the revelation of complex relationships, or the unfolding of an integrated chain of events. Often no particular connection exists between one scene and the next; the film does not have a strong sense of plot and consequently does not build to a climactic conclusion. Canby perceives this as a virtue. In his laudatory review he observes that entire scenes—or even reels—can be rearranged without making much difference in total impact. Canby believes the effect of this structure is to make everything seem "effortless" (Lax 263). Allen's ability to interject new, absurd permeations on the gangster premise without letting the material becoming stale or the audience bored testifies to the vitality of his imagination.

Although not one of Allen's more memorable efforts, *Take the Money* did provide him a propitious beginning in one other crucial respect: Palomar gave him complete artistic freedom. "They never bothered me. I got final cut, everything I wanted to do. It was a very pleasant experience. And from that day on I never had any . . . interference in any way" (*Woody Allen on Woody Allen* 18).

See also **Literary Comedy**; **Little-Man Humor**.

Television.   Allen's television career began in late 1955, when he moved to Hollywood to join the NBC Writers' Development Program. One of his earliest assignments was to write for the *Colgate Comedy Hour*, where he met fellow writer Danny Simon. Allen credits Simon (Neil's brother) with teaching him how to structure a comedy script (Fox 25). In 1956, Allen wrote for the short-lived comedy show *Stanley*, which starred Buddy Hackett, Paul Lynde, and Carol Burnett. During the late 1950s he also wrote for Bob Hope, Kathyrn Grayson, and other popular performers. In the winter and spring of 1958, Allen worked on ABC's short-lived comedy series, *Sid Caesar Invites You*. And in November 1958, he and Larry Gelbart wrote a skit for the *Chevy Show* celebrating Caesar's ten years on television. Starring Caesar, Art Carney and Shirley MacLaine, the piece won a Sylvania Award for the year's best television comedy. Allen and Gelbart later wrote "Strange Strawberries," a take-off on Ingmar Bergman's *Wild Strawberries* that appeared in Carney's special, *Hooray for Love*.

By 1960 Allen was earning $1,700 a week writing for the *Garry Moore Show*. This was his last job as a TV writer; despite the high quality of his work, he lasted only a year because he frequently failed to come to work due to lack of interest. He subsequently took an enormous pay cut to began his career as a stand-up comedian, initially working for free as he honed his new craft. Several of Allen's movies recall this decision to sacrifice a lucrative career in a medium he did not respect in order to pursue work that was personally meaningful and satisfying. In *Manhattan* Ike quits television writing to become a novelist; in *Hannah and Her Sisters* Mickey regains his sanity and purpose in life after quitting his job as television producer, and in *Shadows and Fog* Kleinman leaves his miserable clerking position to assume a worse-paying but more gratifying job as magician's assistant in the circus. Lee in *Celebrity* fails to pursue his real passion for fiction or give up an unsatisfying career writing shallow pieces about celebrities' lives. As a result he remains desperate and lost at the end.

After Allen established a reputation as a comic, he began performing on television. He gained considerable national exposure on the *Tonight Show*, on which he frequently appeared with Jack Paar and Johnny Carson, including New Year's Eve shows in 1963 and 1965. He also hosted the show on several occasions. (Allen was later a guest on the 1969 premier of the Merv Griffin Show, CBS's late-night talk show that was intended to challenge the *Tonight Show*.) Allen also appeared on *Hootenanny*, a musical jamboree that ran on Saturday nights in 1963 and 1964. Featuring mostly folk music, *Hootenanny* was taped live before audiences of college students, who were among Allen's earliest supporters.

While filming *Casino Royale* in London, Allen guest-hosted *Hippodrome*, a television entertainment show featuring European circus acts that aired on CBS for two months in the summer of 1966. While in England he was also on *Chelsea at Nine*, *The Eammon Andrews Show*, and *Dusty*, a variety show featuring singer Dusty Springfield. His comedy routine "Woody Allen Looks at 1967" was featured on the *Kraft Music Hall*, and on September 21, 1969, Allen starred in his own CBS special along with Candice Bergen and the Reverend Billy Graham. Allen also appeared on *Hot Dog*, a television children's show that aired on NBC during 1970–1971. Allen and fellow comedians Jo Anne Worley and Jonathan Winters explained to children how things are made. Created by Frank Buxton and produced by Lee Mendelson, *Hot Dog* won a Peabody Award in 1971.

Allen performed on the highly rated *Ed Sullivan Show* on several occasions throughout the 1960s. While rehearsing for his first appearance, he included a joke about "orgasmic insurance" that deeply offended Sullivan, who declared that attitudes like Allen's were responsible for young men burning their draft cards. Allen had not intended to use the joke on the show, but had substituted it for the one he planned to use, so his material would be fresh later. He apologized to Sullivan, who forgave him. Later Woody declared, "When the storm abated, from that day on I had no better ally in show business." Sullivan invited him to dinner, promoted Allen in his newspaper column, and featured Allen on the show regularly (Lax 189).

In 1962, Allen conceived and wrote a television pilot entitled *The Laughmakers*, with Louise Lasser, Alan Alda, and Paul Hampton. But ABC declined to pick it up because its sophisticated humor appealed to too limited an audience. In 1971, political controversy suppressed Allen's *Men in Crisis: The Harvey Wallinger Story*, a made-for-television satire of the Nixon administration. Allen wrote, directed, and played the title character who is based on Henry Kissinger, then serving as national security adviser. He offered it without charge to the public television station in New York City, WNET, which originally scheduled the film for broadcast in February 1972. But the twenty-five-minute film was never released because Allen refused to cut scenes at the request of PBS, which was fearful of retaliation from President Nixon, who was then running for reelection. When Allen refused to make the cuts, PBS took steps that indirectly ensured *Men in Crisis* would not be shown. Allen later described the incident as an honest disagreement. (See also ***Men in Crisis***.)

In 1991, Allen received $2 million to make a series of commercials in Italy for COOP, the nation's largest supermarket chain. The commercials feature space aliens, the Soho art scene, an upscale cocktail party, and a psychiatrist. In 1994, Allen directed and acted in a television movie based on his original 1966 play, *Don't Drink the Water*. Broadcast on ABC, it costarred Julie Kavner, Michael J. Fox, and Dom DeLuise. Along with Peter Falk and Sarah Jessica Parker, Allen starred in a ninety-minute television performance of Neil Simon's *The Sunshine Boys*, which aired on CBS in April 1996. John Erman directed, and Allen revived the role of a fastidious former vaudevillian that George Burns had performed in the 1975 film.

In addition to his own personal appearances, Allen has been the subject of the following television specials: *Film '78* (May 7, 1978; a BBC interview by Iain Johnstone), *Woody Allen* (December 7, 1978; an interview about *Interiors* by Melvyn Bragg for LWT's *The South Bank Show*), *Woody Allen: Love, Death, Sex, and Matters Arising* (November 13, 1987; a BBC interview by Christopher Frayling), *Woody and Mia* (April 8, 1993; an interview by Steve Kroft for CBS's *60 Minutes*), *Woody Allen* (January 1, 1994; an interview by Melvyn Bragg for LWT's *The South Bank Show*), *Moving Pictures: Woody Allen* (April 2, 1995; a BBC interview by Howard Schuman), and *Film '95* (April 17, 1995; a BBC interview by Barry Norman). Allen's breakup with Mia Farrow was dramatized in a two-part mini-series entitled *Love and Betrayal: The Mia Farrow Story*. Aired by Fox on February 28 and March 2, 1995, it starred Patsy Kensit and Dennis Boutsikaris.

W

Waterston, Sam. A film actor who appears in *Interiors*, *Hannah and Her Sisters*, *September*, and *Crimes and Misdemeanors*. Notable appearances in films by other directors include *The Great Gatsby* (1974), *Friendly Fire* (1979), *Heaven's Gate* (1980), *Hopscotch* (1980), *The Killing Fields* (1984), *Mindwalk* (1990), *Assault at West Point: The Court-Martial of Johnson Whittaker* (1994), and *Serial Mom* (1994). Waterston received an Academy Award nomination for his work in *The Killing Fields*. In 1988, he appeared as Abraham Lincoln in NBC's television special *Gore Vidal's Lincoln*, and his was the voice of Lincoln in Ken Burns's 1990 PBS documentary, *The Civil War*. He has also starred in *Q.E.D.* (CBS, 1982) and the current NBC hit series *Law and Order*.

Waterston's most significant roles in Allen's films are Joey's lover Mike in *Interiors*, Peter in *September*, for which Christopher Walken and Sam Shepherd had been originally cast, and Ben in *Crimes and Misdemeanors*. Mike is a politically-oriented documentary filmmaker; Peter appears as a confused, directionless would-be writer, while Ben is an optimistic rabbi who is filled with religious faith despite his growing blindness.

What's New, Pussycat? (French title: *Quoi de Neuf, Pussycat?*). A 1965 film written by Allen, who also costars as Victor Shakapopolis. It stars Peter O'Toole (Michael James), Peter Sellers (Fritz Fassbender), Romy Schneider (Carol), Capucine (Renée), Paula Prentiss (Liz), and Ursula Andress (Rita). Also appearing are Edra Gale (Anna Fassbender), Louise Lasser (the Nutcracker), Nicole Karen (Tempest O'Brien), Jess Hahn (Perry Werner), Eleanor Hirt (Sylvia Werner), Jean Paredes (Marcel), Michel Subor (Phillipe), Françoise Hardy (secretary), Catherine Shaake (Jacqueline), and

Richard Burton (man in the bar). Clive Donner directed; Charles K. Feldman was the producer, Jean Badal director of photography, Jacques Saulnier production designer, Gladys de Segonzac costumer, and Fergus McDonnell editor. Burt Bacharach wrote the score, and Tom Jones sang the title song, which became a popular hit. Marvin H. Albert adapted the screenplay into a novel by the same title, a practice Allen ridicules in *Manhattan*. United Artists was the North American distributor.

Although not one of Allen's personal favorites, *What's New, Pussycat?* gave him considerable exposure and his first opportunity to work in film. Moreover, its success made possible his subsequent efforts at writing, directing, and acting. The film was a critical failure in the United States, where it was criticized for being "leering" and "oversexed," but it found a kinder reception in Great Britain and France, where it was named the best-directed comedy of the year. Moreover, it succeeded admirably at the box office. The fifth top moneymaker of 1965, *Pussycat* cost approximately $4 million to produce and grossed some $8.7 million in U.S. and Canadian revenues (not including later video rentals and television revenues).

During the filming, Allen received his initiation into cinema's world of the rich and famous. He dined with O'Toole and William Holden, had drinks with producer Darryl Zanuck, was escorted through Paris by Capucine, and attended lavish parties. "I found myself yanked into this *dolce vita* role." Nonetheless, for the most part Allen did not enjoy the filming or his constant fights with Feldman over the script, and he spent much of his time alone in his hotel room, practicing his clarinet. He considered his chance meeting with Samuel Beckett to be the one exciting event of his stay in Paris (Lax 208–209). After the film's release Allen became a frequent guest on television talk shows and was invited to dine with President Johnson at the White House. However, Allen maintained that success did not change him, except that he now failed with "a better class of women" (Lax 218).

Feldman chose Allen to write the script after actress Shirley MacLaine convinced him to see Allen's stand-up comedy at the Blue Angel. Feldman concluded that Allen had an "unusual ability to deal with sexual yearnings and inadequacies with such charm and wit" that he would be ideally suited for writing for film (Fox 29). Feldman, who was looking for a vehicle for his girlfriend, Capucine, paid Allen $35,000 to write a screenplay where they could all go to Paris and chase women (Lax 206). Allen earned an additional fee for his acting.

The original concept was based on *Lot's Wife*, a comedy by Ladislaus Bus-Fekete. Bus-Fekete's story had earlier been purchased for Cary Grant, and several aborted attempts had been made to prepare it for film before Allen came to it, including one by I.A.L. Diamond. Warren Beatty was originally cast for the starring role of Michael James. But Beatty, who later called it "the funniest script I've ever read," backed out of the part reportedly because he felt Allen's part was better than his own and because Feldman would not cast Beatty's girlfriend, Leslie Caron. However, Beatty retained his imprint on the film through the title, which was how he greeted his many girlfriends when he spoke to them on the telephone (Fox 30). Allen had lobbied for Groucho Marx to be cast as Michael's sexually frustrated psychologist, Fritz Fassbender, but Feldman chose another comic actor Allen admired, Peter Sellers. Although he enjoyed the opportunity to work with Sellers, Allen was not happy with alterations to the script that he had to make in order to highlight the main stars, and at one point he asked for his name to be removed from the film. Subsequently, all changes in the script were made by others. Ultimately Allen retained the screen credit and promoted the movie on the advice of his agent, Charles Joffe, who accurately believed it would advance his career. Allen later summed up his feelings: "If they had let me make it, I could have made it twice as funny and half as successful" (Lax 204).

The story is essentially a farce, a comedy of errors replete with jealous lovers and absurd, compromising situations. Memorable scenes include Ursula Andress, clad in a snakeskin jumpsuit, parachuting into O'Toole's car; Sellers trying to immolate himself in a Viking-style funeral, and would-be lovers hiding in unlikely places. It concludes with a chase scene that takes place in go-carts.

The plot centers around O'Toole's character, Michael, a fashion magazine editor who is constantly besieged by beautiful women but wants only to be faithful to his fiancée, Carol. However, given his tremendous sexual allure, Michael has been unable to maintain fidelity, so he seeks the help of psychiatrist Fassbender. One subplot centers around Fassbender's unsuccessful attempts to emulate Michael; another features Victor Shakapopolis, Michael's rival for Carol, in Allen's first cinematic little-man role. A starving artist, Victor works as an assistant in a striptease club, helping the strippers dress between acts. When Michael asks about money the job entails, Victor answers twenty francs a week. "Not much money," Michael observes. "It's all I can afford," Victor replies. According to Maurice Yacowar, Michael and Fassbender "can be seen as alternative fantasies by which the boyish Victor defines the range of his own possible sexual development. Michael is the figure that the emerging man would like to become, Fassbender the embodiment of frightening energies and frustrations. Michael represents the Allen persona's dream, Fassbender his dread" (Yacowar, *Loser Take All* 33).

The movie makes no attempt to offer wisdom or great insight; it tries only to be funny. Nonetheless, Sander H. Lee points out that *Pussycat* introduces several themes that permeate Allen's later work, including "two mutually exclusive models for behavior: the search for sexual satisfaction . . . and the search for romantic fulfillment through marriage" (Lee 18). The film also introduces Allen's propensity for parodying earlier movies that he admires. For instance, Michael's dream in which he is surrounded by adoring women whom he must literally whip into shape plays off a similar fantasy from Federico Fellini's *8½* (1963). *Pussycat* also contains a cameo appearance by Richard Burton that Allen did not write. Burton, who had just costarred with O'Toole in *Becket* (1964), walks up to Michael in a bar and asks, "Don't you know me from someplace?" Allen felt the cameo tried to be too cute, and he objected to the producers' treating something as humorous that he regarded as "garbage" (Lax 213).

Despite Allen's negative sentiments, the film was a popular star vehicle, and it served to establish Allen as a star on-screen as well as a writer off-screen. The exposure helped create a fan base for him, and the financial success earned him the fiscal credibility in Hollywood necessary for establishing his career as a filmmaker.

What's Up, Tiger Lily? A 1966 Japanese film onto which Allen superimposed a new and totally unrelated soundtrack. The original version was released in 1964 as *Kagi No Kagi* (*Key of Keys*); the first U.S. version appeared under the title *A Keg of Powder*. It was directed by Senkichi Taniguchi and produced by Tomoyuki Tanaka and Makoto Morita. Hideo Ando wrote the original screenplay, and Kazuo Yamada was director of photography. The cast includes Tatsuya Mikashi (Phil Moskowitz), Miye Hana (Terry Yaki), Akiko Wakayabashi (Suki Yaki), Tadao Nakamaru (Shepherd Wong), Suzumu Kurobe (Wing Fat). Allen, Louise Lasser, China Lee, Kumi Mizuno, and the band The Lovin' Spoonful also appear in Allen's 1966 revision. Allen, Lasser, Frank Buxton, Len Maxwell, Mickey Rose, Julie Bennett, and Bryna Wilson were the voices in Allen's revised soundtrack. Harry G. Saperstein and Reuben Bercovitch produced Allen's version, and the Lovin' Spoonful sang original music, including the movie's theme song, "Pow." American International was the North American distributor.

The first film to be made under Allen's artistic control, if not exactly under his direction, *Tiger Lily* was a moderate financial success that achieved a small cult following. According to Allen, the film cost so little to produce it could not help but make money. Harry Saperstein bought the rights to the original for $66,000, and Allen received a $75,000 fee to add a new, humorous soundtrack and interject some additional material. Allen and his friends

Len Maxwell, Frank Buxton, and Louise Lasser screened the Japanese original several times in a hotel room and improvised funny lines. The good ones were retained in the final script. Also inserted are some short scenes featuring Allen, Louise Lasser, and The Lovin' Spoonful. In one such interlude we see Allen and Lasser's silhouettes imposed onto the film as though they are standing in front of the projector. As their shadows touch one another, Allen's voice declares that they must stop meeting like this because, "my wife is getting wise" and because it is against union rules to have sex in the projection booth. Allen and Lasser married while they were working on the film.

Fearing the extended joke could not sustain a full-length feature film, Allen wanted to make the movie tighter and more dynamic by cutting it to sixty minutes, but Saperstein insisted that it be drawn out to something closer to standard duration (The final version is seventy-nine minutes.) Allen initiated a lawsuit to halt its release because the producers added new material to fill it out over his objections, but he dropped the suit after the film opened and received generally good reviews. The film's screwball humor achieved a modest following. *Sight and Sound* compared it to a Tex Avery cartoon. But it was also criticized for being too long.

The Japanese original was a sexy action-adventure film along the lines of a James Bond movie. In Allen's version the hero, Phil Moskowitz, a self-described "lovable rogue," strives to thwart a conspiracy to steal the world's best recipe for egg salad. The humor comes from the deflation of the subject matter, along with the incongruity of hearing Japanese actors speak like Jewish New Yorkers, black Americans, and other Westerners, and from the use of American country-western music in a Japanese action film. Allen also employs the technique of the comic equation in which he pairs serious matters with trivial ones and treats them equally. For instance, one character complains that his foes kill, maim, and call directory assistance for telephone numbers they could easily look up in the phone book. Other gags include fake mustaches ("Don't tell me what to do or I'll have my mustache eat your beard") and imitations of James Cagney, Peter Lorre, and Walter Brennan. Typically absurd lines include "two Wongs don't make a white" and the claim by one character to represent a nonexistent but real-sounding country that is on the waiting list to become an actual country—in the interim the entire population is in packing crates.

The film's absurdist spirit parallels the humor in Allen's stand-up comedy and the fiction that he was then just beginning to publish in *Playboy* and the *New Yorker*. Another *Playboy* influence is a striptease in the final scene by centerfold playmate China Lee, wife of comedian Mort Sahl, who was one of Allen's chief comedic influences in his early career. Allen lies behind her on a couch, casually eating an apple as she removes her clothes. To her right on the screen is a standard disclaimer stating that all characters are fictitious. Before she is totally disrobed, Allen declares that "if you have been reading this instead of looking at the girl, then see your psychiatrist or go to a good eye doctor."

What's Up, Tiger Lily? does not stand out as one of Allen's finer films; Allen himself later dismissed it as "a sophomoric exercise" (*Woody Allen on Woody Allen* 15). Nonetheless, it helped establish a fan base among viewers who enjoyed his cultural allusions, word play, and self-conscious, absurdist form of humor that was unlike almost anything else then appearing in American cinema.

Wiest, Dianne. An actress who appears in *The Purple Rose of Cairo*, *Hannah and Her Sisters*, *Radio Days*, *September*, and *Bullets over Broadway*. Notable appearances in films by other directors include *Parenthood* (1989), *Edward Scissorhands* (1990), *Little Man Tate* (1991), and *The Bird Cage* (1996).

Wiest demonstrates a wide range of acting skills in the divergent roles she plays for Allen, spanning the flighty sister Holly in *Hannah and Her Sisters* to love-hungry Aunt Bea in *Radio Days* to an over-the-hill, alcoholic, self-important diva in *Bullets over Broadway*, where her dramatically uttered line, "Don't speak!" caught the public imagination.

Wiest won Academy Awards for her performances in *Hannah* and *Bullets over Broadway* and was nominated for her role in *Parenthood*. Allen regards her as "one of the greatest actresses in America. . . . In any form, comedy, tragedy. She's a truly great actress. . . . She hasn't wanted to work much in the last few years, because she's adopted two children and she's been spending most of her time with them. But they don't come any better than her" (*Woody Allen on Woody Allen* 151–152).

Wild Man Blues. A 1998 documentary film about Allen's 1996 month-long tour of Europe with the New Orleans Jazz Band. Barbara Kopple directed. Jean Doumanian, a close friend of Allen, was the producer, Tom Hurwitz cinematographer, and Lawrence Silk editor. The band members include Allen, Dan Barrett, Simon Wettenhall, John Gill, Cynthia Sayer, Greg Cohen, and Eddy Davis, the banjo player who assembled the ensemble. FineLine Features was the North American distributor.

The film follows Allen, his sister, Letty Aronson, and his girlfriend, Soon-Yi Previn, whom Allen later wed, as they travel through Europe, to England, and back to New York. They arrive first in Paris, so Allen can acclimate himself to Europe in a city where he feels comfortable and whose overcast skies appeal to him. Allen and the band then begin their tour in Madrid, and go on to perform in Geneva and several cities in Italy, including Venice, Milan, Turin, Bologna, and Rome. Finally, they close in London.

Although *Wild Man Blues* highlights Allen's jazz performances on the clarinet, it also attempts to reveal his personality and, to a lesser extent, his relationship to Soon-Yi—Mia Farrow's and Andre Previn's adopted daughter who was at the center of Allen's highly publicized breakup with Farrow in 1992. The film reaffirms and fleshes-out long-standing images of Allen as a neurotic, creative artist more than it reveals new aspects of his personality. We learn, for instance, that he typically experiences at least one bout of depression every day. He accepts the depression without wallowing in it or trying to inflict it others and apparently endures it with the knowledge that it will pass. However, in the initial scene aboard the plane to Paris, Allen seems cranky and demanding as he objects to the presence of a dog accompanying one of the filmmakers. Letty and Soon-Yi try to reassure him, as they do throughout the film, but Allen does not want to be comforted.

The viewer obtains the sense that while Soon-Yi is attentive to Allen, she does not become consumed by his petty complaints. Moreover, Allen seeks out her advice on artistic and other matters pertaining to the tour, and she induces him to take gondola rides, go swimming, exercise, and become more socially engaged than he might otherwise. Allen seems to respect her opinions and care for her comfort and well-being. For instance, when room service fails to include toast with her breakfast and Soon-Yi insists that she does not want to make an issue of it with the attendant, Allen tactfully asks her in the waiter's presence if she would like some. And in Madrid, when Soon-Yi's Spanish omelet is not to her liking, Allen trades meals with her, albeit not without some light-hearted objections and wisecracking. Not surprisingly, he often jokes with her, in a witty but complaining or self-deprecating manner reminiscent of Alvy Singer and Annie Hall in their better days.

Allen clearly would be happier to have his creative work appreciated but be personally left alone. Nonetheless, he appears appreciative of and gracious to his fans, making himself available for photographs by media professionals and fans alike and joking casually with his admirers at receptions. In this respect, he seems very like Sandy Bates, his character from *Stardust Memories* who tries to respond pleasantly to the aficionados who swarm around him. Bad service disturbs him, as do other disruptions to his routine, but when the lights in a concert hall unexpectedly go out while he and the band are playing, Allen continues to perform and retains his good humor throughout the situation. He subsequently received a plaque from the local fire department for preventing a potentially dangerous stampede in the darkened hall, an act of "heroism" he later makes light of with his parents.

The band's music is of professional quality, and despite Allen's fears that he is not good enough to sustain an audience's interest for an hour and a half, the performances are enthusiastically received everywhere but Rome. Allen discusses his preference for the big band music he listened to on the radio as a child growing up in the 1940s, when Benny Goodman and Louis Armstrong were standard fare, and he expresses his pleasure in the simple, "raunchy" New Orleans style of jazz. The band performs such numbers as "Down by the Riverside" and "Home! Sweet Home!" and Allen, who headlines the concerts, performs several solos. The film succeeds in revealing Allen's passion for the music and his respect for accomplished jazz musicians like Sidney Bechet and John Coltrane. Allen seems to be at his personal best when he is performing or trying out a rare virtuoso clarinet that is on exhibit, but not for sale, at a European music shop.

His receipt of a lifetime achievement award in Italy gives Allen a forum for articulating his objections to awards for the arts. To Allen, the subjectivity and quirkiness of the awards process render them suspect, despite the arguments by Letty and Soon-Yi that awards signify that his work has been especially meritorious. But Allen notes how Marlon Brando's incredible performance in *Streetcar Named Desire* failed to receive an award, even though it was clearly the most outstanding of its year. He appreciates the honor he has been given, but wonders how he can deserve an award that has also gone to Ingmar Berman and Akira Kurosawa but not to Federico Fellini, whom Allen had long admired. Appropriately, director Kopple overlays the soundtracks from several Fellini films while depicting Allen's adventures in Italy.

Wild Man Blues has many humorous moments as Allen comments on his circumstances and experiences in Europe. But the funniest part comes when he returns to New York and visits his elderly parents, Martin and Nettie Konigsberg. Allen hands over his awards to his ninety-six-year-old father, who seems much more interested in the quality of the engraving than in the honors implied by the awards. And his mother still maintains that Woody should have become a pharmacist instead of a comedian or filmmaker. She also voices her objection to his relationship with Soon-Yi, on the grounds that intermarriage will eventually lead to the elimination of the Jewish people, a remark that does not seem to faze either Woody or Soon-Yi. Finally, Nettie concludes the movie by abruptly telling the camera crew that they have seen enough and must go now.

Williams, Tennessee. An American playwright who lived from 1911 to 1983. In several of his works, Allen alludes to Williams's plays, especially *A Streetcar Named Desire* (1947). Blanche DuBois, the fading southern belle from *Streetcar*, appears suddenly as a character in Allen's play *God*, and in *Sleeper*, Allen's character Miles Monroe suffers amnesia and believes himself to be Blanche. To snap him out of it, Luna (Diane Keaton) assumes the role of Blanche's brother-in-law, Stanley Kowalski, imitating the renowned performance by Marlon Brando. Like Miles, in *Celebrity* Robin Simon (Judy Davis) delivers Blanche's famous line, "I always rely on the kindness of strangers." And in one of his stand-up comedy routines, Allen recalls playing a five-year-old Stanley in his school play. Moreover, when Allen was writing for television, he and Larry Gelbart authored a parody of *Cat on a Hot Tin Roof* for the *Chevy Show*. *The Hot Tin Cat*, which aired November 2, 1958, starred Art Carney as Big Daddy and Shirley MacLaine as his daughter (Lax provides a detailed description, p. 113).

   Allen's *The Floating Light Bulb* appears to derive from Williams's *The Glass Menagerie* (1944). Both center around dysfunctional families and study the impact of family members' neurotic behavior on a sensitive child who withdraws into a more pleasant artificial world within his or her mind.

Willis, Gordon. A cinematographer who was director of photography for all of Allen's films between 1977 and 1985: *Annie Hall*, *Interiors*, *Manhattan*, *Stardust Memories*, *A Midsummer Night's Sex Comedy*, *Zelig*, *Broadway Danny Rose*, and *The Purple Rose of Cairo*. Among Willis's other credits are Francis Ford Coppola's *The Godfather* Parts I, II, and III (1972, 1974, 1990), Herbert Ross's *Pennies from Heaven* (1981), and Alan J. Pakula's *Klute* (1971) and *Presumed Innocent* (1990).

   Allen maintains that his association with Willis is responsible for his maturity as a filmmaker. He especially credits Willis for helping him develop graphic technique and for pointing out why particular approaches to shooting a scene will or will not work. Allen praises Willis's instincts and compares him to Rembrandt because Willis "loves to paint with light" (Lax 329). He regards Willis as a "master of shadows, the master of chiaroscuro" who has influenced new American cinematographers to employ more sophisticated lighting (*Woody Allen on Woody Allen* 22–24). Julian Fox notes that Allen shares Willis's preference for shooting "a sequence exactly as he wants to see it on screen, offering no alternatives for the editor to play around with. Both men share a propensity for fantasy, conjured photographically rather than with special effects, and each has made something of a fetish of darkly-lit interiors" (Fox 20). Moreover, Allen credits Willis for teaching him the effectiveness of having dialogue offscreen while showing something else onscreen, as well as for educating him about other aspects of filmmaking.

Allen began working with Carlo Di Palma in 1984, when Willis was un-available to film *Hannah and Her Sisters*, and Allen's visual style subse-quently changed. He thinks Willis is better technically than Di Palma, but he admires Di Palma's European style of movement and mobility: "When I started working with Gordon, I knew very little; Gordon was a genius and he educated me. So I was always a little in awe of him. When I was with Carlo I was much more mature and knew what I wanted. And I had devel-oped a style. . . . It's like when you leave your parents' house; now you're grown up and do your own thing" (*Woody Allen on Woody Allen* 153). In particular, Allen moved from using tightly framed, carefully composed shorter shots that Willis preferred to very long sequences that he feels more comfortable with.

Although Willis was finally nominated for an Academy Award for his work on *Zelig*, Allen feels even this nomination was primarily for his tech-nical achievement and not his aesthetic accomplishments. Willis's finest work, including *The Godfather* Parts I and II and *Manhattan*, *Interiors*, and *A Midsummer Night's Sex Comedy*, was passed over by the Academy. Allen points to this slight to Willis as an example of why the awards lack credibil-ity (Lax 282). Willis later received a second nomination for *The Godfather* Part III.

For additional reading about Willis's filming of *Manhattan*, see Willis's interview with Dean Goodhill in *American Cinematographer* (November 1982). Fox provides an extensive discussion of the technical process in-volved in making *Zelig*. See also Michelle Bogre's interview with Willis about *Zelig* in *American Cinematographer* (April 1984) and Willis's inter-view in *L'Express* (September 1983).

Without Feathers. A best-selling collection of Allen's short fiction and plays published by Random House in 1975. Some of the stories are original to this collection, but several first appeared between 1972 and 1975 in *New Yorker*, *New Republic*, *Playboy*, and the *New York Times*. The second of Al-len's three books, it follows *Getting Even* (1971) and precedes *Side Effects* (1980).

The title, which alludes simultaneously to Plato and Emily Dickinson, signals the literary sophistication and word play that characterize many of the stories. Plato described man as a two-legged animal without feathers, while Dickinson's quote, "Hope is the thing with feathers," serves as the epigram for the book. The title is thus provocative: perhaps Allen is making some comment on the human condition or announcing his comical-cynical viewpoint by leaving us "without hope." But taking this line of reasoning very far would simply make us the butt of Allen's joke. Throughout this collection, as well as in much of his other work, Allen spoofs intellectuals who seek too hard for meaning or who push literary interpretation and critical jargon into the realm of the ridiculous.

Allen doubtless was aware of the allusions his title made and its invitation for interpretation. But he treats the subject more playfully than profoundly. This becomes explicit in "Selections from the Allen Notebooks," where he declares, "How wrong Emily Dickinson was! Hope is not 'the thing with feathers.' The thing with feathers has turned out to be my nephew. I must take him to a specialist in Zurich."

Allen's allusions to high culture point back to ancient Greece, progress through the Renaissance, and converge on the anguished nineteenth-century souls who inhabit the fictional worlds of Ibsen and Dostoyevsky and the real worlds of Van Gogh and Gauguin. But the overriding playful tone comes from the energetic, absurd, and quick-witted word play associated with American literary comedy, such as found in the *New Yorker* stories of S. J. Perelman, Robert Benchley, and James Thurber and in Marx Brothers movies. In fact, Allen's ability to play Groucho-like with the great masterpieces of Western culture accounts for much of his appeal to college-educated adults who have had to read, write papers, and take tests about the literature Allen spoofs.

Just as the Marx Brothers dive into the classical repertoire in *A Night at the Opera* (1935) and delight in sabotaging a performance of a Verdi opera and the high-society pretentiousness that accompanies it, Allen immerses himself in the canon of Western fine arts and letters and turns it into a playground for pairing the sublime with the ridiculous. Without demeaning the masterpieces or the existential problems they explore, Allen makes fun of characters who take their lives too seriously or become so obsessed with finding the meaning of life that they cannot enjoy it. The same pleasure in toying with literary and intellectual history informs Allen's other work from the era, including his first book, *Getting Even*, and the films *Bananas*, *Play It Again, Sam*, *Everything You Always Wanted to Know About Sex*, *Sleeper* and *Love and Death* which, like *Without Feathers*, was released in 1975. (See also **Literary Comedy**.)

The collection presents itself in part as the found papers of Woody Allen, reproduced by scholars for posterity in the way the letters, notebooks, journals, story drafts, and essays of important writers and artists from earlier eras have been preserved and reproduced. Allen thus parodies a wide range of public and private writing. The first entry, "Selections from the Allen Notebooks," purportedly from Allen's secret private journal, mimics the real and fictional journals of tortured souls from nineteenth- and twentieth-century literature. Invoking such clichés of romanticism as insomnia and consumption, the journals assume a confessional tone. But instead of grappling with the moral dilemmas, recriminations, and burning passions that torment Dostoyevsky, Allen speaks of absurdities: underwear in the shape of the kaiser on roller skates, a man whose one dream is to sit up to his waist in gravy, and a friend who wants all government officials to dress like hens.

"The Whore of Mensa" is probably the best-known piece from the volume. First published in the *New Yorker* in 1974, the story employs the form of the hard-boiled detective novel, but it derives its humor by reversing prevalent attitudes about beauty and brains. Allen invokes all the clichés about married men who employ prostitutes, but the gratification his character surreptitiously seeks is cerebral, not sexual. Protagonist Kaiser Lupowitz, who first appeared in *Getting Even* as the narrator of "Mr. Big," is closely patterned after Humphrey Bogart's rendition of Sam Spade. Lupowitz's client is being blackmailed because he has secretly been meeting with a college woman. "My wife is great, don't get me wrong," Babcock explains. "But she won't discuss Pound with me. Or Eliot. I didn't know that when I married her. See, I need a woman who's mentally stimulating. . . . And I'm willing to pay for it."

Lupowitz agrees to take the case and arranges to meet with a young redhead to discuss Melville and Hawthorne. Symbolism, he learns, costs extra. Allen inverts a famous image from John Updike's widely anthologized story "A & P," as Lupowitz observes that the woman was packed into her slacks "like two big scoops of vanilla ice cream." (Allen returns to the same simile in "The Condemned" from *Side Effects*.) The woman, who conforms to a type of coed intellectual that Allen indeed found attractive, has long straight hair, a leather bag, silver earrings, and no makeup.

Before he cracks the case, Lupowitz learns that emotional experiences are for sale too: for fifty dollars he could "relate without getting close" or for a hundred dollars watch a woman have an anxiety attack. For fifty dollars more, he could listen to FM radio with twins.

Other notable pieces of fiction include "The Irish Genius," "But Soft . . . Real Soft," "A Guide to the Lesser Ballets," and "If the Impressionists Had Been Dentists." "The Irish Genius," first published in *New Republic* in 1975, spoofs the poetry of William Butler Yeats and the literary commentary about it. "But Soft . . . Real Soft" begins by discussing scholarly claims that the works of Shakespeare were actually written by Sir Francis Bacon, Ben Jonson, Queen Elizabeth, and the Homestead Act. Allen extrapolates from the premise that major writers were assuming the identity of other major writers and goes on to conclude that "Samuel Johnson was Samuel Pepys. Pepys was actually Raleigh, who had escaped from the tower to write *Paradise Lost* under the name of John Milton, a poet who . . . was hanged under the name of Jonathan Swift. This all becomes clearer when we realize George Eliot was a woman."

First published in the *New Yorker* in 1972, "A Guide to the Lesser Ballets" absurdly spoofs the story lines employed by classical ballets. For instance, *Dmitri*, the first dance, opens at a carnival. The spirit is festive, but the trombones "play in a minor key to suggest that soon the refreshments will run out and everybody will be dead." Vaguely alluding to Igor Stravinsky's *Petrouchka* (1911), the plot centers on a girl who spurns her lover in favor of a puppet named Dmitri, who excites her by suggesting they check into a hotel and register as Mr. and Mrs. Joe Doe. The spurned lover, who had wooed her by leaving mixed-green salads at her doorstep every night, naturally goes mad. "A Guide" became the basis for *Dmitri*, a twenty-minute dance-drama that was performed by the Los Angeles Chamber Ballet in 1989. (See **Dmitri**.)

"If The Impressionists Had Been Dentists" presents a series of letters from Vincent Van Gogh to his brother, Theo. Vincent describes his inner anguish, but his artistic medium is now dentistry instead of oil painting. He broods because Degas is critical of his X-ray work and despairs because he cannot even afford Novocaine. He must anesthetize his patients by reading Theodore Dreiser's fiction to them. Most important, Van Gogh's genius is misunderstood and unappreciated by those around him. "Mrs. Sol Schwimmer is suing me because I made her bridge as I felt it and not to fit her ridiculous mouth. . . . I decided her bridge should be enormous and billowing, with wild explosive teeth flaring up in every direction like fire!"

In addition to the prose pieces, Allen includes two one-act plays, *Death* and *God*. *Death*, which later served as the basis for Allen's film *Shadows and Fog*, presents a comically bleak, Kafka-like situation in which Kleinman, a clerk, is roused from his bed by vigilantes who are tracking a killer but will not tell Kleinman what he is expected to do. Kleinman thus enters an uncertain world in which crucial facts are unknown but where he is compelled to act decisively. (See **Death**.)

God seems heavily influenced by the theater of the absurd that flourished in the 1950s. The beginning is especially reminiscent of Samuel Beckett's *Waiting for Godot* (1952), as a writer and actor in ancient Athens are on stage alone, talking interminably about their inability to find a suitable conclusion for the play they are producing. According to the stage notes, these parts should be played by two broad burlesque clowns. Apropos of the absurdist theater that *God* spoofs, the play's opening line is "Nothing . . . just nothing . . ." And like *Godot*, *God* fails to reach a conclusion but returns instead to its beginning, as writer and actor continue to argue about the ending and complain that it is "absurd."

Like other experimental literature of the era, such as John Barth's *Lost in the Funhouse* (1968), much of the play's plot revolves around how to get the story told and reach a satisfactory conclusion to the narration. And like other twentieth-century narratives, such as Luigi Pirandello's *Six Characters in Search of an Author* (1921), Tom Stoppard's *Rosencrantz and Guildenstern Are Dead* (1966), Robert Coover's *Universal Baseball Association* (1968), and, later, W. P. Kinsella's *Shoeless Joe* (1982), *God* depicts overlapping layers between fiction and reality that sometimes become entangled. For instance, when Woody Allen appears in the character of the author, Woody Allen, the traditional demarcation between real people and fictional characters becomes blurred. The levels of reality become confused again when an audience member—a fictional character in *God* but an "outside," "real" person in the play within the play—is called onstage and asked to interact with the characters from the play within the play but without assuming a role. The Jewish coed from Great Neck thus appears as an anachronism on the set from ancient Athens, and she questions what reality "really is." The writer wants to sleep with her but the actor complains that their levels of reality are incompatible: "You idiot, you're fictional, she's Jewish—you know what the children will be like." Allen's sudden introduction of Blanche DuBois from *A Streetcar Named Desire* (1947) as a new character in *God* complicates the layering of realities, as one fictional world intrudes on another. Allen explores this layering of fictional and real characters more fully in his 1985 film, *The Purple Rose of Cairo. God* was performed by the National Radio Theater of Chicago, with Tony Roberts as Hepatitis and Allen as the Voice of the Author.

Without Feathers is a tour de force of literary parody; it imitates almost every kind of literary mode, from private letters and journals to public essays, the poetry of Yeats, the detective novel, German expressionism, and theater of the absurd. At the same time that Allen spoofs the classics, he demonstrates substantial familiarity with and appreciation of them. There is little bitterness in his humor, and no attempt to make profound statements, only comic incongruities that play off the forms, themes, and expectations found in high culture. Like the Marx Brothers, Allen has immersed himself in his cultural heritage and found pleasure in the sounds of words, the rhythms of language, the pairings of images, and the joys of his imagination.

See also *Getting Even*; **Plays**; *Side Effects*.

Z

Zelig. A 1983 film directed by, written by, and starring Allen, who plays Leonard Zelig. It costars Mia Farrow (Dr. Eudora Fletcher), Marianne Tatum (actress playing Dr. Fletcher), Garrett Brown (actor playing Zelig), Stephanie Farrow (Sister Meryl), Will Holt (rally chancellor), Mary Louise Wilson (Zelig's sister Ruth), Sol Lomita (Martin Geist), John Rothman (Paul Deghuee), Deborah Rush (Lita Fox), Patrick Horgan (narrator) and Susan Sontag, Irving Howe, Saul Bellow, Bricktop, Bruno Bettelheim, and John Morton Blum as themselves. Robert Greenhut was the producer, Gordon Willis director of photography, Dick Hyman music director, Mel Bourne production designer, Santo Loquasto costumer, and Susan E. Morse editor. Kerry Hayes and Brian Hamill did the still photography, and Joel Hyneck, Stuart Robertson, and their colleagues at R/Greenberg Associates provided the optical effects. Hyman performed many of the pieces and composed six original songs: "Leonard the Lizard," "Doin' the Chameleon," "Chameleon Days," "You May Be Six People But I Love You," "Reptile Eyes," and "The Changing Man Concerto." Additional music includes "I've Got a Feeling I'm Falling," "I'm Sitting on Top of the World," "Five Foot Two, Eyes of Blue," "Ain't We Got Fun," "Sunny Side Up," "I'll Get By," "I Love My Baby, My Baby Loves Me," "Runnin' Wild," "A Sailboat in the Moonlight," "Charleston," "Chicago, That Toddlin' Town," and "Anchors Aweigh." Orion Pictures was the North American distributor.

Predicated on the introduction of a fictional character into historical events, *Zelig* anticipates Robert Zemeckis's far more successful *Forrest Gump* (1994), a technical tour de force that also interjects newly created images of a fictional person into historical documentary film footage. Apart from Pauline Kael, who characteristically dismissed Allen's effort as much ado about nothing, most critics were enthusiastic about the film. The *New York Times*'s Vincent Canby went so far as to crown Allen "the premier American film-maker of his day." Overall, *Zelig* received the best reviews of any other Allen movie since *Manhattan*, four years earlier. The special photographic effects were singled out for especially high praise, and Gordon Willis received an Academy Award nomination for the cinematography. Santo Loquasto was nominated for the costumes.

Zelig ran for fourteen weeks in New York and reached the number one spot in *Variety*'s box office chart during its second week. But despite the strong opening, *Zelig* only broke even in North America and made a small profit worldwide, costing $6.5 million to produce and earning only $6.8 million in U.S. and Canadian rentals. Julian Fox suggests that its lack of strong dialogue, character development, and strong story line may account for its lack of popularity. Allen's own belief is that most Americans largely missed the point of the movie. "The content of the film has not even to this day been evaluated properly in the United States, because everyone was so focused on the technical aspects. . . . [the technical achievement] was a small accomplishment, but it was the content of the film that interested me" (*Woody Allen on Woody Allen* 141).

To recapture the appearance and feel of a 1920s documentary, Willis shot *Zelig* in black and white, using original lenses and light and sound equipment from the era. He used flicker-mattes to reproduce the flickering of old movies, and technicians scratched the negative to make it seem aged. Although the filming required only about twelve weeks, the preproduction and postproduction work was extensive and time-consuming. According to Willis, "We spent months selecting archival footage, then had to study methods of interpolating Woody's fictional character into real scenes." Willis adds, "We had to work backwards, start with the original historical material, and visualize how it would match our photography. . . . There are only two matte shots in the movie. The rest was intercut, so the intercutting of the material was extremely important" (Fox 146–147).[1]

Allen's reason for so painstakingly recreating the sound and look of an old documentary was to comment "on the specific danger of abandoning one's own true self, in an effort to be liked . . . to fit in . . . and where that leads on a political level." His original idea for the film was "to do a story about a person whose personality changed all the time to fit in everywhere. He wants so badly to be liked that he changes his personality to fit in with every group he's with. Then I thought, it would be very interesting to see the physical changes. He becomes who he is with. Then I thought, it would be very interesting to present him as an international phenomenon and that his story should be told in a very documentary way, as though this was a famous international figure" (*Woody Allen on Woody Allen* 136, 141). Elsewhere, he adds, "One doesn't want to see this character's private life; one's more interested in the phenomenon and how it relates to culture. Otherwise it would just be the pathetic story of a neurotic" (quoted in Pogel 172).

Set in the 1920s and 1930s, *Zelig* tells the story of Leonard Zelig, a "chameleon-man" who involuntarily changes his physical and personal attributes to blend in with the people who surround him.[2] At the same time, the film exposes America's passion for transforming extraordinary personal crises into mass entertainment. Finally, Allen's credible intrusions of cinematic characters into historical documents reminds us that we always operate in shadows and fog: We can never distinguish illusion from reality with complete certainty; we can never fully trust what we think we know, and even sensory-based empirical knowledge is suspect.

The core story is a romance. *Zelig* shows how love cures Allen's ultimate little man, a man whose self-esteem is so low that, like T. S. Eliot's J. Alfred Prufrock, he dares not stand out in any way or express individuality in any manner.[3] Wanting only to be liked, Zelig has totally repressed his sense of self. When his psychiatrist asks, "Who are you?" he replies, "I'm nobody; I'm nothing." He first tries to become someone he is not when he pretends to have read *Moby Dick* in order to avoid censure by his erudite companions. Later, after being ridiculed for not wearing green on St. Patrick's Day, he so desperately wants to conform and become Irish that his nose turns red, and he speaks of the potato famine and "the little people." F. Scott Fitzgerald records Zelig's transformation in a single afternoon from a Harding Republican to a working-class Democrat as Zelig interacts first with the guests at a high-society party and then with the help. In Paris, where intellectuals "see in him a symbol for everything," Zelig's transformation into an Orthodox rabbi is so convincing that certain Frenchmen suggest sending him to Devil's Island—Allen's reminder of the Dreyfus affair and the anti-Semitism that flourished in France before World War II. Although Zelig always remains male, even in the exclusive company of women, among African Americans he turns black, and he is hospitalized after turning Chinese.

The subject of diverse popular and medical theories, Zelig undergoes electric shock treatment and receives experimental drug therapy before finally being entrusted to Dr. Eudora Fletcher, a psychiatrist who shows genuine compassion for him. Initially Zelig's denial mechanisms are too strong for her to penetrate, and he merely mimics her, pretending that he is an esteemed psychiatrist who teaches a course in advanced masturbation at the Psychiatric Institute. Fletcher finally breaks through when she reverses roles, accepting him as the doctor and presenting herself as a pretender who exhibits his symptoms. Thus confronted with himself, Zelig acknowledges that he is not a psychiatrist, an admission that opens the way for serious exploration of who he really is. Once he gains the confidence to express his own preferences and opinions, he becomes cured. He and Dr. Fletcher fall in love and plan to marry.

However, as in other Allen stories, the protagonist must first realize his worst fears before finally exorcising them. Terrified of the smallest expressions of disapproval, Zelig becomes the center of a national scandal that erupts after a woman accuses him of fathering her child while he was a different personality. Subsequently several people file lawsuits similarly accusing him, and the public support he earlier enjoyed turns to universal condemnation.

The entire nation's rejection of him provokes a relapse, and Zelig then disappears, only to turn up occasionally in different guises throughout world. He eventually falls in with Hitler's Nazis, because, as author Saul Bellow observes in the film, "there was also something in him that desired immersion in the mass and anonymity, and fascism offered Zelig that kind of opportunity, so that he could make something anonymous of himself."

But the power of love proves stronger than the pull of fascism. Dr. Fletcher tracks him down at a Nazi rally, where Zelig recognizes her and regains his identity, disrupting Hitler's speech in the process. They flee in a stolen airplane, which Zelig flies while assuming the identity of a pilot, and they return to America as heroes. Zelig tells his adoring crowd, "It shows what you can do if you're a total psychotic," and Bellow concurs, "It was his very disorder that made a hero of him." Zelig and Dr. Fletcher finally marry and live happily together.

Zelig's cure comes from the honest self-confrontation offered by his psychotherapy and from Dr. Fletcher's love and commitment to him. Both enable him to reverse his low self-esteem and accept himself as a worthy individual. As Fitzgerald remarks in a final, bogus journal entry, "Wanting only to be liked, he distorted himself beyond measure. . . . One wonders what would have happened if, right at the outset, he had the courage to speak his mind and not pretend. In the end it was, after all, not the approbation of many but the love of one woman that changed his life."

If the story of Zelig's personal crisis ends happily, Allen's depiction of mass culture is less optimistic, because mass culture inevitably distorts the individual. Fascism represses and absorbs the individual, but Allen shows how American popular culture makes him larger than life, transforms him into an entertainment commodity, and ultimately disposes of him when it loses interest.

Zelig becomes larger than life when the public turns his neurotic tendency to change himself into an occasion for merriment. Zelig becomes the basis for the chameleon dance during the roaring twenties; Josephine Baker performs it to great acclaim in Paris. He is also the subject of numerous songs, including "Reptile Eyes," "You May Be Six People But I Love You," and "Chameleon Days," sung by Mae Questel as Helen Kane. (Questel, who later plays Sheldon Mills's mother in *Oedipus Wrecks*, had been the voice of Betty Boop in the 1930s.) The bespectacled Zelig is also the butt of topical jokes that have spread across the country: "What's brown and white and yellow and has four eyes? Leonard Zelig at the League of Nations."

Moreover, almost everyone who knows him exploits Zelig as a commodity. The most overtly cynical are his sister, Ruth, and her boyfriend, Martin Geist, a carnival con man. They remove Zelig from the hospital before he is cured and take him on tour as a traveling freak show. Geist also arranges for Zelig to endorse products, such as a cigarette ad that features only Zelig's face and the caption, "We smoke Camels."

But more reputable professionals exploit him just as cynically. Even the doctors, except for Dr. Fletcher, regard Zelig more as a medical anomaly and an opportunity for fame and career advancement than as a feeling individual. Retired reporters for the now-defunct *New York Daily Mirror* describe how with Zelig they did not even need to distort the facts in order to create a sensation: "You just told the truth and you sold papers. It never happened before."

Zelig's story can also sell movie tickets, and it becomes the subject of two very different films. Hollywood's *The Changing Man* presents Zelig's life as a sentimental romance, and it projects an Anglicized view of America, in which a tall, handsome, sensitive-looking WASP portrays the very ethnic-looking Leonard Zelig. On the other hand, the "documentary" of Zelig's life, though retaining Zelig's Jewish origins, presents him primarily as a social phenomenon, and it does little to explore his inner feelings or sentiments. For instance, it points out that labor leaders condemn Zelig for initiating a speed-up by holding several jobs, one for each personality. And it notes that the Ku Klux Klan regards this "Jew who was able to transform himself into a Negro or Indian [as] a triple threat." But even the documentary is not able to take Zelig (or itself) altogether seriously, as the audiotrack plays an upbeat chameleon-man song, while the picture shows doctors administering electric shocks to Zelig as he sits passively strapped into a chair.

However, as different groups assign different values and meaning to Zelig, they also actualize his neurotic fantasy, which is to eviscerate his inner self and become solely a projection of what others want him to be. In fact, his public personae completely submerge his inner identity. The mass culture transforms Zelig into songs, dances, movies, and the embodiment of its fears and desires. Literally, he becomes a living legend. Zelig's neurosis encourages his transformation into a commodity and a legend, because it enables him to surrender his private identity and become entirely a public phenomenon. In short, his complete identification with and absorption by the popular culture is another manifestation of his neurotic desire to blend into his environment. At the same time, society's eagerness to embrace Zelig as a commodity demonstrates the tendency of mass culture to trivialize the individual and regard private anguish as a short-term source of mass entertainment.

Ultimately, Zelig proves to be many contradictory things: the personalities he assumes, the images he projects within the popular culture, the symbols he embodies for others, and the "inner personality" that Dr. Fletcher recognizes, responds to, and ultimately coaxes out and loves. This multidimensional picture conforms to Allen's modernist worldview that holds reality to be paradoxical, uncertain, relativistic, and incompletely knowable. The pseudo-documentary format also serves to articulate this worldview, as it challenges our own ability to distinguish between fact and fiction. The value of the film's technical achievement is that it obscures our ability to state with certainty which scenes are true historical documents and which are ersatz. In an era where we rely on photographic documentation to establish and verify facts, Allen's movie diminishes our confidence that any photograph or film documentary is necessarily authentic—indeed, that any form of documentation is entirely trustworthy. Even conventional introductory and closing statements are false, such as the movie's dedication and final expression of thanks. On the other hand, some of the images *are* accurate and the people and events actual. Thus, by intermingling fact and fiction, Allen makes us experience our own reality as uncertain and not fully knowable. Yet within this dicey context, he still insists on the worth of self-knowledge and self-acceptance and on the nurturing value of love.

NOTES

1. Fox provides an extensive discussion of the technical process (145-148). See also Michelle Bogre's interview with Willis in *American Cinematographer* (April 1984) and Willis's interview in *L'Express* (September 1983).

2. Allen chose *Zelig* as the film's title only after discarding several other possibilities, including *The Changing Man*, *The Cat's Pajamas*, and *Identity Crisis and Its Relationship to Personality Disorder*.

Zelig's name means "blessed" or "dear departed soul" in Yiddish, and Nancy Pogel suggests that a possible source for the title is Benjamin Rosenblatt's "Zelig," an obscure short story about a lonely Russian Jewish immigrant. Several critics have noted similarities to Orson Welles's *Citizen Kane* (1941), which also interjects a fictional character into history and mixes fake and real documentary footage. Colin L. Westerbeck, Jr., notes that the interview format plays on Warren

Beatty's *Reds*, which costars Allen's former lover and costar Diane Keaton. Pogel compares *Zelig* to Chris Marker's *La Jetée* (1962), and Sander H. Lee notes similarities to T. S. Eliot's poem "The Hollow Men," Franz Kafka's story "The Metamorphosis" (1915), Jean-Paul Sartre's treatise *Being and Nothingness* (1943), and Eugène Ionesco's play *Rhinoceros* (1959).

For a reading based on the theories of Jacques Lacan, see Richard Feldstein; for a reading based on the theories of M. M. Bakhtin, see Ruth Perlmutter; for a discussion of the film's "poststructural anxiety," see Sam Girgus, *The Films of Woody Allen.*

3. As Nancy Pogel notes, "The little man in *Zelig* remains involved in questions that are central to all of Allen's films—whether identity and personal integrity can survive oppressively dehumanizing and exploitative social circumstances; whether it is possible to find an authentic self in a world where illusion and reality are confused and where truth always appears to be unreliable and self-contradictory" (Pogel 171).

Filmography

Bananas (1971). Costars Louise Lasser. Mickey Rose collaborated on the script. Part farce and part satire, this comedy spoofs Castro's revolution in Cuba and American politics of the Vietnam War era.

Broadway Danny Rose (1984). Costars Mia Farrow and Nick Apollo Forte. One of Allen's finest films from the era, this tribute to borscht-belt comedy focuses on a former comedian, now a personal manager, who becomes involved with gangsters and a gangster's moll.

Bullets over Broadway (1994). Allen wrote and directed but did not act. Stars John Cusack, Dianne Wiest, Chazz Palminteri, and Jennifer Tilly; Douglas McGrath collaborated on the screenplay. Another comedy dealing with gangsters from the prohibition era, this film parodies artists who take themselves and their work too seriously, as it questions the meaning of morality in an absurd universe. The art deco costumes and sets and rich photography are especially noteworthy.

Casino Royale (1967). Directed by John Huston et al. Allen acted but did not direct or write the screenplay, though he made some uncredited contributions to it. Costars include Peter Sellers, Ursula Andress, David Niven, Orson Welles, Jacqueline Bisset, George Raft, William Holden, Charles Boyer, and John Huston. Allen plays James Bond's nephew, Jimmy, who suffers from a complex about his short physique in this spoof of the Bond spy thrillers.

Celebrity (1998). Allen wrote and directed but did not act. Stars Kenneth Branagh, Judy Davis, Leonardo DiCaprio, Winona Ryder, Joe Mantegna, Melanie Griffith, and Charlize Theron. Indebted to Fellini's *La Dolce Vita*, the film exposes the excess and superficiality of America's cult of celebrity as it follows the life of a magazine writer who has lost touch with his true personal priorities.

Crimes and Misdemeanors (1989). Costars Mia Farrow, Martin Landau, Anjelica Huston, Alan Alda, and Claire Bloom. Perhaps Allen's most overt examination of morality, the film echoes Shakespeare and Dostoyevsky as it questions the meaning of ethical behavior and proper action in an absurd, atheistic universe. The story has two plotlines: the serious one deals with blackmail and murder, the more comedic one with pretension, envy, and jealousy.

Deconstructing Harry (1997). Costars Kirstie Alley, Richard Benjamin, Billy Crystal, Judy Davis, Mariel Hemingway, Amy Irving, Julie Kavner, Julia Louis-Dreyfus, Demi Moore, Elisabeth Shue, Stanley Tucci, and Robin Williams. Widely regarded as Allen's bitter, postmodern response to the public treatment of his breakup with Mia Farrow, the film intermingles fiction and reality as it presents the life of Harry, a successful novelist suffering for the first time from writer's block after he has written a thinly disguised autobiographical novel about his unsuccessful personal life. Harry, played by and loosely based on Allen, appears as a caricature who exaggerates all the negative things Allen has been accused of: being mi-

sogynistic, selfish and self-absorbed, anti-Jewish, sexually exploitive and
perverse, and fundamentally unable to connect to other people.

Don't Drink the Water (1969). Directed by Howard Morris, starring Jackie Gleason and Estelle Parsons, screenplay by R. S. Allen and Harvey Bullock,
based on the stage play by Woody Allen. Allen was not involved in the production. Allen directed and starred with Julie Kavner, Michael J. Fox, and
Dom DeLuise in the 1994 made-for-television remake. The Cold War comedy centers on a New Jersey Jewish family vacationing in Vulgaria, an
Eastern European country behind the iron curtain. After the father inadvertently photographs a secret military installation, they take refuge in the
American embassy, which is headed by the ambassador's inept son, who
has been left in charge in his father's absence. Weeks before the daughter is
scheduled to marry, the family is more concerned with the wedding ar-
rangements than with the international incident they have created.

Everyone Says I Love You (1996). Costars Goldie Hawn, Alan Alda, Julia Roberts, John Cusack, and Drew Barrymore. This tribute to the Marx Brothers
is Allen's only musical comedy. It is perhaps his happiest, most uplifting
movie.

Everything You Always Wanted to Know About Sex* (**But Were Afraid to Ask*).
(1972). Costars Louise Lasser, John Carradine, Lynne Redgrave, Burt Reynolds, Gene Wilder, Lou Jacobi, and Anthony Quayle. Loosely based on
the book by David Reuben, the film is composed of seven sketches dealing
with sexual behavior. Notable are a love affair between a man and a sheep,
a Frankenstein parody about an enormous breast that terrorizes the countryside, and a sketch featuring sperm readying themselves for their mission.

The Front (1976). Directed by Martin Ritt, written by Walter Bernstein. Stars Allen, Zero Mostel, Michael Murphy, and Andrea Marcovicci. The writer,
producer, director and many of the actors were blacklisted during the 1950s
red scare, including Mostel, who claimed to be "a man of many faces—all
of them blacklisted." Allen plays a front who submits under his own name
television scripts that were written by talented blacklisted, and hence unem-
ployable, writers during the red scare. He falls under the suspicion of right-
wing agents affiliated with the House Committee on Un-American Activities Committee, and they coerce a blacklisted comedian (Mostel) to spy on
him. The story is based in part on the suicide of comedian Philip Loeb.

Hannah and Her Sisters (1986). Costars Mia Farrow, Michael Caine, Barbara
Hersey, Dianne Wiest, Maureen O'Sullivan, Max Von Sydow, and Carrie
Fisher. This film explores the loving and envious relationships among three
sisters and finds the meaning of life in a Marx Brothers movie.

Husbands and Wives (1992). Costars Mia Farrow, Judy Davis, and Sydney Pollack. One of Allen's bleaker films, *Husbands and Wives* is indebted to
Bergman's *Scenes from a Marriage*. It follows the dissolution of two ostensibly happy marriages.

Interiors (1978). Allen wrote and directed but did not act. Stars Diane Keaton, Geraldine Page, Maureen Stapleton, Sam Waterston, and E. G. Marshall. Allen's first purely serious film, *Interiors* plays off Bergman's *Cries and Whispers* as it explores the manipulations and unwholesome feelings and attitudes that motivate the behaviors of an apparently respectable family.

King Lear (1987). Directed, written, and edited by Jean-Luc Godard, who plays the Professor. Stars Burgess Meredith, Peter Sellars, Molly Ringwald, Leos Carax, and Kate and Norman Mailer. Allen appears briefly as the enigmatic editor who splices the film and then sews the celluloid back together with needle and thread. Very loosely based on Shakespeare's masterpiece and replete with postmodern self-references, Godard's *King Lear* experiments with sound, image, and plot. It is also largely incoherent, perhaps in imitation of Lear's delirium.

Love and Death (1975). Costars Diane Keaton. Set during the Napoleonic Wars and filled with literary allusions, this comedy spoofs the great nineteenth-century Russian novels, the films of Ingmar Bergman, and the big existential questions about the meaning of life.

Manhattan (1979). Costars Diane Keaton, Mariel Hemingway, Michael Murphy, Meryl Streep, and Anne Byrne. Marshall Brickman collaborated on the script. The story centers on a divorced writer who has romantic affairs with a high school girl and a sophisticated art critic. Ironically, the girl proves to be the most mature person in the group, with the highest level of self-knowledge and the greatest capacity for giving and accepting love.

Manhattan Murder Mystery (1993). Costars Diane Keaton, Alan Alda, Anjelica Huston, Jerry Adler, and Lynn Cohen. Marshall Brickman collaborated on the script. In his first film after the Mia Farrow scandal, Allen returned to full-fledged comedy, and Diane Keaton returned as his leading lady. The story centers on a couple who find themselves enmeshed in a murder plot as they investigate the suspicious disappearance of an elderly neighbor. (This was Allen's original conception for *Annie Hall*.) The plot is especially indebted to Alfred Hitchcock's *Rear Window*.

Men in Crisis: The Harvey Wallinger Story (1971). Costars Louise Lasser and Diane Keaton. A made-for-television satire of the Nixon administration and then national security adviser Henry Kissinger, the twenty-five-minute film was never released. Allen refused to cut scenes at the request of PBS, which was fearful of retaliation from Nixon, who was preparing to run for reelection. When Allen refused to make the cuts, PBS took steps that indirectly ensured *Men in Crisis* would not be shown.

A Midsummer Night's Sex Comedy (1982). Costars Mia Farrow, Mary Steenburgen, Jose Ferrer, Tony Roberts, Julie Hagerty. This film plays off both Shakespeare's *A Midsummer's Night's Dream* and Bergman's *Smiles of a Summer Night*. Set around the turn of the twentieth century, it features three couples spending an enchanted weekend in the country. Among other things, it contrasts mysticism and empiricism, detached intellect and pure physicality, animal attraction and passionate love.

Mighty Aphrodite (1995). Costars Mira Sorvino, Helena Bonham Carter, Michael Rapaport, Claire Bloom, Olympia Dukakis, and Jack Warden. This film plays off Greek tragedy as a sports writer seeks out the identity of the parents of his adopted son.

My Favorite Comedian (1979). Allen compiled this sixty-two-minute selection of scenes from Bob Hope movies for a fund raiser for the Lincoln Center's Film Society.

New York Stories (1989). An anthology of short films set in New York directed by Allen (*Oedipus Wrecks*), Francis Ford Coppola (*Life Without Zoe*), and Martin Scorsese (*Life Class*). See *Oedipus Wrecks*.

Oedipus Wrecks (1989). Costars Mia Farrow, Julie Kavner, and Mae Questel (the off-screen voice of Betty Boop and *Popeye*'s Olive). A forty-one-minute short story, *Oedipus Wrecks* appears as part of the anthology *New York Stories* that also includes short films directed by Francis Ford Coppola and Martin Scorsese. Allen's farce is about a successful Jewish lawyer who suffers from ambivalent feelings for his domineering mother. His life changes for worse, and for better, after he wishes her gone and she vanishes, only to reappear in the sky above Manhattan.

Play It Again, Sam (1972). Directed by Herbert Ross. Allen starred and wrote the screenplay, which is based on his stage play. Costars Diane Keaton and Tony Roberts. The movie plays off Humphrey Bogart films, especially *Casablanca* (1942). In one of his little-man roles, Allen is a recently divorced film critic who tries unsuccessfully to emulate Humphrey Bogart's self-assured, controlling manner. He falls for the wife of his workaholic best friend as she tries to help Allen with his love life. The title is a famous misquote from *Casablanca*, which starred Bogart and Ingrid Bergman.

The Purple Rose of Cairo (1985). Allen wrote and directed but did not act. Stars Mia Farrow, Dianne Wiest, Jeff Daniels, and Danny Aiello. The story centers on an abused wife who spends much of her time escaping her troubles at the movies and falls in love with a film character who steps off the screen and into her life.

Radio Days (1987). Allen wrote, directed, and narrated but did not appear on screen. Stars Mia Farrow, Dianne Wiest, Julie Kavner, Michael Tucker, Jeff Daniels, Tony Roberts, Diane Keaton, and Wallace Shawn. *Radio Days* plays off Federico Fellini's *Amarcord* as the narrator recalls growing up in New York during World War II, when the radio was the medium that linked families, communities, and the entire nation.

Scenes from a Mall (1991). Directed by Paul Mazursky, written by Mazursky and Roger L. Simon. Stars Allen and Bette Midler. This comedy shows a middle-aged professional couple working through their marital difficulties in a shopping mall.

September (1987). Allen wrote and directed but did not act. Stars Mia Farrow, Dianne Wiest, Denholm Elliot, Sam Waterston, Jack Warden, and Elaine
Stritch. This film explores the love-hate relationship between a mother and
daughter as it plays off the real-life drama of actress Lana Turner, whose
abusive lover was stabbed to death by her thirteen-year-old daughter.

Shadows and Fog (1992). Costars Mia Farrow, Michael Kirby, David Ogden
Stiers, Lily Tomlin, Jodie Foster, John Cusack, John Malkovich, and Madonna. Based on Allen's play *Death*, *Shadows and Fog* plays off early German expressionist films, such as those by Fritz Lang and Robert Wiene and
even early Hitchcock. Franz Kafka is another strong influence in this story
of disorientation. Allen's character spends the entire story trying to ascertain what his assignment is in a secret plot to capture a mad killer. In the
process, he falls in love with a woman who has run away from the circus
and taken refuge with a bevy of prostitutes.

Sleeper (1973). Costars Diane Keaton, John Beck, Mary Gregory, and Don
Keefer. Marshall Brickman collaborated on the script. One of Allen's pure
farces, *Sleeper* is set two hundred years in the future, when all society is
controlled by a totalitarian regime. Allen stars as a 1970s health food store
owner who is miraculously resuscitated by scientists affiliated with the underground. Because he has no official identity, he is potentially useful and,
in spite of himself, becomes involved in the revolution. One of the funniest
routines features Keaton imitating Marlon Brando playing Stanley Kowalski from *A Streetcar Named Desire*, while Allen plays Blanche DuBois.

Stardust Memories (1980). Costars Charlotte Rampling, Jessica Harper, Marie-
Christine Barrault, and Tony Roberts. One of Allen's most experimental
films in terms of style and structure, *Stardust Memories* plays off Federico
Fellini's *8½* as it portrays the confused life of a harried film director beset
by out-of-control fans and embroiled in unsatisfactory romantic relationships with emotionally unstable women.

The Sunshine Boys (1996). Directed by John Erman. Stars Allen, Peter Falk, and
Sarah Jessica Parker. In this ninety-minute television performance of Neil
Simon's play, Allen revives the role of a former vaudevillian who must
team up with his long-estranged partner. George Burns originated Allen's
role in the 1975 film version; Walter Matthau and Richard Benjamin originated Falk's and Parker's roles, respectively.

Take the Money and Run (1969). Costars Louise Lasser, Janet Margolin, Marcel
Hillaire, and Lonnie Chapman. Mickey Rose collaborated on the script. The
first film Allen directed and starred in, *Take the Money and Run* is a broad
comedy that employs a pseudo-documentary style to present the life of an
incompetent bank robber.

What's New, Pussycat? (1965). Directed by Clive Donner. Allen wrote the
screenplay. Stars Allen, Peter Sellers, Peter O'Toole, Romy Schneider,
Paula Prentiss, and Ursula Andress. Set in France, the film follows three
men whose lives are dominated by their uncontrollable sexual desires. Ac-

cording to Allen, "Left to my own instincts, I could have made the film twice as funny and half as successful." However, although he considers the movie inferior to his later films, *Pussycat* was a huge commercial hit that made his other films possible.

What's Up, Tiger Lily? (1966). Original version, *Kagi No Kagi* (*Key of Keys*), directed by Senkichi Taniguchi, 1964. Allen directed the re-release of this Japanese gangster film onto which he overlaid an incongruously dubbed script. Ben Shapiro received credit for the production conception; Allen was largely responsible for the script. This parody of James Bond movies features Asian actors who speak in the dubbed soundtrack as though they are Jewish, African American, or otherwise Western. Allen's plot centers around the attempts by the Japanese protagonist, Phil Moscowitz, to find the recipe for a great egg salad.

Wild Man Blues (1998). Directed by Barbara Kopple. A documentary film about Allen's 1996 month-long tour of Europe with the New Orleans Jazz Band. Allen was the featured soloist on clarinet. The film provides glimpses of his private life with Soon-Yi Previn and reveals his popularity in Europe. Jean Doumanian, a close friend of Allen, was the producer.

Zelig (1983). Costars Mia Farrow, John Buckwalter, and Marvin Chatinover. Includes cameo appearances by Susan Sontag, Irving Howe, Saul Bellow, and Bruno Bettleheim. The pseudo-documentary follows a man so insecure he adapts himself, chameleon-like, to be just like whomever he is with.

Bibliography

FICTION BY ALLEN

Complete Prose of Woody Allen. New York: Wing Books, 1991. [This volume reprints the fiction from *Getting Even*, *Without Feathers*, and *Side Effects* but does not include Allen's plays from those books.]

Getting Even. New York: Random House, 1971.

The Illustrated Allen Reader. Ed. Linda Sunshine. New York: Vintage, 1994.

The Lunatic's Tale. Illustrated by Etienne Delessert. Minneapolis: Redpath Press, 1987. [First published in *Side Effects*.]

Side Effects. New York: Random House, 1980.

Without Feathers. New York: Random House, 1975.

PLAYS BY ALLEN

Central Park West. In Allen et al. *Death Defying Acts.* New York: Samuel French, 1996. [First performed in 1995.]

Death: A Comedy in One Act. New York: Samuel French, 1975. [First published in *Without Feathers*.]

Death Knocks. [A one-act play first published in the *New Yorker*; rpt. in *Getting Even*.]

Don't Drink the Water. New York: Samuel French, 1967. [First performed in 1966.]

The Floating Light Bulb: A Drama in Two Acts. New York: Samuel French, 1982. [First performed in 1981.]

God: A Comedy in One Act. New York: Samuel French, 1982. [First published in *Without Feathers*.]

Play It Again, Sam: A Romantic Comedy in Three Acts. New York: Samuel French, 1969. [First performed in 1969.]

SCREENPLAYS BY ALLEN

Four Films of Woody Allen. New York: Random House, 1982. [*Annie Hall, Interiors, Manhattan*, and *Stardust Memories*.]
Hannah and Her Sisters. New York: Random House, 1987.
Sleeper. New York: Random House, 1978.
Three Films of Woody Allen. New York: Random House, 1985. [*Zelig, Broadway Danny Rose, The Purple Rose of Cairo*.]

NONFICTION BY ALLEN

"Am I Reading the Papers Correctly?" *New York Times* January 28, 1988: 22.
"Annie Hall." *L'Avant-Scène* December 15, 1977.
"Attention! See Europe with the King of the International Set (me)." *Esquire* (February 1966).
"Everything You Always Wanted to Know About Sex You'll Find in My New Movie." *Playboy* (September 1972).
"Fine Times: An Oral Memoir," *New Yorker* March 17, 1975: 34–35.
"Girls of *Casino Royale*." *Playboy* (February 1967).
"How Bogart Made Me the Superb Lover I Am Today." *Life* (March 1969).
Introduction to Moss Hart's *Act One*. New York: St. Martin's Press, 1987.
"My Speech to the Graduates." *New York Times* August 10, 1979.
"On Love and Death." *Esquire* July 19, 1975.
"Quoi de Neuf, Pussycat?" *L'Avant-Scène*, no. 59 (1966).
"Random Reflections of a Second-Rate Mind," *Tikkun* 5.1 (January–February 1990): 13–15, 71–72; rpt. in *The Best American Essays, 1990*. Ed. Joyce Carol Oates. New York: Ticknor & Fields, 1991. 1–8.
"Through a Life Darkly." *New York Times* September 18, 1988: 30. [Review of Ingmar Bergman's autobiography, *The Magic Lantern*.]
"What's Nude, Pussycat?" *Playboy* (August 1965).
"Woody, the Would-Be-Critic." *New York Times* May 2, 1971.

ALLEN ON PHONOGRAPH RECORDS

The Third Woody Allen Album. Capital, 1968. [Recorded live at Eugene's in San Francisco, August 1968.]
Woody Allen. Colpix, 1964. [Recorded live at Mr. Kelly's in Chicago, March 1964.]
Woody Allen, Volume 2. Colpix, 1965. [Recorded live at the Shadows in Washington, D.C., April 1965.]
Woody Allen: The Nightclub Years: 1964–1968. United Artists, 1976. [A compilation of material from the earlier albums. This has been reissued as a compact disc. See below.]
Woody Allen Stand-up Comic, 1964–1968. Casablanca Records and Film Works, 1978. [A compilation of material from the previous albums.]

ALLEN ON COMPACT DISC

The Bunk Project, Eddy Davis musical director. Music Masters, Inc. 1993. [Allen
    and his band perform New Orleans–style jazz.]
Woody Allen: The Nightclub Years: 1964–1968. 1968; reissued by as compact
    disk by EMI Recordings, London. [Stand-up comedy.]

ALLEN AS A PHOTOGRAPHIC SUBJECT

Champlin, Charles, and Derrick Tseng. *Woody Allen at Work: The Photographs
    of Brian Hamill.* New York: Harry N. Abrams, Inc., 1995.

ALLEN FEATURED AS A CARTOON CHARACTER

Hample, Stuart. *Non-Being and Something-ness.* New York: Random House,
    1978. [Selections from the comic strip *Inside Woody Allen*, with intro-
    duction by R. Buckminster Fuller.]

ALLEN AS THE SUBJECT OF PATIENTS' DREAMS

Burton, Dee. *I Dream of Woody.* New York: William Morrow & Co., 1984

NOVELIZATIONS OF MOVIES

Marvin H. Albert. *What's New, Pussycat?* New York: Harmony Books, 1965.

PLAYS BASED ON ALLEN'S STORIES

Getting Even. Adapted by Afterthought Productions at the Edinburgh Festival,
    August 1990.
"The Kugelmass Episode" and "Mr. Big." Adapted for stage in a series of "plat-
    form" performances directed by Michael Kustow in 1980 at London's
    National Theatre.
Lahr, John. *The Bluebird of Unhappiness*, 1987. [Contains skits of *Death Knocks*,
    "My Apology," "The Kugelmass Episode," and "Mr. Big." Premiered at
    the Royal Exchange Theatre in Manchester, England, in 1987 under the
    direction of Braham Murray. Stanley Silverman composed the music.]

DANCES BASED ON ALLEN'S STORIES

Holden, Stanley, choreographer. *Dmitri* [A 1989 dance drama based on Allen's
    "A Guide to Some of the Lesser Ballets" from *Without Feathers.*]

BIOGRAPHIES OF ALLEN

Baxter, John. *Woody Allen: A Biography*. London: HarperCollins, 1999.

Fox, Julian. *Woody: Movies from Manhattan*. Woodstock, NY: The Overlook Press, 1996.

Guthrie, L. *Woody Allen: A Biography*. London: Drake, 1978.

Lax, Eric. *Woody Allen: A Biography*. New York: Vintage Books, 1992.

Meade, Marion. *The Unruly Life of Woody Allen: A Biography*. New York: Scribners, 2000.

Palmer, Myles. *Woody Allen: An Illustrated Biography*. New York: Proteus, 1980.

INTERVIEWS WITH ALLEN

Allen, Woody. *Woody Allen on Woody Allen: In Conversation with Stig Björkman*. Ed. Stig Björkman. New York: Grove Press, 1995.

Banker, Stephen. "A Conversation with Woody Allen." (1973) In Steven Spignesi, *The Woody Allen Companion*. 20–29.

Didden, Marc. Interview with Allen in *New Musical Express* September 22, 1979.

Ebert, Roger. *Movie Home Companion*. Andrews and McMeel, 1992; rpt. in Steven Spignesi, *The Woody Allen Companion*. 55–59.

Farber, Stephen. "Human Existence with a Penthouse View." *Moviegoer* (May 1985); rpt. in Steven Spignesi, *The Woody Allen Companion*. 30–38.

Geist, W. Interview with Allen in *Rolling Stone* (April 9, 1987): 38–40+; rpt. in Steven Spignesi, *The Woody Allen Companion*. 39–55.

Rich, Frank. "An Interview with Woody," *Time* (April 30, 1979): 68–69.

Shales, Tom. "Woody: The First Fifty Years." *Esquire* 107 (April 1987): 88–95.

SECONDARY SOURCES

Barth, John. *Chimera*. New York: Random House, 1972.

———. *Giles Goat-Boy*. 1966; rpt. New York: Anchor Books, 1987.

———. "The Literature of Exhaustion." *Atlantic* 220 (August 1967): 29–34.

———. *Lost in the Funhouse*. Garden City, NY: Doubleday, 1968.

Benayoun, Robert. *Woody Allen: Beyond Words*, 1986; rpt. as *The Films of Woody Allen*. New York: Harmony Books, 1987.

Bernstein, Mashey, " 'My Worst Fears Realized,' Woody Allen and the Holocaust." *Perspectives on Woody Allen*. Ed. Renée R. Curry. New York: G. K. Hall & Co., 1996. 218–236.

Blair, Walter, and Hamlin Hill. *America's Humor: From Poor Richard to Doonesbury*. New York: Oxford University Press, 1978.

Blake, Richard A. *Woody Allen: Profane and Sacred*. Lanham, MD: Scarecrow Press, 1995.

Blansfield, Karen C. "Woody Allen and the Comic Tradition in America," *Studies in American Humor* 6 (1988): 142–153.

Bogre, Michelle. Interview with Gordon Willis. *American Cinematographer* (April 1984).

Borges, Jorge Luis. "Pierre Menard, The Man Who Wrote the *Quixote*." *Labyrinths*. New York: New Directions, 1964.

Bragg, Helen. "Woody Allen's Economy of Means: An Introduction to *Hannah and Her Sisters*." *Literature/Film Quarterly* 16.1 (1988): 44–48.

Brode, Douglas. *The Films of Woody Allen*. New York: Carol Publishing Group, 1997.

Carroll, Tim. *Woody and His Women*. Boston: Little, Brown and Company, 1993.

Champion, Lauri. "The Kugelmass Episode." *Explicator* 50.1 (Fall 1992): 61–63.

Champlin, Charles, and Derrick Tseng. *Woody Allen at Work: The Photographs of Brian Hamill*. New York: Harry N. Abrams, Inc., 1995.

Culler, Jonathan. "The Uses of Madame Bovary." *Diacritics* 11.3 (Fall 1981): 74–81.

Curry, Renée R., ed. *Perspectives on Woody Allen*. New York: G. K. Hall & Co., 1996.

Desser, David. *Jewish American Film Makers: Traditions and Trends*. Urbana: University of Illinois Press, 1993.

Dickstein, Morris. "Urban Comedy: Chaplin to Allen." *Partisan Review* 52.3 (1985): 271–281.

Didion, Joan. "Letter from Manhattan." *New York Review of Books* August 16, 1979: 17.

Downing, Crystal. "Broadway Roses: Woody Allen's Romantic Inheritance." *Literature/Film Quarterly* 17.1 (1989): 13–17.

Dunne, Michael. "*Stardust Memories, The Purple Rose of Cairo*, and the Tradition of Metafiction." *Film Criticism* 12.1 (Fall, 1987): 19–27.

Ebert, Roger. "Interiors of Woody's Mind," *Chicago Sun-Times* September 10, 1978: sec. 3, p. 1.

Farrow, Mia. *What Falls Away: A Memoir*. New York: Bantam, 1998.

Feldstein, Richard. "Displaced Feminine Representation in Woody Allen's Cinema." *Discontented Discourses: Feminism/Textual Intervention/Psychoanalysis*. Eds. Marleed S. Barr and Richard Feldstein. Urbana: University of Illinois Press, 1989. 69–86.

———. "The Dissolution of the Self in *Zelig*." *Literature/Film Quarterly* 13.3 (1985); rpt. in Renée R. Curry, ed. *Perspectives on Woody Allen*. New York: G. K. Hall & Co., 1996. 71–77.

Girgus, Sam B. *The Films of Woody Allen*. Cambridge: Cambridge University Press, 1993.

———. "Philip Roth and Woody Allen: Freud and the Humor of the Repressed." *Semites and Stereotypes: Characteristics of Jewish Humor*. Eds. Avner Ziv and Anat Zajdman. Westport, CT: Greenwood, 1993. 121–130.

Gittelson, Natalie. "The Maturing of Woody Allen." *New York Times Magazine* April 22, 1979: 30–32.

Green, Daniel. "The Comedian's Dilemma: Woody Allen's 'Serious' Comedy."
    Literature/Film Quarterly 19.2 (1991): 70–76.
Grimsted, David. "The Purple Rose of Popular Culture Theory: An Exploration
    of Intellectual Kitsch." *American Quarterly* 43 (1991): 541–578.
Hample, Stuart. *Non-Being and Something-ness*. New York: Random House,
    1978. [Selections from the comic strip *Inside Woody Allen*, with intro-
    duction by R. Buckminster Fuller.]
Harty, John. "Allen's 'The Kugelmass Episode,'" *Explicator* 46.3 (Spring 1988).
Hill, Hamlin, *Mark Twain: God's Fool*. New York: Harper & Row, 1973.
Hirsch, Foster. *Love, Sex, Death, and the Meaning of Life: Woody Allen's Com-
    edy*. New York: McGraw-Hill, 1981.
Jacobs, Diane. . . . *But We Need the Eggs: The Magic of Woody Allen*. New York:
    St. Martin's Press, 1982.
James, Caryn. "Pointing the Way to *Annie Hall* and Beyond." *New York Times*
    December 4, 1997: B9.
Knight, Christopher J. "Woody Allen's Manhattan and the Ethnicity of Narra-
    tive." *Film Criticism* 13.1 (1988): 63–72.
LeBlanc, Ronald D. "*Love and Death* and Food: Wood Allen's Comic Use of
    Gastronomy," *Literature/Film Quarterly* 17.1 (1989): 18–26; rpt. in
    Renée R. Curry, *Perspectives on Woody Allen*. New York: G. K. Hall &
    Co., 1996. 146–157.
Lee, Sander H. *Woody Allen's Angst: Philosophical Commentaries on His Seri-
    ous Films*. Jefferson, NC: McFarland & Company, 1997.
Liebman, Robert Leslie. "Rabbis or Rakes, Schlemiels or Supermen? Jewish Iden-
    tity in Charles Chaplin, Jerry Lewis, and Woody Allen." *Literature/Film
    Quarterly* 12.3 (1984): 195–201.
Mast, Gerald. "Woody Allen: The Neurotic Jew as American Clown." *Jewish
    Wry: Essays on Jewish Humor*. Ed. Sarah Blacher Cohen. Bloomington:
    Indiana, 1987. 125–140.
McCann, Graham. *Woody Allen: New Yorker*. Cambridge, MA: Polity Press, 1990.
Moor, Jonathan. *Diane Keaton*. New York: St. Martin's Press, 1989.
Morris, C. "Woody Allen's Comic Irony." *Literature/ Film Quarterly* 15 (1987):
    175–180.
Navacelle, Thierry de. *Woody Allen on Location: A Day-to Day Account of the
    Making of* Radio Days. New York: William Morrow, 1987.
Nicholas, Mary P. *Reconstructing Woody: Art, Love, and Life in the Films of
    Woody Allen*. Lanham, MD: Rowman & Littlefield, 1998.
Perlmutter, Ruth. "Woody Allen's *Zelig*: An American Jewish Parody." Andrew
    Horton, *Comedy/Cinema/Theory*. Berkeley: University of California
    Press, 1991; rpt. as "*Zelig* According to Bakhtin" in Renée R. Curry, ed.,
    Perspectives on Woody Allen. New York: G. K. Hall, 1996. 78–90.
Pinsker, Sanford. "Jumping on Hollywood's Bones, or How S. J. Perelman and
    Woody Allen Found It at the Movies." *Midwest Quarterly: A Journal of
    Contemporary Thought* 21 (1980): 371–383.

Place, Janey. "Women in Film Noir." E. Ann Kaplan, ed., *Women in Film Noir.*
    Rev. ed. London: British Film Institute, 1980.
Pogel, Nancy H. *Perspectives on Woody Allen.* New York: Twayne Publishers,
    1987.
Quart, Leonard. "Woody Allen's New York." *Cineaste* 19.2–3 (1992): 16–19.
Reisch, Mark S. "Woody Allen: American Prose Humorist." *Journal of Popular
    Culture* 17.3 (Winter 1983): 68–74; rpt. in Renée R. Curry, ed., *Perspec-
    tives on Woody Allen.* New York: G. K. Hall & Co., 1996. 137–145.
Rosenblatt, Benjamin. "Zelig." Edward J. O'Brien, ed., *The Best Short Stories of
    1915.* Boston: Small Maynard & Co., 1916. 219–225.
Rosenblum, Ralph, and Robert Karen. *When the Shooting Stops . . . the Cutting
    Begins.* New York: Viking, 1979.
Schatz, Thomas. "*Annie Hall* and the Issue of Modernism." *Literature/Film
    Quarterly* 10.3 (1982): 180–187.
Scholes, Robert. *Fabulation and Metafiction.* Urbana, IL: University of Illinois
    Press, 1979.
Spignesi, Stephen J. *The Woody Allen Companion.* Kansas City: Andrews and
    McMeel, 1992.
Stewart, Barbara. "Showering Shtick on the White House." *New York Times* De-
    cember 4, 1997: B1.
Thomson, David. "Shooting the Actor," *Film Comment* (June–July 1998): 12–19.
Vipond, Dianne L. "*Crimes and Misdemeanors*: A Re-Take on the Eyes of Dr.
    Eckleburg." *Literature/Film Quarterly* 19.2 (1991): 99–103.
Wernblad, Annette. *Brooklyn Is Not Expanding: Woody Allen's Comic Universe.*
    Rutherford, NJ: Fairleigh Dickinson University Press, 1992.
Westerbeck, Colin L., Jr. "*Interiors,*" *Commonweal* September 29, 1978:
    630–632; rpt. in Renée R. Curry, ed., *Perspectives on Woody Allen.* New
    York: G. K. Hall & Co., 1996. 28–30. [Review of *Interiors.*]
———. "The Invisible Man: You Are What You Meet." *Commonweal* Septem-
    ber 9, 1983: 468–469; rpt. in Renée R. Curry, ed., *Perspectives on
    Woody Allen.* New York: G.K. Hall & Co., 1996. 34–36. [Review of *Ze-
    lig.*]
———. "A Visual Poem to New York City." *Commonweal* August 3, 1979:
    438–439; rpt. in Renée R. Curry, ed., *Perspectives on Woody Allen.* New
    York: G. K. Hall & Co., 1996. 31–33. [Review of *Manhattan.*]
Winsor, Chris. Online review of *Central Park West.* www.eye.net/eye/issue_
    06.12.97.
Wolcott, James. "How Green Was My Woody," *Vanity Fair* (December 1998):
    150–163.
Yacowar, Maurice. "Beyond Parody: Woody Allen in the 80s." *Post Script: Es-
    says in Film and the Humanities* 6.2 (Winter 1987): 29–42.
———. *Loser Take All: The Comic Art of Woody Allen.* New York: Frederick
    Ungar, 1991.

Index

Boldface page numbers indicate location of main entries.

About the Author

RICHARD A. SCHWARTZ is Professor of English and Fellow of the Honors College at Florida International University in Miami. He has written extensively on twentieth-century fiction, film, and humor.